Understanding Contemporary Strategy

This textbook provides a comprehensive introduction to modern strategy, covering the context, theory, and practice of military strategy in all its different forms.

Covering all the main issues in the field, the book explores the major themes through a combination of classical and modern strategic theory, history, and current practice. It is split into three main sections:

- The first provides the context for contemporary strategy and includes discussions of the human, technological, intelligence, ethical, and grand strategic dimensions.
- The second part explores the theory and practice of strategy in different geographical domains, including land, sea, air, space, and cyberspace.
- The final part engages with three of the most challenging forms of strategy in the contemporary era: nuclear weapons, terrorism, and insurgency.

This second edition brings the book up to date by including discussions of the rise and fall of the Islamic State of Iraq and Syria (ISIS); the emergence of robotics and artificial intelligence; major events in space and cyberspace; and the growing profile of nuclear weapons. Each chapter presents the reader with a succinct summary of the topic, provides a challenging analysis of current issues, and finishes with key points, questions for discussion, and further reading.

This book will be essential reading for upper-level students of strategic studies, war studies, military history, and international security.

David J. Lonsdale is a senior lecturer in war studies at the University of Hull, UK, and author of four books.

Thomas M. Kane is an independent scholar and author of eight academic books.

Understanding Contemporary Strategy

Second Edition

DAVID J. LONSDALE AND THOMAS M. KANE

Routledge
Taylor & Francis Group

LONDON AND NEW YORK

Second edition published 2020
by Routledge
2 Park Square, Milton Park, Abingdon, Oxon, OX14 4RN

and by Routledge
52 Vanderbilt Avenue, New York, NY 10017

Routledge is an imprint of the Taylor & Francis Group, an informa business

First edition published by Routledge 2012

British Library Cataloguing-in-Publication Data
A catalogue record for this book is available from the British Library

Library of Congress Cataloging-in-Publication Data
Names: Lonsdale, David J., author. | Kane, Thomas M., 1969– author.
Title: Understanding contemporary strategy / David J. Lonsdale and Thomas M. Kane.
Description: Second edition. | London ; New York, NY : Routledge/Taylor & Francis Group, 2020. | Kane's name appeared first in earlier edition. | Includes bibliographical references and index.
Identifiers: LCCN 2019039656 (print) | LCCN 2019039657 (ebook)
Subjects: LCSH: Strategy—Textbooks. | Military planning—Textbooks. | Military policy—Textbooks.
Classification: LCC U162 .K268 2020 (print) | LCC U162 (ebook) | DDC 355.4—dc23
LC record available at https://lccn.loc.gov/2019039656
LC ebook record available at https://lccn.loc.gov/2019039657

ISBN: 978-1-138-05946-7 (hbk)
ISBN: 978-1-138-05947-4 (pbk)
ISBN: 978-1-315-16353-6 (ebk)

Typeset in Avenir and Dante
by Apex CoVantage, LLC

This book is dedicated to Colin S. Gray, a great strategic thinker, mentor, and friend.

Contents

Text boxes

Acknowledgements

A book such as this is many years in the making. Developing an understanding of the many subjects occurs through a process of research, teaching, and discussion with colleagues and students. As a result, there are many people to thank. Most importantly, we would like to thank Colin S. Gray, who gave us a wonderful grounding in strategic studies during his PhD programme in the 1990s. It is a sign of his genuine commitment to the subject and his former students that Professor Gray continues to actively inspire and support us to this day. We have been fortunate to work with outstanding colleagues in various departments throughout our careers. In particular, we would like to show our appreciation to colleagues past and present at the Joint Services Command and Staff College, Reading University, and the University of Hull. We would also like to thank the many students who have shared our passion for strategy over the years. Engaging with them on the various topics covered in this book enabled us to develop and hone our ideas considerably. This book would not have happened without the patience and wisdom of Andrew Humphries at Routledge, whom it has been a pleasure to work with over a number of years. Finally, we would like to thank our families and friends. They continue to demonstrate overwhelming support for academic projects that too often dominate periods of our lives.

Introduction

'War is a matter of vital importance to the state; the province of life or death; the road to survival or ruin. It is mandatory that it be thoroughly studied'.[1]

These words, written approximately 2500 years ago by the Chinese general and theorist Sun Tzu, provide a simple but convincing impetus for academic study on the subject of war. Despite this persuasive call to intellectual arms, the study of war in its broader context remained undeveloped for much of history. Until the second half of the twentieth century the study of war had been largely restricted to the military. This, with a few notable exceptions (Clausewitz being the prime example), understandably led to a focus on tactical and operational issues and the development of principles for success. Military scholars and practitioners tended to focus on getting the job done rather than ruminating over war in its broader context. Thus, in the realm of military practice, it is rare to find serious study on the nature of war and its relationship to the other aspects of human sociopolitical activities.

This deficiency has been rectified, to some degree, with the academic discipline of strategic studies. In response to a call from the theorist Bernard Brodie, intellectual engagement with the subject of war has developed since the Second World War. This book seeks to further our understanding of war in both theory and practice. Importantly, it not only addresses the practice of strategy in all its forms but also discusses the context in which this occurs. To fully comprehend how strategy functions, it is essential to understand human, political, social, ethical, cultural, and technological contexts. Importantly, although strategic studies is an academic discipline, it has not become detached from military practice. There continues to be recognition that strategy is a practical subject with substantial consequences in the real world. As Brodie noted, 'Above all, strategic theory is a theory for action'.[2] That being the case, it is hoped that strategic studies has subjected war to rigorous intellectual analysis but at the same time has recognised the limits of theory in the practical and dangerous world of war. This current volume very much seeks to hold true to that tradition.

The nature of strategy is eternal, but clearly the strategic landscape is constantly evolving. Indeed, much has changed in the eight years since the first edition of this book. In 2012, the strategic studies community was focused on irregular war; although drones had gained some notoriety, autonomous lethal weapons had yet to provoke much debate; cybersecurity was prominent, but cyber strategies were not yet fully formed (arguably, they still are not); and some hoped that nuclear weapons would soon be consigned to the dustbin of Cold War history. In 2020, although irregular war still occupies a degree of attention, great power confrontation is rapidly rising on the strategic agenda. This has brought with it a renewed interest in the technologies and operations of regular war and a refocusing of attention on nuclear weapons. Additionally, cyberspace has now been officially recognised as a warfighting domain, with its own dedicated forces and independent command. Thus, while still acting as a general introduction to the eternal elements of strategy, the second edition of *Understanding Contemporary Strategy* reflects recent changes in the global strategic environment. Consequently, it will be of interest and use to those seeking to understand the theory and practice of strategy as we enter the third decade of the twenty-first century.

War and strategy

War and strategy are the subjects of this volume, but what exactly are they, and how does one differentiate between them? War is a political and social activity, which has been most accurately defined by Hedley Bull as 'organized violence carried on by political units against one another'.[3] Important points to note in this definition are that the violence is organised and undertaken by political units. This is not to say that violence in war is always tightly controlled, or that it always has a clear and direct relationship to a political goal. However, Bull's definition does imply that the violence stems from political motives (whatever they might be) and has purpose; it is not random or mindless. The policy objectives that motivate war can be extremely varied, as Clausewitz reminds us: 'Policy . . . is simply the trustee for all these interests against other states. . . . we can only treat policy as representative of all interests of the community'.[4] In this sense, we must regard war not as the failure of politics but as politics through violence: 'War is the continuation of political intercourse with the admixture of other means'.[5]

This work takes a fairly broad approach to the subject of what should be classified as war. For conceptual clarity and validity, this book takes the position that any act of violence undertaken by a political actor for policy effect should be defined as war. Thus, a terrorist car bombing or the large-scale invasion of one state by another is an act of war. The scale of violence is not the determining factor when defining war. Rather, the existence of war is determined by the nature of the actor using violence and the intent underpinning the act. This definition also applies if violence is threatened but not used. This reflects the important point made by Clausewitz when he notes that everything in war relates to battle: 'it is inherent in the very concept of war that everything that occurs *must originally derive from combat*' (emphasis in the original).[6] This broader definition of war applies even to political violence by proxy. So, for example, a state supporting an insurgency (perhaps through the supply of material or the training of forces) against another state is engaged in war. This is so because said actor is using violence against another political unit for policy objectives. There may be political, legal, and security ramifications for taking such a broad approach to the definition of war. However, conceptual clarity requires it.

Such a rational, Clausewitzian approach to the definition of war is not universally accepted. For some, the scale of violence is the key when defining war. From such a perspective, for a conflict to be classified as a war a certain number of combat fatalities must occur. The figure often used in this respect is 1000 in a 12-month period.[7] Clearly, such a numerical fixation is problematic and may lead to ludicrous anomalies. Are we to accept that a politically motivated violent conflict resulting in 999 fatalities is not war, for the sake of one death?

Equally problematic are those occasions when organised violence for political ends is not defined as war for political purposes. A government facing a terrorist or insurgent campaign will often refuse to use the term *war* to describe the security situation. This is done so as not to endow their irregular foes with a sense of legitimacy. In international politics, the idea that states have a legitimate monopoly on violence is a widely accepted norm. Thus, to describe an irregular campaign as war is to give an irregular foe a sense of legitimacy. In contrast, states prefer to describe irregular acts of war as criminal actions. A state actor may also choose not to define violent actions as war in order to limit the political fallout of military adventure. Describing actions as military assistance is less controversial than declaring that the state is going to war.

However desirable a more restricted approach to a war definition may be for political decision makers, it can have negative consequences. It has been convincingly argued that the United States erred by not declaring war during the conflict in Vietnam. Harry G. Summers concludes that this prevented the United States from enacting wartime measures at home and also failed to prepare the US public psychologically for the coming struggle.[8] The Bush administration's approach to the War on Terror presents a striking contrast. Although the labelling of the war against al-Qaeda has received strong criticism, it could be argued that it set the correct mood for the long and costly conflict to come. It can be seen from this brief discussion that how we define certain activities can have significant consequences on how they are perceived and even conducted.

The focus of strategy is the relationship between war and policy objectives, and it can be defined as *the process that converts military power into policy effect*. Strategy, then, is not war. Rather, it is the process by which war functions as a political act. Thus, when a practitioner looks to war to solve their political problems or to pursue political ambitions, they must concern themselves with strategy. After all, it is only through strategy that war can successfully function as a form of politics. Without the process of strategy, military power may become disconnected from the policy that gave rise to it. It is true that the exercise of military power will have strategic effect whether desired or not. This simply refers to the reality that there are political consequences to military actions, no matter how small. However, for military power to have positive policy effect, it must be guided by strategy.

Understanding the complexity of strategy

War has played an important, if tragic, role in human history. The outcome of wars can have substantial consequences for the individual, the state, or the entire international system. Thus, it is wholly sensible for those with responsibilities in this field to seek to understand both the nature of war and best practice. This task is challenging. War is a complex human and social phenomenon, which is influenced by many external factors and internal dynamics. In the modern period, this complexity has increased with the development of technology and associated new forms of warfare. Heavier-than-air flight, nuclear weapons, near-Earth orbit, and cyberspace are four examples of technology opening up new threats and opportunities in the field of conflict.

As war has become more complex, practitioners and theorists have sometimes struggled to understand the sustained implications of new developments. As an example, air power affected almost all existing forms of warfare but also promised to enable revolutionary new methods. Strategic bombing, airborne operations, and close air support (CAS) all promised to radically alter actions in and beyond the battlespace. But, which of these would offer genuinely lasting effects? As military establishments and their political masters sought to understand this new third dimension to warfare, the task was further complicated by the opening up of the space and cyberspace domains. Thus, the arena of strategy was expanded further. This expansion is only part of the challenge, however. Just as important are the implications of social, cultural, and political change in the modern period. The backdrop for strategy has become more prominent. This is nowhere more evident than in the field of ethics. Strategic practitioners are increasingly subject to ethical and legal standards. This creates a substantial challenge in an activity that is, by its very nature, violent and chaotic (if also rational).

Thankfully, at the same time that the challenge of strategy has intensified, intellectual enquiry has also increased. It took the invention of nuclear weapons, and in particular the very real threat of global Armageddon, for humankind to finally take up the mantle handed down by Sun Tzu in a more systematic fashion. The novelty of nuclear weapons, allied to their destructiveness, meant that the military was no better placed than anyone else to comprehend the new epoch. Thus, civilian academics from a wide range of disciplines turned their thoughts to the challenges of modern strategy. Thus, strategic studies began to develop, drawing inspiration and influence from various fields, including economics, history, anthropology, and philosophy.

This all bodes well for the theory and practice of strategy. However, strategic studies still struggles to find a permanent home in the world of academia. There are a few established think tanks and research institutes that specialise in the field. However, in the university sector, centres for strategic studies have largely failed to develop into independent departments.[9] Strategic studies degree programmes emerged in the aftermath of 9/11 but are still far from widespread. Often, subjects in the field of strategy are offered merely as options as part of degrees in international relations or history. Indeed, in recent years, we have witnessed a reduction in the number of specialist degree programmes and student numbers in the United Kingdom. Following the attacks of 9/11 and the subsequent conflicts in Afghanistan and Iraq, there was an understandable surge in interest in strategy as society sought to understand the events unfolding around them. And although the rise and fall of ISIS and the war in Syria have kept war in the public consciousness, other issues have attracted the attention of those of a political mindset. Brexit and the election of President Donald Trump have tended to take the headlines more in recent years.

While most academic disciplines go through peaks and troughs, it is important to maintain an ongoing intellectual engagement with the subject. As Betts intimates, it is important to keep the strategic flame alive, even during times of relative peace.[10] Sadly, there are plenty of potential large conflicts simmering under the surface of the current international system. At the time of writing, North Korea, Iran, Russia, and China all have serious and growing tensions with the United States. Maybe none of these will develop into a significant war. However, geopolitics tends to throw up great power conflicts on a fairly regular basis. Thus, our understanding of strategy must be maintained and developed in each generation.

It is hoped that books such as this will help to further establish a solid intellectual foundation for the ongoing development of strategic studies. By offering a broad introduction to the subject while maintaining a reasonable depth of analysis, this work seeks to help codify and cement the study of war as a coherent, unified field of study. To achieve this goal, this book is divided in to three sections. What follows is a summary of each chapter, with a brief description of the changes for this new edition.

Chapter summaries

The first section contains six chapters that establish the context in which strategy occurs. The first of these six chapters defines strategy in a detailed manner. The chapter begins with an explanation of the various uses of military power. It is shown that despite being a rather blunt instrument, military force is surprisingly flexible if used correctly. From here, the chapter outlines the nature of strategy and then identifies those features that pose substantial challenges for the practitioner. From there, the work seeks to provide various answers and / or aids to help manage these challenges. Especially worthy of note for the 2nd Edition is the theoretical development of the dimensions of strategy. In particular, we introduce the concept of internal and external dimensions and how the former can be used to manipulate the latter.

Chapter 2 deals with what is probably the most basic, but most fundamental, truism in strategy: it is a human activity. That being the case, Chapter 2 addresses the human dimension through two main areas of study: culture and psychology. Discussion of the former takes us into the realms of the strategic culture debate. The literature on strategic culture raises questions regarding the influence that culture has on the practice of strategy. The chapter discusses the validity of the notion of strategic culture and addresses a range of issues, such as the dangers of stereotyping one's opponents. Having discussed culture, the chapter then turns its attention to psychology, in particular the crucial but intangible forces of morale and unit cohesion. The 2nd Edition adds new material on how the use of robotic surrogates in combat may affect the psychology of warfare. Early twenty-first century experience indicates that the personnel responsible for operating crewless combat vehicles experience some of the same stresses as those directly engaged in combat.

Chapter 3 deals with the increasingly challenging area of ethics as applied to war. Since this volume is primarily concerned with understanding the nature of strategy and best practice, this chapter will conclude with an analysis of how strategists can incorporate an ethical dimension into their practice while still seeking to achieve their policy objectives. However, before that can be done, the basic foundations for ethics must be understood. It is also important to understand the realist take on the role that ethics plays in international politics. Since strategic studies is heavily infused by realism, it is important to understand how the latter views ethical issues. It will become clear that tensions exist between some of the core demands of ethics and the realist school of thought. To understand how some of these tensions can be mitigated, the chapter will outline the just war tradition (which for the 2nd Edition includes the developing subject of *jus post bellum*), which seeks to reconcile the need for war in international politics with ethical concerns. The just war tradition is reflected in the modern laws of war. It will be argued that although the laws of war provide a reasonably balanced and sensible approach to the regulation of armed conflict, modern interpretations and use of them has become increasingly problematic from the perspective of best practice. It is this that creates the need for a strategy-centred approach to subject of ethics and war. Strategy is accounted for via the innovative approach: strategic necessity. For the 2nd Edition, we have also included a discussion of a strategy for the common good, as a possible alternative.

Technology provides the tools for strategy; this much is clear. What is less clear is how significant is the role played by humankind's inventions. Chapter 4 seeks to explore this issue through the prism of the revolution in military affairs (RMA)/military transformation debate. At the centre of the RMA hypothesis is the idea that periodically opportunities arise to transform the conduct of warfare. If pursued correctly, these changes may confer significant advantage on those who exploit them, and may even revolutionise the act of war. Perhaps not surprisingly, this hypothesis has not been universally accepted. Thus, Chapter 4 begins by outlining the origins and development of the RMA hypothesis. The chapter will pay particular attention to the ongoing information-age RMA and, for this 2nd Edition, the subsequent rise of unmanned systems – the so-called post-human epoch. The many implications of robotics and artificial intelligence (AI) are discussed as they relate to the different levels of strategy. The chapter also engages with the complex ethical questions surrounding lethal autonomous weapons. The chapter will then discuss the role of technology in strategy, identifying it as an important but not decisive dimension. Finally, the chapter concludes with an assessment of whether the RMA hypothesis has any real utility in the theory and practice of strategy. Throughout the chapter, historical case studies will be used to illustrate the various sides of the debate.

Chapter 5 discusses the surprisingly neglected field of intelligence in the conduct of strategy. The chapter notes that strategists are rediscovering the field of intelligence, and it thus outlines the key issues that have arisen as a result. The first section notes key historical events that aroused contemporary interest in this topic. The second section discusses how theorists have depicted the relationship between intelligence and strategy and how their work may help policymakers organise intelligence services to keep strategists as well informed as possible. These theoretical concepts, however, are not fully satisfying. The third section observes that intelligence agencies perform functions that go beyond passively gathering information. The fourth and final section suggests that despite theorists' attempts to distinguish between intelligence and the strategic planning it supports, intelligence is an organic part of strategy, which raises many of the same moral, political, and operational issues as war itself. The 2nd Edition adds a case study on US intelligence community reforms in the early twenty-first century and a discussion of intelligence in contemporary Russia.

Chapter 6 conceptually lifts the work above the challenges of using military force for policy effect and into the higher realms of grand strategy. The first section of the chapter summarises the reasons why some people question the existence of grand strategy. The second section notes that states and other political actors nevertheless act purposefully at the grand strategic level. The third section explores some of the factors that underpin successful action in this arena and reflects on points to consider when interpreting them. This 2nd Edition acknowledges that contemporary powers now recognise cyberspace as an arena of grand strategy. This chapter also notes developments in the UK aircraft carrier programme and the European Union's progress towards completing the Galileo satellite navigation system.

Having set the context in which strategy is practised, the second section of the work deals with strategy in the main geographic domains: land, sea, air, space, and cyberspace. Chapter 7 focuses on that most basic of geographic expressions of military power: land warfare. It begins by explaining the concept of control, as expressed by Admiral J.C. Wylie. The chapter then goes on to discuss how control is achieved in the modern environment. To that end, it explains the techniques of modern land warfare as follows. An initial section details the problems that soldiers faced as modern weapons and modern industry became widespread. This section focuses on the example of the First World War. The second section discusses the solutions that commanders in that conflict developed. The third section discusses how military thinkers of the 1920s, 1930s, and 1940s integrated new weapons and new tactics into higher levels of planning. The final section asks whether methods that emerged during the world wars of the twentieth century remain appropriate in the wars of the twenty first. The 2nd Edition adds new material on how precision-guided munitions may affect the dynamics of land combat and explores the effect of inexpensive military drones on the land campaign.

Chapter 8 deals with sea power, which is an area of strategy afflicted by definitional problems. The chapter begins by seeking to provide clarity on the parameters of the subject. Much of the existing confusion stems from the interchangeable use in the literature of the following terms to describe strategy at or from the sea: 'naval', 'maritime', and 'sea power'. The chapter opts for the latter term and does so on the basis that it restricts analysis to the use of military assets in the maritime environment, rather than including other maritime issues such as insurance. The chapter also provides conceptual clarity by identifying the differences between command of the sea and control of the sea, both of which seek to explain strategic relationships within the maritime environment. This section is enhanced with a discussion of sea denial (the attempt to deny use of the sea to a maritime enemy). Since strategy is concerned with using military assets to achieve policy objectives, the chapter explores how sea power can be used in this respect. Finally, the chapter closes with an analysis of the most pressing issues in contemporary sea power. For this 2nd Edition, we focus on the growing maritime power of China and Russia; 'good order at sea' (mainly dealing with piracy, human trafficking, and terrorism); the operational implications of new and developing technologies (unmanned systems, networks, and the future of the capital ship); and the latest developments in US maritime strategy in response to these challenges.

Chapter 9 on air power assesses the development and significance of strategy in the third dimension. It is argued that the invention of heavier-than-air flight at the beginning of the twentieth century instigated some of the most significant changes to the character of warfare. To explain these changes, the chapter describes and analyses the development of air power over the last 117 years. This analysis ranges from the surprising diversity of operations in the First World War through the massive bombing campaigns and divisional-scale airborne campaigns of the Second World War, and for this 2nd Edition, it finishes with an assessment of air power in the most recent of conflicts: Afghanistan, Iraq, Libya, Syria, and ISIS. The chapter not only highlights the flexibility of air power but also identifies its weaknesses as an instrument of strategy. In the final analysis, the chapter concludes that air power is an extremely potent form of strategic power, but one that is best used as a supporting arm to surface forces.

Chapter 10 turns our attention to the still-underdeveloped subject of space power. The chapter summarises how space technology affects strategic thought in the early twenty-first century. The first four sections introduce the spacecraft and related technology that have proven most useful in military operations and other strategic activities. These sections outline what currently existing space systems can and cannot do. A concluding section discusses issues that space technology raises for strategists. These range from theoretical questions about whether strategists should treat space strategy any differently from any other form of strategy to more-immediate debates concerning which branches of the armed forces should control space operations. The 2nd Edition adds information on the Galileo satellite navigation system, China's alleged test of a high-altitude anti-satellite (ASAT) in 2013, and India's ASAT test of 2019. This chapter also explores US President Donald Trump's decision to create the independent Space Force and France's decision to create the air force–based Space Command.

Chapter 11 presents a new subject for this 2nd Edition. Although cyber and information warfare matters were discussed in the 1st Edition, it is clear that cyberspace has become ever-more strategically important in the eight years since the original publication. Thus, cyber power needs to be fully explored as an instrument of strategy. The chapter is divided into four sections. It begins with an examination of the existential threat posed by cyberattacks, justifying the rise of cybersecurity in government policy. From here, the chapter provides strategic clarification of the subject at hand. Although the existing literature has made some important contributions to cyber strategic discourse, strategic concepts are too often either misused or ignored. The third section of the chapter discusses the various missions of cyber power: how does cyber power actually function as an instrument of policy? Finally, the limitations of cyber power are examined. The chapter concludes with a call for a unified, comprehensive approach to cyber strategy.

Having discussed the theory and practice of strategy in the main geographic domains, the final section of the book explores some of the most challenging forms of strategy: nuclear strategy and irregular warfare. Arguably, the invention of nuclear weapons has posed the greatest challenge to modern strategists. The destructive power of these weapons, especially when fitted to ballistic missiles, poses substantial challenges to those who have to control them for policy effect. Thus, Chapter 12 begins by describing the basic technological characteristics of nuclear weapons and the core strategic concepts that flow from these. Having established the basic parameters of the subject, the chapter then explores the development of nuclear strategy during the Cold War, making reference to the most important works of theory in the field. It is argued that deterrence was always at the heart of nuclear strategy. However, deterrence was never as simple or easy as some proclaimed. Indeed, in nuclear strategy, the details really matter. While recognising the dominance of deterrence, the chapter also analyses the important work done in the field of nuclear warfighting. Finally, for this 2nd Edition, the chapter closes with a discussion of the contemporary nuclear security environment, focusing on the substantial modernisation efforts and developments in doctrine. And in that connection, it presents a blueprint for nuclear strategy for the current age.

Chapter 13 deals with one of the great challenges of modern strategy: terrorism. The chapter equips readers to analyse how terrorists and their opponents work to achieve political and military objectives. The first section discusses what terrorists have commonly been able to accomplish, the techniques they have commonly employed, and the resources they have commonly required. The second section considers the methods that state governments and others have commonly used against terrorists and the strategic decisions those who fight terrorists must make. The conclusion considers how terrorists fit into broader struggles in world politics and considers the proposition that an exceptionally vicious 'new terrorism' presents an unprecedented threat in the twenty-first century. For the 2nd Edition, we explore the spread of so-called hybrid terrorist threats, using ISIS as a prime example. This chapter also compares ISIS with another well-known hybrid military organisation: the Communist forces that participated in the American phase of the Vietnam War.

Insurgency has dominated strategy on and off since the end of the Second World War. Despite years of experience and theoretical and doctrinal development, counterinsurgency (COIN) remains one of the most challenging pursuits in modern strategy. Chapter 14 seeks to discover why this is the case and what can be done about this state of affairs. To do this, the chapter opens with an analysis of insurgency, focusing on how it functions as an instrument of strategy. From there, the work critiques accepted wisdom on counterinsurgency. Making reference to important theoretical works, alongside historical experience, the chapter provides an alternative approach to the practice of COIN. In particular, the chapter highlights the importance of understanding COIN as war. From this position, while recognising the value and importance of the hearts-and-minds dimension, the chapter refocuses on the defeat of the enemy forces and the coercion of the local populous. Overall, the chapter seeks to reconnect the practice of COIN with the core principles of strategy. For this 2nd Edition, we have further developed our theory that merges both enemy-centric and population-centric approaches. This is supported with even more historical evidence from important case studies and an analysis of recent/current COIN campaigns (including the rise and fall of territorially defined ISIS).

The book concludes by asking, what are the patterns in grand strategy today? Although a thorough answer to that question would require volumes, the concluding chapter of this work sketches the outline of a response and reflects on how studying the contemporary grand strategic environment can help us to understand the broader topic of twenty-first century strategy. In particular, the 2nd Edition notes a number of developments that have occurred since 2012. These include the rush by multiple countries to establish bases around the Horn of Africa, the rise and fall of territorial ISIS, and the renewed spates of belligerent rhetoric from North Korea.

Notes

1 Sun Tzu, *The Art of War*, trans. Samuel B. Griffith (London, Oxford University Press, 1971), p. 63.
2 Bernard Brodie, 'Strategy as a Science', *World Politics* 1:4 (July 1949), pp. 467–88.

3 Hedley Bull, *The Anarchical Society* (New York, Columbia University Press, 1977).

4 Carl von Clausewitz, *On War* (Princeton, Princeton University Press, 1976), p. 606.

5 Ibid., p. 87.

6 Ibid., p. 108.

7 This approach is taken most famously by J. David Singer's, *Correlates of War Project*, www.correlatesofwar.org/

8 Harry G. Summers, *On Strategy: A Critical Analysis of the Vietnam War* (New York, Ballentine Books, 1995).

9 The Department of War Studies at King's College London is a rare exception.

10 Richard K. Betts, 'Should Strategic Studies Survive', *World Politics* 50 (October 1997), pp. 7–33.

Context

PART I

Strategy

1

Reader's guide

The use of military power in politics (offence, defence, deterrence, coercion, and miscellaneous); defining strategy; the levels of strategy; the challenges of strategy (disharmony in the levels, the troubled relationship between war and politics, the enemy, the nature of war, the multidimensional nature of strategy, the polymorphous character of war, and friction); dealing with the challenges of strategy (theory and history, ample and quality forces, appropriate strategic culture, military genius, and effective command process).

Introduction

The conduct of war, regardless of time or place, cannot be meaningfully understood without reference to strategy. This book is divided into chapters that deal with strategy in many contexts. The essence of strategy, however, remains constant regardless of the situation. Strategy, which can best be described as *the process that converts military power into policy effect*, provides purpose and meaning for military activities. This opening chapter seeks to provide an understanding of strategy and the different levels at which it operates. Said understanding will not only define the core features of strategy but also identify those aspects of strategy that create substantial challenges for the practitioner. In particular, the discussion will focus on the troubled relationship between war and politics; the multidimensional nature of strategy; the polymorphous character of war; the nature of war; and friction. The chapter will then discuss how these difficulties can be overcome. However, before the chapter delves into the complexities of strategy, it will consider the place of military power in the world of politics and will in particular discuss the varied uses to which it can be put.

> **Box 1.1 Strategy defined**
>
> Strategy is the process that converts military power into policy effect.

The use of military power

Although military power often appears ill-suited to the nuanced world of politics, war is a political act and at times a necessary one. In conceptual terms, military power can take a number of forms: defence, offence, deterrence, coercion, and miscellaneous. Taken together, these categories represent the many uses to which military force can be put. Although military power is often perceived as a fairly blunt instrument of policy, it is a remarkably flexible tool in the right hands, and especially in relation to its psychological effects, it can be fairly subtle. This chapter will now briefly outline each of these different uses.

Defence is the most basic and important function of military power. Providing physical security for the nation-state is an essential enabler for the proper functioning of society. Indeed, without effective defence, societies and/or states can simply disappear off the map. For example, South Vietnam and Carthage are but two examples of states that no longer exist due to a failure in the defensive function of their military forces. Even if a state survives foreign attack and invasion, the effects of aggression can still be devastating. Millions of Jews in Europe who were outside the borders of Nazi Germany were slaughtered in Nazi concentration camps partly because the military forces of their respective states could not withstand German forces of conquest. Although the notion of security has expanded (to include such dimensions as economic and environmental security), providing basic physical security for its citizens and resources still remains the primary function of the state. Despite the importance of the defensive mission, there are no guarantees that it can be fulfilled in every circumstance. It may be, as was the case for Poland in 1939, that invading forces prove too strong and overwhelm defensive measures taken.

Despite the best efforts of sections of the international community (as expressed through international organisations and international law) to rein in military power, it continues to perform an offensive role. Both sub-state actors (terrorists and insurgents) and nation-states still regard the aggressive use of military power as legitimate and productive in pursuit of their policy objectives. Russian actions in Ukraine, the campaigns of al-Qaeda and ISIS, and the invasions of Afghanistan and Iraq all serve to illustrate this point. Whether or not these particular adventures are regarded as successful is something of a moot point. From the perspective of a strategic analyst, what matters is that certain actors choose offensive military power as an appropriate means to achieve their objectives. Indeed, there are some policy objectives that are only attainable by aggressive military action, at least in a reasonable timeframe. Although the removal of the Taliban (from power in Afghanistan) and Saddam Hussein's regime could conceivably have been achieved via diplomatic and economic pressure (although this is debatable), military power achieved these goals in relatively short order. However, as these and many other examples illustrate, the offensive use of force is fraught with difficulties and dangers. 'Use with care' is a label ideally suited for the offensive use of force.

The offensive use of force is not restricted to large invasions. Raids are a form of offensive action that have far more limited goals, perhaps focused on the destruction of a distinct target or the capture and/or killing of an individual. Examples of successful raids include the Israeli strikes on nuclear reactors in Iraq (1981) and Syria (2007) and the US raid to capture/kill Osama Bin Laden (2011). As will be explained in Chapter 11, the most recent raid against a potentially hostile nuclear programme (the Iranian uranium enrichment site at Natanz in 2010) was conducted via cyberattack (Stuxnet). This was, at least in part, because the Iranians, conscious of the 1981 and 2007 attacks, built the facility underground precisely to secure it against air attack.

In contrast to physically taking or defending something, deterrence and coercion function via the psychological effect of military power. Whereas deterrence has the negative objective of persuading an enemy not to take a certain course of action, coercion seeks to compel an enemy to act in a certain manner. It is tempting to suggest that deterrence differs from coercion in that the former relies solely on the threat of force, not its actual use. Whereas, coercion often requires a demonstration of force (the infliction of some pain) to have an effect. Although there is some validity in this perspective, it is not entirely true. Deterrence can occur once fighting has actually started. In such circumstances, so-called intra-war deterrence may rely on actions taken to increase the potency of threats. Nonetheless, it is generally true that deterrence is seen to have failed if force is actually used. It is also true that coercion can, and often does, function purely on the threat of force to compel. The mere deployment of forces in theatre may sometimes be enough to encourage a change in behaviour.

In conceptual terms, deterrence can operate via two distinct, but certainly not mutually exclusive, methods: punishment and denial. The former relies on the threat of the infliction of unacceptable costs on an enemy. By contrast, denial seeks to deter an enemy by denying them the ability to achieve their objectives. Deterrence grew to prominence during the Cold War, as it appeared to be the most apt defence posture for nuclear weapons. However, deterrence is by no means a product of the twentieth century, nor has it lost its relevance since the end of the superpower standoff. It remains an important element in defence policy and can be general or immediate (tailored) in character.[1]

Coercion, as Thomas Schelling so aptly describes, is based on 'the power to hurt'.[2] If it works well, coercion is an efficient use of force that has the possibility of no actual fighting occurring. Thus, policy objectives may be met simply by a vocal threat or the deployment of forces. As Byman and Waxman note, there is a significant difference in taking something and persuading someone to give it.[3] In terms of costs to oneself, the latter is normally preferable. Although violence may not be needed, cumulative punishment may be required until the enemy changes their behaviour, as in the 1999 Kosovo campaign.

Although potentially efficient forms of strategy, both coercion and deterrence suffer from similar problems and limitations. Most importantly, they cede a certain amount of control to the enemy. Ultimately, it is the enemy that decides if they will accede to one's demands or not. Their pain threshold may be extremely high, or they may not fully believe the threats they face. Both forms of strategy also rely on a reasonable understanding of the enemy. What do they value? How can I hurt them sufficiently? Can I hurt them? How much pain can they withstand? How does their decision-making process work? These are all extremely valuable questions one must pose when constructing a strategy of deterrence or coercion. To provide satisfactory answers to these questions, the intelligence task is substantial and complicated by analytical challenges. For example, accurate analysis of enemy intentions and will is undermined by various cognitive impediments. These include confirmation bias, groupthink, and mirror imaging. Before the attack on Pearl Harbor, key decision makers in the United States saw no advantage for Japan in an attack on Hawaii. As a result, US policy towards Japan, which included economic coercion, underestimated Japanese objectives and will. There is also the danger that a particular enemy may be beyond deterrence and coercion; their will and objectives may be near total in nature. Like all other aspects of strategy, there are no guarantees when using these forms of action.

Despite its rather blunt image, military power has great flexibility as an instrument of strategy. Those roles not mentioned so far can be corralled under the heading of miscellaneous. Under this category are too many uses to discuss them all in detail, but the most significant ones are defence diplomacy, constabulary, disaster relief, and peacekeeping. Defence diplomacy uses military force to grease the wheels of peaceful diplomatic relationships. Port visits by naval vessels and military parades for visiting dignitaries are some of the most obvious examples of this type of activity. The constabulary function covers counternarcotic operations as well as the enforcement of trade embargoes. Disaster relief is rather self-evident, but no less important for that. Due to their range of capabilities and culture of service, military forces are often the first on the scene of a major disaster. Finally, as the post–Second World War era reveals, various international and regional organisations have used neutral military forces in attempts to stabilise and monitor tense security environments, thereby enabling lasting political solutions to be explored.

Defining strategy

It has been established that military power has a substantial and reasonably flexible role in politics. But how does one translate military power into policy effect? The answer is strategy, but the term 'strategy' needs to be defined carefully. The theoretical literature provides many definitions of strategy. Clausewitz prefers a rather straightforward combat-orientated approach: 'strategy [is] the use of engagements for the object of war'.[4] Liddell Hart appears to have a slightly more nuanced understanding of the role that military power can play in the pursuit of policy: 'strategy is the art of distributing and applying military means to fulfill the ends of policy'.[5] Liddell Hart's definition appears somewhat broader than that of Clausewitz, in that it can incorporate acts such as coercion, peacekeeping, and constabulary operations. The French theorist Andre Beaufre draws attention to the competitive nature of strategy: 'strategy is . . . the art of the dialectic of force or, more precisely, the art of the dialectic of two opposing wills using force to resolve their dispute'.[6] Finally, Colin Gray describes strategy as 'the bridge that relates military power to political purpose; it is neither military power per se nor political purpose'.[7] Drawing on all of these definitions for inspiration, to reiterate, this work defines strategy as *the process that converts military power into policy effect.*

It is useful to linger for a moment on the concept of process. Strategy is concerned with the dynamic relationships among ends, ways, and means, whereby ends refers to the policy objectives sought and ways refers to the strategic application of military means in the pursuit of those ends. In this sense, we see that although strategy deals with physical military assets, it is itself immaterial. Like love, strategy does not possess tangible, material form. It is not an entity. However, also like love, the effects of strategy can be seen and experienced and can have revolutionary consequences. Strategy is formed in the mind of the strategist and/or in the discussions that occur between the political and military leadership. Strategy is really concerned with controlling the process of converting military means into positive policy outcomes. Later in this chapter, we will return to the idea of controlling the process of strategy.

Box 1.2 The levels of strategy

Policy – sets the objective to be achieved.
Grand strategy – coordination of all a nation's assets to pursue policy objective.
Military strategy – use of military power in support of grand strategy.
Operational – links tactical actions to military strategy (conceptually and geographically).
Tactical – details relating to combat (deployment and engagement).

For conceptual reasons, and to rationalise the delegation of command, the process of strategy is organised into different levels. Atop the taxonomy of strategy is *policy*: the objective to be pursued. As Clausewitz reminds us, policy objectives can be extremely varied: 'Policy . . . is simply the trustee for all these interests against other states. . . . we can only treat policy as representative of all interests of the community'.[8] Whatever the policy objective in question, it must guide all the actions of the strategist. Since war is merely political intercourse conducted through the threat or use of violent force, military power should never become divorced from the policy that it serves. However, establishing a viable relationship between policy and the military instrument is challenging. Sometimes the conversion of military power to policy effect is direct, as would be the case when the policy objective requires that land or resources be seized. At other times, the relationship between military objectives and political objectives is more abstruse. One can think, for example, of when military power is used for nation building. The challenge that such strategies pose can be referred to as reification: the process of converting something immaterial (security, nation building, etc.) into a material reality (the presence of military forces to provide security).

Once a policy objective has been identified, a method to achieve it must be established. To do this, the strategist must evaluate all of the available means at their disposal in light of the objective sought. For conceptual clarity, these means are normally divided into four categories: diplomatic, intelligence, military, and economic (DIME). For this 2nd Edition, and to account for developments in recent years, we add a *c* for cyber: DIMEC. Taken together, these are the instruments of *grand strategy*, the function of which is 'to coordinate and direct all the resources of a nation, or band of nations, towards the attainment of the political object[ive]'.[9]

Like strategy, grand strategy is a process by which these various means are converted into policy effect. One of the key decisions to be made in grand strategy is what mixture of means is to be used. It may be that military force plays no part in certain contexts. Alternatively, as in the Second World War, military power may be the leading component.

If achieving the policy objective requires the use of military force, then *military strategy* (the focus of this volume) comes into play. The process of converting military power into policy effect is achieved through the *tactical* and *operational* levels. The former is concerned with the details of combat. More specifically, tactics are about deployments, engagements with the enemy, and interaction among the various units at a commander's disposal. Although each contact with the enemy represents a distinct tactical event, it is in the modern period normally the combined effect of tactical actions that has an effect on strategy. How tactical actions relate to strategy is the realm of the operational level, which can be thought of in conceptual and physical terms. Conceptually, it is at the operational level where tactical actions are joined together to create strategic effect. In a physical sense, the operational level represents a large command area in which tactical actions are coordinated towards some operational goal. These goals are varied and may include the capture of a city, the destruction of enemy forces, or the pacification of an area.

More often than not, significant strategic impact will result only from the cumulative effect of many tactical events. The process by which these events are coordinated exists at the operational level. A strategic bombing campaign provides one such example, in which the cumulative effect of a number of bombing raids gradually depletes the enemy's will and capability to resist. However, in some circumstances, it is possible for one tactical event to influence strategy significantly. History is replete with many campaigns that were won or lost on the basis of one battle, lasting perhaps only a few hours. In the modern era, it is still possible for small tactical actions to have serious consequences. Take, for example, the Serb massacre of Kosovo Albanians at Racak, which appears to have been the trigger for NATO intervention in Kosovo.[10]

The challenges of strategy

If a war is conducted with competence (history suggests this is a big ask), actions throughout the different levels of strategy will be coordinated and harmonious.[11] The policy objective should be clear at all levels of command. There should be a clear understanding of how military force can best serve the objective, and a suitable and viable military objective(s) should be established. The operational-level commander should appreciate how the tactical units at their disposal work together to produce positive effect. Finally, these units must perform competently at the tactical level in the face of the enemy. This all sounds fairly straightforward. However, as this chapter will illustrate, there are many obstacles to overcome to produce such a smooth and harmonious process of strategy – not least of which is the real danger of disharmony occurring among actions in the different levels of strategy.[12]

The performance of Nazi Germany in the Second World War provides a vivid example of what can occur when the levels of strategy are out of kilter. Throughout the war, German forces generally performed extremely well at the tactical and operational levels. Indeed, the Wehrmacht has been described as 'one of the most formidable military machines in history'.[13] However, German grand strategy simply asked too much of them. Hitler's ambitions could not be met with the resources available to the German armed forces. As the war progressed, Germany acquired too many powerful foes on too many fronts. Ironically, one of the fronts that Germany acquired it did so as a result of tactical success. North Africa was never intended to be a significant theatre of operations for Germany. However, it became so due to a combination of Rommel's ambitions and outstanding early successes, aided by British errors. In this sense, tactical success can foster ambitions and open up opportunities that do not sit well with the situation at the higher levels. Overall, it can be seen that Germany, despite the quality of its forces, suffered from disharmony among the levels of strategy.

Disharmony among the levels of strategy is but one of the many challenges thrown up by the nature of strategy. Indeed, difficulties for the practitioner are to be found from the get-go, in the core relationship in strategy: between the military world and the policy world. Due to its violent and destructive nature, war can sometimes appear to be a rather clumsy and blunt instrument in the world of politics. This is not to suggest that war is necessarily an inappropriate tool of policy. Rather, it is to note that although sometimes necessary, the very nature of military power produces negative side effects. Take, for instance, modern counterinsurgency (discussed in detail in Chapter 14). Military force is essential for counterinsurgency, both to provide security and authority for other sociopolitical activities to flourish. At the same time, the exercise of military power risks collateral damage, and the mere presence of well-armed foreign troops may alienate a local population. In this sense, the complex process of sociopolitical nation building does not necessarily sit comfortably with the presence of military forces. The introduction of military power can also lead to escalation of a crisis, which often entails a more protracted campaign than first envisaged. The use of military power often unleashes powerful emotive forces and adds an extra layer of interaction, with uncertain outcomes likely to result.

In contrast, military power can often be the most appropriate instrument to fulfil political objectives. The mere presence of military power may coerce an adversary without the actual use of destructive force or the need for protracted economic sanctions and diplomatic manoeuvres. In the face of a powerful and threatening neighbour, the deployment of military forces may be a wholly sensible preparation for self-defence. At the more aggressive end of the scale, military power is the only viable instrument for those intent on conquest or the destruction of foreign powers. However morally repugnant, the Third Reich's ambitious goals could only be pursued through military means. Interestingly, the final outcome of the Second World War (from Germany's perspective) highlights the real dangers of unleashing the military instrument as a tool of policy. Of course, such counterproductive results are not inevitable, as much of the history of the Roman Empire and the campaigns of Alexander the Great testify to. Clearly, though, the rich history of military power suggests that results are uncertain and that the instrument requires careful handling.

The practice of strategy can also be compromised by the cultural mismatch between the military world and the political world. The outlook, agendas, and methods of these two partners in strategy can be far removed from one another. Modern democratic political leaders are often preoccupied with of a range of factors that do not figure so prominently in the military sphere. These include public opinion (which is increasingly shaped by the media, both traditional and social), internal party politics, and election timelines. These will inevitably influence the political atmosphere within which strategic decisions are made. However, these same concerns may be out of kilter with the realities of war. This was especially evident in the Vietnam War. For reasons primarily related to domestic US politics, none of those who occupied the Oval Office during this time (Kennedy, Johnson, and Nixon) fully committed the United States to the war. In the contemporary period, with the decline in mass military service, public knowledge of war has likewise declined. As a consequence, the inevitable violence of warfare rarely plays well with a modern audience. Similarly, uncertainties emanating from interaction with the enemy usually do not tolerate precise exit strategies and dates favoured by political leaders.

These points of tension between the political aspects and the military aspects of strategy can be dealt with only via what Elliot Cohen has described as the unequal dialogue.[14] When producing strategy, both sides in the process must understand, as much as possible, each other's environments, capabilities, and requirements. The political leadership must appreciate what is militarily possible, and the military leadership must appreciate what is politically possible. It is likely that both sides will have to compromise on their respective ideal positions. Hence, we see how the process of strategy should function. Nonetheless, whatever compromise position is reached, the resulting strategy must be in tune with the nature of war. If this is not the case, an enemy may be able to exploit such a deficiency. As a side note, and to emphasise the Clausewitzian nature of strategy, inequality in the dialogue emanates from the fact that military power is a tool of policy; they are not equal partners in the process.

Some of these tensions are not present when the political leadership and the military leadership are combined in one individual. Leaders such as Alexander the Great and Napoleon merged political and military requirements. In many respects, this appears to be the perfect solution to the problems at the heart of strategy's troubled relationship. However, in the absence of a genuine dialogue, there is a real danger that strategic decisions are taken without the benefit of an external audit. In the cases of both Alexander and Napoleon, the result of this was the same: both leaders could not contain their ambitions and eventually outreached themselves. Napoleon was eventually defeated by the range of enemies he had acquired, and Alexander was forced to turn back when his army mutinied in India. Also, on occasions, the separation of political and military leaderships has worked extremely well. Cohen notes that strategic decision-making prospered once President Lincoln found General Grant to lead the Union war effort.[15]

The very nature of war as a physical activity also complicates the task of the practitioner of strategy. The nature of war is complex and may be defined with a number of terms. Excluding the policy rationale, which has already been dealt with in the earlier discussion on the nature of strategy, the following categories appear to capture the main features of war: violence, competition, and uncertainty (largely emanating from human interaction).

War cannot be understood without reference to violence: 'war is a clash between major interests, which is resolved by bloodshed – that is the only way in which it differs from other conflicts'.[16] Although violence may not occur in every strategic situation, it is always possible and indeed is the engine of policy effect: 'it is inherent in the very concept of war that everything that occurs *must originally derive from combat*' (emphasis in the original).[17] The presence of violence produces many challenging effects on those involved in strategy. Most obviously, violence diminishes one's forces. The loss of men and equipment reduces one's physical capability to achieve policy objectives. However, the effects of loss are felt not only at the physical level. The emotional impact of losses may affect the morale of troops and weaken the resolve of the public and/or the political decision makers. Thus, the strategist may have to navigate their way through stormy emotional waters while witnessing a reduction in their military capabilities. While correctly recognising the negative effects of violence on strategic performance, it is important not to present this issue in a simplistic, one-dimensional form. The relationship of violence to resolve and morale is complex. Being on the receiving end of violence can rouse a society into action and greater resolve. The determination of the United States to defeat Japan in the aftermath of Pearl Harbor is but one example of this effect.

The emergence of cyber power somewhat qualifies the omnipresence of violence in strategy. As will be discussed in Chapter 11, cyberattacks such as Bronze Soldier, Shamoon, and BlackEnergy suggest that strategic power can now be exercised in a virtual, nonviolent form. However, the relationship between cyber power, kinetic force, and violence is not so straightforward. The 2010 Stuxnet attack on the Iranian nuclear programme reveals that cyber power can cause physical destruction; the 2007 Israeli raid on the Syrian nuclear facility al Kibar shows that cyber power can be used as a force multiplier to kinetic force; and the 2019 Israeli airstrike on Hamas hackers provides evidence of an escalatory dynamic between cyber and violent kinetic force. Thus, although cyber power does provide the possibility of strategic action without violence, there exists an important relationship between the two. Cyber power does not exist in a nonviolent vacuum; rather, it sits in the violent world of strategy.

The competitive nature of war is self-evident, but no less important for that. Indeed, the role of the enemy must not be underestimated. When asked why the South had lost the battle of Gettysburg, the Confederate General George Pickett replied, 'I think the Union Army had something to do with it'.[18] In strategy, the existence of an intelligent foe substantially complicates the task of the practitioner in numerous ways and at all the levels of strategy. Not only is the enemy seeking to prevent one from reaching one's goals, but also, their objectives must be considered and may have to be countered. The enemy can complicate the nature of one's strategic tasks in many ways. For example, they may change the nature of the challenge entirely, by opening up a new front or acquiring new allies. Indeed, their new allies may include opponents within one's own country, in which case domestic subversion becomes a problem. In extremis, the enemy's existence may all but guarantee failure. Put simply, an opponent may be so powerful, or have such a strong resolve, that one has to rule out any chance of achieving one's objectives.

To note that war is a human activity infused with uncertainty is, in some respects, an unremarkable statement. When limited, error-prone humans are involved in any activity, uncertainty is almost always present. The simple task of getting to work on time is at the mercy of numerous factors that could cause delay. That being the case, there is always a small degree of uncertainty as to whether one will actually arrive on time. Of course, various steps can be taken to reduce this uncertainty. Leaving the house earlier than normal or making one's lunch the night before should enhance the chances of prompt arrival. However, a traffic accident caused by a distracted driver ahead will scupper one's best intentions. If we extrapolate from this simple example and apply the same logic to warfare, the uncertainties multiply. Not only are there more moving parts (both human and technology) involved; they are also under severe pressure from the actions of the enemy and hence are more likely to fail in their appointed tasks. The presence of the enemy also adds to the level of uncertainty since one cannot be sure of the enemy's intentions, the morale of their troops, or sometimes even the possible whereabouts of their forces. Uncertainty also emanates from the unknown results of future interaction among belligerents in a conflict.

Since the arrival of the information age, we have witnessed a host of claims that uncertainty can be significantly reduced in modern warfare.[19] The application of information technology to the battlespace is said to enable the realisation of operational concepts such as dominant battlespace knowledge and total situational awareness. While it is true that the physical assets of warfare are more visible in the contemporary era, uncertainty is still prevalent. Intangible elements, such as morale or levels of training, cannot be seen and quantified by overhead sensors; the enemy's intentions are likely to remain unknown in their entirety; and as the 1999 Kosovo conflict illustrates, enemies have proven adept at deceiving modern reconnaissance assets.[20] Furthermore, certain forms of warfare, such as terrorism and insurgency, are not based on large numbers of physical assets that can be so easily monitored and targeted. Uncertainty, therefore, will remain a feature in strategy.

So not only does the interface between military conflict and policy objectives impose strains on the efficacy of strategy, but the nature of the former also compounds the problem. Above all else, war is a human activity. Although technology plays a crucial role in warfare, the nature of war is largely the result of human involvement. Human involvement in war produces significant levels of uncertainty and unleashes powerful emotive forces in the face of violence and suffering. Within this challenging environment, humankind must strive to achieve its objectives in the face of an intelligent enemy who may be just as determined to reach their goals. The result of such an interaction can be devastating and costly, as was amply demonstrated in the First World War, when strategy stumbled to overcome a range of confounding factors.

The complexity of strategic practice is complicated further by its multidimensional nature. The idea that strategy can be broken down into component parts, or dimensions, can be found in the writings of Clausewitz and, more recently, Michael Howard.[21] However, it is Gray who has produced the most developed work on the multidimensional nature of strategy. In *Modern Strategy*, Gray identifies 17 dimensions, which he divides into three categories: people and politics (people, society, culture, politics, ethics), war preparation (economics and logistics, organisation, military administration, information and intelligence, strategic theory and doctrine, technology), and war proper (military operations, command, geography, friction, the adversary, time). The troubling aspect of this theory for the practitioner is Gray's comment that failure in any of the dimensions may lead to failure for an entire strategic enterprise.[22]

Box 1.3 The dimensions of strategy

Internal
People.
Politics.
Economics and logistics.
Organisation.
Military administration.
Intelligence.
Technology.
Military operations.
Command.
Theory and doctrine.

External
Time.
Geography.
Society.
Culture.
Ethics.
Adversary.
Friction.

In practice, the logical outcome of strategy's multidimensional nature is that the strategist must gain command of a vast range of related activities and concepts. This task is made even more difficult because some of the dimensions are not directly under the strategist's control. Indeed, we can helpfully think of the dimensions as being either internal or external to the process of strategy making. With reference to the internal dimensions, strategy is something one drives forward, something one can seek to control. At the same time, the external dimensions, of which there are seven, ensure that strategy has a dynamic nature beyond the driven process. The internal dimensions are people, politics, economics and logistics, organisation, military administration, intelligence, technology, military operations, command, theory, and doctrine. All of these dimensions, to a greater or lesser extent, are subject to some level of control and internal development. To illustrate, people can be selected and/or trained to ensure better strategic performance; policy can be adjusted to take account of military conditions; appropriate technology can be procured; and theory and doctrine can be studied and developed in a manner that facilitates a flexible and appropriate cognitive approach to likely strategic scenarios.

In contrast, the following external dimensions exist outside the process of strategy making: time, geography, society, culture, ethics, adversary, and friction. All of these dimensions impinge on the performance of strategy but cannot be directly affected by the actions of the strategist. Thankfully, these external dimensions can be influenced or managed, to some degree, via effective action in the internal dimensions. The relationship between the internal and external dimensions is complex, and an example of this process may help further explain the dynamics of strategy.

Time is perhaps the external dimension par excellence. In normal human experience, the linear progression of time is inexorable. The aphorism 'time waits for no one' has real significance in the conduct of strategy. Yet while time itself cannot be manipulated, the politics dimension can influence perceptions of time. Most importantly, politics should set policy objectives that are commensurate with a realistic timeframe. Similarly, action in the economics and logistics dimensions should provide the resources to sustain a war effort over the required period. The Second World War is illustrative of the interplay between time and economics and of how the latter can manipulate the former to create strategic advantage. As time passed, the Allies more effectively mobilised their economic resources. This was especially evident in the Pacific theatre, where from 1944 onwards, the United States deployed maritime resources that overwhelmed fierce Japanese resistance. The time dimension can also be manipulated via the method of waging war. In this way, the dimensions of theory and doctrine, military operations, command, technology, and intelligence all figure prominently (what we might call the warfighting dimensions). When time is against one's campaign, rapidly concluding that campaign may be essential. For those up against tactically and operationally superior foes, a protracted irregular campaign will prove useful.

The complexity of strategy is enhanced further by the polymorphous character of war. Although wars are all things of the same nature, each war differs in its details. These differences can be described in different ways and to varying levels of detail. The most basic taxonomy divides war into regular and irregular forms. The former most often describes warfare that is conducted by large, state-based, uniformed, well-equipped forces that have recognisable formations and command structures. By and large, regular forces attempt to apply the laws of war. In contrast, irregular warfare is the domain of insurgents and terrorists, which is based largely on infantry, are generally regarded as sub-state actors, are fewer in number, operate within less formal command structures, and may eschew uniforms and adherence to the laws of war. Strictly speaking, to the regular/irregular taxonomy, one should also add nuclear and cyber. These two categories of war are not normally given such recognition. This is possibly because, thankfully, nuclear war is not an everyday experience, and cyberwar is still a developing and contested phenomenon (see Chapters 11 and 12 for an exploration of these two distinct forms of strategy).

Although in theory regular and irregular forms of war can be neatly divided, the reality is far more complex. As in Vietnam, regular and irregular forms of warfare often coexist. Indeed, as was the case for Communist forces in Vietnam, it is possible to operate a strategy that is built on these two forms of warfare acting together. The Communists operated a two-pronged approach in their attempts to conquer South Vietnam. The North Vietnamese Army (NVA) presented a regular threat to US and South Vietnamese forces, while the Viet Cong (VC) operated predominately as an irregular insurgent force in the South. By adopting this strategy, the Communists substantially complicated the task of the Americans and their southern ally. In simple terms, defeating the NVA required firepower and the concentration of forces, whereas countering the VC called for a greater dispersal of forces and less aggressive operations to protect the populous and win their support. With NVA and VC forces operating side by side, the challenge posed to US commanders is obvious.

As discussed in Chapter 14, it is also the case that irregular forms of warfare can morph into regular operations and vice versa. This is the premise of Maoist revolutionary war theory, in which the objective is to graduate from irregular guerrilla operations to full-blown conventional warfare. Alternatively, as displayed by Ba'athist forces in Iraq, a regular army may disperse and transform itself into an irregular force when facing a conventionally superior foe.[23] The contemporary term 'hybrid warfare' – used, for example, in relation to Russian operations in Ukraine – attempts to reflect such complex realities, with the additional component of cyber operations. Although it is useful to recognise additional tools in the strategist's toolkit, it is important to acknowledge that these complex challenges have always existed in strategy.

Aside from its basic character (regular, irregular, nuclear, cyber), each war is affected by a range of other factors. These include the geography of the battlespace, the strategic culture of the belligerents, and the available technology. It takes little imagination to understand that with such a range of factors affecting the character of warfare, each conflict will be unique. This poses a substantial challenge for those with strategic responsibility, because each potential form of warfare requires different capabilities and preparations. Worse still, since the future is uncertain, the character of the next war remains unknown in precise detail. In the face of this complex polymorphous reality, defence planners must prepare for a range of possible futures, usually within the confines of limited budgets and competition among the different services for their share of the pie. An analysis of the security environment may give some indication of where the next threat is coming from. However, defence planning is not an exact science, and long procurement cycles may leave a state with capabilities out of kilter with changing security circumstances.

Within the reality of the polymorphous character of war, each strategic community will be more or less prepared to cope with certain forms of warfare. Certain strategic episodes are more suited to a state's strategic culture and sociopolitical sensibilities. For example, modern Western states tend to be more adept at fighting regular, time-limited wars against clearly identifiable enemies. As the recent wars in Iraq and Afghanistan suggest, these strategic actors do less well in protracted irregular conflicts. On the issue of modern Western states as strategic actors, in contrast to some accepted wisdom on the subject, the West does not unduly suffer from sensitivity to casualties. The American Civil War and the world wars of the twentieth century suggest that large sacrifices are sustainable in the right circumstances. What does seem to be true is that Western societies are less comfortable with protracted wars of choice in which progress is difficult to identify. We can conclude that in the face of the polymorphous character of war a strategic community must remain flexible in its capabilities, strategic culture, and indeed its approach to the whole business of strategy.

As an important aside, focusing on the polymorphous character of war should not prevent us from acknowledging commonalities in strategic experience. Many conflicts share certain features. It is this that allows us to learn from history. Despite being over two thousand years apart, Alexander the Great's tactical approach and the German operational concept of blitzkrieg share some important characteristics. Both were based on a combined-arms force, within which infantry supported a rapidly moving spearhead (Alexander's instrument of decision was the heavy companion cavalry). Furthermore, the success of both of these forms of warfare relied on the ability to punch a hole in the enemy's lines and thereby break their cohesion and resistance. Thus, another of the great challenges for the strategist is that they must learn from history, appreciating commonalties in historical experience, but seek to apply these lessons learned in unique strategic episodes.

Much of the discussion concerning the challenges of strategy so far can be corralled within the Clausewitzian concept of friction: 'the only concept that more or less corresponds to the factors that distinguish real war from war on paper'.[24] Friction has been most expertly dissected in the 'unified concept of general friction', as identified by Barry D. Watts. This taxonomy contains danger; physical exertion; uncertainties and imperfections in information; resistance in one's own forces; chance events; physical and political limits on the use of force; unpredictability stemming from interaction with the enemy; disconnects between the ends and the means.[25] One could legitimately edit Watts's taxonomy, adding or subtracting various causes of friction. However, the notion of friction as a master concept in strategy is valid. The idea that strategy on paper is a different beast to strategy in practice is an essential truth. The process of converting military force into positive and successful policy effect has to overcome myriad difficulties. It is thus vital that strategic practitioners expect friction and create systems and capabilities able to deal with it. To use a boxing analogy, in the face of friction, strategy must learn to roll with the punches.

Dealing with the challenges of strategy

The earlier discussion seems ominous for those in the business of strategy. However, those with responsibility for strategic performance can take a number of steps to help alleviate the impact of the difficulties just mentioned. In particular, they can engage in study and reflection on strategy, develop appropriate forces, and foster the correct strategic culture in their respective security communities. Perhaps most importantly, they can seek to identify and foster talented commanders. Alternatively, if natural talent is thin on the ground, they can establish command structures and cultures that enable competent generals to produce good decisions.

In the practical world of strategy, the value of theory is open to discussion. Put bluntly, strategic success is not necessarily premised on the study of strategic theory (although more knowledge and reflection should help). The process of converting military power into policy effect is not abstract or unfathomable, although it is challenging and sometimes subtle. Some of the great practitioners of strategy, such as Alexander the Great and Napoleon, seem to display a natural affinity for strategy. In this sense, they appear to be innately attuned to how military force can be used for policy effect. Alexander enjoyed such outstanding levels of success over such a long period of time (12 years), and in many varied contexts, that it is reasonable to conclude that he must have had some natural ability for strategy. Perhaps he was endowed with a particularly keen intellect and/or with innate leadership qualities. Napoleon was also said to possess outstanding cognitive abilities.[26] Such conclusions should not surprise us. The notion that the great practitioners have a natural affinity for strategy should no more surprise us than the idea that great artists have a natural artistic gift.

Be that as it may, the abilities of Alexander and Napoleon were undoubtedly enhanced by the study of strategy. Napoleon extolled the virtues of historical research on past campaigns, while Alexander must have learned much from his father, Phillip II.[27] Strategy is such a complex activity that serious study must be considered a sensible requirement, especially as the subject matter carries such import. As Sun Tzu noted, 'War is a matter of vital importance to the state; the province of life or death; the road to survival or ruin. It is mandatory that it be thoroughly studied'.[28] Thus, in an attempt to follow the advice of the Chinese theorist, the practitioner is well advised to become a student of both theory and history. The requirement for learning is even more essential when one considers that people of Alexander and Napoleon's ilk are few and far between. The absence of what Clausewitz called military geniuses must be compensated for. It is thus important for the armed services to institute formal educational programmes into their officer training regimes. Unfortunately, while education in theory and history can be found in most modern staff colleges, it still often plays second fiddle to more practical subjects such as procurement and defence management. In tight teaching schedules, Clausewitz is breezed through in order to give more time to understand the workings of the Ministry of Defence. As problematic as the modern military's approach to theory and history is, it is nothing compared to that of their political masters. Although they may occasionally read important books on strategy, there is little evidence to suggest that Western political leaders take the time to attain an understanding of the workings of strategy or its practice in history.[29]

While correctly identifying the importance of an education in strategic theory and history, it is important to note the limits of academic ruminations in the practical field of strategy. Since strategy is a complex pursuit, infused by intangible forces, no work of theory can provide a formula for success. This is not the purpose of theory, as Clausewitz reminds us:

> Theory cannot equip the mind with formulas for solving problems, nor can it mark the narrow path on which the sole solution is supposed to lie by planting a hedge of principles on either side. But it can give the mind insight into the great mass of phenomena and of their relationships, then leaves it free to rise into the higher realms of action.[30]

Theory, then, does not provide the answers, but it does fulfil an invaluable role by identifying the important phenomena in strategy and how they interact. One might say that theory enables us to ask the right questions, or that theory trains the mind. In this way, the teaching of strategy in professional military education (PME) must make use of conceptual frameworks that enable the strategist to better comprehend unique strategic situations through the prism of enduring themes.[31] It is also important to foster the ability to think intuitively.[32]

For theory to be useful, just how closely related to practice must it be? The answer to this question is different depending on whether one is discussing strategic theory writ large or individual works. Brodie is essentially correct when he comments that strategic theory is theory for action.[33] On this basis, strategic theory as a whole must have a strong sense of the possible. However, this does not mean that each work of theory must talk to the practitioner. The value of an individual piece may come from the contribution it makes to the development of thought, even if it has no obvious and direct relationship to practice. From this perspective, the contribution of any particular work to practice may not surface for some time, and indeed the relationship between theory and practice may be indirect. So long as a theorist is contributing to our general understanding of military force as an instrument of policy, their work is valid. Furthermore, in line with Clausewitz's comment that theory works by training the mind of the commander, a work of strategic theory can have value without offering principles or making direct reference to existing issues in the practice of strategy. In this sense, the theorist can make an important contribution merely by stimulating the mind of a practitioner in relation to the nature of strategy.

Moreover, although there is obvious value in theory addressing the issues of the day, there are also inherent dangers in such an approach. Thomas C. Schelling, one of the great strategic thinkers of the Cold War, warned of the dangers of theorists constructing theory solely in response to the practical demands of the day: 'those who have grappled with ideas like deterrence, being motivated largely by immediate problems, have not primarily been concerned with the cumulative process of developing a theoretical structure'.[34] As identified by Schelling, theory that is devoted to the needs of the practitioner runs the risk of being underdeveloped or being developed in such a way that its universality, in both time and space, is endangered.

A talented strategist, hopefully with a decent understanding of theory and history, still requires forces of a reasonable quality and quantity (relative to the task at hand) to succeed. Experienced and/or well-trained forces are better able to deal with the uncertainties and challenges (both emotional and physical) that result from the nature of war and friction. Both Alexander the Great and his father, Phillip II, benefited from having a core of professional troops. The significance of this can be seen most clearly at the battle of Chaeronea, where Phillip's Macedonian forces comprehensively defeated the part-time forces of the Greek city-states. Of course, great commanders usually do not simply inherit good forces. Rather, a great commander is often regarded as such, in part, because of their ability to transform ordinary forces into a well-honed cohesive instrument. This was certainly the case with Phillip II and with Major General John E. Sloan, who is credited for transforming the US 88th Infantry Division during the Second World War.[35]

Just as the quality of forces is important, so it is with the quantity of troops and equipment. Sufficient numbers can enable a commander to pursue their objectives in the face of losses and protracted operations. Reserves and replacements can be crucial to cope with unexpected losses or to exploit new opportunities. The old Russian adage that 'quantity has a quality all of its own' still has much to recommend it. Towards the end of the Second World War, Germany's war effort suffered substantially from insufficient numbers of troops and material. For example, its efforts to defend the Reich from allied bombing raids were hampered by an increasingly small cadre of experienced pilots.[36] Of course, however desirable it may be to have sufficiently large forces, it is not always possible. There may be many reasons (including population trends, cultural attitudes to conflict, and budgetary constraints) why a commander has only limited forces at their disposal. Thus, whatever the situation may be in terms of resources available, it is important for those responsible for strategy to consider issues of quantity, relative to the task at hand and the nature of strategy, as described earlier.

In this discussion of troops and equipment, it is also worth singing the praises of technology. Although, quite correctly, the value of technology has been questioned in the counter-RMA discourse, one must be careful not to throw the baby out with the bathwater. Having superior and appropriate technology in sufficient numbers can confer significant advantage. Although technological advantage will struggle to overcome factors such as poor strategy or incompetent command, all things being equal, it can make a substantial difference at the tactical and operational levels. In terms of technology, the relationship between quantity and quality is complex. In the Normandy campaign, Allied armour came out on top, despite the relative inferiority of its tanks. One-on-one, most Allied tanks could not match the German Panther or Tiger tanks. However, in terms of crude numbers, there were simply too many Allied tanks for the Germans to cope with. A Panther would run out of shells before the Allies ran out of tanks.[37]

Waging war, like all other social activities, is to some degree influenced by culture. Just how much influence culture has, or should have, on strategy is open to debate.[38] In terms of whether or not strategic culture is a valid concept, the debate can be divided between those who perceive cultural differences among security communities and those who give more weight to the notion of a strategic person. The latter suggest that different actors will make similar rational choices given a similar set of circumstances. As with much in life, the truth about strategic culture lies somewhere in between these two differing perspectives, with perhaps the balance leaning in favour of those who subscribe to cultural differences. While security actors often do act on the basis of rationality and an understanding of best strategic practice, their actions may be bounded by cultural considerations. During the sixteenth century, Philip II of Spain, although well informed and capable of sound strategic judgements, was culturally bound by his Catholic faith. Regarding himself as defender of the faith, Philip could not contemplate compromise with his enemies. It was this position that partly led Spain to the ill-fated attempted invasion of the United Kingdom in 1566.

For those seeking ways to deal with the complexities and difficulties of strategy, strategic culture is of supreme importance. As Clausewitz identified, due to its competitive nature, war has an escalatory tendency. That being the case, he provides a warning to those who would seek, for cultural reasons, to moderate war's violent tendency: 'If one side uses force without compunction, undeterred by the bloodshed it involves, while the other side refrains, the first will gain the upper hand'.[39] Thus, an inappropriate strategic culture will leave an actor unprepared to deal with the harsh realities of strategic competition. This was certainly the case for the Greek city-states when they faced the rising power of Macedonia at the battle of Chaeronea. The warfare practised in Greece at that time was quasi-ritualistic in nature; was regulated by shared norms; normally tolerated only light casualties; and had little appetite for pursuit of a defeated enemy. This culturally restrained form of warfare was devastatingly swept aside by the total warfare practised by Macedonia. Thus, it is imperative that modern security communities develop and maintain a strategic culture that accepts the violent and competitive nature of strategy. If this is not achieved, these same communities are likely to struggle in the face of strategy's many challenges. More importantly, they will be at a distinct disadvantage relative to those whose strategic culture is more in tune with the realities of strategy. There is clearly a complex relationship at work between strategy and culture. It would be simplistic to claim either that strategy is all culture or that the rational actor can dispense with cultural concerns and influences.

All of the measures just described can make important contributions when seeking to alleviate the difficulties of strategic practice. Nonetheless, strategy is a human activity, and as such, success requires human judgement, as Churchill noted: '[war's] highest solution must be evolved from the eye and brain and soul of a single man. . . . nothing but genius, the demon in man, can answer the riddles of war'.[40] If nothing else, strategy is concerned with politics, which in turn is about human interactions. In the world of politics, perception is critical. Subtle changes can have significant consequences. Thus, it takes the human mind to understand and deal with human affairs. Even then, misjudgement and misperception are to be expected. How will the enemy react? How will we react? How will the public respond? The answers to such questions as these are never likely to be more than educated guesses. Human participation also brings with it emotive forces and intangible variables. Factors such as morale, intentions, and public perceptions are difficult to predict accurately and/or control. Consequently, despite best efforts to reduce the effect of uncertainty and complexity in modern strategy, predictable and quantifiable outcomes are not possible. It is thus the burden of the strategic practitioner to make their best call on these and many other issues.

The earlier paragraphs have not only identified significant challenges in the practice of strategy but also noted that the potential solution (human judgement) comes with no guarantees. On this basis, one could be forgiven for thinking that success in strategy is rare. And yet history reveals that policy objectives are often met, albeit sometimes at higher-than-anticipated costs. Part of the reason for success can be found in Clausewitz's concept of the military genius. Although the Prussian theorist may have been writing about exceptional individuals, such as Napoleon, we can apply some of his criteria for military genius more generally to competent commanders. In this sense, security communities can ease the challenge of strategy by identifying and/or developing military geniuses. Alternatively, in the absence of naturally talented commanders, they can institute command procedures and training that can provide some compensation. However, as the mistakes made by Alexander the Great and Napoleon testify, there are no guarantees even in the presence of genius. In that case, the other aids to strategic practice may prove their worth.

When considering what constitutes a military genius, Clausewitz identified a number of characteristics: physical and moral courage; incisiveness; presence of mind; strength of will and character; an ambitious nature; determination; and coup d'oeil.[41] Taken together, these traits not only will help the commander identify the route to success but also should enable them to better deal with the inevitable friction that occurs along the way. This applies not only to the mechanics of warfare but also to the aforementioned emotional, intangible aspects of the profession. Leadership, determination, and moral courage are all important in this respect. Concerning the cultural and social dimensions of strategy, in recognition of the limits of human aptitude, it is important that society (including the media and politicians) is tolerant (to a point) of mistakes and failures. Due to friction and the array of challenges encountered, even the most talented of strategists is likely to have setbacks. This is even more likely to occur when we consider that each strategic situation is unique, and therefore, the commander must, to some degree, learn as they go along.

Conclusion

Strategy, *the process that converts military power into policy effect*, is a complex and challenging activity. Military power and policy objectives are not always suitable bedfellows. The former may be too blunt and too costly for the refined tastes of the latter. Similarly, policy may sometimes be too demanding of the military instrument. As troubling as this is for the strategic practitioner, this tense relationship between the military and policy worlds is but one obstacle to success among many. Also note strategy's multidimensional nature; the polymorphous character of war; the nature of war; and Clausewitz's universal concept of friction. Despite these many obstacles to success, military power is a surprisingly flexible tool of policy. It can be used for defence, offence, deterrence, coercion, and various miscellaneous uses. To achieve success in these pursuits, the strategic practitioner should take a number of steps. In particular, they should seek education in theory and history (raising their awareness of the multidimensional nature of strategy and how to control and manipulate relationships among the dimensions); acquire and develop forces sufficient in quantity and quality; nurture an appropriate strategic culture; and develop a command process that enables military geniuses to flourish or compensates for their absence. With these in place, the strategist will be best placed to take on the challenge of strategy in its many environments and forms.

Key points

1 The nature of strategy is unchanging.
2 Strategy is primarily concerned with the process of converting military power into policy effect.
3 Strategy is difficult.
4 Strategy is a multidimensional activity.
5 The internal dimensions can be controlled to manage the effects of the external dimensions.
6 The difficulties of strategy can be mitigated by good theory, good and ample forces, and outstanding commanders.

Questions

1 What is strategy?
2 Why is strategy so difficult?
3 Can the challenges of strategy be overcome?
4 How does the nature of strategy influence the conduct of strategy in different contexts?

Notes

1 Deterrence is discussed in more detail in Chapter 12: 'Nuclear Strategy'. An excellent introduction to the subject is Lawrence Freedman, *Deterrence* (Cambridge, Polity Press, 2004).
2 Thomas C. Schelling, *Arms and Influence* (New Haven, CT, Yale University Press, 1966).

3 Daniel Byman and Matthew Waxman, *The Dynamics of Coercion: American Foreign Policy and the Limits of Military Might* (Cambridge, Cambridge University Press, 2002).

4 Carl von Clausewitz, *On War* (Princeton, NJ, Princeton University Press, 1976), p. 177.

5 Basil H. Liddel Hart, *Strategy: The Indirect Approach* (London, Faber and Faber, 1967), p. 335.

6 Andre Beaufre, *An Introduction to Strategy: With Particular Reference to the Problems of Defence, Politics, Economics, and Diplomacy in the Nuclear Age* (London, Faber and Faber, 1965), p. 22.

7 Colin S. Gray, *Modern Strategy* (Oxford, Oxford University Press, 1999), p. 17.

8 Clausewitz, p. 606.

9 Liddel Hart, *Strategy*, pp. 335–6.

10 Ivo H. Daalder and Michael E. O'Hanlon, *Winning Ugly: NATO's War to Save Kosovo* (Washington, DC, Brookings Institution Press, 2000), p. 64.

11 Williamson Murray convincingly argues in his *Military Adaptation in War* that incompetence is the norm in strategy and other complex human activities. Williamson Murray, *Military Adaptation in War: With Fear of Change* (Cambridge, Cambridge University Press, 2011).

12 The problem of disharmony is well discussed in Edward N. Luttwak, *Strategy: The Logic of War and Peace* (Cambridge, MA, The Belknap Press, 1987).

13 Jurgen E. Forster, 'The Dynamics of Volksgemeinschaft: The Effectiveness of the German Military Establishment in the Second World War', in Allan R. Millett and Williamson Murray (eds.), *Military Effectiveness, Volume 3: The Second World War* (Cambridge, Cambridge University Press, 2010), p. 181.

14 Eliot A. Cohen, *Supreme Command: Soldiers, Statesmen, and Leadership in Wartime* (New York, The Free Press, 2002).

15 Ibid.

16 Clausewitz, p. 173.

17 Ibid., p. 108.

18 Quoted in R.L. DiNardo and Daniel J. Hughes, 'Some Cautionary Thoughts on Information Warfare', *Airpower Journal* 9:4 (1995), p. 76.

19 See Chapter 4 for a detailed discussion of these ideas.

20 Benjamin S. Lambeth, *NATO's Air War for Kosovo: A Strategic and Operational Assessment* (Santa Monica, RAND, 2001).

21 Michael Howard, 'The Forgotten Dimensions of Strategy', *Foreign Affairs* 57:5 (1979), pp. 975–86.

22 Gray, *Modern Strategy*, p. 25.

23 This subject is discussed in more detail in Chapter 14.

24 Clausewitz, p. 119.

25 Barry D. Watts, *Clausewitzian Friction and Future War*, McNair Paper 52 (Washington, DC, Institute for National Strategic Studies, National Defence University, 1996).

26 David Gates, *The Napoleonic Wars 1803–1815* (London, Arnold, 1997), p. 2.

27 David Chandler, *The Campaigns of Napoleon* (London, Weidenfeld and Nicolson, 1966), p. 139.

28 Sun Tzu, *The Art of War*, trans. Samuel B. Griffith (London, Oxford University Press, 1971), p. 63.

29 However, President Bush did read Eliot Cohen's book *Supreme Command*. See John Keegan, 'Servant of a Theory', www.spectator.co.uk/books/20316/servant-of-a-theory.thtml

30 Clausewitz, p. 578.

31 D. Auerswald, J. Breslin-Smith, and P. Thornhili, 'Teaching Strategy through Theory and Practice', *Defence Studies* 4:1 (2004), p. 1.

32 Colin S. Gray, *The Strategy Bridge: Theory for Practice* (Oxford, Oxford University Press, 2010), p. 55.

33 Bernard Brodie, *War and Politics* (London, Cassell, 1974), p. 452.

34 Schelling, *The Strategy of Conflict*, p. 7.

35 I would like to thank Norman Murphy for bringing this example to my attention. For more details, see John Sloan Brown, *Draftee Division* (Lexington, University Press of Kentucky, 1986).

36 Williamson Murray, *The Luftwaffe 1933–45: Strategy for Defeat* (London, Brassey's, 1996), p. 275.

37 John Ellis, *Brute Force: Allied Strategy and Tactics in the Second World War* (London, Andre Deutsch Ltd., 1990).

38 For a detailed analysis of culture in strategy, see Chapter 2.

39 Clasuewtiz, pp. 83–4.

40 Winston S. Churchill, quoted in M. Carver, 'Montgomery', in John Keegan (ed.), *Churchill's Generals* (London, Weidenfeld and Nicolson, 1991), p. 139.

41 Clausewitz, pp. 100–12.

Further reading

Aron, Raymond, *Peace and War: A Theory of International Relations*, trans. By Richard Howard and Annette Baker Fox, (New York: Anchor Press & Doubleday, 1973).

Brodie, Bernard, *War and Politics*, (New York, 1973).

Cohen, Eliot A., *Supreme Command: Soldiers, Statesmen, and Leadership in Wartime*, (New York: The Free Press, 2002).

Freedman, Lawrence, *Strategy: A History*, (Oxford: Oxford University Press, 2013).

Gray, Colin S., *Theory of Strategy*, (Oxford: Oxford University Press, 2018).

Lonsdale, David J., *Alexander the Great: Lessons in Strategy*, (Abingdon: Routledge, 2007).

Luttwak, Edward N., *Strategy: The Logic of War and Peace*, (Cambridge, MA: The Belknap Press, 1987).

von Clausewitz, Carl, *On War*, (Princeton, NJ: Princeton University Press, 1976).

Wylie, J.C., *Military Strategy: A General Theory of Power Control*, (Annapolis, MD: Naval Institute Press, 1967).

Tzu, Sun, *The Art of War*, trans. By Samuel B. Griffith, (London: Oxford Univeristy Press, 1971).

The human dimension   **2**

Reader's guide

How culture and psychology influence strategy; attempts to control these factors; strategic culture; morale; combat motivation and unit cohesion; the psychology of terrorists and suicide attackers.

Introduction

To make strategy effectively, one must account for the culture and psychology of the people involved in the process. At the level of war planning, one must pay attention to the courage and other mental characteristics of military personnel, both friendly and enemy. Iraqi leader Saddam Hussein's 1991 plan to bloody his United Nations opponents in 'the mother of all battles' evaporated when a significant proportion of his troops surrendered without attempting to fight. At the level of grand strategy, one must pay attention to civilian attitudes as well. The Communist leaders of North Vietnam understood that they could never destroy the U.S. Army on the battlefield, but they successfully waged a campaign to defeat the United States by exploiting its own political system.

Culture and psychology influence the types of strategies that people adopt and their willingness to engage in them. While most armies in the Second World War devoted time and resources to avoiding and disarming landmines, Soviet commanders cleared minefields by marching their own infantry through them. Culture and psychology organisation play an equally important role in shaping peoples' economic behaviour – and, thus, their access to strategically significant resources. For these reasons, influential strategic thinkers acknowledge that it is impossible to understand strategy without studying the human context in which it takes place.

When one investigates the role of culture and psychology in strategy, one encounters a third factor: politics. The reason why the North Vietnamese could frustrate U.S. Military policy 'on the streets of New York' is that the United States is a democracy. One of the reasons why Soviet commanders could get away with marching their own troops through minefields is that their country was not. Not only did the fact that the United States is a democracy force national leaders to pay attention to public opinion, but also, as suggested by political thinkers from Immanuel Kant to (among others) Francis Fukuyama, democratic political systems reduce their citizens' willingness to tolerate certain kinds of wars. Undemocratic political systems typically attempt to condition their people to adopt certain attitudes towards war as well, sometimes with more success than others.

Carl von Clausewitz summed up the significance of culture, psychology, and politics in his famous statement that war is 'merely' a 'continuation of political intercourse' in all its social and personal complexity.[1] Elsewhere, he emphasised that 'war should never be thought of as *something autonomous*' (emphasis in original).[2] According to Clausewitz, there is no one phenomenon called war. Different wars waged under different social and political circumstances are fundamentally different things.

Strategists and government

In principle, Clausewitz's politician and commander do not always have to resign themselves to the sociopolitical circumstances that they find themselves in. Leaders may attempt to modify these factors through means such as giving their troops patriotic speeches or instituting new laws designed to prepare the country for war. Certain political movements have even attempted to use the powers of government to reprogramme citizens' minds. The authorities in the Soviet Union, for instance, spoke of creating a New Soviet Man. For these reasons, any discussion of human factors in strategy must overlap with discussions of the role of the armed forces in national government.

There often appear to be strategic advantages in giving the armed forces a large role. Nevertheless, it is dangerous for a country to allow the military to become too deeply involved in broader political issues. States that fail to separate the role of the armed forces from the role of civilian government risk evolving into dictatorships. Perhaps because of US President Dwight Eisenhower's experience as a general, he was acutely concerned that what he called the military-industrial complex would deprive American citizens of their freedom. Undemocratic governments face, if anything, even greater dangers from their own armed forces. Of all Adolph Hitler's enemies, the ones that came the closest to assassinating him were German officers who felt that he was mismanaging strategy.

One may counter that people who lose wars are also at risk of losing their preferred systems of government. For this reason, practically all states grant the armed forces more political influence in wartime. Certain strategic thinkers have gone further by suggesting that no matter how much people might want to have a civilian government with the power to control the military, they cannot afford to. This idea was particularly popular among the total war theorists of the 1920s and 1930s.

British strategist J.F.C. Fuller, whose ideas about how to use tanks and aircraft anticipated the so-called blitzkrieg campaigns of the Second World War, summed up what many of these theorists believed about the relationship between strategy and politics. 'War to-day is total', Fuller begins; 'therefore it includes everything, therefore it influences everything, and therefore, in turn, it is influenced by everything'. This led him to conclude that parliamentary systems of government should be 'rationalised' by being transformed into dictatorships.[3]

Those who believe in liberal democracy (or other political ideals) might respond that even if dictatorships have a military advantage, other systems of government are inherently worth preserving. American revolutionary Benjamin Franklin expressed this point with the line 'Those who would give up essential Liberty, to purchase a little temporary Safety, deserve neither Liberty nor Safety'. Moreover, military governments have not proven as strategically effective as total war theorists such as Fuller expected them to be.

The army officers who governed Argentina from 1976 to 1983 provide an example of how badly military governments can mismanage strategy. Argentina's economy deteriorated under their rule. This undermined the country's ability to maintain its military over the long term. Then, in April 1982, general and head of state Leopoldo Galtieri ordered his armed forces to invade the British-held Falkland Islands.

Galtieri's timing was abominable. When Argentina attacked, the British government had recently announced plans to cut its naval forces. If Galtieri had waited for the cuts to take place, he would have faced a weaker opponent. Moreover, if Galtieri had waited, his own forces would have been better equipped. One of Argentina's most effective weapons systems was the air-launched Exocet anti-ship missile. One of Argentina's key handicaps was that its pilots had only five operational Exocets at their disposal. When Galtieri attacked the Falklands, Argentina was waiting for French technicians to outfit its forces with nine additional Exocets.

Having occupied the islands, Galtieri's regime rejected further opportunities to improve his forces' capabilities. If the general had ordered his troops to extend the airstrip outside the Falkland capital of Port Stanley by 2000 feet, Argentina would have been able to operate a wider range of combat aircraft over the warzone. Extending the runway was unlikely to have required more than a week, and Argentina's armed forces had sufficient materials and trained engineers to carry out this project sitting idly on the mainland. Instead of improving the runway, Galtieri chose to use his country's transport aircraft to garrison the islands with the maximum possible number of lightly armed conscript infantry. The size of this garrison made it difficult to supply, its lack of heavy weapons made it vulnerable, and its reluctant troops proved inferior to British professionals.

Argentina's military government also neglected to prepare its troops for the islands' harsh climate, wasted opportunities to strengthen its army's defences against a British attempt to retake the islands, failed to work out an effective system for achieving cooperation between its navy and air force, and used its resources unimaginatively in combat. Within a month, a British taskforce arrived to recapture the Falkland Islands. Although the British and Argentinean contingents appeared similar in numbers and in the quality of their equipment, the United Kingdom won a decisive victory, retaking the islands and killing approximately three of Argentina's troops for every soldier it lost of its own. Galtieri and his subordinates gave up control over Argentina's government the following year, turning their power over to a democratic regime.

Researcher Samuel P. Huntington argues that Galtieri's failings are typical of military officers who attempt to govern. Huntington's study remains one of the most influential works on the nature of the military profession and on the relationship that military officers should have with civilian politicians. Politics and military strategy demand different skills and reward different mental attitudes. Few people can be effective at both at once. Moreover, when military officers do politicians' jobs, they almost inevitably end up disagreeing over political issues. This undermines their ability to work together in the way that soldiers, sailors, and fliers must.

Another reason why few strategic theorists recommend large-scale programmes to change friendly governments and societies is that few practising strategists have the opportunity to put such programmes into action. Certain well-connected military officers or other officials may be able to take over their own government in a coup. Leaders of a victorious revolutionary movement may be able to force their country's inhabitants to accept a completely new way of life. The majority of all military commanders and civilian strategists go through their entire careers without getting the chance to do either of these things. Moreover, some aspects of human psychology and national culture are impossible to change through political means, even for the most powerful revolutionary leader.

Furthermore, staging a successful coup or revolution is likely to involve enormous costs and risks. Foreign enemies may well take advantage of the new regime's weakness. Therefore, although it is theoretically possible to achieve strategic advantages by transforming one's own political system, strategic thinkers normally find it wiser to take a more modest approach. Few would deny that military officers and civilian strategists need cooperation from their government to do their job effectively. Nevertheless, most contemporary strategic theorists would agree that strategists should accept civilian control.

Nor, most strategic thinkers would add, can means be given priority over their purpose. To do so, as the saying goes, is to put the cart before the horse. For these reasons, the rest of this chapter will focus on relatively fixed aspects of culture and psychology. Although large-scale attempts to re-engineer society by putting the armed forces in charge of its government are part of the human context of strategy, what remains of this chapter will pay comparatively little attention to them.

Culture and strategy

People from different cultural backgrounds appear to have distinctive attitudes towards war and strategy and to behave accordingly. The fifteenth-century political thinker Niccolò Machiavelli lamented that although his fellow Italians were courageous as individuals, they had little aptitude for organised warfare. Five hundred years later, the Italian military suffered from much the same handicap in the Second World War. In a similar fashion, one may generalise that American strategists characteristically rely on overwhelming their enemies with firepower, that Russian military commanders characteristically rely on overwhelming their enemies with superior numbers of troops, and that British national leaders prefer to use their navy rather than their army, simply to pick three examples of frequently valid cultural generalisations.

One may find exceptions to all such claims. Not only is it unfair to judge people based on cultural stereotypes, but it can also be a fatal mistake. Before World War Two, some American military thinkers assumed that the Japanese were nationally incapable of developing effective air forces. Japanese pilots proved them wrong at Pearl Harbor.

Box 2.1 Dysfunctional strategic cultures

One of the most spectacular examples of a dysfunctional strategic culture is that of fifteenth-century China. In the 1200s, the Chinese developed naval forces, shipbuilding technology, and an extensive overseas trading network, partially because Mongol invaders had deprived them of their inland sources of wealth. When the Mongols conquered China, they maintained China's fleet and maritime industry so that they could use it themselves. Mongol ruler Kublai Khan compelled his Chinese and Korean subjects to build the ships for his ill-fated invasion of Japan. The Mongols also used Chinese ships to collect tribute from remote provinces of their empire, and in 1329, these offerings amounted to a record 247,000 tons of cargo.[4]

In 1368, Chinese patriots drove out the Mongols and re-established an independent Chinese state, ruled by the emperors of the Ming dynasty. The first Ming rulers continued to encourage maritime trade and to commission militarily powerful imperial fleets. Chinese ships of this era were more seaworthy and more capable in battle than their European counterparts. China's period of maritime supremacy reached its zenith when Emperor Cheng Zi dispatched a court eunuch named Cheng Ho to lead a fleet of so-called treasure ships on a series of voyages to the Indian Ocean.

Cheng Ho defended Chinese colonists living in Sumatra, convinced the rulers of numerous countries to offer submission to China, and, on one voyage, overthrew the ruler of Ceylon. Each time he returned to China, his treasure ships arrived laden with valuables, medicines, exotic animals, and novelty items for the emperor. Meanwhile, other Chinese admirals suppressed the *wokou* pirates who plagued Asian coasts during this period. Chinese diplomats compelled the Japanese rulers to help them against the *wokou* by threatening to invade Japan. The fact that the Japanese took their threat seriously indicates both that China's fleets were powerful and that Chinese rulers were able to use those fleets to strategic advantage.

Nevertheless, cultural factors made it difficult for China's rulers to embrace their empire's status as a maritime power. Chinese moralists traditionally urged rulers to live simply, avoid warfare, and devote state resources to helping the common people. These moralists also warned against any activities that brought Chinese people into contact with foreign barbarians and encouraged them to take up barbarian ways. Such moralists could easily depict the treasure ships as aggressive, extravagant, and corrupting. Moreover, a faction within the Chinese government had an interest in portraying maritime activities this way.

The scholars who managed China's bureaucracy were traditional rivals of the eunuchs who made up the Emperor's personal staff. Since the eunuchs controlled the treasure ships, the scholar-bureaucrats opposed the treasure ship programme. From the early 1400s onwards, the scholars used the moral arguments just mentioned to convince a series of rulers to impose progressively more restrictive limits on sailing and shipbuilding. In 1525, the scholars convinced the emperor of the time to ban all ships with more than one mast, and in 1555, the imperial court decreed that setting sail in an seafaring ship was a crime equivalent to espionage.

With no Chinese navy to suppress them, the *wokou* flourished. Raiders harried China's coasts practically at will. Over the centuries, China's rulers relaxed the anti-shipping laws, but the population of sailors and artisans who had made China a sea power in the early 1400s had gone. Meanwhile, in other parts of the world, maritime technology had advanced rapidly. By the time of the Opium War during 1839–40, the United Kingdom's Royal Navy was able to defeat the entire Chinese empire with a squadron of 16 medium-sized vessels.[5]

Crude prejudice is a handicap, in strategy as everywhere else. Nevertheless, the fact that cultural generalisations are unreliable does not mean that they cannot be useful. Strategists never get to enjoy perfect information. Those who remember the limits of generalisation may be able to use their knowledge of various peoples' cultures to gain greater insight into what their enemies, their allies, and even their own forces are likely to do in critical situations.

Strategic theorist Colin Gray, a pioneer in the study of strategic culture, uses the battle of Trafalgar to illustrate this point.[6] This battle took place during the United Kingdom's wars with Napoleonic France. The French and their Spanish allies had assembled a larger navy than the British had. This allowed them to threaten the United Kingdom's fleet.

British Vice-Admiral Horatio Nelson decided to strike first. Moreover, he ordered the ships under his command to form columns and sail straight into the opposing Franco-Spanish fleet. This was dangerous, since it allowed the French and Spanish to fire their cannon at the approaching British ships. During the opening phase of the battle, the column formation made it difficult for the British to shoot back.

Nelson's tactic, however, allowed the British to break into the enemy formation and duel Franco-Spanish ships at close range. The British Vice-Admiral guessed, correctly, that his enemies would be unprepared for this type of fighting. Nelson successfully guided his own flagship into combat with the enemy command vessel and crippled it. The captains of the French and Spanish vessels responded individually and ineffectively, allowing Nelson's numerically smaller fleet to destroy them one by one.

Gray notes that the British commander's earlier encounters with French and Spanish sailors had given him reasons to expect that his opponents would react timidly to an aggressive manoeuvre. Nelson could not have been sure that his previous experiences were still valid. The French and Spanish could have learned from their past mistakes. Nevertheless, the British commander had to do something to counteract his enemies' advantages. He took a calculated risk, and it paid off.

Not only do citizens of various countries have recognisable strategic cultures, but so do other groups of people. Those from similar economic backgrounds, for instance, often have similar attitudes even when they come from different parts of the world. Older people often have characteristically different perspectives from those of younger people. Men typically play different cultural roles in war from women. Professional military personnel have a different culture from civilians and short-term conscripts. Officers have a different culture from enlisted personnel. Each branch of the armed services has its own ways of doing things.

One could list many more cultural groups that may have their own ways of thinking about strategy. Moreover, the various forms of strategic culture blend and overlap. Not only is there a French culture, a military culture, and a naval culture, but the French navy has a culture of its own. A French admiral belongs to all of these cultures at once, and many more. There may be times when the fact that a certain strategist falls into one cultural category is important and other times when the fact that that strategist falls into other categories makes more of a difference. Those who wish to study the role of culture in a specific strategic situation must decide for themselves which cultures to investigate.

A history of strategic culture theory

Military commanders and state leaders have used cultural information in every era, some more successfully than others. Classic writings on strategy mention the role of culture. The ancient Chinese theorist Sun Tzu stressed the importance of understanding the 'thing which causes the people to be in harmony with their ruler', and the earlier Chinese thinker T'ai Kung specifically advised strategists to pay attention to various peoples' differing customs.[7] Nevertheless, nineteenth- and twentieth-century strategic theorists tended to downplay the role of culture.

Since weapons have the same effect on the human body in every culture, many theorists assume that the most effective methods of using them must be the same in every culture as well. The same point seems to apply to all other instruments of strategy. If certain groups of people have customs that prevent them from choosing the most effective methods, they are likely to lose wars to less squeamish enemies, and their customs are likely to disappear. For these reasons, military scholar Michael Handel suggests that the 'logic of war' is as universal as the 'laws of gravity'.[8] People from different cultures may learn to apply that logic in different ways and at different speeds, but just as apples fell to the ground the same way long before Newton developed his theories, strategy works the same way everywhere and always.

This way of thinking implied that it was more useful for theorists to figure out how to solve strategic problems effectively than it was for them to spend time worrying about how people from other cultures might approach similar problems. During the Cold War, however, theorists studying nuclear strategy concluded that this might not always be true. Since practically everyone wished to avoid nuclear war, most Western theorists agreed with thinker Bernard Brodie's observation that the main goal of nuclear strategy had to be that of preventing such a war from breaking out in the first place.[9] This meant that the most effective policies for building and deploying nuclear weapons were not automatically the ones that would inflicted the most damage on the enemy; the most effective polices were the ones that convinced potential enemies to do certain things – or not to do certain things – without either side actually needing to fight. To these thinkers, nuclear strategy was primarily psychological.

At first, most strategic thinkers continued to take the position that the principles of strategy were universal. No one, these theorists reasoned, could fail to understand the importance of avoiding nuclear annihilation. As long as state leaders understood that they could not use nuclear weapons without suffering a nuclear attack in return, this logic implied, those leaders would refrain from doing so. There might be exceptions in certain extreme situations – such as one in which leaders in one country feared that if they did not launch a nuclear attack, a potential enemy might strike first and destroy them before they had the chance to respond. There might also be a grey zone of limited warfare in which both sides used nuclear weapons in small numbers while continuing to deter each other from using them in an all-out strike. This way of thinking suggested that in nuclear matters at least, all state leaders would respond to similar situations in similar ways, regardless of their personalities, political ideas, and culture.

Brodie himself rejected this point of view. His belief that human psychology includes complex emotional and cultural elements alienated him from many of his colleagues. By the 1970s, however, increasing numbers of theorists began to write about the importance of culture in strategy. In 1977, for instance, Jack Snyder published a report titled The Soviet Strategic Culture: Implications for Limited Nuclear Operations. Snyder noted that even if Soviet and American leaders shared the same desire to avoid destruction in the realm of theory, their cultural backgrounds led them to interpret political and military situations differently in practice.

That meant that a nuclear policy that would deter the United States from using nuclear weapons might not deter the Soviet Union. That also meant that American leaders who presumed that they could use small numbers of nuclear weapons against the Soviet Union and expect their opponents to respond in an equally restrained fashion might be taking an even greater risk than other theorists had warned. Soviet leaders, thinking from a Soviet cultural point of view, might well interpret the limited American strike as a prelude to an all-out attack and respond accordingly.

Other theorists, notably Colin Gray, David Jones, Carnes Lord, and Kenneth Booth, explored the strategic significance of culture further. Their efforts prompted an academic debate on how to study strategic culture most effectively. China scholar Alastair Iain Johnston warned that it is all too easy to use intangible concepts such as culture as an excuse for fuzzy thinking.[10] Johnston urged theorists to propose specific ways that they believed that specific countries' culturally held ideas would cause those countries to behave. This would make it possible to apply a variety of formal social science research techniques to determine whether strategists from those countries do what the cultural theorists predicted that they would do.

Johnston himself used such techniques to test the widely accepted proposition that Chinese strategists have a cultural disdain for violence that causes them to refrain from aggressive policies even when such policies might help them achieve their goals. Johnston's work indicated that the proposition was wrong and that, in fact, Chinese culture encouraged state leaders to achieve their ends through violence. Johnston was undoubtedly correct to conclude that Chinese strategists have advocated aggressive policies in numerous historical periods.

Other sinologists, however, noted that Johnston's use of painstakingly designed research methods had not made his findings any more definitive than less formal approaches to studying China.[11]

Research methods are only as good as the data one applies them to. China scholar Arthur Waldron pointed out that Johnston had studied only one body of ideas in Chinese political and strategic thought. Had he studied different thinkers and different historical periods, his methods might have produced different results. In fact, Waldron noted, the Chinese themselves have discussed the pros and cons of aggression throughout their history. Although Johnston had hoped his methods would allow him to answer questions about strategic culture objectively and definitively, Waldron found that he had merely contributed one more subjective and partially fuzzy argument to what will probably turn out to be an endless debate.

Other strategic culture theorists added that Johnston's attempt to separate cultural influences from other factors that affect strategy was doomed to fail.[12] Culture, these theorists argued, interacts with all the other components of strategic behaviour. British leaders have not tended to rely on naval power purely because their country has a maritime culture; British leaders have relied on naval power because the United Kingdom is a series of islands, because large land armies are expensive, because they tend to inherit strong navies from their predecessors, and because of a wide variety of other reasons – one of which is, indeed, culture. Culture reinforces British leaders' other motives for choosing to use naval power. The other factors that incline them to choose naval power, in turn, have helped shape British strategic culture.

Johnston was right to say that unless thinkers distinguish cultural influences from the other factors that affect strategy, nothing they say about strategic culture can ever be certain. To this, traditional strategic culture theorists would repeat that nothing in strategy ever is. Traditional theorists doubt that any research technique can replace human judgement. What one calls judgement may be what another calls fuzzy thinking, but traditionalists suggest that it is the only tool for studying strategic culture that we actually have.

What culture can tell us

Although the traditional strategic culture theorists do not believe that it is possible to separate culture from the other factors that influence strategy, they have proposed ways that cultural knowledge may help one to analyse strategic affairs. Gray begins by pointing out that it is impossible to understand anything whatsoever about strategy without considering the cultural element.[13] Strategy is a human activity. Human beings learn everything they know in the various cultures they belong to. Therefore, people choose goals, make plans, respond to new developments, and perform activities in cultural ways. By the same token, anyone who wants to study strategy would be wise to remember that they are doing so from their own cultural perspective and that people from other backgrounds may perceive the same situations differently.

Studying culture also gives analysts specific insights into strategic behaviour. Gray notes that strategic culture 'expresses comparative advantage'.[14] By this, he means that people from one culture may be better at performing certain activities than are people from other cultures, even when both start with the same resources and opportunities. The United Kingdom's Special Air Service, Special Boat Service, and other elite units are consistently more effective than their American counterparts, even though American special forces have similar training and gear. German armies typically perform better than equally sized and equipped ground forces from other countries, to note another example, but German navies tend to be at a disadvantage.

One reason why different peoples develop different cultural strengths and weaknesses is that external factors such as geography reward them for doing so. Germany's location in the centre of Europe, to continue the previous example, has ensured that German states frequently shared land borders with potential enemies. Over time, the organisations responsible for maintaining German states' ground forces had more opportunities to develop effective techniques. German states' most dedicated and capable military thinkers have normally found better career opportunities in the ground forces. These thinkers trained their successors to do the things that worked well for them.

Gray adds that people cannot change their cultural perspective simply because it would be useful for them to do so.[15] It would be impossible for German strategists who learned about war in a culture that emphasises ground forces to rapidly transform themselves into the mental equivalents of British strategists who learned about war in a culture that emphasises navies. German strategists may adapt what they know about land combat to fight at sea, and they may even win naval battles, but they will continue thinking and acting according to their culture. The less time people have to prepare for a culturally unfamiliar strategic challenge, the more likely they are to fall back on traditional approaches.

Dysfunctional strategic cultures

Those who claim that the principles of strategy are universal remain right about certain points. Some approaches to solving strategic problems are more effective than others are. Since culture influences both the approaches that leaders choose and how subordinates put leadership decisions into practice, it would seem to follow that some strategic cultures are inherently superior. The same logic suggests that other cultures are dysfunctional. There are certainly cases in which cultural inclinations seem to have prompted strategists to adopt foolish policies.

Many cultural traits that seem dysfunctional in some circumstances can promote effective behaviour in others. Gray illustrates this point by discussing the widely observed American cultural tendency to seek technological solutions for every problem.[16] When this cultural tendency inspires Americans to develop and use effective new technology, it is functional. When this cultural tendency inclines Americans to neglect the hard work of addressing complex issues that lack a 'quick fix', it is not.

For this reason, it is difficult to assess the overall effectiveness of any strategic culture. The fact that people with seriously dysfunctional attitudes towards strategy tend to lose wars allows one to assume that any strategic culture that has survived for more than a few generations is at least minimally functional. People may also manage to sustain flawed strategic cultures when they possess other advantages that compensate for their dysfunctional cultural attitudes. Gray, for instance, suggests that dysfunctional elements of Russia's strategic culture caused Russian armed forces to collapse in 1917, 1941, and, with less bloodshed, 1989.[17] Non-cultural factors such as Russia's climate, geography, and population allowed the Russian state to recover from these catastrophes.

In the early twenty-first century, some Western military writers started to ask whether their own strategic culture is still functional. The U.S. Army's 2004 Campaign Plan calls on American armed forces to transform their institutional culture in order to take full advantage of what theorists have called the (or a) revolution in military affairs. Retired American Colonel Ralph Peters expresses broader concerns about Western society in general. Peters notes that despite the vast firepower of Western armed forces, warriors from cultures that encourage such practices as suicide bombing can, in his words, 'hamstring' Western nations.[18]

Peters goes on to speculate about a war between the People's Republic of China and the United States. Americans, he warns, 'conditioned to levels of comfort unimaginable to the generation that fought World War II would balk at the sacrifice war with China would require of them'. Elsewhere, he asks, 'which population would be better equipped, practically and psychologically, to endure massive power outages, food-chain disruptions, the obliteration of databases and even epidemic disease?' Although Peters does not prescribe detailed measures for reforming Western culture, he suggests that censorship might help.

Meanwhile, Gray, who in the 1970s and 1980s helped to revive the idea of strategic culture, cautions twenty-first-century military thinkers against taking the idea too far. Culture is only one of the factors that influences strategy, he warns, and it is not always the most important one.[19] Moreover, culture is difficult to interpret effectively. Those who are dissatisfied with a strategic culture – whether their own or somebody else's – will find that culture is normally difficult to change. To ignore strategic culture is to ignore the fact that strategists are human beings, but to look to strategic culture theory for easy solutions is to set oneself up for failure.

Morale and combat effectiveness

Throughout history, epics and chronicles have celebrated the courage of warriors. The earliest writings on strategy recognise that fighters who possess mental attributes such as bravery and willingness to obey orders are invaluable in battle, whereas those who lack them are useless. Ancient Chinese works suggest numerous steps that commanders can take to instil such traits in their troops. These writings advise commanders to win soldiers' trust through personal attention, by paying attention to soldiers' physical needs, and by enforcing consistent standards of discipline.

The ancient Chinese also recognised that people think and behave differently while under the stress of warfare than they would in even the most demanding of civilian activities. Sun Tzu (ca. 500 BCE) suggested that commanders can take advantage of this fact by putting soldiers in situations that force them to fight well: 'For it is in the nature of soldiers to resist when surrounded, to fight to the death when there is no alternative, and when desperate to follow commands implicitly'.[20] Other ancient Chinese writers observed a potential drawback to such methods. Even the bravest and best-trained soldiers, they noted, have a psychological breaking point.[21]

Clausewitz added that it is a mistake to romanticise either the experience of combat or the traits of effective soldiers.[22] It is not, Clausewitz continues, that scenes of glory, bravery, and thrilling excitement are mythical. Such moments occur. Nevertheless, they are rare, and come 'like a medicine, in recurring doses, the taste diluted by time'.[23] Moreover, those who have not experienced war can never fully understand what combat is like. For that reason, they can never fully understand how soldiers will react to it. In battle, 'the light of reason is refracted in a matter quite different from that which is normal in academic speculation'.[24]

Despite Clausewitz's warning, twentieth-century academics in fields ranging from sociology to military history have investigated the psychology of combat. Data from the Second World War suggests that myth-makers are at least partially right to emphasise the importance of heroes. The same data suggest that ancient strategists were right to suggest that military leaders can deliberately cultivate heroism. In World War Two, airborne troops recurrently outperformed soldiers from more mundane branches of the armed forces.

One vivid example of this was the German parachute assault on the island of Crete in 1941.[25] The Greek and British forces defending the island outnumbered the Germans. Greek and British forces also possessed tanks, trucks, and artillery. The Germans, by contrast, were unable to deploy any equipment heavier than a light mortar until they captured an airfield. Moreover, the British had intercepted and decrypted the German troops' orders, which came by radio.

Therefore, the Germans had to drop from the air into the middle of a larger and better-equipped force that knew exactly where they were going to land and had enjoyed ample time to prepare. Nevertheless, the German airborne forces not only captured Crete but inflicted more casualties than they suffered. Airborne troops typically receive more rigorous training than their comrades in other units. Paratroopers perceive themselves as elite and commonly enjoy a high degree of espirit de corps. Parachute units also frequently have the luxury of setting higher standards for their recruits. The case of Crete suggests that these factors make parachute troops braver, fiercer, and more resilient.

Clausewitz was right, however, to warn that the 'taste' for heroism becomes 'diluted' with prolonged or frequent exposure. Data from World War Two also indicated that the stress of combat wears troops out over time. Most people proved able to fight effectively for 200–240 days.[26] After that time, in the words of one study, a soldier becomes 'so overly cautious and jittery that he [is] ineffective and demoralizing to the newer men'.[27] The same study found that approximately 2% of all soldiers resist the stress of combat for much longer periods. Members of the hardy 2% seemed to have a wide range of personalities, but the survey noted that many appeared to be 'aggressive psychopaths'.[28]

Combat motivation and unit cohesion

Since aggressive psychopaths are prone to disobedience and unlikely to cooperate effectively with others, they are of limited use to strategists. Nevertheless, other World War Two–era research highlighted the difficulties in motivating psychologically normal people to fight. Historian and U.S. Army general S.L.A. Marshall presented the results of one particularly influential study in his work *Men Against Fire*, originally published in 1947. Marshall claimed that only 15% of American soldiers fired their weapons at the enemy.[29] The U.S. Army Air Corps observed a similar phenomenon with pilots. Under 1% of American pilots accounted for between 30% and 40% of enemy aircraft destroyed.[30]

The men who failed to shoot were not necessarily cowards. Most obediently marched into places where enemy troops could shoot at them. Nevertheless, even in combat, they were at least subconsciously reluctant to kill. Marshall advised commanders to watch their troops in battle and urge the non-firers to use their weapons, but he recognised that this was only a partial solution.[31] If armies were to achieve higher levels of effectiveness, they needed to find some way of breaking down soldiers' psychological resistance to killing.

Marshall also explored the factors that motivate soldiers to take avoidable risks and make extraordinary efforts. In his view, belief in higher causes and loyalty to 'buddies' played indispensable roles. Belief in higher causes, Marshall argued, encourages troops to remain steadfast over long periods.[32] Personal relationships motivate military personnel in the tumult of combat.[33] Other influential studies based on Second World War data suggested that comradeship outweighed all the other factors that inspire troops to fight. When social scientists Edward Shils and Robert Janowitz interviewed veterans of the German Army, for instance, they found that personal relationships were considerably more important in determining whether a German unit would fight effectively than any soldier's opinions about Adolf Hitler.[34]

The emotional bonds that hold a military unit together became known as *cohesion*. Military personnel form the most cohesive groups with the comrades they know best. Early research into unit cohesion suggested that strategists do not need to place a high priority on convincing their own side's military personnel that their cause is just. Strategists must, however, encourage the processes by which fighters form comradeship bonds.

The studies of unit cohesion seemed to connect with Marshall's findings about the difficulty of getting soldiers to fire their weapons. Military culture often seems harsh, brash, disdainful of outsiders, and resistant to change. Research into unit cohesion suggested that this culture – despite its unpleasantness – might be vital to building effective comradeship bonds. Marshall's work suggested that this culture might be equally vital to encouraging military personnel to do their most important job.

A strategist who accepted these conclusions would probably be sceptical of attempts to change military tradition for social and political purposes – by abolishing brutal training practices, for instance, or by expanding the role of women. Such a strategist would also probably be reluctant to train or use military personnel for operations that threaten to erode aggression and comradeship. Policing former warzones, for instance, requires military personnel to exercise unusually high levels of restraint with their weapons. Such operations are also exceptionally likely to put personnel in a position where they must sacrifice comrades to protect foreign civilians. Traditionalists in the U.S. Army have often used such points to justify an attitude that General John Shalikashvili summarises with the phrase 'real men don't do peacekeeping'.[35]

Shalikashvili himself sees this attitude as misguided. When armed forces become reluctant to 'do peacekeeping' they become less useful to the states and people they serve. This point has attracted special attention since the end of the Cold War, because the powerful states of this period have been more interested in maintaining order in troubled parts of the world than in fighting all-out wars against their military equals. People in these states have also become increasingly reluctant to inflict casualties, even on their enemies. Nevertheless, even in an unrestrained conflict such as World War Two, all combatants faced the task of policing conquered territories, and this required them to achieve some level of cooperation with the population.

Therefore, there may be more than one way to motivate military personnel. In fact, the World War Two–era studies on combat behaviour and unit cohesion may not be as reliable as military commanders initially believed. When Marshall studied the Korean war, he found that almost four times as many American troops – 55% – were firing at the enemy.[36] Later studies showed that between 90% and 95% of American soldiers fired in Vietnam.

One reason why American soldiers proved more willing to shoot in Korea and Vietnam may be that the U.S. Army introduced new training methods designed to make them more aggressive. These methods ranged from having soldiers fire at human-shaped targets when learning to use their rifles and requiring recruits to chant 'kill, kill, kill' while running. One author suggests that these practices had the side effect of making soldiers more vulnerable to psychological damage.[37]

Another reason why soldiers since World War Two appeared more willing to use their weapons may be that Marshall's original study was misleading. Although Marshall claimed to know the percentage of troops who fired at the enemy, he had not attempted to sample a statistically representative cross section of U.S. Army personnel. Instead, he had interviewed somewhat arbitrarily selected groups of soldiers. Moreover, eyewitnesses report that he did not routinely keep detailed records of his interviews. Therefore, one must conclude that he based much of his work on his potentially unreliable memories and impressions.

Immediately after the 2003 Iraq War, a team of U.S. Army researchers interviewed American troops, Western reporters, and Iraqi prisoners of war to test the World War Two findings on cohesion and motivation. Unlike Marshall, these researchers used a structured interview format and kept detailed records.[38] This study confirmed the fact that personal relationships in military units play a critical role in motivating soldiers to fight. Nevertheless, American combat veterans of 2003 also reported fighting for idealistic reasons.

Even in the heat of battle, those veterans claimed that they took courage from their belief that they were liberating the people of Iraq. Research by scholar and former military intelligence officer Paul F. Robinson documents his argument that idealistic codes of honour have motivated soldiers in combat throughout history.[39] This fact is not necessarily reassuring. Robinson adds that these codes have taken different forms in different periods and that many of them encouraged brutality.

Robinson's research, like the studies of combat motivation in 2003, suggests that it would be a mistake to assume that the factors that inspire military personnel to fight well are the same in all times and places. At a minimum, this suggests that strategists must pay attention to the factors that affect personnel in the forces that interest them. This even suggests that it may be possible to inspire military personnel to respond to new forms of motivation. With proper leadership, perhaps, real troops can learn to do peacekeeping. The methods of getting them to do so, however, remain uncertain.

Psychology once removed: remotely operated vehicles

One way to overcome the human reluctance to kill is to automate the process. It is probably easier to discharge a howitzer at a target one knows only by its map coordinates than it is to fire a rifle at a visible human being. It is also harder for artillery crews to refrain from killing without being noticed by their commanding officers. The fact that technological advances make killing progressively easier is disturbing, but from the narrow perspective of a war planner, it would seem to be an advantage.

Dispatching a robot to attack one's enemies might seem like a particularly palatable way to kill. (Chapter 4 discusses this issue in more detail, with reference to all levels of strategy and to the ethical component.) One can only speculate about the psychological dynamics that might come into play should armed forces field fully autonomous fighting machines. The armed forces of the early twenty-first century, however, have typically kept drones and other unmanned combat vehicles under human control. Although drone operators are often thousands of miles from any warzone, a U.S. Air Force study indicates that they experience extreme stress and that they form bonds with the ground troops they support that are similar to those who are physically together on the battlefield.[40] Empathy – for one's comrades and even for the enemies one must kill – appears to be embedded deeply enough in the human condition to operate even through a video link, and although this is an impediment to military operations, it may reveal something encouraging about our species.

Asymmetric psychology? Terrorists and suicide bombers

Where Marshall studied the difficulty of motivating troops to kill, twenty-first-century strategists have become interested in the opposite problem: understanding why followers of transnational movements such as al-Qaeda and ISIS are so eager to commit violence that many are willing to carry out suicide attacks. As Chapters 13 and 14 will discuss, understanding this issue is probably essential to countering such movements. Although those of us who have been raised in relatively peaceful surroundings might be tempted to dismiss those who perform suicidal mass killings as monsters, research indicates that reality is more complex. Evidence suggests that most supporters of transnational militant groups think and behave much like the rest of us. Nevertheless, there are also indications that those who carry out the deadliest attacks commonly have abnormal psychological tendencies – a fact that may tell us as much about war itself as it tells us about terrorism.

Perhaps the most compelling argument in favour of the proposition that militants respond to the same motivations as non-militants is that virtually all societies have condoned mass killings under one set of circumstances or another. This is not to say that all such acts are morally equivalent. As Chapter 3 points out, there are persuasive reasons to accept that large-scale killing may be more excusable in some situations than in others. Nevertheless, the fact that so many Europeans celebrated the outbreak of World War One reminds us that the appetite for bloodshed can be widespread, and the fact that elite military units such as special forces are typically able to fill their ranks with enthusiastic volunteers reminds us that the high possibility of dying does not necessarily deter recruits. There may be an important distinction between the willingness to risk death and the willingness to seek it, but the armed forces of Imperial Japan successfully instituted suicide attacks as a routine tactic in World War Two.

A U.S. Army handbook states simply that there is no single social or psychological profile for predicting terrorist behaviour.[41] Tori DeAngelis, writing for the American Psychological Association, reviews academic research on the subject and concurs that the typical terrorist is not deranged.[42] DeAngelis goes on to note that there is psychological research that links membership in terrorist organisations to widespread human traits, such as the desire to avenge perceived injustices.[43] Those who hope to discredit militant organisations in the eyes of potential recruits or to encourage captive fighters to renounce terrorism may be able to use this research to develop their arguments.

Nevertheless, one recalls that the opposing forces of World War Two found that an exceptionally motivated fraction of their troops accounted for a disproportionately large number of their victories. One also recalls that the U.S. Army discovered that a much smaller percentage of its troops were, by most commonly accepted definitions, mentally ill and that although these soldiers were unmanageable, they had potentially useful traits.[44] The U.S. Army went on to introduce training reforms that may well have improved the general effectiveness of its forces while raising the incidence of mental illness.[45] One may reasonably infer that mentally disturbed individuals also play pivotal roles in transnational militant organisations, even if most militants are within the mainstream.

And indeed, Adam Lankford of the University of Alabama has accumulated evidence suggesting that the suicide attackers who have achieved such prominence in the early twenty-first century frequently display similar tendencies to those who kill themselves without invoking any religious or political cause.[46] Lankford has outlined these arguments in widely read publications and developed them further in his more scholarly work.[47] Lankford has expressed the hope that such findings will help to discredit suicide bombers in the eyes of many who might otherwise admire them.[48] This may indeed be a useful line for counterterrorists to follow. Nevertheless, it is difficult to escape the opinion that war in all its forms is inseparable from possibilities in the human condition that are so horrible that most of us prefer to disown them as madness. Military strategy succeeds to the extent that it harnesses those possibilities in those who are presumably sane.

Conclusion

Studying the human context of military operations can sensitise strategists to possible dangers and alert them to possible opportunities. The nuclear strategists who deliberately ignored strategic culture, for instance, risked catastrophically misunderstanding how Soviet leaders might respond to Western actions. Nelson, on the other hand, assessed his opponents' culture accurately and used his assessment to choose effective tactics in a strategically critical battle. The various studies of combat motivation suggest further ways that armed forces might train and deploy troops to maximum effect.

Just as strategists handicap themselves when they ignore human factors, so too do they risk serious mistakes when they confuse common assumptions about culture and psychology with proven facts. The second error is particularly dangerous for those who are bold – or arrogant – enough to advocate radically changing society and government to achieve strategic advantages. One cannot understand strategy without considering its social and psychological dimensions. Nevertheless, in applying ideas about the human dimensions of strategy, one must exercise caution.

Key points

1   To make strategy effectively, one must account for the culture and psychology of the people involved in the process. These people may include military personnel, the civilian population, and other more specific groups.

2   Governments can coerce people to behave in prescribed ways. Under certain circumstances, governments may be able to motivate people to adopt new ways of thinking. Therefore, attempts to address the cultural and psychological sides of warfare overlap with politics. Nevertheless, it is seldom wise – let alone moral – for military commanders to seek direct control of the government for strategic purposes.

3   People from different cultural backgrounds appear to have distinctive attitudes towards war and strategy and to behave accordingly.

4   Few human beings can perform effectively in combat for more than approximately 240 days.

5   Interpersonal bonds in military units play a powerful role in determining how bravely and aggressively the members of those units fight.

6   Despite the importance of culture and psychology in warfare, strategic thinkers have often overstated and oversimplified their influence.

Questions

1   How can strategists best exploit cultural and psychological factors?
2   How can strategists apply cultural knowledge most effectively?
3   How can strategists best use elite military units?
4   How much should armed forces change to conform to new social expectations?

Notes

1 Carl von Clausewitz, *On War*, trans. Michael Howard and Peter Paret (New Haven, Princeton University Press, 1976), p. 87.

2 Ibid., p. 88.

3 John Fuller, *Machine Warfare: An Enquiry into the Influences of Mechanics on the Art of War* (London, Hutchinson & Co., 1942), pp. 8–10.

4 Joseph Needham, Wang Ling, and Gwei-Djen Lu, *Science and Civilisation in China*, Vol. 4 (Cambridge, Cambridge University Press, 1971), pp. 487–8.

5 Immanuel Hsu, *The Rise of Modern China* (Oxford, Oxford University Press, 1970), pp. 229–33.

6 Colin Gray, *Modern Strategy* (Oxford, Oxford University Press, 1999), p. 140.

7 Ralph Sawyer (trans.), *The Seven Military Classics of Ancient China* (Oxford, Westview, 1993), p. 55.

8 Michael Handel, *Masters of War, Classical Strategic Thought* (London, Frank Cass, 1992; 2nd Edition 1996), p. xii.

9 Kenneth Booth, Bernard Brodie, John Baylis, John Garnett (eds.), *Makers of Nuclear Strategy* (London, Pinter Publishers, 1991), p. 21.

10 Alistair Iain Johnson, 'Thinking about Strategic Culture', *International Security* 19:4 (Spring 1995), p. 33.

11 Arthur Waldron, 'Cultural Realism: Strategic Culture and Grand Strategy in Chinese History by Alastair Iain Johnston', *The China Quarterly* 147 (September 1996), pp. 962–4.

12 Gray, *Modern Strategy*, pp. 138–9.

13 Ibid., pp. 142–3.

14 Ibid., p. 144.

15 Ibid., p. 143.

16 Ibid., p. 147.

17 Ibid.

18 Ralph Peters, 'The Counterrevolution in Military Affairs: Fashionable Thinking about Defense Ignores the Great Threats of our Time', *Weekly Standard* 11:20 (February 2006), www.weeklystandard. com/Content/Public/Articles/000/000/006/649qrsob.asp (accessed August 2, 2006).

19 Colin Gray, 'Out of the Wilderness: Prime Time for Strategic Culture', *Comparative Strategy* 26:1 (January 2007), p. 17.

20 Sun Tzu (Tao Hanzhang, commentator, Yuan Shibing, trans.), *Sun Tzu's Art of War: The Modern Chinese Interpretation* (New York, Sterling, 1987), p. 122.

21 Sawyer, *The Seven Military Classics of Ancient China*, p. 138.

22 Clausewitz, *On War*, p. 113.

23 Ibid.

24 Ibid.

25 Franz Uhle-Wettler, '*Auftragstaktik*: Mission Orders and the German Experience', in Richard D. Hooker (ed.), *Maneuver Warfare: An Anthology* (Novato, Presidio Press, 1993), pp. 236–7.

26 William Miller, *The Mystery of Courage* (Cambridge, MA, Harvard University Press, 2002), p. 61.

27 Ibid.

28 Ibid.

29 Samuel Lyman Atwood Marshall, *Men against Fire: The Problem of Battle Command in Future War* (Gloucester, MA, Peter Smith, 1978), p. 54.

30 Anthony Kellett, 'The Soldier in Battle: Motivational and Behavioral Aspects of the Combat Experience', in Betty Glad (ed.), *Psychological Dimensions of War* (London, Sage, 1990), p. 228.

31 Marshall, *Men against Fire*, pp. 74–5.

32 Ibid., p. 161.

33 Ibid.

34 Leonard Wong, Thomas Kolditz, Raymond Millen, and Thomas Potter, *Why They Fight: Combat Motivation in the Iraq War* (Carlisle, Strategic Studies Institute, 2003), pp. 2–3.

35 Joseph Klein, 'It's Time for Extreme Peacekeeping', *Time*, November 16, 2003, www.time.com/ time/magazine/article/0,9171,543812,00.htm (accessed November 9, 2007).

36 Dave Grossman, *On Killing: The Psychological Cost of Learning to Kill in War and Society* (Boston, Little Brown and Company, 1995), p. 251.

37 Ibid., p. 253.

38 Wong, Kolditz, Millen, and Potter, *Why They Fight*, p. 6.

39 Paul Robinson, *Military Honour and the Conduct of War: From Ancient Greece to Iraq* (Abington, Routledge, 2006), passim.

40 Megan McCloskey, 'The War Room: Daily Transition between Battle, Home Takes a Toll on Drone Operators', *Stars and Stripes*, October 27, 2009, www.stripes.com/news/the-war-room-daily-transition-between-battle-home-takes-a-toll-on-drone-operators-1.95949#.WNGlmTsrLIU (accessed March 21, 2017); Elisabeth Bumiller, 'Air Force Drone Operators Report High Levels of Stress', *The New York Times*, December 18, 2011, p. A8, www.nytimes.com/2011/12/19/world/asia/air-force-drone-operators-show-high-levels-of-stress.html (accessed March 21, 2017).

41 U.S. Army Training and Doctrine Command, *A Military Guide to Terrorism in the Twenty-First Century*, *DCSINT Handbook No. 1*, Leavenworth, August 15, 2007, p. 2/10, www.au.af.mil/au/awc/awcgate/army/guidterr/cover.jpg (accessed March 22, 2017); U.S. Army Training and Doctrine Command, *A Military Guide to Terrorism in the Twenty-First Century*, *DCSINT Handbook No. 1*, Leavenworth, August 15, 2007, www.au.af.mil/au/awc/awcgate/army/guidterr/ (accessed March 18, 2017); U.S. Army Training and Doctrine Command, *A Military Guide to Terrorism in the Twenty-First Century*, *DCSINT Handbook No. 1*, Leavenworth, August 15, 2007, pp. 2/10, www.au.af.mil/au/awc/awcgate/army/guidterr/ch02.pdf (accessed 18 March 2017).

42 Tori DeAngelis, 'Understanding Terrorism', *Monitor on Psychology* 40:10 (November 2009), www.apa.org/monitor/2009/11/terrorism.aspx (accessed March 18, 2017).

43 Ibid.

44 William Miller, *The Mystery of Courage* (Cambridge, MA, Harvard University Press, 2002), p. 61.

45 Wong, Kolditz, Millen, and Potter, *Why They Fight*, p. 6.

46 Adam Lankford, 'Martyr Myth: Inside the Minds of Suicide Bombers', *New Scientist*, July 3, 2013, www.newscientist.com/article/mg21929240-200-martyr-myth-inside-the-minds-of-suicide-bombers/ (accessed March 20, 2017).

47 Adam Lankford, 'Martyr Myth', *Adam Lankford Criminology Professor, the University of Alabama*, http://adamlankford.com/research.htm (accessed March 22, 2017).

48 Ibid.

Further reading

Glad, Betty (ed.), *Psychological Dimensions of War*, (London: Sage, 1990).

Gray, Colin S. , *Modern Strategy*, (Oxford: Oxford University Press, 1999).

Huntington, Samuel P., *The Soldier and the State: The Theory and Politics of Civil-Military Relations*, (Cambridge, MA: Belknap Press, 1957).

Marshall, S.L.A. , *Men against Fire: The Problem of Battle Command in Future War*, (Gloucester, MA: Peter Smith, 1978).

Robinson, Paul, *Military Honour and the Conduct of War: From Ancient Greece to Iraq*, (Abingdon: Routledge, 2006).

The ethics of war   3

Reader's guide

Perspectives in ethics: consequentialism and deontology; realism and ethics; the just war tradition (jus ad bellum, jus in bello, jus post bellum); the laws of war; strategic necessity; strategy for the common good.

Introduction

The subject of ethics, much like culture, holds a somewhat awkward position in the world of strategy. Since humans are moral beings, ethics must have an influence on strategy. And yet since the latter is a rational activity, the seemingly emotive and subjective world of ethics may be regarded as an unwelcome interloper in the process of strategy. Or as Bernard Brodie notes, 'the strategic writer . . . will normally regard moral considerations as tiresome impediments to the flow of one's thoughts'.[1] As noted in the Introduction to this book, strategy is a complex, uncertain, and competitive activity. Ethical concerns merely seem to further complicate the job of the strategist. However, ethics is not something that the modern strategist can ignore. Ethics has become an increasingly important issue as war has come under ever-more-complex legal and moral scrutiny. The laws of war, based on long-standing ethical traditions, have developed substantially since the second half of the nineteenth century. Taken together, ethics and law are central components of what Michael Walzer terms the 'war convention'.[2]

Since this volume is primarily concerned with understanding the nature of strategy and best practice, this chapter will conclude with an analysis of how strategists can incorporate an ethical dimension into their practice while still seeking to achieve their policy objectives. However, before that can be done, the basic foundations of ethics must be understood. Moreover, since strategic studies is heavily infused by realism, it is important to understand how the latter views ethical issues. It will become clear that tensions exist between some of the core demands of ethics and the realist school of thought. To understand how some of these tensions can be mitigated, the chapter will outline the just war tradition, which seeks to reconcile the need for war in international politics with ethical concerns. The just war tradition is reflected in the modern laws of war. Although the laws of war provide a reasonably balanced and sensible approach to the regulation of armed conflict, modern interpretation and use of them has become increasingly problematic from the perspective of best practice. This creates the need for a strategy-centred approach to the subject of ethics and war. This new approach is best described as strategic necessity. In turn, the realist impulse in suggested necessity is somewhat reined in by reference to the common good. The latter, it is argued, provides the rationale for a balanced approach to ethics: one that caters for both moral and strategic needs.

Perspectives in ethics

If strategy seems complex, try ethics. The problem with ethical standards is that, like the proverbial opinion, everyone has one. Moral relativism is a genuine headache for the subject of ethics. In a world of many diverse cultures, it is to be expected that different ethical standards exist. Are they all equally valid, or is it possible to identify a dominant set of ethics that has greater legitimacy? Indeed, is it desirable to attempt to elevate one set of moral standards above all others and then attempt to apply them universally? Such an enterprise has been labelled 'ethical imperialism'.[3] Despite the challenge of moral relativism, certain writers have identified a set of common values that appear to apply across most cultures. This 'overlapping consensus', to use John Rawl's terminology, includes key principles, such as a prohibition against murder and torture and the innocence of children.[4]

Box 3.1 Ethical perspectives

Consequentialism
The moral value of an action is based on balance of consequences.
Choose actions that produce the greatest good.
Torture may be valid if it saves lives.
But are some actions intrinsically wrong?
How does one judge the balance of outcomes?

Deontology
This theory is based on duties.
Certain actions are right or wrong, regardless of consequences.
Human beings should not be regarded as mere means to an end.
Who defines what is right and wrong?
What if rights or duties clash?

Although some form of consensus can be identified, how it is constructed, interpreted, and applied is not necessarily straightforward or universally agreed on. There are differing approaches to this question, two of which dominate discussions on the ethics of war: consequentialism and deontology. The former judges the moral value of an action based on its consequences. Generally speaking, if the consequences of an action produce greater good (or happiness, in utilitarian terms) then it will be regarded as the right thing to do. From such a perspective, it may be legitimate to sacrifice one innocent life to save five, assuming that it is the only way to achieve said outcome. In the field of security, a consequentialist may argue that it is right to torture a terrorist suspect to extract information from them if it will prevent a future atrocity. While there is much to recommend this approach to ethical dilemmas, there are some obvious problems. To return to our first example, it seems intrinsically wrong to value human life in such stark quantifiable terms. One could argue convincingly that the innocent human life sacrificed to save others has as much value and right to existence as any other. Therefore, on what moral grounds can the basic right to life be removed? Another problem with the consequentialist position is that it is not always easy to predict the balance of outcomes. In the terrorist example, how can we know in advance that the information extracted from torture will prevent an attack and save lives?

In contrast to consequentialism, based as it is on the balance of outcomes, deontology rests on the notion that certain actions are right or wrong, regardless of their consequences. Deontology is a duty-based approach to ethics. One of the most important proponents of this approach is Immanuel Kant. For Kant, certain duties were unconditional and absolute. On this basis, Kant argues that there are categorical imperatives, or commands to act in certain ways. One of the most important of these imperatives is to treat other humans as ends in themselves, not as mere means to an end. So to stick with our examples, it is always wrong to take an innocent human life or to engage in acts of torture, even if in doing so many other lives are saved. To put it another way, the action is judged on its own merits: the ends can never justify immoral means.

Upon initial examination, the deontological approach appears to be clear and straightforward. However, some difficulties can be identified. An obvious question relates to the source of fundamental principles: who decides what is inherently right and wrong? For some, the answer to this question is God, but this answer will not convince everyone. In the absence of God, who should take the role of moral architect? Another flaw in deontology is that ignoring the consequences of an action potentially allows evil to triumph. For example, during the Second World War, a deontological perspective may have prohibited certain Allied military operations (such as strategic bombing, especially when targeted against civilian areas). However, if such actions played an important part in the defeat of Nazi Germany, then disallowing them would have risked ceding victory to Hitler and his allies. In this sense, deontology promotes or denies choices based on right intention, regardless of the context and subsequent consequences. Finally, how does deontology cope with conflicting duties? Nigel Warburton poses the following dilemma for a duty-based approach to ethics. If we have a duty not to lie, but also a duty to protect the life of an innocent, what should we do if a murderer asks us for the location of their next innocent victim?[5] In the strategic bombing example, which is the greater duty – the defeat of Nazi Germany or the duty to protect innocent German lives?

In war, where decisions are often made in difficult, complex, and uncertain circumstances, it is problematic and limiting for a commander to tie themselves to either of the these approaches. In this sense, they will benefit from a form of decision-making that considers both consequentialism and deontology. This is well illustrated in the doctrine of double effect (first articulated by St Thomas Aquinas), which permits actions that are well intentioned and necessary yet still have foreseeable negative consequences. For example, a bombing mission targeting an important military facility would be permissible even though civilian casualties could be anticipated. In the making of such a decision, the deontological approach is evident in that there may be a duty to act and the intention is right (civilians are not the intended target). However, consequentialism also plays its part, in that for such a mission to be considered legitimate, the civilian losses must be proportionate to the expected gains. If proportionality can be achieved, then the cause of greater good can be served. Although the doctrine of double effect has a certain moral logic, it is still open to different interpretations. Michael Walzer, for example, argues that it is not sufficient merely to apply the principle of proportionality. Rather, he calls for evidence of positive steps taken to avoid civilian casualties.[6] Invariably, making decisions such as this, especially when they include such concepts as proportionality, is an act of judgement rather than the result of a scientific or quantifiable process. For this judgement to be valid, the commander must consider the context that they find themselves in.

Realism and ethics

Having to make an ethical judgement, taking into account context and considering both consequentialist and deontological approaches, is challenging. And as noted earlier, the whole enterprise is somewhat undermined by moral relativism. Thus, there appears to be some merit in taking a realist stance and dispensing with serious ethical ruminations altogether.

Realism operates on the basis that the international system is competitive and anarchic, with no governing authority to regulate behaviour. To prosper and even survive in such an environment, state actors must be pragmatic and seek power: 'the capacity of a political unit to impose its will upon other units'.[7] In such a world, especially in the absence of a legitimate governing authority to provide a secure environment, limiting one's options for abstract ethical reasons is dangerous. For the traditional realist, a state's actions must be governed by self-interest, not by some moral code: 'states in anarchy cannot afford to be moral'.[8] In this sense, when evaluating the legitimacy of a war, a realist would 'use prudential rather than moral considerations'.[9]

On the surface, it seems that realism has no room at all for ethics. And yet it has already been noted that ethics plays a part in strategy and international politics simply because humans are moral beings. This would suggest that for realism to deserve its title, it must take some account of ethics. And indeed, it does. When realism is further analysed, it becomes apparent that it deals with ethics in at least three main ways. First, although the realist version of the international system is described as anarchic, it is not without notions of acceptable forms of behaviour (rules and norms). As Snyder argues, certain norms underpin the state-centric realist paradigm and act as system modifiers.[10] One example is state sovereignty. Although these norms may not be inviolable, and are likely to be overridden in times of extreme emergency, they do have a place within the realist paradigm. In fact, Hans Morgenthau (a leading thinker in the realist school) goes further by suggesting that state actors recognise certain absolute moral barriers in international politics. Morgenthau argues that from a purely pragmatic perspective, it would be expedient for states to diminish the population of their potential rivals. Reducing a rival's population would diminish an important source of their relative power. However, certainly in peacetime, and even in most wars, states do not enact such a policy. The reason for this, Morgenthau argues, is that there is an agreed-on moral position among states on the value of civilian life.[11]

Second, some of the basic assumptions underlying strategic studies (which is closely associated with realism) also suggest that behaviour cannot be judged on purely pragmatic grounds. The core Clausewitzian idea that war is a continuation of policy is at one level an ethical principle. The notion that military power is valid only if it serves the interests of the community can be regarded as a moral statement. In this way, one might argue that realism operates in a consequentialist manner, by regarding war as a necessary evil to serve the greater needs of the community. Finally, in the service of self-interest, many realist authors accept that ethical concerns do have an impact on the practice of strategy and therefore have to be taken into consideration. Take, for example, the following statement by Colin S. Gray, who argues that war 'should be waged militarily in such a manner as not to sabotage its political goals'.[12] It is also worth noting that the more embedded ethics becomes in military affairs, the more it becomes part of military culture.

In the final analysis, realism can be said to share some of the features of naturalism in the field of moral philosophy. This philosophical approach is based on the principle that values should be based on facts. To put it another way, we ought to behave in such a manner as is consistent with the way the world is. Although realism may regard itself as empirically based, in that it merely describes the way the international system operates, it also has normative elements. Some realists, especially those in strategic studies, proffer advice based on their perspective on the workings of the system. So, for example, realist authors may reject the importance of ethics as a dimension of strategy on empirical grounds, because it contradicts how the system functions. And yet, ironically, this is a normative statement.

Just war

Despite some statements to the contrary, it is clear that a relationship exists between ethics and realism. However, that relationship, especially in times of war, is a troubled one. Difficulties in the relationship emanate from a number of factors, including the balance between competing ethical perspectives (consequentialism and deontology), the nature and subsequent demands of strategy (which is complex, rational, uncertain, and competitive), and the fact that moral concerns are likely to be overridden in times of emergency (which are most usually found in times of war). Despite these substantial obstacles to a coherent relationship, ethics and war have to coexist, if for no other reason than the fact that humans are moral beings. One of the most notable attempts at reconciling ethics and the use of force is the just war tradition.

The just war tradition is based on the premise that violent conflict is likely to occur. In this tradition, war is accepted as a social fact, abhorred but tolerated as a lesser evil. Indeed, within the just war framework, war can be considered in a more positive light, as a moral necessity in certain cases: an answer to injustice.[13] However, though necessary and legitimate, war must be regulated, both in terms of its outbreak and conduct. This approach to ethics and war has a long history.[14] It is difficult to precisely identify a start point for just war, but one can identify preliminary features of the tradition in ancient Greece. Before the rise of Macedonia, the Greek city-states waged war between themselves in a quasi-ritualistic manner. To use Plato's language, their conflicts were defined as 'discord' rather than 'war', the latter being far more total and unregulated. The former was characterised by a range of restrictions, including no pursuit of a defeated enemy and prohibition against attacks on civilians and their property. It is actually from ancient Greece, Aristotle in particular, that we get the term 'just war'.

The just war tradition developed further in Rome, where the Roman politician Marcus Tullius Cicero outlined many of the features that we today associate with just war. In particular, he was concerned that Roman military adventures should be perceived as a last resort to correct some injustice (right intention); that there was a formal declaration of war by a legitimate authority; that prisoners of war were treated fairly; and that in the conduct of war a distinction should be made between combatants and non-combatants.

These early notions of the legitimate use of force found resonance in a growing Christian dialogue on the subject, led by such moral authorities as St Augustine, St Thomas Aquinas, Gratian, Vitoria, Suarez, and Grotius (the latter wrote from a Christian standpoint even though he was not a member of the clergy or a religious order). Christian theologians sought to reconcile Christ's message of forgiveness and pacifism with the virtues of charity and love, which could be interpreted as producing a duty to protect one's neighbour from harm. Dominating the Christian approach to just war was the notion of right intention. For writers such as Aquinas, right intention was crucial, not only because it justified the recourse to war but also because it should influence the conduct of military operations. The argument was that a war fought on the basis of Christian virtues would be conducted in a manner consistent with those same principles. Out of this line of reasoning came the important principle of proportionality.

The modern interpretation of just war, although largely couched in secular philosophical language, is directly built on this tradition. Just war is now most commonly divided into two distinct but related components: jus ad bellum (justification for going to war) and jus in bello (justice in how war is conducted). The former is subdivided into six further categories, all of which represent a criterion that must be met for the war to be judged as legitimate: just cause; right intention; last resort; legitimate authority; proportionality; and reasonable prospect of success. Jus in bello is divided into discrimination and proportionality. These criteria will now be further explored. As this analysis progresses, it will become clear that although just war provides a common language through which we can debate the legitimacy of wars, the application of the theory is problematic and specific to each case.[15] The section will end with a brief excursion into a developing third component of the just war taxonomy: jus post bellum (justice after war).

Box 3.2 Just war

Jus ad bellum
Just cause.
Right intention.
Last resort.
Legitimate authority.
Proportionality.
Reasonable prospect of success.

Jus in bello
Proportionality.
Discrimination.

Jus post bellum
Rights vindication.
Proportional political rehabilitation.
Economic reconstruction.
Proportional punishment of war criminals.

Jus ad bellum: just cause

Just cause is most commonly associated with self-defence. It is commonly recognised, and indeed is enshrined in the United Nations Charter, that every individual, group, or state has an inherent right to defend itself in the face of an imminent or actual armed attack. This principle has been developed further to include the idea that one can act in the defence of others and perhaps even in the defence of certain rights. In modern times, this principle has been applied to UN and NATO operations in defence of Kuwait in 1991 and the Kosovo Albanians in 1999. The latter, although not authorised by the United Nations (the campaign was conducted by NATO), was important because it indicated that an ethnic community within a sovereign state could be protected by external powers. In essence, outside powers could act in self-defence on behalf of a group that was powerless to do so itself. Indeed, at a 2005 World Summit, member states of the United Nations committed themselves to the principle of Responsibility to Protect (R2P). The latter is aimed at preventing genocide, war crimes, ethnic cleansing, and crimes against humanity.

Self-defence and the defence of others seem fairly straightforward cases of just cause. However, the issue has been clouded in recent years with the notion of pre-emptive or preventive self-defence. Following the 9/11 terrorist attacks on New York and Washington, the Bush administration outlined a doctrine that sought to legitimise this broader interpretation of self-defence. Under Bush, the United States argued, with some legitimacy, that it was irresponsible for a state to wait for an attack to form before responding. Especially in an age of weapons of mass destruction (WMDs) and international terrorism, such an approach could leave a state vulnerable to devastating levels of destruction. Upon careful examination, pre-emptive self-defence appears to be logical and legitimate. It seems justified for a state to pre-emptively respond to an imminent attack, thereby potentially reducing the damage that may be suffered had the attack gone ahead unhindered.

The legitimacy of such actions rests on one's definition of 'imminent', however. Few would argue with a state acting pre-emptively on the basis of enemy forces moving into attack positions or reliable intelligence showing that terrorists were in the final stages of launching an attack. Problems arise with the notion of preventive self-defence. This notion tends to relate to actions taken against a threat in the earlier stages of its development. For example, preventive self-defence could be used as the grounds for attacks against a rogue state's nuclear programme, for fear that at some later stage, nuclear weapons could be developed and targeted against others. The legitimacy of such an attack would be open to question, certainly if it is sold as an act of self-defence. With no direct evidence to indicate that any weapons would be used in anger, a basis for self-defence would be difficult to justify. In a world of intelligence reports of uncertain reliability, deciding when to act on a perceived threat will always be a difficult judgement call and something of a gamble. If a politician gets it right and pre-empts an obvious enemy attack, their actions will be regarded as legitimate and will likely attract international support. However, if they get it wrong and act prematurely, they may simply be regarded as an aggressor. Of course, waiting too long for evidence of a threat to mature may ultimately leave a state as the victim of an unhindered attack.

Jus ad bellum: right intention

Associated with the notion of just cause, resort to war must also be undertaken with right intention. Generally speaking, a war must seek to produce an obviously better and more just outcome than if it had never been fought. So, for example, a war fought for humanitarian reasons (perhaps to prevent or limit ethnic cleansing) would seem to pass the test of right intention. In contrast, a war fought to increase the power and territory of a state (even if said state perceived itself as a force for good) would struggle to fit comfortably into this category. Clearly, as this last example reveals, whether or not right intention has been satisfied is very much in the eye of the beholder. In our example, a state that perceives itself as a force for good may regard its aggrandisement as an act befitting the notion of right intention. However, other international actors are unlikely to agree with such a judgement. Perhaps just as importantly, such a war would likely breach international law (which will be discussed in more detail later on).

Jus ad bellum: last resort

Resort to the use of force, although perceived as legitimate under certain circumstances, should not be undertaken lightly or in haste. Indeed, for a war to be universally declared just, military action must be considered the last resort. Before war is initiated, even in a case of obvious just cause and right intention, all other reasonable peaceful methods must have been exhausted to resolve the issue in question. How this responsibility is fulfilled depends on the circumstances. In the case of an imminent attack or extreme humanitarian emergency, it would clearly be inappropriate to spend weeks to allow the wheels of diplomacy and/or sanctions to produce a fruitful outcome. In such circumstances, nonviolent means would have to be explored rapidly and perhaps even bypassed entirely. However, under less than extreme circumstances, diplomatic means must be leveraged to solve a dispute or correct an injustice. Normally, in the post-war period, this would involve using the mechanisms of the United Nations. Economic sanctions are slightly trickier from a moral standpoint. Although they have often been regarded as a more ethical response than military action, this viewpoint is increasingly being questioned. The effects of sanctions, especially when targeted against totalitarian regimes, often fall most heavily on the poorest sections of society.

Jus ad bellum: legitimate authority

It is not only the decision to wage war that incurs scrutiny in the just war tradition; who makes that decision is also of import. The decision-making body must be regarded as a legitimate authority. As Whetham notes, the one exception to this rule is those acting in self-defence.[16] Since self-defence is regarded as an inalienable right, one does not require authority to enact that right. However, in most other circumstances, legitimate authority must be recognised. This is another area of the just war debate open to differing interpretations. How does one define 'legitimate authority' in a way that attracts a reasonable level of consensus? In the modern international system, legitimate authority almost exclusively lies with the recognised governments of nation-states or international organisations acting on their behalf. The latter, in particular the United Nations, have become increasingly central to this issue. Aside from self-defence and cases of urgent humanitarian intervention, resort to war is considered legitimate only if it is authorised by the UN Security Council. However, in contrast to the views of some commentators who regard the United Nations as a neutral arbiter, the United Nations is a construct of the nation-state system. It is true that the United Nations holds a degree of legitimacy and authority somewhat beyond the states from which it is made. Nonetheless, states in the Security Council, and especially the Permanent Five who hold the power of veto, ultimately decide whether or not the United Nations acts on issues of war. Therefore, in a practical sense, one could argue that legitimate authority still ultimately resides with the nation-state.

Do non-state actors have any standing on the issue of legitimate authority? There are certainly cases, especially those involving state-based injustices, when it may be argued that a non-state actor enjoys some legitimacy in its use of force. There are many who would regard the African National Congress's (ANC) military campaign against the South African government as an example of just cause and legitimate authority. Such examples suggest that non-state legitimate authority is possible in cases were the legitimacy of the standing government or political system is questioned. In contrast to the case of the ANC, few would regard the leadership of the Irish Republican Army (IRA) as legitimate authority in a just war sense. Because the Irish Republican movement had access to, and representation in, the democratic political system, a self-proclaimed Republican leadership would not be regarded as having the legitimate authority to undertake violent military action in pursuit of its goals.

Jus ad bellum: proportionate response

Even if all of the criteria so far have been met, the resort to war must be proportionate to the issue at stake. Some cases are fairly clear-cut in this respect. If massive human rights abuses are occurring (as in Kosovo), especially if civilian casualties are the result, then military action would seem a proportionate, if regrettable, response. Likewise, if an actor represents an existential violent threat to the regional and international order (as did the territorially defined ISIS), then military action would again seem proportionate. One could also argue, although it is a more problematic case, that war would be a proportionate response to massive disruption to the global economy, perhaps through the seizure of oil fields (as in the 1991 Gulf War). It would be more difficult to justify the resort to war over the affections of a woman (Troy), however.

The 2003 invasion of Iraq offers an interesting case study on the issue of proportionality. If one rejects the argument that the 2003 war can be legitimised as an act of preventive self-defence or a humanitarian intervention (to overthrow the regime of Saddam Hussein), then one is left with the notion that the war was fought in response to Iraq's failure to fulfil its obligations under UN resolutions relating to its WMD programme. When the United Kingdom and the United States failed to get a second UN resolution authorising military action against Iraq in 2003, reference was made to the 1991 resolutions, which authorised military action should Iraq fail to destroy and account for its WMD programme and stockpiles. However, in the absence of an imminent threat from Iraq's WMD (if indeed it had any), an invasion would seem a disproportionate response to Iraq's failure to completely account for its previous activities. Alternatively, one could argue that the reputation of the United Nations was at stake and that this could be regarded as enough of a cause to justify resorting to war. Clearly, the Iraq case indicates that the issue of proportionality is a subjective area of debate.

Jus ad bellum: reasonable chance for success

Finally, for resort to military action to be regarded as just, there must be a reasonable chance for success. At first glance, this seems a rather odd criteria for just war and seems more at home in a strategic assessment. However, its inclusion makes sense because to incur the terrible costs of war without any hope of success could be regarded as unnecessary suffering. When assessing a war against this final criterion of jus ad bellum, the word 'success' has to be clearly understood. It should not necessarily be equated with outright victory in the sense of defeating the enemy or achieving one's ultimate policy objective. Rather, success may be defined as achieving a more favourable settlement from a conflict. Such an approach can be seen in Japan's continued resistance towards the end of the Second World War. Although defeat was looking increasingly inevitable, the Japanese continued to resist, hoping to inflict such costs on the United States that the latter would offer terms more favourable than unconditional surrender. As a final point, if the enemy is hell-bent on the destruction of one's nation or race, then self-defence may be regarded as legitimate even in the face of certain defeat.

From this discussion, it appears that under the doctrine of just war, legitimate recourse to arms is not easy to achieve. War can be legitimately initiated only by a legitimate authority (increasingly understood to be the United Nations or an equivalent body), as a proportional response, in the service of a just cause, with the right intention, when other avenues of peaceful resolution have been exhausted, and where there is a reasonable prospect of success. And as noted, the challenge of meeting these criteria is complicated by the fact that many of them are open to subjective interpretation. Despite the challenges involved, war continues to be regarded as a legitimate tool of policy. This is especially the case as an act of self-defence, which is regarded as an inalienable right and as a response to significant levels of injustice, especially extreme humanitarian crises. However, the complexity of the subject is evident in the controversies surrounding the definition of 'self-defence' as it relates to pre-emption and preventive forms of action.

Jus in bello: discrimination

For a war to be regarded as just, meeting the criteria of jus ad bellum is not sufficient. How the war is conducted is just as important. Walzer warns against the temptation to ignore jus in bello if jus ad bellum has been satisfied.[17] As noted, the criteria for jus in bello are discrimination and proportionality. Discrimination is unambiguously based on the notion that there is a clear distinction between combatants and non-combatants and that the latter do not represent legitimate targets of military force. In turn, non-combatants are not permitted to take up arms in a conflict. Discrimination refers not only to civilians but also to combatants who have become hors de combat (outside the fight). This status applies most commonly to prisoners of war and the wounded. Importantly, discrimination applies also to objects, including buildings and infrastructure. Attacks against civilian objects are prohibited under Rule 7 of the handbook on the customary law of war. This rule is designed to prevent civilians suffering as a result of attacks against such things as food and water supplies.

Although discrimination may be regarded as an absolute principle in just war, its application is somewhat complicated by a number of issues.[18] In the first instance, distinguishing between a combatant and a non-combatant may not always be so straightforward. This is especially problematic during insurgencies and counterterrorism campaigns, when an irregular enemy may deliberately hide among the general population. However, this difficulty is somewhat overcome by the 1977 Geneva Protocol I, which states that regular military forces should assume a person is a non-combatant unless proven otherwise.[19] The problem of defining 'non-combatant' is even more pronounced in relation to objects. Take, for example, the electricity grid of a nation. While it clearly underpins much of civilian life, it also may be an important component of military command and control and the enemy's war-making potential. Therefore, is power generation a legitimate target or not?

The principle of discrimination (in terms of both people and objects) is also clouded by military necessity and the aforementioned doctrine of double effect. Although military necessity can never be used as a justification for the deliberate targeting of civilians, it does, in combination with double effect, permit the foreseen but unintentional killing of civilians for military purposes. This point may seem to dilute much of the intended effects of the principle of discrimination. However, military necessity should not be regarded as a permissive notion. Rather, as Henry Shue indicates, under the principle of military necessity, a military operation can be undertaken only if it is physically necessary and indispensable and/or unavoidable in order to achieve military objectives. Also, even under the principle of military necessity, all actions must be lawful.[20] Hence, military necessity can never be regarded as an excuse for actions that are unnecessarily brutal or indiscriminate, even if they are carried out in the pursuit of legitimate military goals. Finally, the principle of discrimination is supported by, and works alongside, the principle of proportionality.

Jus in bello: proportionality

Both discrimination and proportionality are concerned with preventing unnecessary suffering in war. The principle of proportionality seeks to limit suffering by demanding that the human costs of military operations be reasonable in relation to the expected military gains. Thus, although unintended civilian casualties are permitted under the notion of double effect, they cannot be disproportionate to the goals sought. For example, destroying an airbase in a populated area with a nuclear warhead, although it would almost certainly achieve its military goal, is likely to be regarded as a grossly disproportionate use of force.

Henry Shue argues that a military operation must also have a clear and achievable objective that creates significant military advantage for any costs involved to be considered proportionate. He argues that it is insufficient to undertake an action with only some vague hope or idea that it will at some stage deliver military advantage.[21] Although it is difficult to argue with Shue's general point, one can take issue with his understanding of the nature of war and the examples that he uses. For example, he argues that the attritional battles of the First World War should not be regarded as legitimate on these grounds. Although in retrospect many of the battles of this conflict appear problematic on the grounds of military necessity and proportionality, the commanders at the time were genuinely seeking a breakthrough. And even in their failures, they were relearning the art of war in the face of modern technology. The results of this costly learning experience can be seen in the remarkable gains achieved by both sides in 1918. Also, some attritional battles were fought precisely because they seemed to offer the best prospect for a positive outcome. For example, at the battle of Verdun, the Germans thought they could crush the resistance of the French by bleeding the French army dry. The fact that they were wrong does not diminish the fact that they initially perceived attrition to be a war-winning strategy. Finally, Shue is unnecessarily harsh on campaigns that rely on cumulative effects. The Germans were finally defeated, at least in part, by the cumulative attritional effects of big battles such as the Somme and Verdun. Thus, we can conclude that many of the battles of the First World War were necessary to achieve overall victory and that they were proportional relative to the scale of the war and the character of warfare at that particular moment in history.

Proportionality also relates to the methods and weapons of war. Again, the principle behind this is preventing unnecessary suffering. Thus, certain weapons and methods of warfare are prohibited because they cause unnecessary suffering that is disproportionate to any military gains that could be made. Weapons that are designed to maim rather than kill are often prohibited on the basis that they inflict unnecessary suffering. Such a prohibition applies to laser-blinding weapons, for example. In terms of methods, atrocities such as rape are prohibited. Although such methods could be used to terrorise and coerce a population, they too are prohibited on the grounds of proportionality and causing unnecessary suffering.

One set of weapons that seems completely at odds with the principles of jus in bello are nuclear weapons. However, the ethics of nuclear strategy are less clear than one might imagine. It is theoretically possible for nuclear weapons to pass both the discrimination and proportionality tests. A small nuclear device could be used against enemy forces (perhaps a naval vessel) in a remote and unpopulated area (sea or desert). In such circumstances, it is entirely possible that no civilians or civilian infrastructure would be harmed or damaged. Still, the residual radiation from a nuclear device, which can last for many years, could result in a breach of both proportionality and discrimination at some later date. However, outputs from a nuclear device can be altered to limit the amount of residual radiation (this was the basis for the infamous neutron bomb of the Cold War) and thus realign nuclear weapons with jus in bello.

Despite the fact that one can construct a scenario in which nuclear weapons can be used in a proportionate and discriminatory manner, this is hardly the norm in nuclear strategy. Historically, nuclear strategy has been based, in part, on the delivery of massive amounts of destruction against urban areas. In those cases where civilian centres have not been targeted – so-called counterforce missions that focus on the enemy's nuclear forces and command and control – the proximity of military targets to areas of human habitation almost guarantees substantial civilian losses. Thus, in most circumstances, nuclear weapons appear to fail important aspects of just war theory. And yet even in its traditional guise, when large-scale use can be anticipated, nuclear strategy resides in somewhat of a grey area in the ethics of war debate.

Ambiguity over the ethics of nuclear strategy emanates from two main sources: nuclear deterrence and supreme emergency. As Chapter 12 of this book argues, nuclear strategy has been dominated by the concept of deterrence. And because nuclear deterrence seeks to prevent war, and thereby create a positive outcome, a consequentialist would regard nuclear deterrence as morally valid. Although it works on the basis of threatening vast amounts of suffering and unhappiness, it actually is intended to produce happiness by promoting a stable security relationship devoid of war and its attendant suffering.[22] However, this carefully balanced position is clearly undone if deterrence fails and the threat is enacted. What, then, for the consequentialist position?

Deontology presents a similarly complex position. On the one hand, one could argue that since nuclear deterrence has as its intended goal the prevention of war, nuclear strategy is morally valid due to having sound intentions. In this sense, we have a duty to prevent war, and if nuclear threats are the only means to achieve this, then they are perceived as morally legitimate. Such an argument is premised on the idea that we can distinguish between the threat of nuclear annihilation (deterrence) and fulfilling that threat. On the other hand, a deontologist may take the position that it is immoral to threaten that which it is immoral to do. This is especially the case because nuclear deterrence, by holding entire populations hostage, is using human beings as mere means to an end.[23]

From the perspective of the just war tradition, nuclear weapons appear morally unsound because in most cases, although not all, they appear to fail the tests of both discrimination and proportionality. However, on the issue of nuclear deterrence, Walzer proposes that supreme emergency (the threat of nuclear war) requires us to adjust our ethical position. In particular, as with the consequentialist position outlined earlier, he argues that threatening evil may be morally defensible because it seeks to prevent that same evil from occurring.[24] While there is a recognisable logic in this position, it still suffers from the problem of what happens if deterrence fails, by deliberate act, miscalculation, or accident. Indeed, deterrence may fail precisely because the threats on which it is based provoke fear and instability in a security relationship. What Schelling described as 'the reciprocal fear of surprise attack'.[25] At this point, the just war argument appears to break down in relation to nuclear weapons. However, with a more liberal interpretation of discrimination, proportionality, and double effect, nuclear war itself may be defensible under the umbrella of supreme emergency.

If we accept the position that the threat of nuclear war creates a supreme emergency, then it seems reasonable to argue that the state of supreme emergency continues to exist after nuclear war has begun. In this case, rather than simply submit themselves to global Armageddon, decision makers have a moral duty to wage war in such a way as to limit damage and suffering. This is one of the arguments in support of adopting a nuclear warfighting doctrine.[26] Damage limitation is most directly achieved via counterforce strikes against the enemy's nuclear forces and his command and control infrastructure. Attacks against the civilian population (countervalue attacks) would be difficult to justify on moral grounds. Although it is possible that countervalue attacks could support intra-war deterrence, and thereby fit into the consequentialist position, they would clearly fail any deontological test and the just war principle of discrimination. However, civilian losses as a consequence of counterforce missions could be justified under the principle of double effect. And since there is a state of supreme emergency, one could argue that the anticipated heavy losses are proportionate to the objectives sought, namely the survival of the nation-state and perhaps even the human race as a viable species. This scenario is undoubtedly horrific, but there is a certain logic to it from an ethics perspective – certainly, from one that is based on the just war tradition and accepts the principles of supreme emergency and double effect. Of course, as with so many of the debates just outlined, this argument is based on subjective interpretations of proportionality. Are the deaths of 200 million people, for example, proportionate to the objective of saving an entire nation and perhaps the vast majority of the human population?

Jus post bellum[27]

Jus post bellum is a developing area of the just war tradition. It is concerned with establishing a lasting just peace in the aftermath of conflict. Actions within war, and the purposes for which the war is fought, clearly have an impact on how just peace is established. Thus, there exists an important relationship among all three sections of the just war tradition. For example, for right intention to be effectively realised, the principles of jus in bello must be respected. To coin a phrase, it is no use creating a desert and calling it peace. As Emily Pollard argues, 'the intentions of a country going to war cannot be "right intentions" if they do not intend to fight morally, or if they do not intend to act morally in victory'.[28] Equally, the post-conflict phase must be a prime consideration in the war-planning phase. The 2003 invasion of Iraq, and the tragic events that followed, provides evidence of the consequences of treating the post-conflict environment as an afterthought.

Jus post bellum places certain responsibilities on belligerents, especially victor powers. For writers such as Walzer and Orend, it is not sufficient to merely seek a return to the status quo ante. As Orend notes, 'that situation was precisely what led to armed conflict and war in the first place'.[29] Rather, the post-war environment must be more just. In this sense, jus post bellum identifies characteristics that appear to support key components of the common good. These include rights vindication, proportional political rehabilitation, economic reconstruction, and the proportional punishment of war criminals. How a war is waged and for what policy objectives have important impacts on the realisation of these characteristics and hence on perceptions of legitimacy.

Rights vindication is concerned with addressing the injustice that led to conflict but is also concerned with limiting the ambitions of the victor. The rights referred to include the right to life and liberty and entitlements to territory and sovereignty.[30] This principle also seeks to prevent the victor from adding objectives that go beyond the original just cause. In this way, it provides guidance on the just termination of conflicts. Proportional political rehabilitation seeks to address the political structures and cultures that led to conflict and to provide a more stable political environment for the future. Measures can include demilitarisation, human rights education, and even structural reforms to overturn the pre-war political system. Such an approach worked well in post-war Germany and Japan but is far more controversial in cases such as Iraq. This is clearly a contentious area that potentially leads us into the realms of regime change and the legitimacy of that objective. To prevent abuses by the victor powers, Mark Evans has suggested, sovereignty should be returned as quickly as possible once stability has been established.[31] Moreover, political rehabilitation must be guided by right intention, so that the interests of all are promoted, not just the interests of the victors.

As a consequence of war's destructive nature, economic reconstruction is essential for a just post bellum environment. As Williams and Caldwell note, 'without the rehabilitation in some small measure of war-torn economies, it may be difficult to secure the most basic of human rights'.[32] Economic wellbeing also contributes to the prospects for post bellum stability. An example of such an approach is the Marshall Plan, enacted by the United States in 1948. Under the European Economic Recovery Program, the United States provided over $12 billion to European countries ravaged by war. The recipients included the recently defeated West Germany, which received 12% of the aid programme. More controversial, perhaps, is the issue of reparations. How much should defeated aggressor powers be made to pay for their aggression? At the conclusion of the First World War, the Treaty of Versailles and the 1921 London Schedule of Payments instructed Germany to pay reparations totalling $33 billion. As a result of political and economic instability, Germany struggled to meet the payments. Over the years, various adjustments were made to the repayment scheme, which was finally settled in 2010. It is also suggested that the humiliation and burden of the reparations and War Guilt Clause in the Treaty of Versailles contributed to the rise of national socialism in Germany. Although it would be ludicrously reductionist to claim that the reparations were primarily responsible for the rise of the Nazi Party, the emergence of a totalitarian fascist state is clearly counter to the objectives of jus post bellum. This merely underlines the importance of a well-thought-out post bellum programme that is premised on a just and stable post-war order, not on revenge.

Finally, we turn to the issue of proportional punishment for war crimes. In the search for a just and stable peace, proportional punishment serves a number of purposes. In the first instance, it enables reconciliation and closure for the victims of war crimes. As Orend argues, 'failing to punish the aggressor degrades and disrespects the worth, status, and suffering of the victim'.[33] It also acts as a deterrent to dissuade others from breaching the precepts of just war in the future. In this way, it enhances the standing of just war. As Bass notes, a post-war judicial process 'represent[s] a powerful instantiation of the principles of just war theory, formally calling leaders to account for their violations of those tenets at the heart of *jus ad bellum* and *jus in bello*'.[34] It is, however, important that punishment be based on universal accountability and due process. All sides in a conflict must be held to the same standards, and the accused must have fair representation. If these important legal and moral principles are absent, a lasting just peace is more difficult to ensure.

The laws of war

Although the ethics of war and laws of war are distinct, the modern legal system for regulating conflict is based on the just war tradition.[35] In this sense, the laws of war are divided into those that cover the resort to force (jus ad bellum) and those that regulate the conduct of hostilities (jus in bello). This chapter will now outline the main laws in both cases, before discussing the efficacy of the legal framework for conflict.

During the interwar period of the twentieth century, there were two main attempts to prohibit recourse to war in international politics: The League of Nations and the 1928 Kellogg–Briand pact. The absence or withdrawal of key states doomed these attempts to failure, as was evidenced in the outbreak of the Second World War. However, the shock of a second devastating global conflict inspired a third attempt at regulating war as a tool of policy. Thus, resort to war in international politics is now largely governed by Article 2 (3) (4) and Chapter VII of the UN Charter. Article 2 (3) stipulates that 'All members shall settle their international disputes by peaceful means'. This is supported by Article 2 (4): 'All members shall refrain in their international relations from the threat or use of force against the territorial integrity or political independence of any state, or in any other manner inconsistent with the purposes of the United Nations'. Chapter VII of the UN Charter contains two exceptions to this general prohibition against the use of force: individual and collective self-defence and actions authorised by the UN Security Council for the maintenance or restoration of international peace and security. These provisions are endowed with the character of jus cogens, which is defined as 'a peremptory norm of general international law . . . accepted and recognised by the international community of states as a whole as a norm from which no derogation is permitted'. At one level, this prohibition looks fairly robust. However, some of the terminology is open to interpretation. How does one accurately define 'the threat of force'? Does such a threat need to be overt and direct? Similarly, how does one define 'peace and security'?[36]

The various laws that apply to jus in bello are now commonly referred to as international humanitarian law (IHL), although they can be subdivided into Geneva Law and Hague Law. The former is primarily concerned with protecting the victims of armed conflict, while the latter relates to the methods and means of warfare. The Geneva Law is based on the four Geneva Conventions of 1949 and additional protocols. The four conventions, signed and ratified by 194 states, deal with the victims (sick and wounded) of (I) land warfare; (II) sea warfare; (III) prisoners of war; and (IV) civilians. In 1977, the Additional Protocol II, which deals specifically with civil wars, was signed. Hague Law is based on the Hague Conventions of 1899 and 1907 and the 1977 Additional Protocol I to the Geneva Conventions. Hague Law seeks to regulate the conduct of warfare in general, and it includes specific areas such as maritime and aerial bombardment, chemical munitions, and bullet design.

Although much effort has been expended on the development of the laws of war, producing an extensive and complex legal framework for hostilities, the efficacy of international law (including the laws of war) often comes under attack. It is argued that states abide by the law only when it is in their interests to do so, disregarding laws as and when they need. This perception is no better illustrated than by the famous comment by the German Chancellor Theobald von Bethmann-Hollweg on the eve of the First World War: 'We are now in a state of necessity, and necessity knows no law'. This statement can be interpreted in a number of ways. Justin Morris argues that it is significant for the status of international law that Germany invaded neutral countries 'not in disregard for the law, but rather in conscious breach of it'.[37] Thus, even though in breach of the law, there is some recognition of its status in the workings of the international system. Although there is clear merit in Morris's interpretation, his position is perhaps too generous towards the status of international law. A different reading of the chancellor's statement might emphasise the point that in certain circumstances (supreme emergency) the law is not consciously breached; rather, it is considered defunct. To put it another way, 'in time of war the law is silent'.[38] This is particularly important in relation to the laws of war, as it is precisely in moments of conflict that the law is arguably most needed and tested.

Although at times the law is disregarded, this is the exception rather than the norm. The vast majority of the time, states abide by the laws of war. Even when the laws have been ignored in relation to jus ad bellum, those pertaining to jus in bello are largely applied. Why is it that states normally abide by international law, even in times of war? There are a number of reasons why states respect and apply the law. These reasons can be grouped under the headings of self-interest (which can be subdivided into stability, legitimacy, and reciprocity) and shared norms. For the most part, self-interested states benefit from stability and predictability within the international system. The law clearly helps to facilitate these goals. It is also generally beneficial for states to be well regarded by their peers. In particular, it is important for a state to be trusted and to be seen to play by the rules. By fulfilling their obligations under international law, a state is likely to be perceived as a legitimate actor within the system. Finally, on the issue of self-interest, for the most part, international law protects the interests of the state system. This covers many aspects of state relations, including trade and communications, to name just two. Thus, a state may abide by the law on the understanding that others will do the same: 'do unto others as you would have them do unto you'.

Thus far, this discussion represents a realist take on states' behaviour in relation to international law. However, there may be other, less-pragmatic reasons underlying attitudes towards the law. As noted earlier in relation to the work of Morgenthau, it may be that states, which at some level reflect the moral beings they represent, hold certain norms to be valid. This may apply to individual laws, such as non-combatant immunity, or it may relate to the validity of the rule of law in general. In this sense, states may abide by international law simply because they perceive it to have intrinsic value beyond the interest of the state.

Thus, in relation to the fortunes of international law, it seems that most of the time, states are happy to abide by a legal code. However, it is also evident that state actors will breach, ignore, or redefine the law if required, especially when facing a supreme emergency. As noted earlier, in the aftermath of the 9/11 attacks, the United States released a new security doctrine that seemed to broaden the definition of self-defence, to include pre-emptive and preventive action. This expanded interpretation of self-defence partly formed the basis for the 2003 invasion of Iraq.

For those who put much value on the rule of law as it pertains to jus ad bellum, the prospect of states acting in a minority to redefine aspects of international law may seem like a retrograde step. Indeed, one might argue that such a reinterpretation of international law is nothing more than a cover for an act of realist power politics. However, it has also been argued, particularly by the Blair government at the time, that the invasion of Iraq was undertaken to maintain the integrity of international law. In this sense, the invasion was launched to uphold the authority of the United Nations and was actually justified in law by Iraq's failure to fulfil its legal obligations under Security Resolutions dating back to 1991. Again, this might be regarded as a cover for naked power politics, but there is some basis for such claims to legitimacy. In the final analysis, the invasion of Iraq, and its consequences for international law, can be read in many ways. It can be seen as upholding international law (the 1991 UN resolutions); as a redefinition of the inherent right to self-defence, much needed in the changing security environment; or as naked power politics reflecting no respect for the laws of war. However one sees it, the invasion of Iraq still represents an exception rather than the norm. The laws pertaining to jus ad bellum may be open to some debate in the aftermath of 9/11, but they are still very much in effect.

At the same time that jus ad bellum is being challenged, the principles of jus in bello appear to be more eagerly applied and monitored. The legal profession now has much greater influence in the conduct of military operations. This is matched by a substantial increase in ethics training in military services. This increase in ethical and legal awareness has been partially brought about, and monitored, by global 24/7 media and the growth of non-governmental organisations (NGOs) dedicated to the promotion of human rights and the rule of law. These so-called norm-entrepreneurs, such as Human Rights Watch, have become increasingly well organised and influential in compiling reports and naming and shaming states that breach established principles on the use of force.[39] This increased awareness has brought to light such abuses as those carried out at Abu Ghraib prison in Iraq. There have also been developments in the enforcement of international law. Most importantly, the International Criminal Court was established in 2002. This permanent tribunal can hear cases relating to genocide, crimes against humanity, and war crimes. At the time of writing, 122 states have ratified or acceded to the Rome Statute of the International Criminal Court. However, important actors in the international system, including the United States, Russia, and China, either have not signed the treaty, have withdrawn from it, or have yet to ratify it.

While these developments in the application of jus in bello are to be welcomed by those interested in the regulation of armed conflict, the story is not wholly positive. The conflicts in Kosovo, Syria, Sudan, and Rwanda, and many more besides, reveal that brutality and even genocide still plague humanity. However, negative developments are not just related to cases in which the laws of war seem impotent. It is also possible to identify areas where a legal approach may have overstepped the mark and become overly intrusive and complex. In the United Kingdom, coroners' courts now routinely investigate the death of British troops in combat zones and in doing so make judgements on the competence of military operations. While it is useful from the perspective of best practice to examine past military operations, it is less easy to see the benefit of a coroner ruling that a combat death was unlawful. Is this the right forum for such analysis and discussion? In one hearing, the coroner concluded thus: 'It is my belief that it is imperative that our forces, whether they be in Iraq or Afghanistan, are given the best available equipment'.[40] While this is a sentiment that most would agree with, it takes little account of the complexities of defence planning and military operations in the face of the enemy. This is not to deny that military failures and the deaths of servicemen could often have been avoided with more careful preparation. Rather, it is merely to note that those making a judgement on such issues should be cognisant of the nature of war and the challenges of defence planning.

The laws of war are also becoming increasingly complicated. One commentator who is generally supportive of the legal approach has admitted that 'Mastering the body of IHL and related areas is a challenge for any military or civilian lawyer'.[41] If we remind ourselves of the complexity and uncertainty intrinsic to war, then we have to conclude that introducing further complexity through the medium of the law is problematic. It certainly seems to go against the advice of Clausewitz: to keep things simple. If applied and interpreted with too much vigour, there is a real danger that the laws of war will begin to conflict with the demands of strategy. Indeed, in a remarkable statement, Christopher P.M. Waters argues that 'Strategy should not trump law when the two depart'.[42] Is Waters really arguing in favour of accepting defeat to uphold the laws of war? He may not be thinking in terms of victory or defeat, but if the practitioner denies themselves certain strategies, defeat may be the outcome. At best, the costs of a campaign may increase. Although Morris and Brodie are largely correct when they note that the laws of war are not especially prohibitive from the standpoint of military effectiveness, there is a sense that legality and ethical concerns are beginning to take precedence over strategic efficacy.[43]

Strategic necessity

In such an emerging reality the practitioner of strategy is left with a substantial dilemma. How does he achieve his policy objectives (victory) against an intelligent foe in a complex environment, whilst at the same time having to meet ever more complex and intrusive legal and ethical demands? The answer to this challenge may be strategic necessity, which puts policy considerations first, but by doing so also takes into account ethical and legal concerns. However, before this chapter details exactly what this entails, it is important to outline the significance of victory and the means to achieve it.

As noted earlier, there are those who regard the laws of war and ethical principles as inviolable but who do not regard strategy (the process of achieving victory) as so sacred. From this perspective, certain methods, those that breach valued norms and laws, should be rejected, even if they represent important means to victory. In response, it is important to remind ourselves just how important victory actually is. At best, failing to achieve one's objectives means that the lives sacrificed in a campaign are lost for little, if any, gain. Defeat, however, can be far more serious. The Jews of Europe, aside from those already trapped inside Nazi Germany, were slaughtered in part because their respective states were defeated. The citizens of Carthage faced a similar fate at the hands of the Roman Republic. In this sense, Brian Bond is convincing when he argues that 'terrible and destructive as war is, victory is usually sharply differentiated from defeat'.[44] Should victory be sacrificed in the name of legal and ethical principles? This is a legitimate question to ask on both strategic and ethical grounds. In relation to the latter, it is an example of the clash of duties identified earlier in the deontological position. If there is a moral duty to defeat evil or to defend the interests of the community, should we deny ourselves certain methods to achieve those goals? In this sense, Walzer argues that each war must be judged twice according to jus ad bellum and jus in bello. It also raises the prospect that there may be a hierarchy between the two components of the just war tradition. If a war passes the jus ad bellum test, should it be given an easier ride in relation to jus in bello?[45]

This question is complicated by the methods (means and ways) available to a strategist. Ideally, a strategist will have at their disposal a method that achieves the objectives and fulfils the demands of law and ethics. Indeed, the laws of war demand that a commander choose the method that achieves their military goals in a manner that causes the least harm. However, that may not always be possible or easy to calculate. As noted earlier, nuclear strategy may require an approach that sits uncomfortably with the just war tradition. Coercion presents similar problems. Coercion is regarded as an efficient and effective form of strategy: 'The power to hurt can be counted among the most impressive attributes of military force'.[46] For strategic effect, it relies on the threat of, or indeed the actual infliction of, pain on others. Coercion seeks to change the enemy's behaviour via the threat of punishment. Often this punishment is directed against the civilian population, who in turn may put pressure on their political leadership to accede to the enemy's demands. Although coercion can involve the direct targeting of civilians, coercion in the modern era mostly occurs by attacking infrastructure that supports the functioning of society. Is this an appropriate method for waging war?

How one answers this question will reflect one's ethical approach. A deontologist, assuming that they took the Kantian position that people should be regarded as ends rather than as mere means, would denounce coercion since it uses the pain and suffering of others to reach desired objectives. In contrast, a consequentialist may regard the suffering of coercion as acceptable if it led to the greater good. Since coercion is regarded as an efficient and effective use of force, it is entirely possible that consequentialist demands could be met by ensuring a rapid end to hostilities with minimal loss of life and pain. In contrast, the just war tradition would most likely reject coercion if it relied on the deliberate infliction of pain on a population (which it often does) and thereby failed the discrimination test. The most logical position, although not necessarily the most ethical one, is strategic necessity, which will now be defined.

In contrast to military necessity, which is a legal concept that recognises military requirements, but does so within the confines of IHL, strategic necessity takes a more pragmatic approach to the subject. The difference between these two concepts may be subtle, but it is significant. Strategic necessity takes account of ethical and legal considerations but is not shackled by them. Most importantly for the purposes of this chapter, strategic necessity actively incorporates the ethical dimension into the process of strategy, although it does this in an instrumentalist manner. Under the terms of military necessity, a commander must take account of ethics and the laws of war. This is achieved by the commander's legal responsibility to ensure that any actions are necessary and do not breach IHL. In particular, any operations must comport with the principles of proportionality and discrimination. However, under military necessity, IHL may be regarded as essentially an external framework for action rather than an integral part of the decision-making process. Within strategic necessity, ethical and legal considerations potentially carry as much weight as those relating to military needs.

Exactly how much influence each set of considerations will have in any particular scenario should be determined by the process of strategy. Strategy is driven by policy. Any actions must be judged on how they affect the achievement of the policy objective. Thus, within strategic necessity, it is entirely possible that a military operation that is regarded as necessary and fulfils the requirements of proportionality, discrimination, and double effect (and abides by IHL) could still be cancelled if achieving the policy objective is hindered by anticipated moral outrage. In this sense, within strategic necessity, decision-making has gone beyond mere legal and ethical checks to incorporate these dimensions into an overall vision of strategy. Although this approach might result in even greater regulation and limits on the use of force, this is not necessarily the case. Strategic necessity would also permit actions that breach the war convention if the policy objective demanded it. Although in most cases, it will be in the interests of the state to abide by the law, cases of supreme emergency may call for a more liberal interpretation of aspects of war convention.

With the policy objective as the guiding principle, ethical and legal issues can be dealt with in a more pragmatic fashion, since they have now become part of the process of strategic decision-making. This is not to suggest that strategic necessity invariably simplifies the process of strategy in relation to ethical issues. There are still likely to be some difficult judgements involved in this process. For example, it may be difficult to gauge the likely moral response to certain military actions. What strategic necessity seeks to avoid are complex, intrusive, and sometimes irresolvable legal and ethical debates.

For the most part, abiding by the war convention equals good strategy. However, strategic necessity, which gives the user more flexibility in how they apply and interprets the convention, is a sensible response to Waters's position that the law should trump strategy. Instead, the opposite should be true. War is not the continuation of legal intercourse. War only has meaning and validity if it is used in the service of policy. The process by which this is achieved is strategy. That being the case, how can a war be valid if strategy is made impotent by strict interpretations and adherence to the war convention?

Strategic necessity is not a radical departure from existing positions. Rather, it merely seeks to rebalance the debate back towards the demands of strategy. It represents a pragmatic approach to war-making. However, it is also cognisant of modern attitudes to ethics. And although it fundamentally deals with ethical issues in an instrumentalist manner, it still gives them great respect. Indeed, strategic necessity ascribes value to the war convention because it reflects prevailing ethical norms, which must be respected in the name of good strategy.

There may be no watertight method to fulfil the demands of strategy while meeting the increasingly stringent demands of ethics and the laws of war. Attempting to limit unnecessary suffering in warfare is a positive step in the development of human rights. In this sense, the principles of jus in bello have undoubted value. However, seeking to achieve victory is also a positive goal. In the question about which should take precedence between ethics and victory, strategic necessity suggests that the answer is victory (achievement of the policy objective), although ethical restraints should be respected as far as is practicable. While suffering in warfare should be moderated as far as possible, war should still be allowed to serve its ultimate purpose: achieving the policy objective in the service of the interests of the community. If methods can be found that fulfil the criteria of both strategy and the war convention, then they should be encouraged. However, the strategist's already difficult job should not be complicated further by forcing them to jump through complex legal and ethical hoops. Indeed, it has already been recognised that enemies of the West have identified as a weakness our efforts to apply strict ethical and legal standards, and they are exploiting it. This so-called lawfare, which uses the law to degrade our strategic options, has to be countered at some level.[47] And although at times the best method of neutralising an enemy's strength is to abide by the laws of war and claim the moral high ground, at times it may serve us to be more flexible in how we apply ethical norms and values. Clausewitz is certainly clear on the danger of ceding the enemy an advantage in relation to how law and ethics are applied in war: 'If one side uses force without compunction, undeterred by the bloodshed it involves, while the other refrains, the first will gain the upper hand'.[48]

Strategy for the common good

There is another approach to marry the seemingly conflicting needs of strategy and ethics. It involves using the common good as a meta-narrative. The common good has a long history in political thought, stretching back to Aristotle and ancient Rome and finding expression in the works of St Augustine and St Thomas Aquinas, with notable contributions in the modern period from British idealism (especially T.H. Green), Kant, the contractual approach (found in Rawls and Rousseau), and Catholic social doctrine. In essence, the common good seeks the creation of a sociopolitical environment that enables the individual and the community to flourish and reach their full potential.

Box 3.3 Components of the common good

Sociopolitical conditions that enable the community and individual to flourish:

Respect for the person (including right to life).
Social wellbeing and development.
Peace.
Solidarity.

The common good is best understood as the social and community dimension of the moral good.[49] Since war is a social activity, it is appropriate to understand the conduct of strategy through the prism of the common good. There are numerous ways to perceive the common good. From a security perspective, it is most usefully perceived as being composed of four elements: respect for the person (exemplified by the right to life), social wellbeing and development, peace, and solidarity.[50] The exercise of military power has clear implications for each of these components. Most obviously, war threatens the most basic of human rights (the right to life); by destroying infrastructure and diverting resources, it often wreaks havoc with social development; and it can undermine solidarity via the damaging sociopolitical effects of violence. At the same time, peace, security, and development require protection. As a consequence, within common good discourse, participation in social life, including military service, is perceived as a good.

To ensure that military power serves the common good, rather than undermining it, strategy must be perceived in a positive light. Rather than seeking merely to limit the damage and suffering from military action, the process of strategy can be ordered in a way that promotes the universal good. This is to be achieved in a number of ways. Since war is the continuation of policy, the first step is to ensure that the latter is commensurate with pursuing the common good. Some policy objectives, such as genocide, to cite an extreme example, would make it difficult for the process of strategy to serve the common good.

To be in tune with the common good, strategy should be centred on the minimal, not just proportional, use of violence. As previously mentioned, proportionality may permit excessive levels of violence if military circumstances require it. Thus, a minimal violence approach is more likely to serve the common good. Moreover, minimal violence is extolled in certain forms of strategy. It can be found, for example, in coercion, deterrence, counterinsurgency, and cyberwar. Indeed, minimal violence has a strong theoretical basis. This is expressed most notably in Sun Tzu's *The Art of War*: 'For to win one hundred victories in one hundred battles is not the acme of skill. To subdue the enemy without fighting is the acme of skill'.[51] For those concerned that the common good approach shuns the realist underpinnings of strategy, note that Sun Tzu's preference for nonviolence was motivated primarily by realist considerations. The great theorist and practitioner regarded violence as unpredictable, wasteful, and potentially counterproductive.

One of the great challenges of strategy, from the traditional realist perspective and from the common good perspective, is the difficulty of exerting control over the process. War's natural impulse to escalate, allied with the fact that it is competitive, non-linear, multidimensional, and prone to friction, creates a genuine problem for the strategist seeking to promote the common good. In such an environment, the consequences of political violence may be hard to predict and contain. Thus, to achieve the policy objective at reasonable cost, as well as to minimise damage to the common good, the strategist must strive for military efficacy and the mitigation of the effects of friction. Both of these objectives require, but are not limited to, ample and good equipment, professional forces, good intelligence, experienced forces, good command, historical knowledge, good doctrine, and so on. In this way, the pursuit of the common good and effective strategy are built on the same foundations.

Since solidarity is an essential component of the common good, military operations must be perceived as legitimate. In the absence of legitimacy, rancour and division are likely to result from the exercise of military power. How is legitimacy ensured? The just war tradition, in all three of its guises – ad bellum, in bello, post bellum – provides an appropriate checklist for judging the legitimacy of military actions. And as noted earlier, in relation to strategic necessity, in most circumstances, military operations that are seen as legitimate support good strategy. Clausewitz notes that war is never (more accurately, rarely) the final act. That being the case, the strategist must be conscious of the post bellum environment if the policy objectives pursued and/or won are to have longevity. Policy objectives that result from legitimate military actions are more likely to be perceived as legitimate and therefore more likely to be accepted once the fighting has stopped.

To enhance the chances of legitimacy, military strategy must be integrated within a coherent grand strategy that is itself guided by the common good. With the concepts of development and solidarity in mind, the tendency of military action to break things and kill people has the potential to undermine the unity of grand strategy. Consequently, those responsible for military strategy must be conscious of the impact that their actions have on the broader project. This thought should, of course, inform the planning and conduct of operations. For their part, the other instruments of grand strategy must be employed to negate the negative impact of violent force. Ideally, for every violent action, there must be a positive act of development or solidarity to counterbalance the negative effects of war. In this way, and guided by the policy objective, the different instruments of grand strategy must complement one another in a coherent, holistic process.

This produces an enormous challenge that can be met only on the basis of excellent intelligence. Sun Tzu's call for the most efficacious use of force is premised on his axiom: 'If you know the enemy and know yourself, you need not fear the result of a hundred battles'.[52] The knowledge required to use force minimally, and legitimately, within a coherent grand strategy, achieving one's policy objectives while respecting post bellum considerations of development and solidarity, is substantial. Moreover, the whole project is viable only if the common good acts as a meta-concept that exists above the formation of policy and its realisation through grand strategy, military strategy, operations, and tactics.

The astute reader will note that the two new approaches outlined here, strategic necessity and the common good, are somewhat in conflict. It is true that they both demand the efficacious use of force guided by an overarching objective (policy and/or the common good). The key difference between them is that strategic necessity is driven by a pragmatic focus on the policy objective of one belligerent. In contrast, the common good is driven by a focus on a universal and intrinsically benevolent objective. As a consequence, force is potentially less restrained under strategic necessity. In conclusion, as aspirational as the common good approach is, it may be too challenging for the strategist. In the complex, competitive, and unforgiving world of strategy, strategic necessity is the superior approach, less prone to inviting strategic failure.

Conclusion

War cannot be understood holistically without reference to the ethical dimension. Ethics is intrinsic to human activities. Thus, strategy must take account of this dimension. And yet making sense of ethics in the rational, competitive, and complex world of strategy is challenging. This is largely because ethics is anything but straightforward. How one judges the moral worth of an action will be significantly determined by whether one is operating from a consequentialist or deontological position. Moral relativism adds further complexity to the endeavour. However, while there is undoubtedly much complexity and subjectivity inherent in ethical discourse, in the field of military ethics, a consensus of sorts can be identified. Built on this consensus, the just war tradition seeks to mitigate the tension between ethics and the demands of strategy. Importantly, just war accepts the need for military action under certain conditions. In the contemporary environment, the right to resort to war (jus ad bellum) tends to be limited to self-defence (including the defence of others), the associated notion of responsibility to protect (humanitarian intervention), and the cause of international peace and security. The great challenge in the complex contemporary security environment is to adequately define some of these terms. The term 'self-defence', in particular, has been subject to redefinition. This relates primarily to pre-emptive and preventive forms of self-defence.

When it comes to the conduct of war, the principles of discrimination and proportionality (jus in bello) lie at the heart of ethical discourse. The distinction between combatant and non-combatant is fairly well established, although it is not clear in every situation. In contrast, proportionality is open to a great degree of interpretation. Having to spend valuable time and energy sorting through the differing possible interpretations of proportionality is an unwelcome addition to the complex process of strategy.

Although jus post bellum adds another layer of analysis onto the already-stretched mind of the strategist (since post bellum objectives must be considered in both the planning and active phases of war), the search for a just and stable peace equates with a rational, and therefore strategic, approach. Rights vindication, proportional political rehabilitation, economic reconstruction, and proportional punishment of war crimes all coincide with Clausewitz's notion that war is rarely the final act. For a policy objective to be realised and maintained, the consequences of political violence and war termination must be part of the process of strategy.

Increasingly, the war convention has developed a substantial legal dimension. As in the field of ethics, the laws of war are organised around jus ad bellum and jus in bello. Although there are clear cases of the law being breached and ignored, sometimes on a genocidal scale, for the most part, the laws of war are respected and serve their purpose of regulating armed conflict to reduce unnecessary suffering. While it is generally recognised that the war convention does not significantly prohibit strategic efficacy – indeed, it can be an important component of success – a more zealous application of the law may be developing. There is a danger that obedience to the war convention may begin to take precedence over the quest for victory. The latter (which equates to achieving the policy objective) has to remain the primary consideration. Otherwise, war makes no sense. In addition, increased legal interference in the process of strategy could begin to hinder the freedom of the strategist and add an extra layer of complexity onto an already-challenging activity. That being said, legitimacy, which is often served by legality, is often an important component of effective strategy.

Clearly, the relationship between effective strategy and ethics is complex, at times complementary, but sometimes in a state of tension. One way to overcome possible tensions between the war convention and the demands of strategy is the approach described as strategic necessity. By placing the achievement of the policy objective as the main focus, strategic necessity ensures that all of the dimensions of strategy are given due respect. In the modern environment, ethical concerns demand significant attention. Thus, in most circumstances, the laws of war will be respected and applied. However, strategic necessity is tolerant of the idea that the war convention can be interpreted in a more liberal fashion when circumstances (achievement of the policy objective) require. This position is not wholly different from Walzer's notion of supreme emergency. However, it differs on the grounds that strategic necessity treats the war convention in a more pragmatic, instrumentalist manner. Also, Walzer's definition of supreme emergency (the point at which the war convention can be legitimately ignored) is more restrictive.[53]

In some important respects, the common good also acts as an attractive meta-concept for merging strategic efficacy and ethical demands. With its focus on respect for the person, social wellbeing and development, peace (which needs defending), and solidarity, the common good is potentially a positive driving force for strategy and one that respects all three sections of the war convention – including especially the post bellum environment. Importantly, the promotion of the common good demands military operations be both controlled and effective. Strategic efficacy is served by these same principles. However, striving for the universal good, especially with minimal force (so as not to undermine solidarity), is challenging in the realist and competitive domain of strategy. Clausewitz's warning about ceding advantage for reasons of moral outrage should be taken seriously.

In the final analysis, there are no easy answers to the dilemmas faced by strategists when dealing with ethics in strategy. As with much in strategic studies, Clausewitz provides an outstanding insight into the complexity of the challenge:

> We can thus only say that the aims a belligerent adopts, and the resources he employs, must be governed by the particular characteristics of his own position; but they will also conform to the spirit of the age and its general character. Finally, they must always be governed by the general conclusions to be drawn from the nature of war itself.[54]

Key points

1 There are different perspectives on military ethics, but an overlapping consensus appears to have been reached.
2 Realism appears to reject ethics but actually engages with the subject.
3 Just war seeks to reconcile the demands of ethics with the need for war.
4 The laws of war, though reasonably balanced, can be used in such a way as to interfere with the quest for victory.
5 Victory is a crucial and positive goal.
6 Strategic necessity incorporates ethical and legal demands but gives primacy to the policy objective.
7 The common good seeks to provide a positive, pro-ethics framework for strategy.

Questions

1   Is ethics a suitable subject for strategy?
2   Do the laws of war inhibit strategic performance?
3   Can discrimination and proportionality be accurately judged?
4   Is it right to ignore ethics and the laws of war in the quest for victory?

Notes

1   Bernard Brodie, *War and Politics* (London, Cassell, 1974), p. 47.
2   Other elements of Walzer's war convention are customs, professional codes, and reciprocal arrangements. Michael Walzer, *Just and Unjust Wars: A Moral Argument with Historical Illustrations* (Harmondsworth, Penguin, 1980), p. 44.
3   David Whetham, 'Ethics, Law and Conflict', in David Whetham (ed.), *Ethics, Law and Military Operations* (Basingstoke, Palgrave Macmillan, 2011), p. 16.
4   Quoted in ibid., p. 17.
5   Nigel Warburton, *Philosophy: The Basics* (London, Routledge, 2004), p. 46.
6   Walzer, p. 156.
7   Raymond Aron, *Peace and War: A Theory of International Relations*, trans. Richard Howard and Annette Baker Fox (New York, Anchor Press/Doubleday, 1973), p. 44.
8   Art and Waltz, quoted in Jack Donnelly, 'Realism', in S. Burchill et al. (eds.), *Theories of International Relations* (Basingstoke, Palgrave Macmillan, 2005), p. 31.
9   David Kinsella and Craig L. Carr (eds.), *The Morality of War: A Reader* (London, Lynne Rienner, 2007), p. 55.
10 G.H. Snyder, 'Process Variables in Neorealist Theory', *Security Studies* 5 (1996).
11 Hans J. Morgenthau, 'Political Power and International Morality', in David Kinsella and Craig L. Carr (eds.), *The Morality of War: A Reader* (London, Lynne Rienner, 2007), pp. 24–31.
12 Colin S. Gray, *Strategy and History: Essays on Theory and Practice* (London, Routledge, 2006), p. 86.
13 The various positions to be found in the just war tradition are discussed in Alex J. Bellamy, *Just Wars: From Cicero to Iraq* (Cambridge, Polity, 2006); Kinsella and Carr, p. 55.
14 For more details on the history of the just war tradition, see David Whetham, 'The Just War Tradition: A Pragmatic Compromise', in David Whetham (ed.), *Ethics, Law and Military Operations* (Basingstoke, Palgrave Macmillan, 2011), pp. 68–75; Gregory M. Reichberg et al., *The Ethics of War: Classical and Contemporary Readings* (Oxford, Blackwell, 2006), Alex Bellamy, and Kinsella and Carr.
15 Bellamy, p. 229.
16 Whetham, 'The Just War Tradition', p. 78.
17 Walzer, p. 230.
18 Whetham, 'The Just War Tradition', p. 81.
19 Henry Shue, 'Civilian Protection and Force Protection', in David Whetham (ed.), *Ethics, Law and Military Operations* (Basingstoke, Palgrave Macmillan, 2011), p. 137.
20 Ibid., p. 136.
21 Ibid., p. 142.
22 Srinath Raghavan, 'The Ethics of Nuclear Deterrence', in David Whetham (ed.), *Ethics, Law and Military Operations* (Basingstoke, Palgrave Macmillan, 2011), p. 210.

23 Ibid.

24 Walzer describes supreme emergency in the following terms: 'do justice unless the heavens are (really) about to fall'. Walzer, p. 231. For his discussion of nuclear weapons, see Walzer, Chapter 17.

25 Thomas C. Schelling, *The Reciprocal Fear of Surprise Attack* (Santa Monica, RAND, 1958).

26 See Colin S. Gray, 'War-Fighting for Deterrence', *Journal of Strategic Studies* 7:1 (1984), pp. 5–28.

27 I would like to thank Philip Mayne for his help and advice in the production of this section.

28 Emily Pollard, 'The Place of *Jus Post Bellum* in Just War Considerations', in Fritz Allhoff, Nicholas G. Evans, and Adam Henschke (eds.), *Routledge Handbook of Ethics and War: Just War Theory in the Twenty-First Century*, (New York, Routledge, 2013), pp. 93–104, 95.

29 B. Orend, 'Jus Post Bellum', *Journal of Social Philosophy* 31:1 (2000), p. 122.

30 B. Orend, 'Just Post Bellum: The Perspective of a Just-War Theorist', *Leiden Journal of International Law* 20:3 (2000), p. 580.

31 Mark Evans, 'Balancing Peace, Justice and Sovereignty in Jus Post Bellum: The Case of Just Occupation', *Millenium: Journal of International Studies* 36:3 (2008), pp. 533–54, 542.

32 R.E. Williams and D. Caldwell, 'Jus Post Bellum: Just War Theory and the Principles of Just Peace', *International Studies Perspectives* 7 (2006), p. 318.

33 Orend, 'Just Post Bellum: The Perspective of a Just-War Theorist',, p. 580.

34 Gary J. Bass, 'Jus Post Bellum', *Philosophy and Public Affairs* 32:4 (2004), pp. 384–412, 406.

35 Justin Morris, 'Law, Politics, and the Use of Force', in John Baylis et al. (eds.), *Strategy in the Contemporary World: An Introduction to Strategic Studies* (Oxford, Oxford University Press, 2007), p. 108.

36 Ibid.

37 Ibid., p. 109.

38 Cited in Walzer, p. 3.

39 Christopher P.M. Waters, 'War Law and Its Intersections', in David Whetham (ed.), *Ethics, Law and Military Operations* (Basingstoke, Palgrave Macmillan, 2011), p. 99.

40 Michael Evans, 'Coroners Blame Soldiers' Deaths on an Acute Lack of Equipment', www.timesonline.co.uk/tol/news/uk/article3376542.ece

41 Waters, p. 101.

42 Ibid., p. 91.

43 Morris, p. 109; Brodie, p. 49.

44 Brian Bond, *The Pursuit of Victory* (Oxford, Clarendon Press, 1998), p. 1.

45 Walzer, p. 230; Bellamy, pp. 127–30.

46 Thomas C. Schelling, *Arms and Influence* (New Haven, Yale University Press, 1966), p. 2.

47 Waters, p. 91.

48 Clausewitz, p. 83.

49 Pontifical Council for Justice and Peace, *Compendium of the Social Doctrine of the Church* (Vatican City, Libreria Editrice Vaticana, 2004), p. 164.

50 *Catechism of the Catholic Church* (Vatican City, Libreria Editrice Vaticana, 1994), pp. 1906–9.

51 Sun Tzu, pp. 77–9.

52 Ibid., p. 129.

53 Walzer, p. 268.

54 Clausewitz, p. 718.

Further reading

Bellamy, Alex, *Just Wars: From Cicero to Iraq*, (Cambridge, MA: Polity Press, 2006).

Brodie, Bernard, *War and Politics*, (London: Cassell, 1974).

Fisher, David, *Morality and War: Can War Be Just in the Twenty-First Century*, (Oxford: Oxford University Press, 2011).

Gray, Colin S., *Perspectives on Strategy*, (Oxford, Oxford University Press, 2013).

Kinsella, David and Craig L. Carr, *The Morality of War: A Reader*, (London: Lynne Rienner, 2007).

McCoubrey, H., *International Humanitarian Law*, 2nd Edition, (Aldershot: Dartmouth, 1998).

Norman, Richard, *The Moral Philosophers*, (Oxford: Clarendon Press, 1998).

Reichberg, Gregory M. et al., *The Ethics of War: Classical and Contemporary Readings*, (Oxford: Blackwell, 2006).

Walzer, Michael, *Just and Unjust Wars: A Moral Argument with Historical Illustrations*, (Harmondsworth: Penguin Books, 1980).

Whetham, David (ed.), *Ethics, Law and Military Operations*, (Basingstoke: Palgrave Macmillan, 2011).

Technology

4

Reader's guide

RMAs and military transformation; the information age, robotics and AI; Clausewitzian future; the role of technology in strategy; the RMA hypothesis as an aid to theory and practice.

Introduction

From the 1991 Gulf War until the terrorist attacks of September 11, 2001 shifted attention to irregular forms of warfare, the defence profession was dominated by the Revolution in Military Affairs (RMA) hypothesis. Even with an increased emphasis on counterterrorism and counterinsurgency, the RMA did not disappear. Rather, it matured into the concept of military transformation.[1] This in turn taps into an older impulse in military discourse that lends emphasis to the technological dimension of strategy. At the centre of the RMA hypothesis is the idea that opportunities arise periodically, usually driven by technology, to transform the conduct of warfare. If pursued correctly, these changes may confer significant advantage to those who exploit them and may even revolutionise the act of war.

Perhaps not surprisingly, this hypothesis and the general applicability of military transformation have been challenged. This chapter will begin by outlining the origins and development of the RMA hypothesis. The chapter will pay particular attention to the ongoing information-age RMA and associated developments in robotics, unmanned systems, and AI. Indeed, the latter has been described as the real revolution, with information-age developments seen as but a precursor to the robotics RMA and the coming 'post-human history'.[2] The chapter will then discuss the role of technology in strategy, identifying it as an important, but not decisive, dimension. Finally, the chapter concludes with an assessment of whether the RMA hypothesis and discussions of the technological dimension have any real utility in the theory and practice of strategy.

RMAs and military transformation: origins, development, and core concepts

The modern origins of the RMA debate can be traced back to Soviet writings in the 1980s and historical analysis of European military innovation in the sixteenth century. In the early 1980s, Soviet military writers, published under the name of Marshal Orgarkov, expressed concern at the growing sophistication of NATO conventional forces. In particular, they were worried about the coming together of a number of developing technologies: precision munitions, reconnaissance assets, and command, control, and communication technologies. The Soviets feared that these developments, brought together in a new system, would provide a leap in tactical and operational performance that would bring an end to Soviet conventional superiority.[3] In an unrelated development, historical research appeared to validate these concerns. Geoffrey Parker, in his seminal work *The Military Revolution: Military Innovation and the Rise of the West 1500–1800*, argued that Western colonial dominance could be attributed to the exploitation of advanced military technologies.[4]

These nascent ideas seemed to become reality during the Gulf War of 1991. Before hostilities began, Iraq possessed the fourth largest army in the world. Moreover, elements of the army were battle-hardened following the 1980–88 war with Iran. Although few commentators expected anything but a victory for the United States–led Coalition, it was generally assumed that coalition casualties would be in the tens of thousands. In the event, the Iraqi army was decimated, and the war culminated in a remarkably short hundred-hour ground campaign. Most strikingly of all, the Coalition suffered fewer than four hundred fatalities. This seemed to fit perfectly with one of the two main drivers for predictions regarding the future of war. Lawrence Freedman has noted that discussions about the future character of war are motivated primarily by either fear of an enemy surprise attack and the measures that must be taken to avoid it or the desire for quick and cheap victory. The 1991 victory over Iraq appeared to fulfil the latter.[5]

In a bid to explain this remarkable victory, much attention focused on the technological disparity between the belligerents. This technocentric view of the war was fuelled by television images from the conflict and a number of influential books and articles. The former included clips showing precision-guided missiles entering buildings through windows and Tomahawk cruise missiles navigating low over central Baghdad. Of the latter, one of the most influential was Alvin Toffler and Heidi Toffler's *War and Anti-War: Survival at the Dawn of the 21st Century*. The Tofflers argue that the scale of the Coalition victory can be explained by the fact that the belligerents were operating in different waves of civilisation. For the Tofflers, human history can be divided into three waves of development: agricultural, industrial, and informational. Each of these waves has attendant methods for waging war, and generally speaking, the more advanced form of warfare (in wave terms) will prevail. Thus, in 1991, the Iraqi approach to warfare, which was grounded in the industrial wave, was understandably swept aside by the Coalition's use of third-wave warfare. This third wave of civilisation is more commonly referred to as the information age.[6]

Armed with the idea of an information-age RMA, theorists looked back through history in an attempt to identify other instances of revolutionary change in the conduct of warfare. In an early influential article, 'Cavalry to Computer', Andrew Krepenivich identified ten RMAs.

These included the infantry, fortification, and naval RMAs, to name but three. However, it was less his list of earlier candidate RMAs that made the article standout. Rather, it was his identification of four key elements that an RMA must possess. These were technological change, organisational adaptation, operational innovation, and an identifiable leap in military efficacy. In most instances, technological advances act as the prime catalyst for revolutionary change. However, Krepenivich did recognise that political and social change could sometimes achieve the same results. The most obvious example of the latter, one that appeared in Krepenivich's list, is the Napoleonic RMA. Finally, Krepenivich's work contained a warning for contemporary defence professionals: those who exploited an RMA first gained considerable advantage when it came to conflict.[7] Failure to invest in the information-age RMA could lead to disastrous results. This feeds into the fear of the enemy surprise advantage driver identified earlier, albeit with a technological focus.

In this sense, prediction and discourse on technology and war often contain a degree of advocacy. Certain technological innovations are discussed, not in an objective manner but as a preferred vision of the future.[8] The opposite is also true: technologies that threaten established ways can be stymied by vested interests. The latter is evident in the early development of unmanned systems after the Second World War, when pilot interests, so-called white-scarf bias, prevented the full exploitation of unmanned variants of aircraft.[9] As with any intensely hierarchical institution, the fate of any innovation heavily depends on key individuals. Successful innovation requires supportive and enthusiastic leadership, especially because the military is often conservative and bureaucratic.[10] Moreover, the strategic and military cultures involved also play a part, as does the developing security environment. As an example, Rosen notes that the development of radar fit perfectly with the Royal Air Force's (RAF) increasing interest in command and control for air defence. Similarly, the technological maturation of the helicopter coincided with an increased need for mobility in an age of irregular and nuclear war.[11] It is, then, perhaps, no coincidence that the current rapid development of unmanned systems comes at a time when post-heroic Western powers desire quick cheap victories in wars of choice.

> **Box 4.1 Krepenivich's four characteristics of an RMA**
>
> Technological change.
> Organisational adaptation.
> Operational innovation.
> Leap in military effectiveness.

A well-worn example of the need to get on board the RMA train early (and of course correctly) is the German development of blitzkrieg during the interwar period. Blitzkrieg certainly ticks all of Krepenivich's boxes. New technology came in the form of armoured forces, mechanised infantry, CAS aircraft, and wireless radio. These were brought together in a new organisational form: the Panzer division. The doctrine of blitzkrieg, although not entirely new, melded the new technologies together and gave them operational function.[12] Finally, an increase in military effectiveness appeared to have been achieved in the early years of the Second World War. The conquest of France in six weeks stood in sharp contrast to the four years of indecisive slaughter of the First World War. Equally impressive were the early stages of the campaign in the Soviet Union, when German forces captured and killed millions of Soviet troops and reached the outskirts of Moscow by late 1941. In support of the RMA hypothesis, these successes are partly explicable by differences in approach to the new means of warfare. In contrast to the German approach, which used armoured forces as a concentrated spearhead for their offences, the allies tended to regard their tanks within a traditional mindset, using them as dispersed mobile artillery.

The German development of blitzkrieg appears to fulfil Krepenivich's RMA criteria. And yet, the observant reader will point out that the war did not end terribly well for Germany. This speaks to the fallacy of the first move. Despite the fact that the fear of enemy surprise advantage is often a driver for military innovation, surprise attack often does not lead to strategic success. Pearl Harbor and Barbarossa (the 1941 invasion of the Soviet Union) are just two examples of this truth. In fact, the early triumphs of the Axis Powers were matched in scale by the tragedy of the final moments of the war. What does this tell us about RMA? Is it the case that interwar developments did not amount to a genuine revolution? The latter position is difficult to justify. As noted, new or maturing technology was evident and was used to great effect through the combination of new forms of operational art and innovative organisational structure. Therefore, it may be the case that there are fundamental problems with the RMA hypothesis. More specifically, it may be that the concept of revolutionary (or certainly rapid evolutionary) change has validity, but much like strategic air power, it has been oversold as a decisive factor in war. This chapter will now explore the problems associated with the RMA hypothesis.

Criticisms of the RMA and military transformation

Since its early inception, the conceptual basis for the RMA has been questioned. Some questioned whether it was merely a construct of the United States' military establishment, designed to justify increased investment at a time of potential retrenchment following the end of the Cold War.[13] In a less Machiavellian way, the RMA could be an academic construct with no basis in reality. Academics tend to codify the world. This is understandable, since codification is a legitimate means to intellectually order complex phenomena. Nonetheless, codification can go too far and identify phenomena that do not exist. Even if there is some legitimate empirical basis for identifying the existence of said phenomena, academic codification may oversimplify or exaggerate the boundaries between phenomena. The Tofflers' division of human history into three waves of civilisations appears to be a good candidate for oversimplification. This is not to suggest that these theories have no utility or validity. Identifying broad trends, or grouping phenomena together under umbrella concepts, is a useful means for recognising similarities among seemingly distinct events and/or phenomena.

Another criticism of the RMA hypothesis is concerned with semantics. The term 'revolution' suggests a radical break with the past, which in the case of some of Krepenevich's historical examples may seem unfounded. In this way, the RMA may be guilty of distorting the reality of evolutionary developments, instead emphasising moments of discontinuity in order to support the concept of revolutionary change. In the field of economic and social history, the term 'Industrial Revolution' has fallen increasingly into disuse. Rather, historians now recognise that the shift from an agricultural-based economy to an industrial one occurred over a long period of time. Indeed, agriculture continued to play a substantial socioeconomic role in the United Kingdom well into the twentieth century.

In light of these challenges to the RMA hypothesis, how do the various candidate RMAs fare under scrutiny? Some, such as the infantry and artillery revolutions identified by Krepinevich, appear to be more evolutionary in nature. Indeed, Krepinevich acknowledges that elements of the artillery revolution took as many as 160 years to mature.[14] Some more recent RMAs also appear less radical upon closer inspection. The interwar RMA (described earlier) looks less like a revolutionary change in the conduct of war in light of the similarities between the First World War and the Second World War. Despite being advertised as a war of manoeuvre, the Second World War often resembled its predecessor, in which dismounted infantry attacked fortified positions across open ground.[15] The introduction of mechanised warfare did not render impotent that which went before. Indeed, during the early years of success, the German army was powered as much by equine power as the internal combustion engine.

The fate of the interwar RMA, and in particular Germany's development of blitzkrieg, provides a fascinating example of the limitations of the RMA hypothesis. As previously noted, Germany's outstanding success in the early years of the war did not translate into final victory. A number of factors help to explain why this was so. Germany faced resilient enemies with substantial resources at their disposal. For example, although victory over the Soviet Union may have been close on occasions (especially in late 1941 and 1942), no matter how many battlefield successes Germany had, the Soviets were always able to put another army into the field. To make matters worse, some of those supplying the Soviets (particularly the United States) with resources were beyond Germany's reach. Even though Germany was able to reach the United Kingdom with its bomber force, its main instrument of decision, the army, was blocked by the English Channel and the Royal Navy. Without a rapid end to the war, Germany's enemies were increasingly able to mobilise their global resources. In addition, as the war progressed, the allies developed their own versions of Germany's RMA. War is a great teacher, especially for those who have been defeated but remain in the game. In this way, a monopoly on innovation may be relatively short-lived. There are many reasons why Germany lost the war in Europe.[16] Most importantly, it failed at the higher levels of strategy and in the most important dimensions of strategy. These issues will be discussed in greater detail in the section on technology and the dimensions of strategy.

A final criticism of the RMA hypothesis, in particular its undue focus on technology, relates to the concept of control in strategy. As previously noted, control can be truly exercised only by the man on the scene with a gun. Although advanced technology may help facilitate his performance their role, he still need to be present to execute it effectively. For example, although modern air power played the dominant role in coercing Serbian forces to leave Kosovo, the Albanian refugees would not return to their homes in the absence of NATO ground forces. Moreover, as will be discussed later in this chapter, the increasing presence of unmanned systems is tactically and operationally significant but still falls strategically short when one considers the need for control and the sociopolitical dimensions of war. Strategy is fundamentally about human interaction. Technology, even when used to great effect, plays only a supporting role in that interaction. In this sense, Fuller's comment that the technological drive in war has the aim of removing humankind from the front line, though it may be accurate, is problematic in relation to achieving policy objectives.[17]

Genuine RMAs?

The RMA hypothesis may be flawed, and it may primarily speak to only one aspect of strategy: technological innovation. However, it is difficult to deny that certain technological advancements have exerted substantial influence on the conduct of warfare. Two candidate RMAs of the twentieth century are especially prominent in this respect: air power and nuclear weapons. Within approximately 15 years of the first heavier-than-air flight, during the First World War, aircraft were being used for reconnaissance, ground attack, strategic bombing, and carrier-borne operations. By the Second World War, according to such notable practitioners as Field Marshals Montgomery and Rommel, air power had become the arbiter of success on the battlefield.[18] In its airborne role, it also facilitated the capture of the Belgian fortress at Eban Emel and the island of Crete. At sea, the Battle of Midway was won and lost by actions in the third dimension. Finally, air power had arguably changed the geostrategic environment. The United Kingdom, which had traditionally relied on the English Channel to provide protection from its continental enemies, was now open to direct attack from the air. And as the 1991 Gulf War and Kosovo conflict reveal, in certain contexts, air power has become the leading edge in modern warfare. Among other things, modern standoff air power provides a means of intervention for states that have commitment-phobia. Although it is correct to note that all of the wars mentioned in this brief survey of air power had to be concluded by ground forces, they were all shaped dramatically by air power.[19]

The invention of nuclear weapons has had no less a dramatic impact on strategy than air power. Although nuclear weapons have not been fired in anger since August 1945, they dominated strategy during the Cold War. If nothing else, nuclear weapons promoted the age-old concept of deterrence to a new level of development and prominence. In this sense, their presence in large numbers also appears to have curtailed the direct utility of other military instruments in certain contexts. The conflicts in Korea and Vietnam, tensions over Berlin and Cuba, and more recent border clashes between India and Pakistan could have escalated were it not for the threat of nuclear mutually assured destruction (MAD). There were undoubtedly other factors involved in preventing the Cold War from going hot. Nonetheless, the threat of nuclear annihilation was undoubtedly an important factor.[20]

Nuclear weapons still appear to play this role in the post–Cold War environment. The Head of Iraqi Intelligence during the 1991 Gulf War identified US nuclear forces as the reason Iraq did not employ its chemical arsenal during the conflict. Similarly, there is evidence to suggest that the threat of nuclear release eventually helped to deescalate the conflict between Pakistan and India over the Kargil region in Kashmir.[21] Nuclear weapons, due to their expense and inaccessibility, have not permeated warfare to the same degree as air power. Nonetheless, in the hands of the superpowers, they did reach into almost all areas of military activity. For battlefield use, they were deployed as mortars, artillery shells, short-range missiles, and air-delivered bombs and missiles. Nuclear weapons were also deployed at sea as anti-ship missiles and anti-submarine depth charges. Finally, small mobile weapons were developed for insertion by special forces. Replace the latter with terrorists, and nuclear weapons may have a new role in the future. Finally, as this book goes to print, nuclear weapons drive some of the main events that dominate the geopolitical landscape. The nuclear weapon programmes of North Korea and Iran, alongside Russian force modernisation, dominate the agenda of the Trump administration.

The information age and the rise of robotics and AI

For all of its faults, then, in certain cases, the RMA hypothesis has a role to play in explaining the causes and implications of significant changes to the conduct of war. Since the 1991 Gulf War, the concept of an information-age RMA has been developing. From the perspective of its supporters, the information RMA may be the most far-reaching and important RMA to date, culminating in the rise of unmanned systems and AI.[22] In this respect, the information RMA has two stages. The first stage is concerned with the application of information technology and the power of networks in military affairs. The second stage is enabled by the nascent robotics revolution and associated developments in AI. A related strategic development of the information age, cyber power, is discussed in detail in Chapter 11.

Extraordinary claims have been made concerning the significance of contemporary military innovation. Some commentators have even gone as far as to suggest that with the scale and range of the changes to the character of warfare, the nature of war itself is changing.[23] While this may be hyperbole, it is certainly true that, much like air power, information technology and increasingly robotics (and eventually AI) reach into every aspect of warfare. Thus, the following analysis of the information RMA will provide an important test of the RMA hypothesis per se. If the current RMA, with its reach and high profile, falls short of revolutionary change, this will raise further questions about the validity of the RMA hypothesis writ large.

The first stage of the current RMA gains its potency from the integration of various technologies to form systems and networks. Two concepts that typify this approach are William Owens's 'system of systems' and the associated 'network centric warfare'.[24] The foundations of information-age military systems are advanced C⁴I (command, control, communications, computers and information), precision munitions, and reconnaissance assets. These components are brought together via the digitisation of the battlespace, and they offer the promise of assured kill. With the end result (the kill) all but guaranteed, the competition in information becomes the deciding factor. Various operational concepts developed from this idea. Among the most notable are dominant battlespace knowledge (DBK), situational awareness, and information superiority. Beyond the battlespace, the digitisation of logistics offers greater efficiency, leading to cost savings and higher operational tempo.

As a consequence, in an age of abundant information, a section of the defence profession concluded that these changes signalled the demise of Clausewitz (with his emphasis on battle and uncertainty) and the rise of Sun Tzu (who appears to advocate a knowledge-based approach to warfare).[25]

With the rise of the virtual domain and the information in it, direct human involvement in strategic affairs may be reduced. Even if, as is argued in Chapter 11, cyberattack proves somewhat strategically disappointing, human presence in the battlespace is already being reduced by robotics and the increasingly necessary application of AI (necessary to take advantage of high-tempo and/or swarming unmanned systems). In this sense, the second stage of the information RMA may indeed take us into the post-human age of war. Should this occur, technology would become an increasingly dominant dimension in strategy, in that tactical and operational outcomes would be decided not by human interaction but by machine-on-machine warfare.

Unmanned military systems have a surprisingly long history. David Hambling reports that in the 1849 siege of Venice, the Austrian army remotely dropped small bombs from hot air balloons via a copper-wire control method. Other notable developments in unmanned systems include the British Aerial Target, a First World War wooden biplane with an explosive warhead; the 1918 American Aerial Torpedo, which, using a gyroscope and barometer, was able to fly a preset route before engaging its target; the Second World War TDR-1, which could fly at 150 mph and deliver a 2000-pound munition, guided via television by an operator flying in another plane up to 8 miles away; the tracked German Goliath, which remotely delivered 132 pounds of explosives against enemy tanks or bunkers; converted F6F Hellcat fighters, which were again controlled by television images to attack static targets in the Korean War; the 1960s QH-50 DASH, a US Navy remote-controlled helicopter, which among other things was designed to drop nuclear depth charges; the Fire Fly reconnaissance drone, which flew over 3000 missions in Vietnam; Israel's successful 1982 Suppression of Enemy Air Defences (SEAD) campaign against Syria, in which Mastiff and Scout UAVs helped locate, deceive, and jam Syrian Surface to Air Missile (SAM) sites; and the Hunter & Pioneer reconnaissance drones, used in the Gulf War of 1991. The Pioneer is notable because a group of Iraqi troops attempted to surrender to one during the conflict.[26]

Despite this surprisingly long history, the meteoric rise of unmanned systems had to wait for the coming together of technological development and geostrategic opportunity. The technological development was Predator, the geostrategic context was the War on Terror and contemporary counterinsurgency campaigns. The origins of Predator can be traced back to the 1970s with DARPA's long-endurance drone, Amber, and the cheaper export version, GNAT-750. With a 48-hour loiter capability, the GNAT-750 met the Central Intelligence Agency's (CIA) requirement for a low-level endurance reconnaissance asset during the Bosnian conflict. With help from the Pentagon, the GNAT-750 was enlarged and fitted with satellite communications. Now designated the RQ-1 Predator, the new reconnaissance drone first saw service in 1995. With the addition of a laser designator, the Predator gained an offensive role guiding precision weapons launched from manned aircraft.

The wars in Afghanistan and Iraq provided a conducive environment for the further operational development of Predator. With no effective enemy air defences, and the need to reconnoitre large hostile areas for extended periods, unmanned systems came into their own. Predator was well suited to the task, with a nose camera and a sensor ball with thermal and night vision capability, Lynx radar, signals intelligence (SIGINT) capability, and a laser designator. As a strike asset, Predator had one problem: the delay between the drone identifying a target and the delivery of the munition from a queued-in crewed platform. The obvious answer to this dilemma was to arm the drone with a Hellfire missile. The first Predator strike mission, controlled by the CIA, occurred in October 2001 in Afghanistan. In 2007, a strengthened, more powerful version of Predator was deployed, the MQ-9B Reaper. The Reaper is capable of carrying 14 Hellfire missiles and has been the mainstay of the targeted killing campaigns against al-Qaeda and ISIS around the world.

Now proven in action over an extended period, unmanned systems are developing and proliferating rapidly. In 2018, Paul Scharre reported that global annual spending on military robotics had reached $7.5 billion. That figure is not surprising given that 90 countries operate drones and 16 deploy armed unmanned systems. Moreover, although we tend to think of unmanned systems as aircraft, the United States deployed over 6000 ground robots in Iraq and Afghanistan. Although many of these unmanned ground vehicles (UGV) were Packbots, a non-offensive multipurpose robot, they also included armed systems such as Talon SWORDS. The latter, a tracked vehicle, can carry various weapons, including automatic rifles and grenade launches. In addition to the United States, Russia is developing a variety of unmanned vehicles, including robot tanks, and South Korea has deployed the Samsung SGR-A1 sentry gun along the demilitarised zone with North Korea. The United Kingdom is also rapidly developing its unmanned capability. This includes the Zephyr S, a high-altitude reconnaissance drone with an endurance of over 26 days. In addition, in line with its Force Modernisation Programme, and following the 2018 exercise, Autonomous Warrior, on Salisbury Plain, the United Kingdom is fast-tracking investment in UAVs and UGVs. This includes investment in swarm technology.

If unmanned systems are potentially revolutionary, the addition of AI acts as a potent catalyst. In some respects, this apes the marriage of nuclear weapons and ballistic missiles, signifying that when two or more technologies come together, they can radically change the tactical and operational environment. Along the way, they pose difficult ethical, social, and political questions. Aside from the difficulty, one might say impossibility, of humans controlling swarms of unmanned vehicles, there are other drivers for the adoption of AI in warfare. One of the most obvious at the tactical and operational levels is tempo. A human pilot takes 0.3 seconds to respond to a stimulus and 0.6 seconds to make a choice; AI can do the same in a millionth of a second.[27] In some tactical situations, such as ship anti-missile defence and cybersecurity, human decision-making and response is simply too slow. These systems have to be automated to function effectively. AI and autonomous weapons also substitute for a workforce. This is especially important for contemporary Western powers who increasingly struggle to recruit and retain personnel. As previously noted, it also fits with the post-heroic strategic culture of some modern states. However, it also solves the problem of the surprisingly large workforce requirements to operate unmanned systems. A Reaper 24/7 orbit requires seven to ten pilots, 20 people to operate the sensors, and many analysts to sift through the collected data.[28] AI reduces these workforce requirements to zero.

But what is AI, and what are the implications for war and strategy? For the purposes of this discussion, intelligence can be defined as the ability to understand a changing environment, learn, and adapt accordingly. On this basis, AI is the ability of a machine to perform in such a manner: to understand its environment, learn from interacting with its surroundings, then behave appropriately to the changing circumstances. Or, as the Merriam-Webster Dictionary defines it, AI is 'The capability of a machine to imitate intelligent human behaviour'.

Box 4.2 Levels of autonomy for AI

Semiautonomous – human in the loop.
Supervised autonomous – human on the loop.
Full autonomous – human out of the loop.

Regardless of the precise definition that we use to describe AI, the important thing militarily is that it enables machines, or weapons, to act autonomously. Most importantly, this means ceding some level of control over engagements to machines. The application of political violence ceases to be an entirely human decision. However, when it comes to autonomous weapons, control over the application of violence is not an all-or-nothing choice. Three levels of autonomy are available: semiautonomous, supervised autonomous, and full autonomous. The first of these is described as human in the loop, in which the machine goes through the observe, orientate, and decide steps of the Observe, Orient, Decide, Act (OODA) Loop but must receive human approval to act. In supervised autonomous mode, or human-on-the-loop mode, the machine is able to act, with a human operator supervising the procedure with the ability to intervene if required. In full autonomous operation, or human-out-of-the loop operation, the machine is free to fully perform the OODA loop independently.[29]

All three of these levels of weapons autonomy are extant in various weapon systems around the world, often within the same system. The U.S. Navy's Aegis Combat System has various settings, including one in which a human decision is required to engage a target and Auto-Special, with a human on the loop. The United Kingdom's Brimstone air-launched fire-and-forget anti-surface missile also has various levels of autonomy. In full millimetre-wave (MMW) radar mode, once launched into an area by a pilot, a salvo of Brimstones can choose and engage targets autonomously, even sorting among themselves which targets to attack so as to avoid overlap in effect.[30] Full autonomy is found in Israel's Harop, a six-hour loitering anti-radar drone that detects enemy radars and engages automatically.

As with any technological development, we must avoid being dazzled by the technical characteristics of unmanned systems and AI. Rather, we must assess the tactical, operational, and strategic implications of these developments. Only then can we begin to understand whether the character, and even more so the nature, of war will be significantly affected. Perhaps the most obvious change in an era of AI unmanned systems will be an increase in operational tempo. Akin to flash trading (high-frequency trading) on the financial markets, freed from human cognitive limits, warfare will be able to operate at the speed of computer decision-making. This certainly represents a quantitative change in warfare, but whether it represents a qualitative change is open to question. Over two thousand years ago, Sun Tzu wrote that 'speed is the essence of war'. The need to be first also lies at the heart of Boyd's human-centric OODA Loop. Thus, another increase in operational tempo does not automatically change the core relationship between time and the other dimensions of strategy.

That being said, concern has been expressed regarding the impact of increased operational tempo on crisis stability. The fear is that automated weapon systems may rapidly engage each other as the logical consequence of the need to go first in a high-operational-tempo environment. In such circumstances, the political rational control of war, as enunciated by Clausewitz, would cease to be an effective limit on war's natural tendency to escalate. When discussing such concerns, commentators often cite the 2010 Flash Crash on Wall Street, when automated trading algorithms sent the US Stock Market spiralling downwards, losing 9% of its value in approximately 20 minutes. While it is sensible to highlight the need to retain policy control over the technology of war, it is important to remember that similar, but ultimately unfounded, concerns have been expressed before. Despite the compression of time (the Pershing 2 intermediate range ballistic missile [IRBM] had a flight time of six minutes) and levels of destruction made possible by nuclear weapons and ballistic missiles and despite the tension of the Cold War, policy still retained control over the nuclear arsenals of the two superpowers. Moreover, the narrative that the First World War was caused by the inescapable logic of the railway timetables must be rejected. Again, the causes of the Great War are to be found in German policy, not in technological determinism. As the Cold War demonstrates, policymakers are reluctant to cede control over war and peace to their military commanders. They establish mechanisms that ensure that the unequal dialogue continues to function. In this way, the most likely scenario is that AI will be set up in such a way as to act as an aide to human decision-making, not to usurp it. In this way, machine autonomy may exist at the tactical level but will be curtailed or severely monitored at the operational and strategic levels.

Unmanned systems should provide greater tactical freedom. When human lives are not at risk and human physical limits have been removed from warfighting, new tactical and operational possibilities open up. This is evidenced in US drone campaigns against al-Qaeda and ISIS, when enemies were engaged who otherwise may have been beyond reach. Although essentially a tactical and operational innovation, the drone campaigns have had strategic effect. The capabilities of al-Qaeda and ISIS have been slowly eroded, and their training and organisational activities have been substantially compromised. Moreover, one of the strategic mainstays for irregular groups, the 'body-bag' approach, is becoming less effective. As state forces increasingly rely on unmanned systems, there are fewer human targets (in uniform) for irregular actors to target.

It is also possible that drones, especially when swarming, may bring mass and attrition back to battlespace. Since the Korean War, we have witnessed an increasing move to smaller, professional militaries, equipped with fewer high-tech weapon platforms. But as Martin C. Libicki predicted in 1994, this trend may change with the coming of the 'small and many'.[31] As unmanned systems become smaller and cheaper, and controlled in large numbers by AI, they may come to dominate the battlespace.[32] That being said, we must be mindful of the paradoxical logic of strategy. While many are lauding the possibilities of swarms, defences against them are being developed. In one US exercise, a laser-armed buggy brought down 45 swarming drones.[33] AI can also be spoofed (i.e. deceived). Moreover, we must again be mindful of the danger of technological determinism. As noted in Chapter 1, strategy is about control. And although unmanned systems can exert a degree of control over territory (terrain denial), Wylie's man on the scene with a gun is still likely to play an important part in the human drama of war. Thus, the strategic implications of robotics and AI are not clear. It will take time for the tactical, operational, and strategic possibilities to fully emerge.

There is also a complex legal and ethical component to the discourse on unmanned systems and AI. On the one hand, severe objections have been raised to the delegation of lethal force to machines. These objections include concerns about robots running amok, as in the Terminator or RoboCop films. Such misgivings are not without merit. The software code for modern military equipment is so complex that errors are inevitable. The F-35 fighter requires 24 million lines of code to operate. Even after rigorous testing, typically there are 0.5 errors in every 1000 lines of code.[34] Moreover, the coding behind deep neural nets, which form the basis for modern AI, is both complex and not fully understood by those who create them. Put simply, AI will sometimes produce unanticipated novel outputs or results that are beyond human comprehension.

There are other objections besides practical concerns about the reliability of machines in the lethal business of war. Some object, on philosophical grounds, to humans being killed by machines. Such concerns rest on the basis that robots are not legal agents and cannot engage in moral reasoning. They cannot be held accountable for their actions (although those who make them maybe can), and in this sense, there is an 'accountability gap'. Moreover, there is the notion of inherent human dignity. If life is to be taken at all, it should be taken by another human being, who in turn risks their own life. This is akin to the warrior ethos and code of honour. Others have expressed concerns that machines cannot make judgements in tune with IHL (which has a moral component). When is military need a genuine necessity; in what circumstances does the doctrine of double effect apply; how much force is proportional; and so on? These and other questions call for judgement, judgement that machines, with no moral centre, are not well suited to make. A cold, rational, calculating machine will have no emotional feelings towards its victim.

Finally, the use of unmanned systems may fundamentally affect civil–military relations. In a modern democracy, the military are often honoured and esteemed precisely because they risk injury and death on behalf of the community. This would surely change if fighting was the sole preserve of robots and the difficult decisions were taken by AI. Clearly, in such circumstances, not only would civil–military relations change but the military itself would be unrecognisable.

In contrast to these naysayers, there are moral arguments in favour of deploying lethal unmanned systems and AI. Humans make mistakes in targeting, often because they are tired, hungry, and stressed and are operating on limited information in a complex, fast-moving environment. They may lose sound moral judgement in the face of danger and psychological trauma. In contrast, AI could be programmed with clear rules of engagement and the ability to decide and act consistently without the depredations suffered by humans. Computers can process much more information than humans can and thus can make decisions on a more solid informational basis. Moreover, because unmanned systems tend to be more precise, they can carry smaller warheads, thereby reducing collateral damage. Similarly, 24/7 surveillance, enabled by unmanned systems, produces more intelligence and hopefully fewer mistakes in targeting.

So, what are implications of these changes to the character and agents of war? At the risk of sounding too analytically cautious, it is too early to make any specific predictions. Certainly, as with the arrival of air power and mechanised forces, the character of the battlespace will change with the employment of robotics and AI. This is already occurring to a limited degree. And we can apply our analogy to the colossal campaign on the Eastern Front of World War Two. Interwar doctrine, inspired by the technological developments of the time, promised decisive rapid victories. And indeed, these promises seemed to have been fulfilled in the German successes of 1939 to mid 1941. And yet the new wars of manoeuvre ground to a bloody halt outside Moscow, Leningrad, and Stalingrad. The interwar RMA was spent, and attrition returned to the battlefield.

Clausewitzian future?

With these thoughts on the Second World War still fresh in our minds, we must consider the broader conceptual implications of the current technological epoch. Taken together, the developments that reduce the direct involvement of humans have led some theorists to conclude that we may be moving into a period of post-human warfare: humans' '5000-year-old monopoly over the fighting of war is over'.[35] Not only could humans be removed from the sharp end of war, as the value of information rises, the necessity for violence also diminishes, as conflict becomes decided by the competition over information and networks.[36]

If these visions of near-future warfare come to pass, there may be some justification for the claims that the nature of war is changing. War with little or no violence, and with minimal physical human involvement, would be a different beast to that which Clausewitz wrote about. Indeed, the absence of humans and violence, with the addition of elevated levels of information, would remove many of the main sources of friction from warfare. In this sense, there would be some justification for sidelining Clausewitz's work. An RMA would certainly have occurred; perhaps the most significant in the history of human conflict.

Despite the volume of work promoting the contemporary RMA, the reader is advised not to dispense with their copy of *On War* just yet. As with previous RMAs, the information-age variant is unlikely to develop entirely as its ardent supporters have envisaged. Perhaps even more damaging is the fact that in practice it already looks far from universal in its applicability. We must remember, for example, that recent drone campaigns have largely occurred in permissive environments with limited or no effective air defences. One of the most significant criticisms levelled against the information-age RMA is that it was configured for regular forms of warfare. In the context of the wars against Iraq in 1991 and 2003 (the initial invasion), American information superiority and the abundant use of precision munitions certainly appeared to fulfil the promise of rapid low-cost victories. However, the insurgencies in Iraq and Afghanistan have clearly revealed the limits of digitised forces. By avoiding the use of large concentrations of uniformed troops, insurgents and terrorists are able to bypass many of the capabilities that are the engine of change in the information age.

Although unmanned systems, largely in the form of armed drones and intelligence, surveillance, reconnaissance (ISR) platforms, have acted as an important force multiplier in the irregular conflicts in Iraq, Afghanistan, and Syria, the sociopolitical issues still rumble on. A precision-guided Hellfire missile, though tactically impressive, cannot interact with the local population to gain their trust. And although an armed drone can deny safe terrain to massed enemy forces, it cannot exert 'control' over that same territory and its inhabitants and thereby address the more fundamental sociopolitical issues. Remember that strategy is multidimensional and multileveled.

The continued role of violence

Clearly, then, as the ongoing conflicts in Iraq, Afghanistan, Syria, and Ukraine reveal, although information networks and unmanned systems have proliferated, the aim of removing humans from the sharp end of war is far from a reality. In consequence, violence and suffering will continue to play a central role in the human drama of war. For example, it is estimated that in Syria there have been over 300,000 combat deaths. In Ukraine, in what is a limited conflict, approximately 10,000 combatants have been killed in the Donbass region in the five years from March 2014. The continued presence of violence is due to a number of factors, but for our purposes here, four stand out. First, as many events since 9/11 clearly demonstrate, the enemy has a vote on whether violence is to be removed or not from war. It is naïve and egocentric to believe that one has a monopoly on the direction that future war will take. Certain sections of the Western defence establishment may yearn for humane warfare, but others may have a different vision of the future. In fact, as irregular campaigns since 9/11 amply reveal, certain strategic agents may seek to achieve objectives via especially violent forms of war. Killing British teenagers as they watch a pop concert, slaughtering Yazidi civilians, or beheading hostages on social media are designed precisely to amplify the effects of violence, to terrorise and break the will of the other.[37] Technology can be used in different ways. High explosives can be delivered with precision to limit civilian deaths; alternatively, they can be detonated in a densely populated area to maximise the slaughter of non-combatants.

Indeed, such strategies may be designed precisely to exploit post-heroic perceptions of war. Freedman argues that the RMA-driven high-tech approach, combined with small professional armies, has made the West especially vulnerable to the effects of casualties. This merely serves to magnify the strategic impact of violent forms of war favoured by insurgents. Additionally, enemies are able to exploit the West's increasing fixation on victimhood, which when combined with a technologically driven emphasis on precision renders collateral damage unacceptable. This so-called lawfare approach enables the West's opponents to wage violent forms of warfare while restricting the military operations of more casualty-sensitive states. In contrast to the West, some strategic cultures, notably some irregular forces, extol the virtues of violence and self-sacrifice and are therefore perfectly willing to accept the violent reality of war.

Additionally, it is reasonable to assume, on the basis of historical experience, that we may witness a return to large regular conflicts characterised by massive amounts of firepower and destruction of the enemy's fielded forces and infrastructure. Indeed, the geopolitical relationships among the great powers (the United States, Europe, Russia, and China) have undeniably deteriorated in the last few years. As a warning from history, the unprecedented destruction of the First World War and the Second World War was preceded by a century of limited conflict in Europe. The populations of Europe were not used to killing each other by the millions; and yet that came to pass. Should an enemy akin to Nazi Germany appear, we may once again see instructions along the lines of those given to General Eisenhower before D-Day: You will enter the continent of Europe and . . . undertake operations aimed at the heart of Germany and the destruction of her armed forces'. On this basis, Eisenhower notes that 'This purpose of destroying enemy forces was always our guiding principle'.[38]

Third, as argued in Chapter 11, cyberattack, the most potent means to remove violence from war, does not fare well under close scrutiny. For this new form of warfare to initiate change in the nature of war, it has to produce independent strategic effect. If it does not achieve the latter, it will act merely as a supporting arm for more traditional forms of military power. Despite various warnings concerning the imminent arrival of cyberattack as the next big thing, no campaigns of any real note have occurred. Bronze Soldier, Stuxnet, Shamoon, and BlackEnergy are all significant developments in the character of war, but their strategic effects have been limited.

Finally, we must not neglect the impact of friction on military operations. A wide range of factors stand between any military instrument and the realisation of its full potential. For unmanned systems or cyberattack to affect the nature of war (rather than just its character), they must operate nearly flawlessly. Otherwise, their transformative powers are likely to be severely curtailed. When we consider the range of the sources of friction, it is clear that like all other supposedly transformative technologies, unmanned systems and cyberattack will fall well short of decisive operational and strategic effect. As a reminder, the taxonomy of friction includes danger; physical exertion; uncertainties and imperfections in information; resistance from one's own forces; chance events; physical and political limits on the use of force; unpredictability stemming from interaction with the enemy; and disconnects between the ends and the means.[39] It is true that an unmanned and/or cyber future would essentially eliminate the first two sources of friction. Nonetheless, the remaining six categories are so ubiquitous that operational performance is still likely to be retarded. It must not be assumed that autonomous robots are beyond friction. Of US factories with robotic systems, 4% have suffered major accidents.[40] At the time of writing, Boeing's entire fleet of 737 Max airliners are grounded because it is alleged that a bug in the flight control software may have led to the loss of two aircraft over five months.

The fate of uncertainty

It is not just in the realm of violence that the current RMA is unlikely to deliver. Another element of Clausewitz's theory of war that is likely to survive is uncertainty. This is particularly troubling for the proponents of the contemporary RMA because abundant information is the engine of change in the current epoch. Without regular and reliable access to information, DBK does not materialise, devastating cyberattack becomes much more challenging, and unmanned systems lose their precision and force multiplier effect and may even cease to function altogether. As with violence, a number of factors limit the level of certainty possible in future war. This chapter will now discuss the most important of these: intangible elements of war; interaction with the enemy; human interpretation; and information overload.

The current RMA contains a hidden but important assumption. It assumes that seeing every item in the battlespace is tantamount to knowing everything of value. There is certainly great advantage to be gained from possessing an accurate picture of the battlespace. However, war is not conducted solely by inanimate objects. Military units have a number of intangible features that cannot be seen or quantified to any degree of accuracy. Morale, leadership, intent, and level of training are all important factors that contribute to the final outcome of a mission. The interception of communications may give some insight into these features, but they cannot be gauged with much accuracy.

As with the presence of violence, the levels of uncertainty in war will be influenced by the actions of the enemy. It should not be assumed that information-age assets will function unimpaired. An enemy facing such capabilities has various options to offset them. They may adopt a form of warfare (irregular) that does not play to the strengths of a digitised force. And although unmanned ISR drones have proven reasonably effective in certain irregular environments, the enemy has the option of moving into the urban environment, where the intelligence picture becomes much more complex. Alternatively, as the Serbs did in Kosovo, the enemy may conduct successful acts of deception to undermine an information campaign. They may also have the option of attacking the very assets and platforms that gather and transmit information. We have already seen how directed-energy weapons are being used to counter drone swarms. More significantly, ASAT weapons are back in development. India conducted its first successful ASAT test in March 2019. Such developments are especially problematic for high-tech forces, as satellites underpin much of our digital world.

Of course, it is unlikely that an enemy would be able to entirely shutdown a state-of-the-art military force, crippling its unmanned, information, and cyber systems. Nonetheless, they may be successful enough to offset the relative advantage of such a force. This certainly appears to have been the case in Kosovo, and it continues to be the case in Afghanistan, where the situation in 2019 is best described as a stalemate, albeit with signs that the Taliban is gaining some ground.

In Clausewitz's writings on uncertainty, he identified human interpretation as a factor that reduced the utility of information.[41] This is an important point that reminds us once again that war is composed of rational and non-rational forces. A study of intelligence organisations reveals that the process of turning information into knowledge is fraught with difficulties. Some of these difficulties emanate from human frailties. Groupthink, confirmation bias, mirror imaging, and cognitive rigidity are just some of the reasons why good information can be misused or misinterpreted. Not only does this reduce the value of the information gathered, but it may also actually increase the levels of uncertainty through the input of false knowledge. In this sense, there is a big difference between data, information, and knowledge.

It is tempting to suggest that AI would eliminate many of these human-dependent impediments to the use of information and thereby should increase levels of certainty. It is certainly true that AI is free from human subjectivity and can process vast amounts of data quickly. However, the use of AI alone in decision-making is likely to be restricted to the tactical level, when split-second decisions may be essential. At the higher levels, AI is likely to operate more as an aide to a human commander. This would assuage concerns regarding machine autonomy in crisis stability. Moreover, although AI is good at number crunching, purely logical forms of thinking, it cannot yet replicate abstract human thinking. In this way, AI cannot appreciate the complexities of sociopolitical interactions. In this way, there is a 'democratic deficit' in AI.[42] Just as importantly, AI cannot replace humans as the moral agents in war. Thus, we can conclude that although AI, like advanced ISR systems, will increase certainty in some areas, it does not address some of the most important intangibles inherent in the process of strategy. The future of information processing is likely to be a hybrid system, using the strengths of both human and artificial forms of intelligence.

Another area where AI will mitigate, but not solve, difficulties with processing information is information overload. If we assume that humans will continue to make the ultimate decisions at the higher levels of strategy, a commander may be swamped by a constantly, and rapidly, updating view of the battlespace. Too much information, especially if it contains contradictions, can add to uncertainty. Also, in an age of information plenty, a commander may become too reliant on information and thus fail to act while they wait for a particular knowledge gap to be filled. Alternatively, an AI-aided commander may suffer from 'automation bias', whereby the system is assumed to be correct even when it is not. Such a bias was evident when Patriot air defence batteries mistakenly shot down allied aircraft during the invasion of Iraq.[43] Merely gathering information is not enough. It has to be processed and communicated effectively.

It is also worth noting that having good, ample, and timely knowledge does not guarantee success. Lifting the fog of war does not automatically lead to victory. Knowledge must be acted on. During the campaign in North Africa, after the battle of El Alamein, General Montgomery was in possession of Ultra intelligence that made him aware of Rommel's severe supply difficulties. However, Montgomery's natural caution prevented him from pursuing Rommel's forces with sufficient offensive spirit, and thus the opportunity to destroy Rommel's forces was lost.[44] The gathering and processing of information is but one task in the multidimensional activity of strategy. Accurate information is good to have, but as Colin Gray notes, alone it does not destroy a single piece of enemy equipment.[45]

This brief analysis of the fate of violence and uncertainty in contemporary warfare suggests that the current RMA, although it will affect the character of war, will fail to transform its nature. This is an important conclusion, because the fate of the information-age RMA has implications for the entire RMA hypothesis. Not since the maturation of air power has a group of technologies reached into so many aspects of strategy. Indeed, it is the ubiquitous reach of information technology that underpins many of the ambitious claims regarding changes to the nature of war. A major enhancement of knowledge in the battlespace could destabilise the foundations of Clausewitz's work, based as it is on uncertainty, chaos, and the ensuing violence. Thus, if the Clausewitzian nature of war remains largely intact, the transformative capabilities of the RMA have to be questioned. That being the case, the defence profession may need to rein in its promotion of technology, RMAs, and military transformations as means to understand success and failure in war. Other explanations need to be sought beyond the development and successful application of new technology.

One can go further. It is not just the case that RMAs have failed to transform the nature of war. In fact, the balance of power in this relationship seems to favour the latter over the former. Core elements of the nature of war influence the possible direction that RMAs can take. In this way, the nature of war curtails the implications of a potential RMA. Purported RMAs come and go, but the nature of war is constant. There are four elements of the Clausewitzian nature of war that most heavily influence how changes to the character of war may develop: policy (which itself develops from geostrategic conditions), interaction with the enemy, the climate of war, and war's polymorphous character. Individually, these four elements are not so dominant, but taken together, they produce an inescapable reality.

Since war is always a rational act in the service of policy (however irrational the policy objectives may seem), a developing RMA will be shaped by policy requirements. Military innovation is rarely contained to just one actor. Thus, different variants of an RMA may develop from the same technological basis. As previously noted, during the interwar period, various European powers perceived armoured forces differently. These differences can be partially explained by the different policy objectives and geostrategic circumstances of each state. Nazi Germany, which had an aggressive outlook and the need for rapid victories, concentrated their armoured forces into penetrating spearheads. Whereas France, with an understandable defensive outlook, saw tanks more as mobile artillery that could shore up their defensive positions where needed. In the information age, it is no surprise that the United States, with a range of missions of choice for its dominant conventional forces around the world, should perceive information technology as primarily providing an enhancement to those forces. For the United States, the current RMA is really about the digitisation of forces and an increased reliance on standoff, unmanned capabilities. Those facing the conventional superiority of the United States may understandably adopt a different approach to the modern epoch. In particular, smaller actors may look towards cyberattack as their version of the information-age RMA. Alternatively, they may opt for more primitive forms of irregular warfare, cherry-picking the technology of the information age where it can enhance their operations. In this vein, irregular forces, including Hezbollah and ISIS, have already made use of unmanned systems and modern communications and encryption to better coordinate their operations.

Also, as the security environment changes, or perhaps in response to changes in the domestic political context, the policy objectives of a state may change. In turn, new policy objectives may call for different missions or approaches to warfare. Such a change was clearly evident in the aftermath of 9/11 and the end of regular hostilities in Iraq. Counterinsurgency operations in Afghanistan and Iraq required a shift from a platform- and technology-heavy approach to one centred on dismounted infantry, albeit enhanced by the support of air power (manned and unmanned).

So disparate are the potential uses of most new technologies that it may be disingenuous to identify a unified, coherent version of an RMA. Much like the multiverse theory in physics, there may be infinite possible RMAs from the same technological basis. Which one we experience will depend on our choices.[46] This even applies to candidate RMAs that on initial viewing appear one-dimensional. For some, the nuclear RMA was characterised by nonuse and the dominance of deterrence. However, at different times and in different contexts, nuclear weapons were regarded as instruments of warfighting. In addition, it is plausible that these expensive weapons, which were once the preserve of the great powers, could come into the possession of terrorist organisations. Similarly, for much of its history, air power was used solely by state actors, albeit in a number of different roles. However, from the 1970s onwards, terrorists began to exploit the potential of the third dimension. Their use of air power began with hijackings, and culminated with the attacks of 9/11. Thus, a particular RMA can serve many policy objectives and in different ways.

War is invariably an interactive pursuit. Clausewitz accurately describes it as a duel on a larger scale. Each side has the objective of throwing the other off-balance.[47] As noted in relation to both violence and uncertainty, the enemy has various options to offset or circumvent RMA-based capabilities. Edward Luttwak's concept of the paradoxical logic of strategy suggests that any identified strength eventually will be neutralised or will reap diminishing rewards over time.[48] Even Krepinevich notes that innovation sometimes begets further innovation as a countermove. For him, the artillery revolution was eventually negated by a revolution in fortification.[49] With the war in Afghanistan dragging on at the time of writing, almost 18 years since it began, it becomes increasingly difficult to identify any substantial and lasting strategic advantages to be gained from digitised forces.

The supposed reasons for the overwhelming victory of 1991, which heralded the true arrival of information-age warfare, appear to have been quickly negated. In 1999, Serbia found simple but effective means to reduce the potency of American air power. In 2001, the events of 9/11 demonstrated that American conventional military power could be bypassed entirely. In 2003, Iraqi forces quickly melted away and continued their resistance via an irregular style of warfare. In 2014, ISIS rapidly captured 110,000 square kilometres of territory in Iraq and Syria, partly due to failures in strategy and policy by the West and its allies. To respond to the challenges from 2001 onwards, the United States and its allies have been forced to rely more heavily on infantry-based operations, albeit with support from aerial ISR and strike assets. In this respect, the RMA of 1991 looks increasingly like a meteorite falling to Earth. For a brief period, it lit up the strategic horizon, only to disintegrate when it met resistance.

Clausewitz identified conditions common to all wars, which he classified as the climate of war. The conditions in question are danger, uncertainly, exhaustion, and chance.[50] They are of interest to a study of RMAs because they complicate military operations in a negative fashion. Thus, optimal operational performance cannot be achieved. Again, this is important because an RMA-equipped force may not be able to achieve the leap in performance that has been identified as a characteristic of an RMA. The first three elements of the climate of war particularly affect humans. The physical and mental trauma of battle reduces the performance levels of those engaged in military operations. When uncertainty is added to the mix, along with chance events such as poor weather or the unexpected death of an accomplished commander, operational performance may fall well below what was anticipated. The purpose of discussing these aspects of the nature of war is to inject a degree of realism into debates concerning the contemporary RMA. This does not mean that forces with an innovative edge cannot achieve remarkable results. Nonetheless, the polymorphous character of war, allied to the continued tactical, operational, and strategic need for human presence and interaction, will ensure that the climate of war remains largely valid.

The fourth feature of the nature of war, the polymorphous character, has already been hinted at on a number of occasions in this chapter. War is often equated with the game of chess. However, the two activities are vastly different. Chess is conducted within known and unchanging parameters. Each game uses the same board layout and the same number of playing pieces. These pieces have unchanging capabilities, and each player begins the game with the same mixture of pieces. The whole of the game board and all of the pieces are visible to both players throughout the game. In contrast, each war occurs in unique and changing circumstances. The field of battle is likely to be different on each occasion. Changing climatic conditions may also have an impact on terrain, so that a known field of battle can change dramatically. Also, different environmental conditions will have varying effects on different units. Although some information is likely to be available on the number and composition of the enemy's forces, unexpected reinforcements often arrive at some stage in the battle. More importantly, the forces engaged are rarely symmetrical and will include unidentified units and/or units with indeterminate capabilities. Not only can war take numerous forms, but also the character of any particular war may change over time. Thus, the idea that war will develop along the lines dictated by any one actor and its chosen approach to warfare is fanciful. The character of future war will be complex, reflecting a range of different styles and strategic needs.

Technology, war, and strategy

The debate surrounding RMAs invariably raises questions about the relative importance of technology in the conduct of war and strategy. However, this fixation with new technology is not unique to modern RMA enthusiasts. J.F.C. Fuller, the noted theorist and military historian, is alarmingly definitive on the role of technology in warfare: 'Tools or weapons, if only the right ones can be discovered, form ninety-nine per cent of victory'.[51] Fuller's comment perfectly illustrates one of the main problems with the RMA hypothesis and the emphasis on technology in particular: reductionism. Strategy is a complex activity, so to reduce success or failure to one of its 17 dimensions is highly misleading. Nonetheless, it has to be conceded that history is replete with instances when one side in a conflict appeared to gain important advantage from a technological edge.

The most obvious modern example of this phenomenon is the 1991 Gulf War, the poster boy of the RMA generation. The Iraqi forces were clearly outgunned in almost every department. Any Iraqi aircraft that attempted to challenge the Coalition's air supremacy did not last long. On the ground, Iraqi tanks were outranged by their opposite number, and any shells that they did manage to fire in range could not penetrate the protective armour on Coalition tanks. Iraqi technological disadvantages are well demonstrated by the battle for Medina Ridge on February 27. The 2nd Brigade of the United States 1st Armoured Division engaged Iraq's 2nd Brigade of the Republican Guard Medina Luminous Division. Although the Iraqi forces were well dug in behind a ridge, they still lost 186 tanks and 127 armoured fighting vehicles. In sharp contrast, the Americans suffered only one fatality and four damaged tanks.[52]

Similarly disproportionate kill ratios can be found further back in history. At the Battle of Omdurman, on September 2, 1898, 19,000 technologically superior British and Egyptian forces defeated 52,000 Mahdists. For the loss of 402 casualties, the British and Egyptians inflicted over 20,000 casualties on their enemy. Technology was also important for the Portuguese in their successful attempts to control the Indian Ocean during the fifteenth and sixteenth centuries. Arab vessels in the region had no answer to the firepower of the Portuguese broadside batteries. In 341 BCE, the Chinese state of Ch'i heavily defeated the state of Wei, inflicting tens of thousands of casualties on the latter. This decisive victory was significantly enabled by the former's use of crossbows.[53]

Box 4.3 Technological advantage and the outcome of wars

Technological advantage translated into success
China 341 BCE – Ch'i defeat of Wei.
Fifteenth/sixteenth century – Portuguese domination of Indian Ocean.
1898 – Battle of Omdurman.
1991 – Gulf War.

Technological advantage offset or misused
Nazi Germany in Second World War.
1960s/1970s – US war in Vietnam.
1980s – Soviet war in Afghanistan.
2001–Present – Coalition war in Afghanistan.

These cases are undoubtedly impressive, but for every example of technological superiority contributing to victory, there is a case in which the technologically superior side experienced failure. The Soviets in Afghanistan and the United States in Vietnam are obvious modern examples of when technological superiority could not be translated into success. However, these are both examples of counterinsurgency, which is a notoriously difficult activity for regular forces. More telling, then, is the aforementioned case of Nazi Germany, which led the field in many areas of technological, organisational, and operational development. These examples speak to the strategic truism that deficiencies in one dimension can be compensated for in others. Indeed, it has been suggested that the longer the war, the more important non-technological dimensions become, especially those that are socioeconomic and political in nature.[54]

Moreover, even if our analytical focus is limited to technology, we cannot consider it as a homogenous whole. A strategic agent may be proficient in one form of technology but not in others. Alternatively, a technological system may confer advantage in one context but not in others. In our example of the Second World War, while Germany enjoyed some tactical technological advantage in armoured forces, these same forces (due to the narrow width of their tracks) were ill-suited to the operational demands of the Soviet theatre of operations. Narrow tracks meant that German tanks would get bogged down in soft Soviet terrain. Technology is not a one-size-fits-all solution. Indeed, as with all things strategic, context is everything. In this way, it is misleading to discuss technological superiority in an abstract manner. Superiority – or more accurately, advantage – is relative to the enemy, policy objectives, geography, and so on.

If Fuller is incorrect on the significance of technology, how do we explain the tendency to overinflate this one dimension? It is most likely the case that analysts responsible for this mistake are focusing too narrowly on the tactical and operational levels. This reflects a tendency to equate military success with long-term political success. There is an assumption that the defeat of the enemy's forces, or perhaps control of key terrain, will inevitably translate into an overall positive war outcome. Therefore, having more advanced technology, especially if it is possessed in sufficient numbers, should enable military victory, which in turn should enable political victory. However, there is more to achieving military victory than technology. This is even truer for translating military success into lasting positive political outcomes.

As noted by Gray, strategy is a gestalt. To succeed in strategy requires competence in all of the 17 dimensions of strategy.[55] To reiterate, these dimensions are divided into three categories: people and politics, preparation for war, and war proper. Technology exists as its own dimension in the second category, although it can claim to play an important role in five other dimensions: economics and logistics, information and intelligence, strategic theory and doctrine, military operations, and command. And as noted in Chapter 1, the interactive relationships among the dimensions are complex and changing.

The following analysis illustrates just how complex and multifaceted these interactions are. Clearly, technology underpins the economic basis for military power and plays a central role in both the supply and demand sides of logistics. Certain technological innovations facilitate new forms of economic activity and/or enable more efficient logistic operations. In the modern era, technology has also played an increasingly important role in information and intelligence operations. To cite just one example, the exploitation of microwave radiation provides a form of all-weather reconnaissance. Likewise, although doctrine is influenced by many factors (including history, culture, and ethics, to name just three), technology sets important parameters; it dictates what is possible. The details of doctrine can only be established once it is clear what technology can deliver. Similarly, command in the modern era is heavily dependent on technology. Indeed, as a consequence of the rise of the network, technology is influencing command in the search for greater levels of delegation.

Yet economics and logistics are just as much about management as they are about technology. Human intelligence (HUMINT) continues to play an essential role in strategy (especially in irregular warfare). And as the history of strategic bombing illustrates, theory often helps to mould the development of technology. Belief in the offensive power of aerial bombardment substantially shaped the development of Allied air power in the interwar years. Additionally, although technology significantly shapes all military operations, it is not alone in performing this function. Terrain, doctrine, time, command, ethics, culture, logistics, adversary, and friction also have roles to play, to a greater or lesser degree. Finally, although enabled by technology, much of command is concerned with human interaction, the very human quality of leadership, and the personality traits of the commander.

Thus, even in those dimensions where technology has more obvious influence, other non-technological factors are still at play. Moreover, this still leaves 11 dimensions without a significant technological aspect. More significantly, these 11 dimensions include some of the most important ones: people, politics, society, culture, geography, adversary, and time. It is true that technology may have an impact on these dimensions as well. However, it does not shape them in any substantial way. For example, technology certainly influences the process of politics and even helps to create political issues. The latter can obviously be seen in the field of bio-medics. However, politics is really concerned with first-order issues, such as the value of human life, equality, and freedom. Technology impinges on these issues, but it is not at the core of these debates. In this sense, technology reaches far and wide but does not heavily influence why wars are fought. This is left to politics and thus to people.

If we use the dimensions of strategy to try to understand success and failure in war, technology does not feature especially prominently. Why did Germany fail in the Second World War? To answer this question, one would need to look to the personal politics of the Nazi leadership and conclude that Germany bought into an unreachable political vision. In addition, although Germany fought hard in defence of Nazi ideology, the latter was a potent motivating factor for the Allies from an ethical standpoint. Nazi Germany was simply too ambitious and too dangerous to be left intact.[56] Thus, the Allies were able to overlook their differences and bring together their massive economic resources to overwhelm their common enemy. These dominant dimensions were powerful enough to overcome astute tactical, technological, and operational performances by the Germans.

Even from a narrow technological perspective, the Second World War is complex. Germany led in a number of fields: tank design, jet aircraft, and cruise and ballistic missiles. However, partly due to an emphasis on advanced technology, Germany did not have enough technology. To cite one crude example, during the Normandy campaign, the Allies had sufficient numbers of inferior tanks to exhaust the rounds of the much-less-common German Tiger and Panther tanks.[57] Thus, it seems that in trying to explain the outcome of the Second World War, it is more profitable to focus on those dimensions that concern human issues rather than focus on the technological balance of the war.

Even if we restrict our analysis to the lower levels of strategy, a focus on technology is still inadequate. As important as technology can be in the battlespace, other important factors that influence performance include command, logistics, morale, and training, to name just four. So, even at the lower levels of strategy, technology provides an inadequate explanation for the outcome of events. This conclusion suggests that as a means to understand war and improve performance, the RMA hypothesis is insufficient. Its focus on technology, even if it includes operational and organisational factors, is far too narrow. Success in strategy requires mastering many dimensions, the most important of which have human concerns at their core. Such concerns are often intangible and therefore difficult to quantify and control. This may be one reason why some find it preferable to focus on technological parameters, which can be quantified and controlled to a far greater degree.

Conclusion – the RMA as a methodological and practical tool

One could be forgiven for thinking that the serious flaws identified in the RMA hypothesis leave it empty of value. However, that is not the case. The RMA hypothesis has both methodological and practical value. Although the exploitation of new technology can neither create a uniform style of future warfare nor transform the nature of war, it is important. The previous emphasis on the higher levels of strategy is justified, but it is not designed to reduce the importance of the tactical and operational levels. Actions on the battlefield can have important outcomes. As Clausewitz noted, the enemy can change everything with a successful engagement.[58] Good strategy can be undone by failure in the battlespace. For example, although ambitious, the strategic rationale behind the Gallipoli landings was logical enough. Perhaps this bold move could have changed the complexion of the First

World War. However, we will never know, because the tactical execution was so poor. It is also worth considering what might have occurred had D-Day gone badly for the Allies. At minimum, the war in Europe would undoubtedly have lasted much longer. Even if tactical success cannot completely overturn disadvantage at the higher levels of strategy, it may reduce the costs of war or perhaps even force the winning side to make some concessions. That being the case, it is worth exploring innovations that promise tactical and operational advantages. As Gray succinctly notes, 'technology drives tactics, shapes operations, and enables strategy'.[59]

Also, although less significant than the RMA enthusiasts would have us believe, change in the character of warfare does occur. In addition, history also suggests that adapting quickly to change, or even leading said change, can confer significant advantages. Even if these relative advantages do not last long and do not directly lead to outright success, it is surely preferable to exploit them while one can. This assumes of course that the costs are not too high and the efforts will support one's policy objectives. Thus, from both a methodological and practical position, it is wise to hold onto the notion that change occurs and may be advantageous. The RMA hypothesis should also be congratulated for identifying the means to sensibly exploit innovation. Simply bolting new technology onto existing capabilities is unlikely to confer substantial advantages. It is important to explore new organisational and operational forms to fully realise the potential of new technology. In the First World War, tanks were initially hindered because their advances were preceded by artillery bombardment; this was the standard practice at the time. It took some time to realise that this merely churned up the ground and made an armoured advance more difficult. In this sense, tactics had to adapt to the new technology.

From an academic perspective the RMA hypothesis may be useful. Although continuity may be more empirically compelling than moments of revolution, it is useful to intellectually accept that the latter can occur. In our efforts to explain how the conduct of warfare has changed from the age of the Hoplite (to pick an important but far from definitive starting point in classical history) to the complex joint operations of the current age, it is tempting to focus on relatively slow evolutionary change. For much of the time, this would be accurate. However, there have undoubtedly been moments of genuine and quite dramatic change. The two most likely candidates for this have come in the twentieth century. The invention of heavier-than-air flight and nuclear weapons both have had a rapid and dramatic impact on warfare. Perhaps autonomous unmanned systems will have a similar effect.

We are left to conclude that innovation is real and that technology is important. The problem arises when those promoting the significance of these oversell them as a means to change the nature of war, or as an excuse for iconoclastic writings. Those promoting the contemporary RMA are particularly guilty of these faults. Despite the many claims to overturn the Clausewitzian nature of war, history, ongoing conflicts, and the sensible application of strategic theory all suggest that war will continue to be characterised by uncertainty and violence. In particular, policy, the enemy, the climate of war, and war's polymorphous character together ensure that no innovation will transform war's true nature. Ironically, changes in the character of war do not alter the nature of war. Rather, they are shaped by it. In this way, the nature of war is self-preserving.

Key points

1 The modern RMA hypothesis has diverse origins, but the 1991 Gulf War stands out.
2 RMAs are driven primarily by technology and associated operational and organisational adaptation.
3 The information-age RMA promises a change to the nature of war but falls short of this lofty goal.
4 Autonomous unmanned systems will play an increasing role in warfare but will not fully replace the strategically vital role of humans.
5 Technology is only one of the many dimensions in strategy, and not a decisive one.
6 Whether valid or not, the RMA hypothesis has utility for both the theorist and the practitioner.

Questions

1 Are RMAs merely academic constructs?
2 Will the information-age RMA change the nature of war?
3 In what contexts will autonomous unmanned systems prove especially useful?
4 How significant is technology in the practice of strategy?
5 Does the RMA hypothesis have value?

Notes

1 Thomas L. McNaugher, 'The Real Meaning of Military Transformation: Rethinking the Revolution', *Foreign Affairs*, January/February 2007, www.foreignaffairs.com/articles/62285/thomas-l-mcnaugher/the-real-meaning-of-military-transformation-rethinking-the-revolu#
2 Christopher Coker, quoted in P.W. Singer, *Wired for War: The Robotics Revolution and Conflict in the 21st Century* (New York, Penguin Books, 2009), p. 194.
3 For a discussion of the development of the RMA see James R. Blaker, *Understanding the Revolution in Military Affairs: A Guide to America's 21st Century Defense*, Progressive Policy Institute, Defense Working Paper 3 (Washington, DC, January 1997).
4 Geoffrey Parker, *The Military Revolution: Military Innovation and the Rise of the West 1500–1800*, 2nd ed. (Cambridge, Cambridge University Press, 1996).
5 Lawrence Freedman, *The Future of War: A History* (London, Allen Lane, 2017).
6 Alvin Toffler and Heidi Toffler, *War and Anti-War: Survival at the Dawn of the 21st Century* (London, Little Brown, 1994).
7 Andrew F. Krepinevich, 'Cavalry to Computer: The Pattern of Military Revolutions', *National Interest* 37 (1994).
8 Freedman, *Future of War*.

9 David Hambling, *Swarm Troopers: How Small Drones Will Conquer the World* (Archangel Ink, 2015).

10 Stephen Peter Rosen, *Winning the Next War: Innovation and the Modern Military* (Ithaca, Cornell University Press, 1994).

11 Ibid.

12 One could argue that important elements of blitzkrieg were evident towards the end of the First World War, especially in relation to combined-arms operations. Perhaps more controversially, it may be claimed that Alexander the Great operated a form of blitzkrieg at the tactical level, with the Companion Cavalry acting as the armoured penetration force.

13 A.J. Bacevich, 'Preserving the Well-Bred Horse', *National Interest* 37 (1994).

14 Krepinevich, p. 31.

15 For this argument, see John Ellis, *The Sharp End of War: The Fighting Man in World War Two* (London, Book Club Associates, 1980).

16 For an interesting discussion of these, see Richard Overy, *Why the Allies Won* (London, Pimlico, 1995).

17 J.F.C. Fuller, *Armament and History: A Study of the Influence of Armament on History from the Dawn of Classical Warfare to the Second World War* (London, Eyre & Spottiswoode, 1946), p. v.

18 See Chapter 9 on Air Power.

19 This is even the case for Kosovo, which some commentators have argued was decided by air power alone. See Chapter 9.

20 For discussion of the nuclear revolution in statecraft, see Robert Jervis, *The Meaning of the Nuclear Revolution: Statecraft and the Prospect of Armageddon* (Ithaca, Cornell University Press, 1989).

21 Keith Payne, *How Much is Enough? A Goal-Driven Approach to Defining Key Principles* (Washington, DC, National Institute for Public Policy, 2009); Rodney W. Jones,Minimum, *Nuclear Deterrence Postures in South Asia: An Overview Final Report* (Reston, VA, Policy Architects International, 2001), www.globalsecurity.org/wmd/library/report/2001/south_asia.pdf

22 See Paul Scharre, *Army of None: Autonomous Weapons and the Future of War* (New York, W.W. Norton & Company, 2018); Singer, p. 192.

23 This sentiment can be found in many works, including the following: Francois Heisbourg, *The Future of Warfare* (London, Phoenix, 1997); John Arquilla and David Ronfeldt, 'Cyberwar Is Coming', in John Arquilla and David Ronfeldt (eds.), *In Athena's Camp: Preparing for Conflict in the Information Age* (Santa Monica, CA, RAND, 1996); Robert R. Leonhard, *The Principles of War in the Information Age* (Novato, CA, Presidio Press, 1998).

24 Admiral William Owens (with Ed Offley), *Lifting the Fog of War* (Baltimore, John Hopkins University Press, 2001); Vice-Admiral Arthur K. Cebrowski, 'Network-Centric Warfare: An Emerging Military Response to the Information Age', Command and Control Research and Technology Symposium, June 29, 1999.

25 For example, see John Arquilla and David Ronfeldt, 'A New Epoch- and Spectrum- of Conflict', in John Arquilla and David Ronfeldt (eds.), *In Athena's Camp: Preparing For Conflict in the Information Age* (Santa Monica, CA, RAND, 1996), p. 18; James Adams, *The Next World War: The Warriors and Weapons of the New Battlefields in Cyberspace* (London, Hutchinson, 1998), p. 93.

26 For further details on these developments, see Hambling, pp. 11–25; Singer, pp. 46–59.

27 Singer, p. 127.

28 Scharre, p. 16.

29 Ibid., pp. 29–30.

30 Ibid., p. 104.

31 Martin C. Libicki, *The Mesh and the Net: Speculations on Armed Conflict in a Time of Free Silicon* (Washington, DC, National Defense University Press, 1994), pp. 19–51.

32 This is the central argument in Hambling's work.

33 George Allison, 'U.S. Army Exercise Sees 45 Drones Defeated by Energy Weapons Fired From Fantastically Named "Laser Buggy"', *UK Defence Journal* (March 26, 2018), https://ukdefence journal.org.uk/us-army-exercise-sees-45-drones-defeated-by-energy-weapons-fired-from-fantastically-named-laser-buggy/?no_cache=1

34 Scharre, p. 157.

35 Singer, p. 194.

36 An early discussion of these trends can be found in Edward Luttwak, 'Towards Post-Heroic Warfare', *Foreign Affairs* 74:3 (1995). See also Martin C. Libicki, 'The Emerging Primacy of Information', *Orbis* 40:2 (1996).

37 Charles Dunlap describes such an approach as neo-absolutist war. See Charles J. Dunlap, '21st-Century Land Warfare: Four Dangerous Myths', *Parameters* 27:3 (1997).

38 Dwight D. Eisenhower, *Crusade in Europe* (London, William Heinemann, 1948), p. 247. For those readers who think it highly unlikely that we will see an enemy like Nazi Germany in the future, it is worth remembering that in 1918 it seemed just as unlikely to happen in the first place.

39 Barry D. Watts, *Clausewitzian Friction and Future War*, McNair Paper 52 (Washington, DC, Institute for National Strategic Studies, National Defence University, 1996).

40 Singer, p. 195.

41 Clausewitz, p. 117.

42 Josh Cowls, 'Deciding How to Decide: Six Key Questions for Reducing AI's Democratic Deficit', https://medium.com/josh-cowls/deciding-how-to-decide-six-key-questions-for-reducing-ais-democratic-deficit-2b7a12d922bd

43 Scharre, pp. 137–45.

44 Ralph Bennett, *Behind the Lines: Intelligence in the War with Germany 1939–1945* (London, Pimlico, 1999), pp. 109–10.

45 Colin S. Gray, *Modern Strategy* (Oxford, Oxford University Press, 1999), pp. 38–9.

46 However, unlike the multiverse theory, the different RMAs can interact with each other.

47 Clausewitz, p. 75.

48 Edward Luttwak, *Strategy: The Logic of Peace and War* (Cambridge, The Belknap Press, 1987).

49 Krepinevich, 'Cavalry to Computer', p. 31.

50 Clausewitz, p. 104.

51 Fuller, *Armament and History*, p. V.

52 For details on the various battles in the 1991 Gulf War, see Michael R. Gordon and General Bernard E. Trainor, *The Generals War: The Inside Story of the Conflict in the Gulf* (Boston, Little, Brown and Company, 1995).

53 For further details on the cases discussed, see Philip Ziegler, *Omdurman* (London, Pen and Sword Books, 2006); Ralph Sawyer, *The Seven Military Classics of Ancient China* (Boulder, Westview Press, 1993), p. 11, 15.

54 Freedman, p. 16.

55 Colin S. Gray, *Perspectives on Strategy* (Oxford, Oxford University Press, 2013), p. 155.

56 Richard Overy, *Why the Allies Won* (London, Pimlico, 1996).

57 The significance of this disparity in numbers is discussed in John Ellis, *Brute Force: Allied Strategy and Tactics in the Second World War* (London, Andre Deutsch, 1990).

58 Clausewitz, p. 97.

59 Gray, *Perspectives on Strategy*, p. 168.

Further reading

Freedman, Lawrence, *The Future of War: A History*, (London: Allen Lane, 2017).

Gray, Colin S., *Perspectives on Strategy*, (Oxford: Oxford University Press, 2013).

Krepinevich, Andrew F., 'Cavalry to Computer: The Pattern of Military Revolutions', *National Interest*, Vol. 37 (1994).

Lonsdale, David J., *The Nature of War in the Information Age: Clausewitzian Future*, (London: Frank Cass, 2004).

Owens, Admiral William (with Ed Offley), *Lifting the Fog of War*, (Baltimore: John Hopkins University Press, 2001).

Parker, Geoffrey, *The Military Revolution: Military Innovation and the Rise of the West 1500–1800*, 2nd Edition, (Cambridge, MA: Cambridge University Press, 1996).

Rosen, Stephen Peter, *Winning the Next War: Innovation and the Modern Military*, (Ithaca: Cornell University Press, 1994).

Scharre, Paul, *Army of None: Autonomous Weapons and the Future of War*, (New York: W.W. Norton & Company, 2018).

Toffler, Alvin and Heidi Toffler, *War and Anti-War: Survival at the Dawn of the 21st Century*, (London: Little Brown, 1994).

van Creveld, Martin, *Technology and War*, (New York: The Free Press, 1991).

Intelligence

5

Reader's guide

Intelligence bureaucracies are a new historical phenomenon; theoretical work has focused on improving the process by which intelligence agencies support strategic planners; intelligence agencies as direct actors in strategy; intelligence agencies cannot avoid involvement in politics.

Introduction

Over 3000 years ago, Pharaoh Amenhotep III of Egypt boasted of his ability to collect information about the Babylonian army.[1] Over 2000 years ago, Chinese strategic thinker Sun Tzu proposed methods for integrating intelligence operations into the rest of strategy, adding that a commander who neglects such matters 'is no general' and that a ruler who tolerates such an incompetent is 'no master of victory'.[2] Nevertheless, by the nineteenth century, what former CIA director Allen Dulles called the craft of intelligence had become a lost art. Strategic thinkers have only begun the process of reinventing it.

This chapter outlines key issues which have arisen as strategists rediscover intelligence. The first section notes key historical events that aroused contemporary interest in this topic. The second section discusses how theorists have depicted the relationship between intelligence and strategy and how their work may help policymakers organise intelligence services to keep strategists as well informed as possible. These theoretical concepts, however, are not fully satisfying. The third section shows that intelligence agencies perform functions that go beyond passively gathering information. The fourth and final section suggests that despite theorists' attempts to distinguish between intelligence and the strategic planning it supports, intelligence is an organic part of strategy that raises many of the same moral, political, and operational issues as war itself. One should also note that this chapter focuses on intelligence operations in the physical world. Chapters 4 and 11 delve deeper into the issues of electronic intelligence and intelligence in cyberspace.

The rediscovery of intelligence

Spies, scouts, cryptographers, cryptanalysts, military cartographers, and other intelligence practitioners have been active in every historical era. Strategic thinkers, however, have not always fully appreciated their uses. Moreover, governments have not always maintained institutions to perform the combinations of functions typical for modern intelligence agencies. The rediscovery of intelligence is not so much the rediscovery of any particular practice as it is the rediscovery of the value of those practices and the emergence of organisations dedicated to employing those practices for strategic purposes.

Carl von Clausewitz noted several of the key reasons why strategic thinkers have historically been reluctant to devote too much attention to these matters. The fact that 'many intelligence reports in war are contradictory; even more are false and most are uncertain' was only the first of Clausewitz's concerns.[3] Worse yet, in Clausewitz's view, this barrage of dubious but frequently alarming information may actually make it harder for commanders to assess situations rationally. 'The senses make a more vivid impression on the mind than systematic thought', the Prussian warns, and war 'has a way of masking the stage with scenery crudely daubed with fearsome apparitions'. Such 'apparitions' frighten commanders into wavering at precisely the moments when it is most important for them to be resolute, and the more information commanders attempt to process, the more of these 'apparitions' they will have to contend with.

The scholar John Ferris, who has explored Clausewitz's writings on this topic in depth, reminds us that the Prussian accepted that intelligence could be more useful under favourable circumstances. For instance, Clausewitz suggested that intelligence reports might be more valuable for higher-level planners, who have less need for boldness and more time to reflect.[4] Other early-nineteenth-century strategists, notably Jomini and the Duke of Wellington, promoted more optimistic views of intelligence even for officers in the field.[5] Although strategic thinkers of the nineteenth and earlier centuries commonly recognised that intelligence reports could be useful under appropriate circumstances, most would have concluded that such reporting was not consistently useful enough to justify great investments of either resources or attention. Those who followed Clausewitz's line of reasoning would have added that overinvestment in intelligence can easily become counterproductive.

Despite such scepticism, an increasing number of nineteenth-century political actors formed intelligence-gathering organisations. In 1866, shortly before Prussia invaded Austria, the Prussian king established a bureau known as the Secret Field Police to collect militarily valuable information by spying on foreign governments. Approximately four years later, when revolutionaries attempted to assassinate Tsar Alexander II of Russia, the Tsar founded an agency called the Okhrana to hunt down his political enemies throughout the world. In 1881, a patriotic Japanese citizen named Kotaro Hiraoka took it upon himself to help his country develop up-to-date military and industrial capabilities by forming a secret organisation known as the Black Ocean Society to perform espionage abroad. Similar events took place in numerous other countries.

There was nothing new about spy networks or undercover police forces. Queen Elizabeth I of sixteenth-century England and her contemporary Toyotomi Hideyoshi, to pick but two examples, maintained secret services. Their successors, however, allowed those services to wither. The states and other political actors of the late nineteenth century not only preserved their information-collecting organisations but used them for an increasing variety of purposes.

One of the reasons why such agencies flourished in this era was that new forms of technology were providing them with new kinds of information to collect. By the late 1800s, for instance, diplomats around the world had begun to send much of their most sensitive correspondence by telegraph. Russia's Foreign Ministry cooperated with the Okhrana to intercept such messages.[6] Older forms of spying supported the newer ones. Because many diplomatic telegrams were encrypted, the Okhrana turned to its global network of informers and undercover agents to acquire codebooks and cipher keys. This process allowed the Okhrana, which had been powerful enough when its primary function had been crushing revolutionaries, to acquire a role in virtually every aspect of Russia's foreign policy.

Box 5.1 Types of intelligence data

The intelligence community classifies the sources of strategic information into six widely recognised categories.

Signals intelligence (SIGINT)

SIGINT is a broad category that encompasses attempts to eavesdrop on the various signals one's targets emit in the course of going about their activities. The most prominent types of SIGINT are communications intelligence (COMINT) and electronic intelligence (ELINT). COMINT consists of intercepted messages. Methods for obtaining it range from satellite eavesdropping on radio transmissions to the old-fashioned equivalent of opening mail. ELINT consists of other information gained through electronic monitoring. Locating a radar site by tracing its emissions back to their source is a classic example of this practice. Indeed, some practitioners refer to a sub-category of ELINT known as radar intelligence (RADINT).

Imagery intelligence (IMINT)

IMINT means taking pictures, typically from aircraft or satellites. These pictures may be photographs in visible light. They may also depict targets as seen by radar, infrared cameras, or other types of sensors.

Measurement and signature intelligence (MASINT)

This is another broadly defined category, which covers data from all technical sources other than SIGINT and IMINT. Examples of MASINT include collecting air samples to monitor industrial activity, using microphones to detect the footsteps of people moving through given areas, and using seismographs to gather information on underground nuclear explosions.

Human intelligence (HUMINT)

HUMINT includes all information derived from human sources. These sources may be spies working undercover in enemy organisations, but they may also be diplomats reporting on what they have observed while doing their jobs, scientists explaining their research, travellers offering information on things they have seen while visiting other countries, or prisoners responding to interrogation, to name but a few possibilities.

Open-source intelligence (OSINT)

OSINT consists of legally available information taken from the media, the Internet, museums, published books, telephone directories, national archives, corporate reports, government policy documents, and other publicly accessible sources. Sherman Kent famously estimated 'of the things our state must know about other states, some 90% may be discovered through overt means'.[7]

Geospatial intelligence

Geospatial intelligence consists of information gained by making and using maps.

The telegraph, the telephone, and the wireless radio also accelerated the speed with which intelligence bureaucracies could take in information from far-flung sources and send it back out in a useful form. Theorist Michael Handel suggests that this development made Clausewitz's doubts about intelligence obsolete.[8] By the time of the First World War, intelligence organisations routinely provided strategic planners with information that made it easier – not, as Clausewitz feared, more difficult – for military commanders to make critical decisions with confidence. An example of this point comes from the 1914–18 war at sea, where British naval commanders had to decide how many of their ships to use on missions to distant parts of the world and how many to hold back to counter raids by Germany's surface fleet.[9] One of the main reasons why British admirals succeeded at balancing these conflicting demands was that the naval intelligence organisation known as Room 40 was able both to warn them of coming German attacks and to reassure them during periods when it was relatively safe for them to send their forces elsewhere.

Meanwhile, the tools and methods of warfare grew ever-more complicated. Chapter 2 discusses the increasing complexity of land warfare in detail. Similar processes were underway on the sea, in the air, and, later, as Chapter 3 discusses, in space. The new ways of waging war brought new ways of collecting and processing intelligence. Radar, sonar, aerial photography, sound ranging equipment for locating enemy artillery, and direction-finding equipment for locating enemy radio transmitters are but a few well-known examples. As armed forces made increasing use of the wireless, they provided eavesdroppers with an increasing volume of messages to intercept, and many other new forms of technology had side effects such as radiating heat, emitting radio waves, producing distinctive sounds, or otherwise generating signals for enterprising intelligence organisations to detect.

The increasing complexity of warfare also increases planners' need for information, profoundly and at every level of strategy. In the realms of tactics and operations, the deadliness of modern weapons has made it more vital than ever for commanders to learn where their enemies are and how their own forces might obtain some sort of advantage. In a similar vein, modern weapons systems allow one to strike one's opponents from a great distance away – if one knows where to aim. At higher levels, the increasing importance of new weapons and other technological improvements has made it more important than ever to monitor other strategic actors' technical research. Information about other actors' plans and political relationships has been invaluable in every era, and it remains so today.

If World War One reminded strategic thinkers of the uses of intelligence, World War Two reminded them of the importance of handling it skilfully. Although Soviet leader Joseph Stalin received reports suggesting that Adolf Hitler planned to attack the Soviet Union in the summer of 1941, he refused to believe these warnings, and the German invasion caught Russian forces woefully unprepared. A few months later, Japan inflicted a devastating surprise attack on the American Pacific Fleet at Pearl Harbour. US policymakers later realised that various branches of their country's military and diplomatic establishment had possessed pieces of information that might have predicted the coming raid but that they had collectively failed to recognise the significance of that data. British strategists, meanwhile, enjoyed a historically unprecedented awareness of their enemies' plans and capabilities, not merely because Polish cryptanalysts had provided them with knowledge and technology that allowed them to break many versions of Germany's widely used Enigma cipher but also because they established an exceptionally efficient organisation for decrypting and processing great volumes of intercepted enemy transmissions at Bletchley Park and because this organisation was unusually successful at establishing cooperative relationships with combat commanders. Such failures and successes underscored the need for research to identify effective ways to use modern intelligence organisations as an instrument of strategy.

One of the most fundamental issues that arises in structuring a nation's intelligence community is the question of how centrally organised that community should be. This issue has risen repeatedly in the United States. US experiences illustrate the organisational challenges that all countries that maintain intelligence agencies face. One of the US government's most dramatic attempts to reform its intelligence community began in the aftermath of al-Qaeda's 2001 attack on the World Trade Center and the Pentagon.

Following the 2001 attack, evidence surfaced suggesting that if the various US intelligence agencies had worked together more effectively, they might have been able to prevent the incident.[10] In response, the American government appointed a director of national intelligence (DNI) to supervise the entire US intelligence community.[11] Other reforms redefined 'national' intelligence as all intelligence, regardless of its source, presumably making it easier for branches of the intelligence community that collect intelligence outside US borders to cooperate with domestic law enforcement agencies.[12]

Although centralisation appears to make cooperation easier, critics have responded that it also creates new problems. Critics note, for instance, that different branches of the intelligence community have different objectives. Therefore, they may need a greater degree of autonomy to pursue them. Another is that uniting all intelligence agencies into a single structure breaks down the institutional barriers that might otherwise prevent those agencies from using the ruthless methods that they practice abroad against their country's own citizens. Moreover, an individual or committee with authority over a country's entire intelligence establishment may be too powerful for a government to control.

Box 5.2 The intelligence cycle

The intelligence cycle is a concept that summarises the steps that intelligence agencies must take to provide strategists with enabling information. According to common definitions, the intelligence cycle consists of the following five activities.

Planning and direction

In this phase of the cycle, authorities determine what strategists need to know and how intelligence organisations can best provide them with that knowledge. These authorities need to prioritise intelligence operations and allocate resources to support them. On occasion, they may need to make judgements about the degree of risk that they are willing to accept to achieve certain goals.

For planning and direction to be effective, intelligence professionals must work closely with the political and military leaders they serve. If intelligence officers do not know what strategic planners require of them, they are unlikely to produce useful material, and if strategists do not thoroughly understand intelligence operations, they may not know what to ask for. The fact that intelligence agencies must often restrict information about their operations to those with a clear 'need to know' further complicates communication between information producers and information consumers. The tensions between the ideal of intelligence agencies as politically neutral reporters of fact and the reality that practically everything that intelligence agencies do involves political judgement dominate this phase of the intelligence cycle. Therefore, decisions about exactly who should be involved in this phase of the intelligence cycle and what their roles should be are both critical to strategic success and highly controversial.

Collection

In the planning and direction phase, strategists attempted to ask useful questions. In the collection phase, intelligence professionals gather information that they believe will help them provide meaningful answers.

Collection is most dramatic part of the intelligence cycle. It can also be the most dangerous and expensive. Nevertheless, without effective planning and direction, even the most productive collection programmes can be a waste of effort. Strategists and intelligence analysts have access to far larger quantities of information than they can absorb. The challenge of intelligence collection does not normally lie in obtaining a greater volume of facts; rather, it lies in obtaining key bits of information that make the rest of the data make sense.

Processing and exploitation

In this part of the cycle, intelligence professionals convert the data acquired in the collection phase into a usable form. Processing includes activities such as decrypting enciphered material and explaining scientific measurements in terms that the typical intelligence analyst can understand. The processing and exploitation phase also involves determining which pieces of information are worth considering further, how much faith to put in their accuracy, and who should have access to them. Decisions on these matters may be hotly contested and may involve far-reaching political issues.

Analysis and production

In this phase, intelligence professionals review the processed data and attempt to determine what it actually reveals about issues of strategic interest. A common problem in this stage of the cycle is that different branches of a country's intelligence services may have learned different things about matters of national importance and that analysts working for those different branches may fail to share their knowledge. For this reason, reformers often campaign to centralise intelligence organisations as much as possible, so that a single set of analysts gets to see all the available information. Centralisation, however, can never be more than a partial solution. No matter how unified a nation's intelligence community may appear on paper, no single team of analysts will be able to cope with more than a tiny fraction of the information that its collectors produce.

Even the most centralised agency will need to divide itself into numerous departments, which will eventually fail to communicate with one another. Moreover, different consumers of intelligence may have a legitimate need for specialised agencies dedicated to producing the types of information they require. The problems of generating information to support naval operations, for instance, may be quite different from the problems of generating information to support a nation's diplomatic services. No single organisation can be expected to produce both kinds of information equally effectively.

Dissemination

At this point in the intelligence cycle, analysts report their findings to political and military leaders outside the intelligence community. The dissemination phase involves similar judgements and controversies as exploitation, often on a larger scale. After strategic planners have read the intelligence community's reports, they may decide that they need further information or that they need to monitor the situations that they have already investigated in order to keep their knowledge up to date. In other words, they may return to the planning and direction phase, beginning the intelligence cycle once again.

Informing strategists

In 1951, a student wrote to American intelligence analyst Sherman Kent and asked him for information about his work. 'People who know about spy systems', Kent replied, 'do not write about them'.[13] Over the next few years, however, Kent took a leading role in changing that situation. Kent urged his colleagues to record what they had learned about intelligence work and to collect their writings into a coherent body of literature. Not only would this literature help newcomers to the intelligence services learn what had worked best in the past, but it would also help more innovative members of the profession analyse earlier methods in order to improve on them.

One of the most important functions of this literature, Kent suggested, would be to reflect on the 'fundamental question of what we [in the intelligence profession] are trying to do. What is our mission'?[14] Although Kent noted that this question might have many valid answers, he suggested a widely accepted one in his book *Strategic Intelligence for American World Policy*. Michael Herman, also a veteran intelligence officer and also a leading thinker on the role of intelligence in strategy, recapitulates Kent's position in his more recent classic *Intelligence Power in Peace and War*. Intelligence, Kent and Herman agree, is 'a kind of knowledge'.[15]

The main reason why this knowledge is valuable, Herman elaborates, is that it can serve as an 'enabling facility, helping the world of action exercise power and influence'.[16] Indeed, Herman adds, there are times when simply possessing certain information may allow one to exercise power over others. The mission of the intelligence services, then, becomes that of providing political and military leaders with the most 'enabling' information possible. Elsewhere Herman refers to strategically useful information as 'product', suggesting the image of intelligence services as a sort of knowledge factory, churning out material for others to consume.

Herman emphasises that real intelligence agencies do many other things too. Nevertheless, it is often useful to think of intelligence services as knowledge factories, because this helps one identify ways for them to serve their consumers more efficiently. Workers in ordinary factories mass-produce complex items by performing a sequence of clearly defined tasks along an assembly line, and theorists commonly model the process by which intelligence services provide strategists with large quantities of complex information as a sequence of clearly defined tasks known as the intelligence cycle. Theorists may then go on to look for ways that intelligence agencies might change their methods of performing these tasks to 'enable' strategists to the maximum degree possible.

If intelligence agencies exist to 'enable' strategists, intelligence professionals must resist the temptation to meddle with strategy itself. The knowledge factory model also implies that intelligence professionals must resist all pressure to distort their findings for political reasons, even if the strategic planners who employ them are the ones applying the pressure. To the contrary, intelligence professionals must produce a thorough, objective analysis of the available facts and let others decide how to act on it. An engineer who believes that an airliner designed to certain specifications would be unsafe has a duty to say so even if their superiors want to manufacture such an aircraft, and an intelligence analyst whose work suggests certain conclusions about strategic matters has a similar duty to report them even if decision makers find those conclusions inconvenient.

The knowledge factory model also suggests a restrained approach to dealing with opposing intelligence organisations. Most states devote at least some of their intelligence resources to gathering information about others who may be trying to gather information about them. Terrorist organisations and other non-state strategic actors do the same. This process is known as counterintelligence, or CI. Since opposing intelligence agencies are likely to be adept at keeping their secrets, counterintelligence is among the most difficult activities intelligence organisations perform. In Herman's words, 'this raises the question of how much effort it is worth'.[17]

If the primary purpose of intelligence is to supply higher-level strategists with an information 'product', counterintelligence operations can easily become a wasteful distraction. One will always need to perform a certain amount of counterintelligence as part of one's efforts to protect one's own secrets. Nevertheless, great volumes of detail about opposing intelligence agencies and their practices may not seem particularly useful. Certainly, strategists from beyond the intelligence community are unlikely to know what to do with it.

Manipulating enemies

Other researchers observe that the model of intelligence services as ideologically neutral knowledge factories is idealistic at best. Intelligence professionals, like the rest of us, face political pressures of many kinds. Individuals must develop their careers. The agencies that employ them must manoeuvre for influence and resources within larger bureaucracies. These bureaucracies must respond to politics at the national and international levels.

Some might be willing to sacrifice their jobs for their principles, but they will never purge intelligence of politics. In intelligence work, the full truth is almost never obvious. Practically all intelligence reports include a substantial amount of interpretation, and since there is no sure way to know which interpretations are correct, there is no sure way to tell the difference between integrity and mere stubbornness. For the same reason, there will seldom be any way for even the most self-sacrificing intelligence professionals to prove that they are right. Indeed, those who adroitly practise office politics may be more effective at providing strategists with 'enabling' information than those who remain aloof, because they will find it easier to get strategic planners to listen to them.

These facts limit what one can expect from intelligence organisations. Intelligence professionals may strive for objectivity wherever they can, but they will never truly attain it. Intelligence reports will always be vulnerable to political influence – and thus to politically influenced mistakes. Uncertainty will always dominate intelligence work, just as it will always dominate war.

Moreover, strategists can take advantage of the political dimension of intelligence. One may attempt to manipulate the decision-making processes within opposing organisations, including opposing intelligence organisations. Under most circumstances, the people who possess the most useful skills and resources for such intrigues will be the members of one's own intelligence services. For an example of how this works in practice, one might examine the methods Anglo-American forces used to deceive German commanders about Allied plans to invade Western Europe in 1944.

Although the British, Canadians, and Americans had committed the bulk of their available resources to an amphibious landing in Normandy, they convinced German decision makers that they were preparing much larger forces to attack elsewhere. The Germans assigned 22 divisions to guard against the imaginary threat. Other Allied deception operations helped persuade the Germans to hold back another 30 divisions in the Mediterranean. German commanders continued to waste resources protecting themselves from the fictitious forces for over a month after the Normandy landings had taken place.

The Allied deception campaign is noteworthy because they fooled their enemies on such a vast scale. Although the Allies made full use of ruses such as dummy tanks and misleading radio traffic to make their phony army appear real, it would have been almost impossible for these tricks alone to have influenced so much of the German command structure about such major issues for so long. To begin with, decoys only work if one's enemies can see them, and by 1944, Germany's' long-range reconnaissance capabilities were severely limited. Moreover, as Clausewitz noted, military officers in combat continually receive great volumes of alarming and frequently conflicting reports. Competent commanders grow accustomed to this, learn to weigh the reports against each other, and steel themselves against the urge to overreact. One may always hope to dupe individual opponents at a critical moment, but if the Allies had merely provided their enemies with a few spurious radio intercepts and a few spurious sightings of troop positions, the German leadership would have been unlikely to alter its overall plans in any dramatic way.

To influence Germany's overall strategy, the Allies had to find a way to transmit lies directly to the leaders of the Third Reich. The lies had to convince sceptical listeners to believe them and to help those listeners override the others who would inevitably choose to believe other things. The lies had to include details that would maximise the chances that the German commanders would respond in ways that the Allies wanted them to respond. Moreover, as time passed, the Germans would almost certainly obtain increasing amounts of accurate information. Therefore, the Allies needed to embellish their lies in ways that would make them appear plausible for the longest possible time.

Advocates of the knowledge factory model of intelligence might note that the Allied deception programme depended on large volumes of 'enabling' information. The programme's organisers needed to know which German officers and institutions they most needed to deceive. They needed to know what accurate information their targets possessed, they needed to know what sort of false information their targets would be most likely to find believable, and they needed to know how their targets were reacting to previous deceptions. Allied intelligence services combined data from many sources to provide such information, finding their ability to decrypt key enemy ciphers particularly valuable.

Not only did Allied intelligence organisations indirectly support the deception programme by providing its planners with relatively accurate information, but they also played a direct and vital role in delivering false information to the Germans. the United Kingdom's internal security service, MI-5, had identified all of the German spies operating in the United Kingdom. Rather than merely arresting the Germans, MI-5 had offered them the opportunity to become double agents.

A few of the German agents refused, and the British executed them. The rest of the Germans were available to support Allied deception operations by sending the Germans whatever reports their British controllers wished. the United Kingdom's intelligence services had acquired yet more moles in the German intelligence apparatus through a variety of means, including pure luck. One of the most valuable double agents in the deception programme, a man named Juan Pujol Garcia and known to his British handlers as 'Garbo', was a Spanish citizen who had volunteered his services to the United Kingdom's MI-6 intelligence agency out of personal opposition to Nazism. When MI-6 proved reluctant to accept him, he independently persuaded the Germans to use him as a spy, so that he would be more useful to the British.

During earlier phases of the war, the German High Command had been dubious about HUMINT. In that period, German officers had normally checked the accuracy of spy reports by comparing them to information from other sources. Therefore, the Germans of that era had been harder to fool. By 1944, however, the Allied air forces had largely driven German reconnaissance aircraft from the skies. The Allies had also significantly improved the security of their communications systems. Therefore, German leaders turned increasingly to HUMINT as their only means of acquiring information from within their enemies' homelands, and the United Kingdom's networks of double agents became increasingly useful for misinforming them.

MI-5, MI-6, and their sister agencies put themselves in a position to manipulate the Germans through a combination of tight security measures, effective information collection, and the masterful practice of counterintelligence. The British success required planning and sustained effort. By the time of the Normandy invasion, MI-5 had been developing its network of double agents for over ten years. The British security service began the process while the United Kingdom and Germany were still at peace. (The Germans were already spying on the United Kingdom at that time.) MI-5's work undoubtedly consumed resources that other agencies might have used to collect greater amounts of 'enabling' information, but British planners determined that the opportunity to turn Germany's own spy network against its creators was worth the investment.

If it is possible to infiltrate and control enemy organisations, it is equally possible that enemies will use similar methods against their own enemies. The most reliable way to unmask enemy secret agents is to conduct espionage against the opposing intelligence agencies that operate them. Thus, spies end up spying on spies. The side that manages to place 'moles' in the highest positions within the opposing side's institutions will enjoy the best ability to uncover enemy plots and will also be able to manipulate its opponents most effectively.

Since the process of convincing enemy personnel to become double agents begins with effective counterintelligence, the counterintelligence branches of opposing organisations become particularly attractive targets for subversion. The knowledge factory model suggested that counterintelligence was useful as a protective measure but secondary to the intelligence services' main purpose of acquiring information. Those who view intelligence agencies as tools for actively manipulating one's opponents see things differently. To them, counterintelligence is the most important function that those agencies perform.

The Okhrana was known for its use of manipulative techniques, and later generations of Russian organisations have followed its example. In the twenty-first century, Russia provides an example of how an intelligence community that emphasises the manipulation model might evolve. Vladimir Lenin's first intelligence service, the Cheka, distinguished itself through its active use of infiltration and deception both within the Soviet Union and abroad. This gave it considerable power within the Soviet political establishment – so much power that in 1991, its leaders felt confident enough to attempt a coup.

The coup failed, but not utterly. Boris Yeltsin, president of the Russian Republic, rallied opposition to the KGB's usurpation. Yeltsin went on to dissolve the Soviet Union and found the contemporary Russian state. At this point, one might have presumed that Yeltsin would use his authority as the presumably democratically elected president of a new country to create a new intelligence community reflecting the values of a new Russia. Reality was more complex. Yeltsin repeatedly reorganised the security and information-gathering apparatus of Russia.[18] Nevertheless, when the transformations were complete, former KGB directorates continued to perform their historical functions in new parts of the bureaucracy, and substantial numbers of former KGB personnel continued to do the same jobs they had been doing all along.[19]

The most prominent intelligence agencies in early-twenty-first-century Russia are the Foreign Intelligence Service, abbreviated as SVR, the internally focused Federal Security Service (FSB), and the military intelligence organisation known as the GRU. There are also numerous state bodyguard services, undercover law enforcement organisations, and so on. These agencies appear to retain the KGB's taste for manipulation operations, and they appear to interpret their prerogatives broadly. The FSB, for instance, is nominally tasked with preserving domestic security within Russia, but its leaders appear to have concluded that this mission required them to recruit computer criminals for an operation to collect compromising information on American users of Yahoo Internet services in 2014.[20] One may hope that the contemporary Russian government is more responsive to its citizens than the Soviet regime was and that its relations with other powerful states are more peaceful than the Soviet Union's Cold War interactions with the West, but its approach to using intelligence agencies as instruments of strategy appears to be essentially identical.

The manipulation model also conflicts with the knowledge factory model in more basic ways. Those who assume that an intelligence agency's main purpose is to generate 'enabling' information will wish to disseminate as much 'product' to as many 'consumers' as rapidly as possible. Those who assume that an intelligence agency's main function is to conspire against opposing conspirators will want to scrutinise every new report as a possible enemy deception, even at the cost of discarding interesting findings. Moreover, those who emphasise the manipulation model will wish to restrict information to the smallest number of people possible, in order to minimise the chances of betrayal. Although practically all who subscribe to the knowledge factory model will agree in principle that it is important to guard against deception and practically all who subscribe to the manipulation model will agree in principle that intelligence services must, at some point, provide useful information to outside political and military leaders, adherents of these two views often find it frustrating to work together in practice.

Conclusion

Herman compares debates over the most effective ways to use intelligence agencies to debates over the most effective ways to use aircraft.[21] Navy and army commanders commonly want planes to support operations by ships and ground forces. Air force commanders would usually prefer to fight opposing air forces for control of the skies, arguing that once they secure air supremacy, they will be able to fly where they like, bomb what they wish, and perform grander strategic feats than they could ever accomplish as mere adjuncts to other branches of the armed services. In a similar fashion, advocates of what this chapter has called the knowledge factory model wish to use intelligence services in a support role, whereas advocates of aggressive counterintelligence wish to use intelligence services against other intelligence services as a first step towards perpetrating grand feats of subversion.

Although Herman ends the analogy with this point, one may take the comparison further. Strategic bombing raises profound ethical dilemmas, particularly when it involves targeting civilians. Intelligence strategy poses even broader moral and political questions. Moreover, those who answer these questions wrongly risk outcomes such as embarrassing media exposure and military defeat. Legend has it that intelligence professionals refer to the unwanted side effects of their work as blowback. Even milder versions of blowback may have far-reaching effects on one's political relations and strategic options.

The risk of blowback is particularly obvious when intelligence agencies use clandestine methods in attempts to manipulate other organisations. Although few now object to MI-5's use of undercover agents to influence German military strategy in World War Two, many may question the American CIA's use of secret contacts within Italian political parties to influence the outcome of elections in the early years of the Cold War. More recently, journalists have criticised the CIA's covert support for the Afghan guerrillas who fought Soviet forces in the 1980s, alleging that one of the so-called freedom fighters who benefited from American aid was none other than Osama bin Laden. These journalists' claims remain unproven but troubling.

Although many covert operations appear dubious in hindsight, it is difficult to come up with a simple rule for distinguishing between wise and unwise uses of clandestine influence. Even the United Kingdom's successful and morally palatable campaign to manipulate the German intelligence services began at a time when future relations between the United Kingdom and Germany remained in doubt. UK planners correctly determined that the Germans were destined to be their enemies, but American intelligence officers of the 1950s and 1980s might equally well have determined that the Soviet Union was dangerous enough to justify the CIA operations in Italy and Afghanistan. One cannot make intelligence strategy without making political judgements, and one cannot implement intelligence strategy without incurring political consequences.

Since intelligence strategists must work in secret, it is difficult for governments of any type – including democracies – to control them. Most countries have instituted oversight procedures designed to allow legislators to scrutinise clandestine activities without compromising security. Such procedures, however, inevitably involve uneasy compromises. Intelligence officers will always find that oversight procedures limit their capabilities. Other citizens will always live with the risk that their country's intelligence services may act outside the law.

These illegal actions may violate individuals' rights, undermine constitutional processes, and commit the nation to dangerous policies.

These risks are most obvious when intelligence agencies use force and subterfuge to manipulate those whom they have deemed to be enemies. Thus, Sherman Kent urged the US government to prohibit such operations in peacetime.[22] Nevertheless, even when intelligence agencies limit themselves to the role of knowledge factories, their work intertwines with political debates that shape the destiny of nations. Strategic thinker Roberta Wohlstetter developed this point in her classic comparison of US intelligence before the 1941 Pearl Harbour raid and the 1962 Cuban Missile Crisis.

Between 1941 and 1962, the US government repeatedly overhauled its intelligence services to maximise their efficiency. US intelligence services also acquired valuable new technology, notably the U-2 reconnaissance aircraft. Nevertheless, the intelligence 'product' regarding the missile crisis originally contained gaps and ambiguities as serious as those that misled American planners in 1941.[23] The reason why American strategists performed more effectively in 1962 has less to do with the initial quality of their information than with the fact that they acted more decisively on it. One of their most important decisions was a decision of intelligence strategy: they increased the frequency of U-2 flights over Cuba in order to clarify uncertain points in their knowledge.[24]

In 1941, the US government had been unwilling to acknowledge the likelihood that Japan would attack and hesitant to provoke the Japanese excessively.[25] US leaders in 1962 were reluctant to believe that the Soviet Union would place missiles in Cuba and did not wish to risk a confrontation that might precipitate nuclear war. Nevertheless, during the missile crisis, US leaders chose to question their assumptions and adopt risky new policies. US strategists of 1962 made better choices, not on the basis of superior knowledge but on the basis of what proved to be superior political judgement. Clausewitz's observation that war is merely a continuation of political intercourse with the admixture of other means seems to apply equally well to intelligence, and if the interaction between civilian governments and the armed forces has always been complex, the interaction between civilian governments and their intelligence services may be even more so.

Throughout much of the world, the events of the early twenty-first century have given intelligence services a greater strategic role than ever. Thus, these events have added urgency to debates about precisely what this role should be. As precious as information may be in open warfare, it is even more basic to campaigns against terrorists, insurgents, and others who operate in secret. As of 2010, many of the most powerful states perceive such opponents to be among their most dangerous enemies.

Moreover, in the aftermath of al-Qaeda's September 11, 2001, strike on the United States, Americans learned that US agencies had uncovered clues that might have warned them about the coming attack but that these agencies had failed to appreciate the significance of those clues. Sixty years after Pearl Harbor, the United States' intelligence community was still struggling with the basic problem of processing raw data into 'enabling' information. The September 11, 2001, attack also forced strategists in the United States and elsewhere to confront – yet again – the comparative advantages of using intelligence services primarily as knowledge factories and of using them more aggressively to infiltrate and perhaps subvert opposing organisations.

The most effective – and often the only – way to learn about terrorist plans is to plant informers among the terrorists. This involves similar techniques to planting double agents in opposing intelligence organisations. The risk of blowback is, perhaps, greater. Much of the time, the only way to recruit agents within a terrorist organisation is to rely on members who can be persuaded to betray their comrades, and this involves working with exceptionally unsavoury people, even by the low standards of the espionage profession. The fact that many terrorist groups test their members' loyalty by requiring them to carry out attacks further increases the moral and political difficulties of operating undercover agents within such organisations.

The political judgements involved in intelligence work against terrorists are also at least as profound as those involved in operations against opposing states. Terrorists commonly operate inside the nations they plan to attack. This means that intelligence agencies must face the moral, legal, and public-opinion complexities of working in their home countries. Since terrorist movements often develop out of ethnic and religious conflicts, they confront intelligence strategists with questions of race and religion. The challenge of integrating intelligence into strategy remains alive, as does the challenge of integrating both into the political life of a free country.

Key points

1   National intelligence agencies became commonplace only in the late nineteenth century.
2   Clausewitz warned that intelligence reports can actually undermine a military commander's ability to implement strategy.
3   As war has grown more complex, strategists have become increasingly dependent on intelligence.
4   Nevertheless, the process by which intelligence agencies provide strategists with useful information periodically fails in spectacular ways.
5   Theorists have tried to identify ways to make this process more efficient and reliable.
6   Meanwhile, intelligence agencies have proved to be effective instruments for coordinating campaigns to manipulate opponents.
7   Intelligence, like war itself, seems to be intertwined with politics at every level.

Questions

1   Pick a currently important strategic issue. Which sources of intelligence are most likely to prove useful for understanding it?
2   Should intelligence agencies subvert opposing organisations in peacetime?
3   Should intelligence agencies employ analysts with radical political views?

Notes

1 Raymond Cohen, 'Intelligence in the Amarna Letters', in Raymond Cohen and Raymond West-brook (eds.), *Amarna Diplomacy: The Beginnings of International Relations* (Baltimore, Johns Hopkins University Press, 2000), p. 86.

2 Sun Tzu (Tao Hanzhang, commentator, Yuan Shibing, trans.), *Sun Tzu's Art of War: The Modern Chinese Interpretation* (New York, Sterling, 1987), p. 126.

3 Carl von Clausewitz, *On War*, trans. Michael Howard and Peter Paret (New Haven, Princeton University Press, 1976), pp. 117–18.

4 John Ferris, *Intelligence and Strategy: Selected Essays* (Abingdon, Routledge, 2005), p. 241.

5 Ibid.

6 Christopher Andrew and Oleg Gordievsky, *KGB: The Inside Story of Its Foreign Operations from Lenin to Gorbachev* (London, Hodder and Stoughton, 1990), p. 10.

7 Robin Winks, Cloak and Gown: Scholars in the Secret War 1939-1961 (New Haven, Yale University Press, 1996), p. 456.

8 Michael Handel, *War, Strategy and Intelligence* (London, Frank Cass, 1989), p. 26.

9 Patrick Beesly, *Room 40: British Naval Intelligence 1914–18* (London, Hamish Hamilton, 1982), pp. 308–9.

10 Commissioners, *The 9/11 Commission Report: Final Report of the National Commission on Terrorist Attacks Upon the United States Executive Summary*, pp. 2–3, www.npr.org/documents/2004/9-11/911report exec.pdf (accessed April 10, 2017).

11 Michael Warner and J. Kenneth McDonald, US Intelligence Community Reform Studies Since 1947 (Washington DC, Center for the Study of Intelligence, 2005), available on-line at https://www.cia.gov/library/center-for-the-study-of-intelligence/csi-publications/books-and-monographs/US%20Intelligence%20Community%20Reform%20Studies%20Since%201947.pdf, accessed 27 October 2019, p. 39.

12 Ibid.

13 Robin Winks, *Cloak and Gown: Scholars in the Secret War 1939–1961* (New Haven, Yale University Press, 1987), p. 449.

14 Sherman Kent, 'The Need for an Intelligence Literature', *Studies in Intelligence*, September 1955, www.cia.gov/library/center-for-the-study-of-intelligence/csi-publications/books-and-monographs/sherman-kent-and-the-board-of-national-estimates-collected-essays/the-theory-of-intelligence.html (accessed October 12, 2009).

15 Michael Herman, *Intelligence Power in Peace and War* (Cambridge, Cambridge University Press, 1996), p. 1.

16 Ibid., p. 198.

17 Ibid., p. 172.

18 Amy Knight, 'Yeltsin's KGB', *The Washington Post*, February 13, 1994, www.washingtonpost.com/archive/opinions/1994/02/13/yeltsins-kgb/10892e53-1098-47bb-9b4f-9f353c875228/?utm_term=.f70a0bce2128 (accessed April 10, 2017).

19 Ibid.

20 Ellen Nakashima, 'Justice Department Charges Russian Spies and Criminal Hackers in Yahoo Intrusion', *The Washington Post*, March 15, 2017, www.washingtonpost.com/world/national-security/justice-department-charging-russian-spies-and-criminal-hackers-for-yahoo-intrusion/2017/03/15/64b98e32-0911-11e7-93dc-00f9bdd74ed1_story.html?utm_term=.3c42ec1a4354 (accessed April 10, 2017).

21 Herman, *Intelligence Power*, p. 180.

22 Winks, *Cloak and Gown*, p. 451.
23 Roberta Wohlstetter, 'Cuba and Pearl Harbor: Hindsight and Foresight', *Foreign Affairs* 43:4 (July 1965), p. 705.
24 Ibid., p. 707.
25 Ibid., p. 702.

Further reading

Berkowitz, Bruce D. and Allan E. Goodman, *Best Truth: Intelligence in the Information Age*, (New Haven: Yale University Press, 2000).
Ferris, John Robert, *Intelligence and Strategy: Selected Essays*, (Abingdon: Routledge, 2005).
Handel, Michael I., *War, Strategy and Intelligence*, (London: Frank Cass, 1989).
Herman, Michael, *Intelligence Power in Peace and War*, (Cambridge: Cambridge University Press, 1996).
Howard, Michael, *British Intelligence in the Second World War, Volume Five: Strategic Deception*, (London: HMSO, 1990).
Wohlstetter, Roberta, 'Cuba and Pearl Harbor: Hindsight and Foresight', *Foreign Affairs*, Vol. 43, No. 4 (July 1965), pp. 691–707.

Grand strategy

6

Reader's guide

Grand strategy defined; grand strategy involves a wide range of factors; questionable validity of the concept; historical support for the concept; thinking about grand strategy effectively.

Introduction

The art of strategy goes beyond the immediate problems of winning wars. Over the course of years, a wide range of social, economic, political, and cyberspace-based factors help determine which political communities overcome their opponents and thrive. The same factors help determine which communities suffer setbacks and, occasionally, annihilation. Governments cannot fully control these factors, but they can often influence them, and logic suggests that political leaders who can integrate their policies on such issues in order to provide consistent support for their deepest goals are most likely to succeed. This art of coordinating policies over the long term, in peace as well as in war, is known as grand strategy.

This towers over all the strategic issues that this book has discussed. One reason is that policy – whether this means state policy or the policies of some other type of organisation – determines the goals that strategists seek to achieve. Another is that practically all of the policies that governments and comparable organisations enact affect their strategic options in one way or another. Even policies on social issues – such as education or health care provision – help determine what sort of recruits will be available for the armed forces and what sort of support a government can expect from its population. Moreover, one may use policies of all types, including violence, to alter the policies of others. Therefore, if a state or other political organisation is to enjoy the benefits of sound strategic planning at any level for any length of time, its leaders must attempt to combine all their activities in ways that support their most fundamental aspirations.

Examples of these points abound throughout every chapter. Insurgents, for instance, defeat better-armed state governments by undermining political support for the policies that allow those governments to use their armaments. Nuclear strategists attempt to integrate WMDs into their foreign policies in such a way as to render war not merely unnecessary but impossible. Intelligence agencies are meant help friendly strategic planners to integrate policies and armaments most effectively. Some might note that they are also capable of interfering with other planners' abilities to do the same. Even in open combat between state armed forces, grand strategic decisions about the integration of policies and armaments powerfully influence such basic matters as when war is to occur, where war is to occur, what the objectives of war are to be, and what sort of equipment each side will have at its disposal.

In short, one must understand grand strategy in order to understand any kind of strategy at all. At this point, however, one encounters an obstacle. In the eyes of many scholars, grand strategy is a myth. Many theorists find the concept of grand strategy problematic in principle. Many who follow history and practical politics would note that it can seem impossible to integrate long-term policies in practice. This chapter acknowledges these difficulties but seeks, nevertheless, to set out a method for thinking about grand strategy usefully.

The first section of this chapter summarises why some question the existence of grand strategy. The second section notes that states and other political actors nevertheless act purposefully at the grand strategic level. The third section explores some of the factors that underpin successful action in this arena and reflects on points to consider when interpreting them.

The case against grand strategy

The founders of contemporary international relations theory sought, in the words of Hans Morgenthau and Kenneth Thompson, 'objective laws' governing politics.[1] Such laws cannot merely be detailed descriptions of what political actors have done in various situations: not only would such descriptions risk becoming too complicated to work with, but they would also not necessarily reveal anything about any issues other than the ones the authors had decided to describe. The fact that something happened in a certain way once is no guarantee that it will happen the same way on any other occasion. Most international relations scholars are interested in understanding a wide range of events, some of which may still be in the process of unfolding and some of which lie in the future. Therefore, such scholars need general theories that explain what to expect in easily recognisable and commonly recurring types of situations. The simpler and more abstract these theories are, the more useful scholars find them.

Thinkers from the influential realist school of thought, for instance, typically simplify international political issues by assuming that states are the only important actors in world politics, and the key to understanding what states will do lies in understanding that states are competing for power. Different realists have proposed different ideas about how states compete. Defensive realists, such as Kenneth Waltz, suggest that some states are content with enough power to protect their own interests, whereas offensive realists, such as John Mearsheimer, suggest that all states aggressively seek as much power as possible. Neither defensive realists nor offensive realists involve themselves in the more complex political ideals that political leaders claim to pursue; nor do they scrutinise those leaders' ideas about how to pursue them; nor do they study the organisations those leaders work through; and nor do they linger over details about the weapons, industry, transportation infrastructure, and other physical media through which power is exercised.

Realism is highly compatible with the concept known as rational choice theory. This body of thought assumes that people and organisations normally try to make decisions in ways that maximise their chances of achieving their goals. Many theorists would add that even if this is not always true, rational decision makers will defeat and replace their fuzzy-minded competitors over time. Therefore, according to rational choice theory, it is possible to predict the decisions that others will make in almost any situation. If one knows who the actors in a particular situation are, what their goals are, what their options are, and what each one expects the outcomes of choosing the various options to be, one will know which option that actor will select.

Realism reveals who the actors in international politics are (states), what their goals are (power) and, with only a little more embellishment, what their options for gaining and holding on to power are likely to be. Therefore, it is easy to construct rational choice models to explain what states that behave according to some variant of realist principles will do. In other words, this combination of realism and rational choice theory seemingly allows one to predict the future. Other schools of thought in the international politics discipline have sharply challenged both realism and rational choice theory, but most of them tend to reduce world affairs to simple abstractions as well, for much the same reasons as the realists do. Alexander Wendt's highly regarded *Social Theory of International Politics*, for instance, offers a particularly complete theoretical alternative to realism, but it also intentionally screens out such factors as individual leaders, their ideologies, their resources, and their plans.[2]

Those who practise strategy at any level sink these well-ordered theoretical models into swamps of detail. Theorists may prefer to gloss over peculiarities such as the capabilities of particular weapons systems and the terrain found in particular geographical locations, but combined-arms operations of the sort which dominate land warfare take advantage of precisely these sorts of factors to win wars. The very existence of insurgents and terrorists reminds us that states are not the only actors in international politics. German leaders might have wished to make rational decisions in the later years of World War Two, but the Allied intelligence services turned their very attempts to inform themselves about their options against them. A rational choice theorist who was unaware of the secret Allied deception operation would have been as baffled as the German commanders themselves.

As one rises from tactics and operations towards the grand strategic level of planning, the simplifications of formal international relations theory become increasingly difficult to justify. Grand strategy consists largely of integrating different activities to shape the circumstances of future political issues before they have come to the fore. Strategies of this nature may unfold over decades, if not centuries, and great numbers of them may be at various stages of completion at any given time, all affecting political issues through a wide variety of avenues in a wide variety of ways. The reasons why the Allies were able to carry out their deception operation during World War Two – to pick but one small example – are that, years before the war, a committee within the British intelligence bureaucracy decided to recruit German spies as double agents and that the Allies went on to coordinate this programme with initially unrelated operations such as their campaign to break Axis ciphers and their campaign to win air supremacy over Western Europe. Few theories of international politics even discuss these types of activities, and no manageable theory could account for the mind-boggling variety of ways grand strategists might conceivably combine them.

For these reasons, academics from many of the most influential schools of thought deliberately ignore the parts of grand strategy which threaten their theories. Scholar Nicholas Kitchen documents this point in some detail and notes other authors who explore the issue.[3] Most theorists would acknowledge that this practice makes their models less realistic, and most would add that it is precisely what allows them to develop general theories with meaningful levels of predictive power. Therefore, they would claim that the sacrifice in detail is worthwhile. Many theorists would add that whatever grand strategies individual leaders may dream of following, most will find that they have little choice but to do what theory predicts that they must do.

Many veterans of military and political practice would agree. The idea that a state – or any other large political institution – can actually manage to coordinate all its activities over generations in order to carry out subtle and elaborate plans is naïve. Researchers such as Graham Allison and Philip Zelikow remind us that the actual process of strategic planning in most real-life states involves continuous negotiation among a wide range of bureaucracies and other government institutions, none of which has complete authority over the full range of policies it is involved in and none of which bears direct responsibility for the ultimate outcome.[4] This process is more likely to produce an endless series of momentarily workable compromises than a coherent plan to realise the highest purposes of the nation. As former British prime minister Harold Wilson observed, a week is a long time in politics, and as his predecessor Harold MacMillan noted, the main force that shapes the policies of nations is not strategic cunning but 'events, dear boy, events'.[5]

Of grasshoppers and ants

Nevertheless, governments – and other political organisations – have no choice but to act at the grand strategic level. They may do so haphazardly, they may do so under all manner of constraints, but they do so nevertheless. Such a basic administrative procedure as drawing up a budget may have grand strategic consequences. Decades may pass between the time policymakers allocate funds to develop a new weapons system and the time when armed forces rely on that system in war.

The British government, for instance, identified a need for two new aircraft carriers in its Strategic Defence Review of 1998. Construction began in 2009. One of the ships began air operations in 2018, but as of 2019, the other is not yet ready for action. Once in use, the carriers may serve for at least 30–50 years. In other words, British politicians in office today will knowingly make decisions that shape their country's options for integrating policies and armaments in the 2060s.

Throughout history, there have been leaders who have used such moments of grand strategic decision to advance relatively coherent long-term programmes. Others have taken the shorter view at their own peril. One can find a particularly vivid example of this process in the Warring States Period of ancient China. During this era, China was divided into many feuding kingdoms. One of these kingdoms, the state of Ch'in (Qin), reformed its laws to maximise its military power and went on to conquer its neighbours one at a time, taking opportunities as they presented themselves over a period of approximately two centuries.

In 247 BCE, a 13-year-old prince named Cheng inherited Ch'in's throne. By that time, Ch'in had already extended its borders to both the north and east, annexed approximately half a dozen weaker states and reorganised the captured territory into provinces under its direct control. The young ruler had only to continue this programme in order to crush Ch'in's six remaining rivals and unite all of China into an empire. Over the following 20 years, Cheng – who has gone down in history as Shih Huang-ti (Shi Hunagdi), the First Sovereign Emperor – did exactly that. The last of Ch'in's opponents surrendered in 221 BCE.

One can find further examples of effective long-term policy in seventeenth-century and eighteenth-century Europe. Frederick William I of Prussia, for instance, devoted much of his life to reforming his country's armed forces. Nevertheless, his military endeavours often seemed more like a hobby than a foresighted strategy. For a soldier king, Frederick William waged surprisingly few wars. To this day, popular history presents him as a peculiar man with such odd traits as an obsession with organising a regiment of unusually tall soldiers.

The online reference work Wikipedia, for instance, features anecdotes about how Frederick William I painted the tall troopers' portraits from memory, claimed to love the oversized soldiers more than the most beautiful of women, and arranged marriages among his larger subjects in the hopes of breeding more giants.[6] Since Wikipedia gets its information from its users, one may presume that this is how a wide sample of contemporary history enthusiasts remembers the Prussian king. Wikipedia and its contributors fail to mention that Frederick William I may have had more practical reasons for his affectations.

Like many eighteenth-century rulers, the Prussian king wrote a political testament to help his successors continue his policies:

> Throughout my life, I have been careful not to draw down the envy of the house of Austria [a dangerous rival] on my head. This has forced me to pursue two passions which are really alien to me, namely unbounded avarice and an exaggerated regard for tall soldiers. Only under the disguise of these spectacular eccentricities was I allowed to gather a large treasury and assemble a powerful army. Now this money and these troops lie at the disposal of my successor, who requires no such mask.[7]

The second Frederick William, known as Frederick the Great, did indeed wield his father's army openly and with devastating effect. Approximately two hundred years later, as the empire that the two Fredericks began found itself facing the 'envy' of an enemy alliance that included such powerful nations as France, the United Kingdom, and the United States, its leaders resorted to masks once more. German policymakers began secret preparations to rearm their country for a second world war before the ending of the first.[8] Adolf Hitler, like the 13-year-old king of Ch'in in a different millennium, inherited the work of generations of strategists.

Although Hitler was chillingly frank about his ambitions, he managed to continue Germany's rearmament programme throughout the 1930s, partially because many of his intended victims refused to acknowledge how systematically the German state was proceeding against them. As late as 1938, the United Kingdom's chancellor of the exchequer opposed deploying British troops to France on the grounds that Germany was extremely unlikely to violate Belgian neutrality and that the French, protected by the Maginot Line, could presumably take care of themselves.[9] On May 13, 1940, with German forces already fighting in Belgium, the editors of a US newspaper still felt they could publish the line 'it seems that the Germans are not interested in France at this time'.[10] Within days, German forces had driven deep into French territory. France surrendered the following month.

Ch'in, eighteenth-century Prussia, and twentieth-century Germany were all subject to internal machinations and external 'events'. Prince Cheng inherited the throne amid an intrigue involving the queen, a wealthy merchant, and a virile male attendant. Frederick William I may have left Prussia with an exceptionally well-organised army, but it was an act of fate – the unexpected death of the Austrian emperor in 1740 – that gave his son a suitable opportunity to use it. Twentieth-century Germany sustained its rearmament programme throughout coup attempts, street battles, and the onset of the Great Depression.

This leaves one to ask how these states – and many others – have managed to pursue apparently coherent long-term policies despite all the 'events' that threatened to intervene. A variety of factors commonly shape war and politics at the grand strategic level. Those who pay attention to them improve their chances of recognising points at which they may act to achieve enduring results. An awareness of these factors may also improve one's chances of noticing the grand strategic acts of potential opponents while there is still time to respond.

Box 6.1 Strategic backfilling

Those who criticise the concept of grand strategy note that the process by which states and other large political institutions make policy is inevitably plagued by contradictions. No single leader can personally manage all of a country's strategically relevant activities. Seldom will anyone involved in the process have the leisure to think comprehensively about the long-term implications of their decisions. Instead, a wide range of overworked people responsible for a wide range of different agencies must solve problems related to their own duties as they arise. Even when these officials are not deliberately competing with each other, they will have different views and take different approaches. Their policies will conflict.

Nevertheless, the fact that strategic policymaking is full of day-to-day incongruities need not guarantee that the ultimate results will be equally muddled. The researcher Deborah Stone notes that all political processes are permeated with contradiction. This includes both the processes by which governments choose policies and the processes by which they put them into effect. Stone proposes that we view this not as evidence of mismanagement but as an essential feature of politics itself. The art of politics, Stone implies, consists of 'creat[ing] paradoxes and resolv[ing] them in a particular direction'.[11]

One of the paradoxical features of this art is that one can perform it backwards through time. Stone illustrates this with the following example from US domestic politics.[12] In 1987, Ronald Reagan, who was president at the time, vetoed a spending proposal. The president and his supporters lobbied to prevent the legislature from overriding the veto. Despite their efforts, both houses of Congress voted to reverse the president's decision.

If one judged this event by the standards of the president's initial speeches, Reagan had suffered a defeat. Nevertheless, after the veto was overridden, the president and his supporters – successfully – re-created the event as a political step forward. Reagan, they maintained, had taken on a noble cause despite knowing that the cause was doomed. Those who had opposed his courageous decision, they suggested, would now find it politically necessary to support the president on future issues.

Grand strategists may also be able to give policies coherence in hindsight. One can see a recent example of this in the People's Republic of China's (PRC) space programme. In 2007, after the PRC successfully tested an anti-satellite missile, China scholars Bates Gill and Martin Kleiber wrote an article in the journal *Foreign Affairs* claiming that those who feared that China was pursuing a long-term strategy to increase its military capabilities had dangerously misunderstood the incident.[13] The two scholars quoted then–US vice-president Richard Cheney, who had noted that China's missile test was 'not consistent with China's stated goal of a peaceful rise'.[14] Gill and Kleiber explained this inconsistency by suggesting that the various branches of the Chinese government, including those responsible for such major acts of policy as the decision to test a provocative new weapons system, had become 'rogues' acting in a reckless and uncoordinated fashion.[15] The real danger, Gill and Kleiber warned, was not that the Beijing government had an insidious plan but that the Beijing government had lost control.

Although Gill and Kleiber did not mention it, there were other apparent paradoxes in China's space policy of the early twenty-first century. During this period, China was cooperating with the European Union on the project to develop the Galileo satellite navigation system. This system was to perform the same functions as the American Global Positioning System, and although the European Union maintains that Galileo will be purely for peaceful purposes, the fact that a Sino-European coalition was constructing an alternative to one of the United States' most valuable strategic assets suggested a shift in the balance of power, with political implications for all concerned.

Meanwhile, the PRC also invested in developing a separate satellite navigation system of its own, known as Beidou. Space programmes are not cheap, and developing two different satellite networks to perform the same function would appear to be a poor use of resources. Only Chinese policymakers truly know why the PRC engaged in this apparently wasteful policy. One may easily infer that well-connected officials responsible for collaborating with the European Union on Galileo fought to continue their project, that equally well-connected officials responsible for Beidou fought to continue their project, and that the central authorities found it impossible to cancel either programme.

Beijing's European partners, however, turned out to have inconsistencies of their own. When the Galileo consortium ran short of money, its members restructured their organisation. This restructuring reduced the PRC's influence over Galileo. Moreover, as of 2019, Galileo has yet to achieve its planned operational capabilities.

Beidou has been functioning in various forms for approximately a decade. Whatever factors originally led the PRC to pursue both satellite navigation systems at once, the decision has turned out to be sound. Moreover, Beidou broadcasts on some of the same frequencies as Galileo. This means that, even when Galileo becomes fully operational, it will be difficult for anyone to use it for military purposes unless China agrees. By pursuing initially inconsistent policies, the PRC has gained a working navigation system, independence from its fickle European partners, and some ability to control those partners if Galileo ever becomes a reality.

The author has researched the PRC's involvement in the Galileo project jointly with Dr Xiudian Dai and gratefully acknowledges Dr Dai's contribution to his arguments.

Continuity, change, and strategic options

Perhaps the most widely recognised factor influencing grand strategy is geography. Such influential strategic thinkers as A.T. Mahan, Halford Mackinder, and Nicholas Spykman have paid special attention to its role. These thinkers' works have helped to establish a school of thought in foreign policy analysis devoted to its study, known as geopolitics. The logic behind the geopolitical approach to grand strategy is compelling. Geography, after all, affects one's access to resources, one's exposure to potential enemies, one's ability to cooperate with potential allies, and the sort of climatic conditions one will operate under, not to mention many other factors that may be more or less important at various times.

The fact that most of strategy involves material things means that it matters where those things are. Since cities, rivers, oceans, mountain ranges, and other strategically important parts of the landscape tend to remain in roughly the same places, the geopolitical approach is particularly useful for analysing long-term strategic issues. One of the reasons why Ch'in was able to invade one neighbour after another for two hundred years was that conveniently placed mountain ranges helped protect it from those who might have wished to put an end to its conquests, and one of the reasons why Frederick William I had to disguise his intentions was that Prussia lacked such defences.

Strategists would find it convenient if theorists could come up with universal rules explaining how to take advantage of geography to achieve political goals. So far, theorists have failed to come up with such principles. The Austrian empire of the eighteenth century was Prussia's antagonist, whereas the weaker Austria of the twentieth century became an appendage of Hitler's Third Reich. Geography ensured that the Austrian region would be critical to

German strategy in both periods, but over the course of centuries, the role of the Austrian state practically reversed itself. Important as geography is, one must look at other factors as well.

As society, technology, economics, and political relationships change, the significance of geographical features changes along with them. Accordingly, the British strategic thinker B.H. Liddell Hart identified 'financial pressure', 'diplomatic pressure' and 'ethical pressure' as key 'instruments' of grand strategy.[16] Hart emphasised that a grand strategist must pay attention to the long-term implications of using these instruments 'to avoid damage to the future state of peace'.[17] Decades later, the widely respected historian Paul Kennedy adapted Hart's list as the basis for his own writings on the subject.[18]

Kennedy's expanded definition of grand strategy drew attention to '[t]he critical importance of husbanding and managing national resources', along with the issue of 'national morale and political culture, which is of importance not only on the battlefield but also in a population's willingness to support the purposes and the burdens of the war – or the cost of large defense forces in peacetime'.[19] Other writers on the subject have emphasised a range of other issues. In 2010, for instance, the international relations theorist Nicholas Kitchen pointed out that our ideas about strategy are part of the very strategies that we use to explain them.[20] If we think Hart was right, we will tend to behave the way we think Hart would have advised us to behave.

To understand how any one of these factors affects any particular actor's grand strategic capabilities at any particular time, one must examine it in the context of as many others as possible. One must look for patterns, systems, and relationships. Above all, one must look for ways that strategic actors may take advantage of these convergences of circumstance. One must also look for ways that strategic actors may promote the very developments that they may later wish to exploit.

Here, grand strategy overlaps with the most fundamental questions of politics. If, for instance, managing resources and national morale is important, the organisation of the institutions which manage them must be equally important. Thus, the founders of the United States explicitly designed the US Constitution to 'insure domestic tranquillity' and 'provide for the common defence'. A constitution is, in large part, a blueprint for long-term strategy, and writing one is among the most significant grand strategic activities that political leaders can undertake.

This point about constitutions also applies to international agreements. A treaty is also a grand strategic document, and its terms may shape how its signatories wage war. The same is true of decisions in international institutions and court cases that establish precedents in international law. The fact that some may flout such restrictions does not change the fact that most states attempt to conform to most international laws most of the time, nor does it change the fact that even the most powerful actors may find that a reputation as a so-called rogue state itself limits their future options.

Moreover, if Kitchen is right and ideas matter, then the substance of those ideas must also matter. There may, for instance, be a fundamental difference between making grand strategy for a liberal democracy and making grand strategy for an authoritarian regime. What works well for one type of government may not work as well for another. In many cases, this may simply mean that different regimes must adopt different approaches. Nevertheless, this also raises the possibility that some political systems may be inherently more capable than others. We must hope that the most benign forms of government and the most powerful forms of government ultimately prove to be the same.

Conclusion: a grand strategic compass

The challenges of understanding – and making – grand strategy are fundamentally similar to the challenges of working with strategy at any level. Macmillan's events and Allison's organisational politics are, after all, no more than manifestations of what Clausewitz called friction. Deception is a universal tool in strategy, and self-deception is a universal risk. The reason why grand strategy seems unusually elusive in both theory and practice rests in the fact that it seldom appears purely as itself. Most of the time, it lies beneath the surface of all the other things that states and people do.

As the first paragraph of this chapter noted, education policy may have long-term military implications. Nevertheless, when political leaders consider this issue, training future soldiers is seldom the first thing on their minds. Moreover, it seems unlikely that the citizens of their countries would be better educated if it were. A later paragraph described a constitution as a blueprint for grand strategy – but only in a certain type of state would a constitution be only a blueprint for grand strategy. The word for that type of state is totalitarian.

To think about grand strategy effectively, one must learn to find points at which the strategic significance of various policies has risen closer to the surface – or could be made to. This chapter has suggested that one may look for these points by looking for patterns among the various factors that most commonly influence political destiny. The section that discussed these factors concluded with a discussion of political ideas. Those with an interest in grand strategy have at least two reasons for paying particular attention to this topic.

The first is the one emphasised in the earlier section. Looking for strategically important ideas is often a useful way of recognising the patterns that this chapter has been discussing. The fact that one's own country is adjacent to another state does not constitute a pattern, and even the fact that the neighbouring state happens to have a powerful military remains open to multiple interpretations. Knowing the additional fact that one's powerful neighbour is ruled by fanatics bent on territorial expansion clarifies the situation in a way that few other pieces of information could have done.

The second reason is that political ideas serve not only as landmarks but also as a compass. To make strategy effectively at any level, one needs to know what one is trying to accomplish. Thus, according to British military doctrine, the first principle of war is the selection and maintenance of the aim. This is particularly true at the grand strategic level, where leaders must routinely ask themselves whether to choose policies that maximise short-term to medium-term military capabilities or whether some other issue should take priority. To make such decisions effectively in an environment where grand strategy will seldom be more than one consideration among many, one must cultivate an acute understanding of what is worth fighting for.

Key points

1   Grand strategy combines military activities with other forms of policy to maximise a community's chances for success in war and other undertakings.
2   Scholars have questioned whether states and other political actors ever actually integrate their policies in this fashion.
3   The policymaking process is certainly more complex than a superficial understanding of grand strategy might make it seem.
4   Nevertheless, political leaders have no choice but to act at the grand strategic level – and some do so more effectively than others.
5   A variety of factors commonly shape international politics over the long term.
6   By looking for patterns among these factors, one may discern points at which political leaders may practise grand strategy successfully.

Questions

1   Is a democratic system of government a grand strategic asset or a grand strategic handicap?
2   Are certain geographical regions uniquely important to achieving political power?
3   What factors are most important in grand strategic planning?

Notes

1   Hans Morgenthau and Kenneth Thompson, *Politics among Nations: The Struggle for Power and Peace* (New York, Alfred A. Knopf, 1948), p. 4.
2   Alexander Wendt, *Social Theory of International Politics* (Cambridge, Cambridge University Press, 1999), p. 5.
3   Nicholas Kitchen, 'Systemic Pressures and Domestic Ideas: A Neoclassical Realist Model of Grand Strategy Formation', *Review of International Studies* 36:1 (January 2010), pp. 120–2.
4   Graham Allison and Philip Zelikow, *Essence of Decision: Explaining the Cuban Missile Crisis* (New York, Longman, 1999), pp. 5–7.
5   Thomas Kane, *Emerging Conflicts of Principle: International Relations and the Clash between Cosmopolitanism and Republicanism* (Aldershot, Ashgate, 2008), p. 138.
6   Multiple anonymous authors, 'Potsdam Giants', 2010, http://en.wikipedia.org/wiki/Potsdam_Giants (accessed May 4, 2010).
7   Christopher Duffy, *Frederick the Great: A Military Life* (London, Routledge, 1985), pp. 3–4.
8   Harold Rood, *Kingdoms of the Blind: How the Great Democracies Have Resumed the Follies That So Nearly Cost Them Their Life* (Durham, NC, Carolina Academic Press, 1980), p. 22.
9   Ibid., p. 47.
10   Alistair Horne, *To Lose a Battle: France 1940* (London, Macmillan, 1969), p. 230.
11   Deborah Stone, *Policy Paradox and Political Reason* (London, Harper Collins, 1988), p. 4.
12   Ibid., pp. 3–4.

13 Bates Gill and Martin Kleiber, 'China's Space Odyssey', *Foreign Affairs* 86:3 (May/June 2001), pp. 2–6.
14 Ibid., p. 4.
15 Ibid., p. 3.
16 Basil Liddell-Hart, *Strategy* (New York, Meridian, 1954), p. 322.
17 Ibid.
18 Paul Kennedy, 'Grand Strategy in War and Peace: Toward a Broader Definition', in Paul Kennedy (ed.), *Grand Strategies in War and Peace* (New Haven, Yale University Press, 1991), pp. 2–6.
19 Ibid., pp. 4–5.
20 Kitchen, 'Systemic Pressures', p. 119.

Further reading

Allison, Graham and Philip Zelikow, *Essence of Decision: Explaining the Cuban Missile Crisis*, (New York: Longman, 1999).
Earle, Edward Mead, 'Introduction' in Edward Mead Earle (ed.), *Makers of Modern Strategy: Military Thought from Machiavelli to Hitler*, (Princeton: Princeton University Press, 1943), pp. 7–11.
Gill, Bates and Martin Kleiber, 'China's Space Odyssey', *Foreign Affairs*, Vol. 86, No. 3 (May/June 2001), pp. 2–6.
Kennedy, Paul, 'Grand Strategy in War and Peace: Toward a Broader Definition' in Paul Kennedy (ed.), *Grand Strategies in War and Peace*, (New Haven: Yale University Press, 1991).
Kitchen, Nicholas, 'Systemic Pressures and Domestic Ideas: A Neoclassical Realist Model of Grand Strategy Formation', *Review of International Studies*, Vol. 36, No. 1 (January 2010), pp. 117–44.
Liddell Hart, Basil Henry, *Strategy*, (New York:, Meridian, 1954).

The geographic domains

PART II

Land power

7

Reader's guide

Ground troops determine which side in a war will be capable of controlling people and places; modern weapons make it problematic for ground troops to survive; the tactical solutions that emerged during World War One; the operational solutions that emerged since; the question of whether these solutions will remain valid under twenty-first-century conditions.

Introduction

'The ultimate determinant in war is the man on the scene with the gun. This man is the final power in war. He is control'.

– Admiral J.C. Wylie[1]

There are exceptions to Wylie's point, but not many. Military history includes occasional examples of armed forces that managed to exert control in specific situations with minimal numbers of ground troops. During the 1920s, for instance, numerically small British colonial forces managed to suppress revolts in what was then known as Mesopotamia by bombing rebellious villages from the air. Even in that campaign, however, the British had to combine air attacks with ground operations to achieve lasting success.

Far more common is the situation that developed approximately 80 years later in the same part of the world. In 2003, a US-led coalition invaded Mesopotamia – by then known as Iraq – using the most advanced military technology then in existence. Although the coalition overran Iraq in a matter of days, its forces became bogged down in years of costly and inconclusive fighting, largely because the original invasion force had not included enough ground troops to impose order on the conquered territory. As of the twenty-first century, no amount of firepower and no form of technology can substitute for Wylie's man on the scene.

To place ground troops 'on the scene', one must get them there alive. One must also keep them alive after they have arrived. These obvious points raise some of the most complex problems in contemporary military operations. A direct frontal attack against enemies equipped with modern firearms is suicidal. Attempting to hold a position that comes under fire from contemporary weapons is also problematic, although, amazingly, it has remained possible. These tactical realities have implications for every level of military planning. Whenever military operations involve the possibility of ground combat, strategists must provide troops with means and opportunities to work around these difficulties.

The problem of overcoming modern weapons in a single firefight would be challenging enough by itself. To win a battle or a war, it is only a first step. To achieve anything of lasting importance, higher-level commanders must enable their forces to win many such firefights and to go on doing so. Moreover, higher-level commanders must coordinate these firefights in such a way as to develop small victories into larger ones. This is true for a captain who must decide how to manoeuvre three or four platoons in an attack on an enemy pillbox, and it is equally true for the leader of a country, who must make decisions about the type of military forces to invest in and the circumstances under which to commit those forces to war.

Military thinkers developed techniques to cope with the lethality of modern weapons over the course of the First World War. Germany demonstrated what armed forces can accomplish when they apply these techniques in a coordinated manner when it overran Poland and France in the Second World War. Germany's enemies, notably the Soviet Union, developed those methods of coordination still further as they recovered from the initial German onslaught and went on to dismember the Third Reich. Despite all that has happened since, the tactical methods that evolved during World War One and the operational methods that evolved during World War Two remain the foundation stones of land warfare.

Thus, returning to Wylie's point about the man on the scene, these methods remain basic to all military planning. This chapter explains the techniques of modern land warfare as follows. An initial section details the problems that soldiers faced as modern weapons and modern industry became widespread. This section focuses on the example of the First World War. The second section discusses the solutions that commanders in that conflict developed. The third section discusses how military thinkers of the 1920s, 1930s, and 1940s integrated new weapons and new tactics into higher levels of planning. A final section asks whether methods that emerged during the world wars of the twentieth century remain appropriate in the wars of the twenty first. Later chapters will return to this question in more detail.

Facing firepower

When Germany invaded Belgium and France in August 1914, commanders on both sides hoped to crush their opponents by aggressively taking the offensive. The Germans, in particular, believed that they needed a quick victory for strategic reasons. German commanders hoped to overcome France in time to shift their forces eastward to meet an expected attack from Russia. Certain German strategists had also written about the danger that a long war under modern conditions would bankrupt the countries that fought in it, possibly undermining their governments and reducing their societies to anarchy. Moreover, military thinkers on both sides commonly assumed that the side which attacked more energetically would enjoy a tactical advantage over the side that found itself forced onto the defensive.

This assumption appears logical. Attacking commanders have the luxury of deciding when and where to stage their assault. This gives them greater freedom to fight on their preferred terrain. This also allows them to concentrate their own forces against positions where they believe the enemy to be weak. French military thinkers, in particular, would have added that attacking troops gain a psychological advantage simply from knowing that they are gloriously charging forward. Moreover, attackers have the more general advantage of taking positive action to achieve new things, whereas defenders can only hope that they will eventually exhaust their opponents by holding onto things they already possess.

Despite the apparent logic in favour of aggressive action, this 'cult of the offensive' proved catastrophic in practice. When Germany attacked, France promptly launched a counteroffensive known as the Battle of the Frontiers. In the ten days between August 15 and August 25, 1914, the French lost over three hundred thousand troops in futile attacks on German defensive positions. This amounted to almost one-quarter of their strength. French forces in this battle suffered a higher rate of casualties than any other army in any other major operation throughout the First World War.

Meanwhile, the German forces attacking through the Low Countries advanced almost to Paris before the French and British Allies drove them back. As the German army recovered from the initial battles, its troops halted their retreat and entrenched themselves to resist further French and British attacks. At this point, the Germans still controlled over one-tenth of France, including practically all of France's coal and iron resources. Since the Allies could not overrun the German positions in a frontal attack, they dug trenches of their own, and since the industrial economies of early-twentieth-century nations allowed both sides to field armies of millions, both were able to extend their defensive lines from the Swiss border to the North Sea. This created a situation in which neither side had any obvious way to advance other than to stage direct attacks of the sort that had proven so bloody and difficult in the Frontiers.

If commanders on either side hoped to proceed beyond stalemate, they had to find a more effective way to attack. A variety of factors combined to make this difficult. The first was simply that defenders have always enjoyed certain tactical advantages and probably always will. Defenders have greater opportunity to take advantage of natural cover and to improve it with fortifications such as trenches. This gives them some protection from the attackers' weapons. Attackers, by contrast, must leave whatever cover they have found and advance towards the enemy, taking fire the whole time.

Over the course of the nineteenth century, firearms technology improved dramatically. The most highly trained troops of Napoleon's time would have done well to fire two shots a minute with their muzzle-loading muskets. The troops of the British Expeditionary Force (BEF) managed to deliver ten times that rate of fire in 1914 with their considerably more accurate rifles.[2] Although the BEF's performance was exceptional, it illustrates what the improved shoulder arms could do. Even less-accomplished troops could easily fire five rounds per minute with World War One–era rifles.[3] These developments made advancing against enemy defensive positions bloodier and more difficult than ever before.

Furthermore, the armies of the First World War fielded entirely new types of weapons. Any one of these weapons would have been formidable on its own. Moreover, their capabilities complemented one another, so that they were even more effective in combination than they would have been separately. The best known of these weapons is the machine gun. A single well-placed machine gun could halt hundreds of enemy troops.

Machine guns also had limitations. These weapons are, for instance, difficult to move. Heavier models also require support from crews of up to ten men. These factors were particularly important early in the war, before armies introduced lighter and more mobile machine guns. Moreover, although a single machine gun can fire as many bullets as 20 or 30 soldiers armed with rifles, it also presents a more compact target. When one disables a machine gun position, one instantly neutralises all its firepower. Overcoming 30 individual soldiers will normally be a slower and less-certain process.

The deadliest new weapon of the early twentieth century was modern artillery. Artillery caused approximately 60% of the casualties in the First World War. Just as small arms had grown more accurate and longer ranged, artillery had as well. Meanwhile, gunners worked out techniques to fire shells at a high angle, so that they would rise, pass over whatever obstacles might happen to be in their path, and descend on a target that might happen to be over 10 miles away.

This technique, known as indirect fire, allows commanders to position artillery behind their other forces' positions, keeping the guns relatively – although not completely – safe from enemy action. Indirect fire also allows artillery to strike behind such obstacles as trees, hills, and both sides' troops. By making the enemy more vulnerable in more places, indirect-fire artillery gives commanders a greater range of tactical options. If, for instance, enemy troops take cover from direct-fire weapons by hiding behind trees, hills, or other terrain features, one may use artillery to keep them under fire. If they abandon their cover to escape the shells, they expose themselves to direct-fire weapons again. When commanders succeed at positioning their various types of weapons so that one can hit the targets the other cannot, they leave their enemies with no place to hide.

Indirect fire also allows artillery to strike behind enemy lines without going through the intermediary step of defeating the opposing troops in the middle. This makes it possible for artillery to attack such targets as enemy headquarters, enemy supply depots, and the enemy's own artillery. Roads, bridges, and other components of the enemy transportation network are equally vulnerable, as are wires for field telephones and other line-based communications systems. Thus, modern artillery using indirect fire has the potential to cripple opposing forces before they ever reach the so-called front line.

As is ever the case in war, numerous factors complicate indirect artillery fire in practice. Historically, one of the most important complicating factors has been one of the most obvious ones: gunners using indirect fire cannot see what to aim at or see whether they are hitting it. Speaking broadly, gunners have two options for targeting indirect fire. First, they can drop shells on preplanned locations at predetermined times or in response to prearranged signals. This system is often referred to as map fire. Second, they can rely on friendly troops to inform them about the location of valuable targets and provide them with feedback about where their shells are falling.

For the second method to work, the gunners and the troops directing their fire need a fast, reliable method of communicating. The second method also requires high levels of skill and teamwork. Troops directing the fire (often known as forward observers, or FOs) must have some confidence that the gunners will not hit them instead of the target. Moreover, FOs, gunners, and their commanders must generally agree on which targets to attack. There will normally be far more places in which friendly troops need artillery support than there are guns to provide it, so those responsible for artillery operations need to be able to prioritise.

In 1914, the technology of aiming indirect fire from defensive positions had reached a higher stage of maturity than the technology for aiming indirect fire on the attack. Although gunners had developed basic techniques for working with FOs, their methods remained crude. Moreover, wireless communications systems were also in their infancy. This meant that FOs had to rely on field telephones, and troops on the defensive typically have more opportunities to connect their positions with telephone lines than troops pressing forward under fire. In battle, both sides tended to lose their telephone lines to enemy artillery quickly, but defenders, once again, had a greater opportunity to protect their lines by burying them.

For these reasons, the artillery of 1914 relied heavily on map fire. Again, this favoured the defender, since it is easier for defenders to identify the routes that their enemies will have to take to approach their lines than it is for attackers to pinpoint the spots at which distant opponents have taken positions. The fact that both sides had settled into immobile trenches made it somewhat easier for attackers to figure out where the defending troops would be. Nevertheless, commanders who attempted to hammer opposing trench lines into submission with prolonged artillery bombardments seldom achieved the results they might have hoped for.

Troops under cover can and do survive even the heaviest shelling. Moreover, a well-prepared defensive position consisted of as many as seven trenches, one behind the other. Attackers that overcame the front trench – which their artillery would find easiest to target – would merely have to deal with the next. A well-prepared position also included communications trenches linking the lines of defence. This allowed defenders from the rear trenches to advance under cover as they moved to counterattack. Attackers attempting to continue their advance enjoyed no such luxury. To compound the problems of using massive bombardment as an offensive tactic further, prolonged artillery fire warned defending forces both that an attack was imminent and where it was likely to fall. This permitted defenders to withdraw forces from the most exposed positions, bring in reinforcements, and take other steps to prepare a devastating response.

Yet another new defensive weapon of the early twentieth century was barbed wire. When one thinks of wire obstacles in World War One, one should not picture the vertical fences common on farms. Armed forces in defensive positions string broad nets of wire at ankle height, making it virtually impossible for troops on foot to pick their way forward. If enemy infantry wishes to advance, it must endure enemy fire while painstakingly cutting its way through the barbed wire nets, one strand at a time. The fact that fire from so many types of weapons had grown so much more effective magnified the importance of such obstacles in the First World War.

Artillery could clear wire obstacles by blasting them to shreds. Shellfire, however, pounded the ground into a moonscape of rubble and craters, which also slowed down attackers as they attempted to advance towards the enemy's guns. This problem became all the worse as rain turned shell craters into lakes where wounded or merely overburdened foot soldiers might slip in and drown. Thus, even where the firepower of early-twentieth-century weapons seemed to help the attacker, it proved a mixed blessing.

Little things count

Defending armies, equipped with modern small arms and artillery, occupying multiple layers of fortified and mutually supporting positions, backed by reserve forces, and sustained by the human and material resources of economically developed modern states, proved impossible to overcome, at least in the period from 1914 to 1917. Nevertheless, the factors that favour the defender in modern ground combat are invincible only in combination. Defenders never enjoy all these factors fully at all points and all times. Moreover, attackers can often find ways to complicate their enemies' efforts to coordinate the various elements of an effective defence. Therefore, even in the trenches of World War One, there were always times and places at which commanders could manufacture opportunities to attack.

Here and there throughout the combat zone, attacking troops may simply get lucky. They may find themselves opposing troops who are exhausted or short on ammunition. Their enemies may have positioned themselves poorly, perhaps because of incompetence or perhaps because they have been too busy fighting to prepare defences. The defenders may not have enough artillery within range to support front-line soldiers by providing indirect fire.

The longer armies engage in combat and the larger the areas they happen to be fighting over, the more frequently both sides will encounter fortunate – and unfortunate – flukes of circumstance. These flukes will help the defenders as often as they help the attackers. Neither side can expect to succeed by relying on luck. Nevertheless, troops that watch for opportunities may occasionally find it possible to do things that they would not normally be able to do.

Attackers may also be able to take advantage of the terrain. Even with modern weapons, troops find it difficult to hit targets that they cannot see. Although artillery can shoot over obstacles, the gunners need to know when to fire and where to direct their rounds. Moreover, unless artillery receives prompt, accurate feedback about where its shells are landing, it will have to expend prodigious amounts of ammunition to have any reasonable chance of destroying its targets.

Defenders naturally try to take positions where they will have a clear view of – and clear shot at – approaching enemies. If the defenders have time, they will cut down trees, demolish buildings, and take other measures to improve their fields of fire. Nevertheless, even in deserts and apparently flat fields, there are practically always places in which attackers can find cover. During the 1970s, for instance, Western military analysts estimated that troops holding typical defensive positions on the appropriately named North German Plain would be able to see only 35% of the ground within 1000 metres in front of them.[4] Barely perceptible folds in the Earth can shield troops that lie low and keep the ridgelines between themselves and their enemies. Although troops may have to cross open ground to reach this cover, they may be able to take advantage of fog, smoke, darkness, or other conditions to do so.

Moreover, although it is difficult for attackers to annihilate enemy defensive positions purely through long-range bombardment, artillery – along with all other types of weapons – can still prevent one's opponents from performing at full effectiveness. Troops cannot fight as well while they are under fire. Unless they are exceptionally well protected or exceptionally lucky, they will suffer casualties, and although many of them may survive, the losses will disrupt their activities and weaken them at particular points. Unless they are recklessly brave – and willing to take even heavier losses – they will have to crouch behind cover, withdraw from positions that have come under effective fire, and take other measures to protect themselves. The more troops must concentrate on saving their own lives, they less they will be able to concentrate on killing their oncoming enemies. Even those that manage to return fire will find that smoke, noise, and flying debris make it harder than ever for them to hit their targets or to perform any other functions.

As World War One went on, commanders on both sides became increasingly aware of the importance of finding weak points in enemy lines, of the use of cover to help troops survive long enough to attack those points, and of the value of firepower as a tool for disrupting enemy performance. This awareness helped First World War commanders develop a range of techniques for overcoming the combination of developments that had so often made defensive trenches so impregnable. For instance, the opposing forces of 1914–18 introduced methods for using indirect fire that took full advantage of what artillery could accomplish, as opposed to what it seemed capable of accomplishing in principle. Instead of bombarding enemy positions for days before an offensive, cratering the ground and sacrificing the chance of surprise in hopes of blasting the enemy into oblivion, commanders learned to use artillery in sudden barrages at the moment their troops attacked.

Artillery crews developed techniques to drop rounds just ahead of their own side's infantry and to move the line of falling shells forward as the friendly infantry advanced, so that the enemy would have to deal with both the bombardment and the oncoming foot soldiers at the same time. (This type of artillery fire was known as a creeping barrage.) Both sides also improved their methods of locating enemy artillery and using their own artillery to fire back at it. (This practice is known as counterbattery fire.) Most importantly of all, armed forces developed relatively reliable methods for using FOs to bring artillery to bear against specific targets, making indirect fire a much more efficient tool for attackers and defenders alike.

Meanwhile, commanders learned to move their troops across the battlefield in ways that paid greater respect to the capabilities of modern weapons. Even as military thinkers came to accept that large-scale attacks by large numbers of soldiers had become little more than a form of mass suicide, they became increasingly aware of the fact that smaller teams of soldiers attacking the enemy's weak points could still succeed. Such local attacks could not overrun the enemy's defensive lines, but they could penetrate them in isolated places. The attackers could then send more troops to mop up the stronger points in the enemy's lines while the troops that had successfully infiltrated either assisted them by turning to strike the enemy strong points from behind or continued to advance even deeper into the enemy's position.

Even where defending forces are weak enough to attack, they practically always remain capable of inflicting horrendous casualties. Although writers on strategy often contrast infiltration tactics with the bloodier and presumably less imaginative system of large-scale assault, both depend on sending groups of soldiers towards enemy guns. Therefore, early methods of infiltration required soldiers to attack in a series of waves, so that there would be more troops to continue advancing after the ones in front had been killed.

As previously noted, troops cannot perform as effectively while they are under fire. Therefore, if one group of attackers can fire at the enemy, soldiers in other groups have a better chance of surviving as they advance. At some point, the two groups can exchange roles, with the soldiers who had been advancing pausing to shoot at the enemy while the troops who had been firing move forward. Thus, the two groups can leapfrog past each other, deeper and deeper into the enemy position. Military thinkers often refer to this as moving in 'bounds'. These principles of combining fire with movement have become basic to most methods of moving troops from point to point in combat.

When armed forces first adopted these methods as routine practice, commanders intended to use them with relatively large units in a simple way. In February 1917, for instance, the British army issued a manual known as SS 143, *Instructions for the Training of Platoons for Offensive Action*.[5] This manual advised platoons (units of approximately 60 troops) to divide themselves into sections devoted to manoeuvre and sections devoted to providing firepower.[6] When the platoons came under effective fire, the firepower elements were to pause and shoot back while the manoeuvre elements attempted to move forward and attack the enemy at close range, preferably from a flank. Nevertheless, the manual seemed to envision large numbers of platoons performing this procedure mechanically as they all advanced steadily forward with their troops spread out in lines facing the enemy.

Experienced soldiers immediately recognised that the process was likely to be far more complicated in practice. Different units inevitably found themselves dealing with different terrain, different levels of visibility, differently positioned opponents, and many other differences in fortune as well. Moreover, since gathering large numbers of troops or other military assets in one place presents the enemy with a lucrative target for area-effect weapons such as artillery, these small units must disperse out and conceal themselves as well as they can. By the time of World War Two, this process of spreading out and hiding had continued to the point at which soldiers often found themselves seemingly alone in an apparently deserted landscape, although they were involved in operations involving combat between tens of thousands of soldiers.

Even in 1916–17, platoon commanders found it most practical to, as one British army pamphlet put it, 'dribble' troops forward in 'blobs' of whatever size could best cope with the situation they found themselves in.[7] Individual 'blobs' could end up fighting miniature battles of their own. Later, British regulations formally established the 'blobs' as sections of one non-commissioned officer (NCO) and six troops.[8] Meanwhile, German forces learned to base attacks on similar tactics involving so-called storm wedges of an NCO and nine troops.[9]

If small units were to fight their own isolated battles, they needed weapons that would allow them to apply the principles of fire and movement as independently as possible in as wide a range of situations as possible. Wherever possible, such units needed to be able to carry these weapons with them rather than rely on their comrades elsewhere for support. Therefore, as World War One went on, armed forces introduced a continually expanding range of specialist weapons designed for small-unit combat, distributed them in continually increasing numbers, and entrusted them to troops at ever-lower levels of the chain of command.

In 1914, for instance, the British army issued its troops two heavy machine guns per battalion (a battalion consists of approximately 500–1000 troops). The battalion commander – typically a lieutenant colonel – was responsible for deciding where to position them to support the entire unit's operations.[10] Certain military thinkers advocated creating independent machine gun units, to place the valuable weapons even more firmly under central control.

The opposite approach, however, turned out to be the effective one: by 1916, the British army had begun distributing lighter Lewis guns to individual platoons, and this proved so critical to small-unit tactics that General Sir Ivor Maxse subsequently declared '[a] platoon without a Lewis gun is not a platoon at all'.[11] The German army took this process to its natural conclusion by equipping selected troops with the submachine gun, an automatic weapon small enough for an individual soldier to handle almost as easily as they might handle a rifle.

Other new weapons included trench mortars, which allowed infantry brigades (units of a few thousand) to support local battles with indirect fire without going through the uncertain and time-consuming process of requesting support from distant artillery. Rifle-fired grenades gave each platoon a limited indirect-fire capability of its own. Meanwhile, the opposing armies introduced improved models of the hand grenade. This made it possible for every soldier to carry a few short-range indirect-fire munitions on their belt. The fact that grenades are also area-effect weapons made them useful for clearing numbers of enemies out of confined areas such as trenches, and the flamethrower offered an even more lethal tool for dealing with multiple opponents at close range.

Meanwhile, the opposing armies developed more spectacular new forms of technology, such as tanks, armed aircraft, and poison gas. These innovations seldom achieved lasting results on their own. To make these inventions consistently useful, commanders had to use them in combination with other weapons to support the process by which smaller units exploited local opportunities to win local victories. The development of the tank provides a particularly instructive case study of this point.

The British introduced tanks at the battle of Flers on September 15, 1916. Although the experiment excited journalists and optimistic British officers, the tanks performed differently on the battlefield. Subsequent tank attacks were debacles. At one engagement the following April, the tank forces arrived a day late for the battle and suffered 100% casualties.[12] At another battle, a force of 190 tanks sank into deep mud, while the survivors found themselves forced to advance ineffectually in single file along the few available roads. Only at the battle of Cambrai in November 1917 did tanks finally accomplish anything meaningful.

At Cambrai, tanks led an infantry advance over 2 miles into the German defences. One of the main reasons why the tanks achieved this result was that Cambrai happened to be one of the places at which British forces enjoyed a local advantage. Only a weak German force of two divisions opposed them there, and those two divisions had only 34 artillery pieces.[13] Moreover, British artillery managed to neutralise the enemy guns promptly, depriving the Germans of their most effective weapon for stopping the tanks.

When the tanks advanced at Cambrai, they helped other parts of the British army function more effectively. The tanks, for instance, flattened German barbed wire defences. Not only did this make it easier for the British infantry to advance, but it also freed the British artillery – which would normally have had to destroy the wire with shells – to concentrate its fire on other targets. Just as the power of modern defences depends on a variety of weapons that complement each other's effects, tactics for overcoming such defences must also involve mutually supporting combinations of arms. Although tanks have become considerably more reliable over subsequent decades, this principle remains valid today.

Moreover, tanks themselves must often use the same fire and movement procedures as infantry to advance against enemy defences. Just as tanks proved most consistently effective when integrated into the tactical system that emerged in the middle years of World War One, so too have all the other new weapons and new techniques that have become available for ground combat in later decades, from helicopter gunships to rocket-propelled grenades (RPGs). Many of these innovations are capable of inflicting brutal losses on unprepared opponents, but none have altered the basic logic of the modern battlefield, which includes that it is fatal to expose oneself to effective fire and that those who wish to engage their opponents successfully must go through a torturous process of contriving circumstances in which their enemies' fire will not be effective at opportune points. New weapons have offered troops new options for creating favourable circumstances while forcing them to take new counter-measures against the opposing forces' capabilities. The process of working out how best to coordinate the continually expanding array of weapons and other military assets available in modern ground operations has become mind-boggling.

Box 7.1 Stone, paper, scissors

In the game of stone, paper, scissors, two players extend their fists. Then, at the same moment, they gesture to indicate whether they have chosen to be stone, paper, or scissors. A player who chooses scissors beats a player who has chosen paper, because scissors can cut paper. If, however, one chooses scissors and one's opponent chooses stone, one's opponent wins, because a stone can break scissors. A player can defeat stone, however, by choosing paper, because paper can cover a stone.

The art of combining different types of forces to maximise their combat power resembles this game. Each type of weapon and weapons system has distinct advantages and disadvantages. One tries to deploy them so that they can compensate for each other's drawbacks while confronting enemies with the specific types of weapons that they will find most difficult to deal with. For those unfamiliar with the forces that take part in modern land warfare, the boxes on the following pages provide an introduction.

Infantry

Advantages: Infantry can operate in practically all forms of terrain, can disperse to take advantage of cover, are cheap to field and deploy in large numbers, are relatively easy to conceal, have a relatively high ability to discriminate between enemies and bystanders, have a relatively high ability to interact with human beings, and can use portable missiles and other specialist weapons to inflict casualties on high-value targets such as tanks and aircraft. They can also assist aircraft and indirect-fire weapons in finding targets.

Although individual soldiers are vulnerable, infantry units dispersed in protective terrain can often withstand heavy bombardment while remaining effective in combat – if the troops have sufficient morale.

Disadvantages: Infantry are slow and vulnerable when exposed to enemy fire and most of their weapons have relatively short ranges and relatively little firepower.

One can move infantry from place to place faster by providing troops with motor transport. Normally, however, infantry will have to dismount in order to use its special combat advantages. Infantry mounted in trucks are highly vulnerable, with no compensating advantages except for their ability to travel faster on passable terrain. Infantry mounted in infantry fighting vehicles (or, perhaps, in the armed civilian lorries known as technicals) can duplicate the combat functions of light armour. Main battle tanks, however, outmatch infantry fighting vehicles in both protection and firepower.

Tanks

Advantages: Tanks are fast, have armour protection and substantial firepower in a direct-fire role. 'The best defence against a tank is another tank'.

Disadvantages: Tanks have mobility in rough terrain, poor visibility, require substantial maintenance and substantial fuel and ammunition, and are relatively difficult to conceal.
  Most tanks have vulnerable points, such as treads and radio antennas. Most tanks have thinner armour on the sides, rear, and roof. Moreover, tank commanders prefer to open a hatch and sit with their head outside the vehicle whenever possible, for better visibility. All these things make tanks more vulnerable to snipers, artillery bombardment, infantry anti-tank weapons, and aircraft than they might appear.

Artillery

Advantages: Artillery inflicts substantial casualties and even greater disruption over a broad area. It can strike at targets anywhere within a broad radius of the guns, making it relatively easy for commanders to shift fire to the points where they believe it will do the most good. It can use indirect fire. It can fire back at enemy artillery, a practice known as counterbattery fire. It can interfere with enemy movements and resupply efforts behind the main line of resistance.

Disadvantages: Although artillery can bombard broad areas, it has historically had difficulty ensuring the destruction of point targets within those regions. Not only has this allowed infantry units to remain combat effective despite heavy bombardment, but it has also helped tanks to survive artillery attack. Precision munitions of various kinds have partially overcome this disadvantage of artillery. As methods and techniques of counterbattery fire improve, artillery units must disperse over wider areas, move their guns more frequently, and devote more of their own efforts to firing at enemy artillery, thus reducing their ability to perform other functions. Artillery also consumes large quantities of ammunition. It cannot cooperate with other units effectively unless all are linked by an effective communications network. Towed artillery is slower than tanks and other vehicles.

Airborne/airmobile units

Airborne troops are those that land by parachute or glider. Airmobile troops have vehicles that allow them to land and take off repeatedly during a battle. These vehicles are normally helicopters but may be light planes or, in hypothetical future conflicts, personal jet packs.

Advantages: They can travel rapidly to any point aircraft can reach, bypassing enemy ground defences, and can land behind enemy positions. Airborne troops are typically exceptionally fit, exceptionally well-trained, and psychologically ready for exceptionally challenging missions.

Disadvantages: These units are vulnerable to anti-aircraft fire when travelling to the landing zone. They are highly vulnerable to both anti-aircraft fire and ground fire when landing. They are likely to suffer casualties from landing accidents, especially at night or in rough terrain. Although contemporary airborne/airmobile forces can land with heavier equipment than their World War Two predecessors could, even they cannot deploy heavy artillery or main battle tanks by air. When operating behind enemy lines, airborne/airmobile forces must usually depend on further air operations for reinforcements and fresh supplies.

Tactical air forces

Advantages: They can perform similar functions to artillery across even wider swathes of the battle space. They can travel rapidly. They can perform reconnaissance far behind the enemy's defensive lines. They can attack point targets such as tanks and specific infantry positions with cannons, rockets, missiles, or guided bombs. Appropriate types of tactical aircraft can engage enemy aircraft in air-to-air combat.

Disadvantages: Aircraft require secure and well-equipped bases relatively near the combat zone. Individual aircraft are costly. Not only are pilots expensive to train, but they also require long periods of time to develop their skills. Therefore, air forces find it particularly difficult to afford casualties. For the same reasons, commanders seldom have access to as many aircraft as they might like. The fact that individual aircraft cannot carry enough fuel to remain over the battle space for extended periods of time further limits their availability, and the farther they must fly to reach their targets, the less time they will be able to spend there. Air defences force pilots to waste time and fuel on evasive manoeuvres even when they do not actually shoot down any aircraft. Air defences may also force pilots to fly at altitudes that reduce their ability to find and target opponents on the ground. Weather and terrain may also conceal ground targets from aircraft. Ground troops may further deceive enemy aircraft by using camouflage, dummy equipment, and similar measures.

As attackers learned to use the new tactics to fight their way through enemy defences, defenders found that the most effective response was to adopt similar methods of their own. Just as troops on the offensive do not need to charge forward heedlessly in one great line, troops on the defensive do not need to sit passively in lines waiting for the attackers to come. Defending troops can also spread out in small units, positioning themselves to take full advantage of terrain and other local circumstances. Defenders can conceal themselves and attempt to lure their enemies into ambushes. Most importantly of all, they can seize the nearly inevitable moment at which their enemies run into difficulties to counterattack.

Controlling irregularity

By 1918, both the Germans and the Allies had learned techniques for breaking through the once-invincible trenches – and for fighting back when enemy troops broke through their own. During the middle years of the war, attacking commanders had measured their success at gaining ground in yards. Between March and July of 1918, the Germans advanced over 40 miles. The Allies then counterattacked, recaptured their lost territory, and pushed the Germans back approximately 60 more miles in the opposite direction. Nevertheless, neither army managed to destroy the other. The Germans surrendered for a combination of reasons, in which the British navy's success at blockading Germany's ports, the outbreak of a Communist revolution in Germany, and the German Chief of Staff Erich von Ludendorff's hope that American president Woodrow Wilson would force the other Allies to grant Germany favourable peace terms played roles as great as the summer's battles.

The innovations that allowed platoons to win firefights complicated the problem of using entire armies to win wars. As battles fragmented into myriads of tactical engagements among myriads of small units, it became increasingly difficult for higher-level commanders to direct their forces' activity in any purposeful way. Part of this problem was technical. When officers who wanted to communicate with their superiors, their subordinates, or comrades who were meant to be supporting them had to rely on human runners carrying written messages, it was impossible for small units to support each other in a coordinated fashion.

By 1918, the signalling corps of the opposing forces had developed effective systems for combining flares, lanterns, sirens, messenger dogs, messenger pigeons, messenger aircraft, and field telephones to overcome this problem. As the wireless became more common, it largely supplanted the other techniques. One of the key reasons why German Panzer forces proved so unstoppable in the first years of World War Two was that German officer and armoured warfare theorist Heinz Guderian had insisted on providing every tank in the German army with a radio.[14] As a side note, each of these new communications techniques presented opposing forces with new opportunities to block, intercept, or tamper with each other's messages, giving planners yet another set of continually evolving measures and countermeasures to account for.

Even with improved communications, the process of sending small units to fight semiautonomous battles remains slow and unpredictable. The more one subdivides one's forces, the longer one waits for a perfect opportunity, and the more one insists on securing fire support to cover one's movements, the slower the entire process becomes. Moreover, small units can sustain only small numbers of casualties. Even when larger units must accept greater losses, they may stand a better chance of completing their missions. This means, among other things, that soldiers practically never have the luxury of using all the new techniques fully. Instead, commanders at every level of the military hierarchy must continually make judgements about the losses that they can afford to take and the amount of time they can afford to spend minimising them.

Box 7.2 A closer look at Panzer divisions

As earlier sections have noted, success in modern warfare depends not on any one type of weapon but on using different forces together in effective combinations. Units composed only of tanks would be limited in their capabilities and vulnerable in common combat situations. Armoured vehicles are not, for instance, the optimal tools for establishing control over a civilian population. Moreover, the fact that tank crews have relatively poor visibility makes it possible for enemy infantry to ambush unprotected armoured vehicles and destroy them, especially in woods, towns or other close terrain.

The German Panzer divisions proved so effective not merely because they contained a large number of tanks but rather because the Panzer division packaged armoured vehicles with other types of forces in useful proportions. The Panzer division also equipped infantry and artillery with motor transport so that all could travel at the tanks' speed. Air forces provided an even swifter source of fire support while also scouting ahead of advancing tank forces and shooting down enemy reconnaissance aircraft that might otherwise have spotted the Panzers. Heinz Guderian, who played a critical role in organising the Panzer divisions, discussed these principles at length in his work *Achtung-Panzer*.[15]

As armies introduced new equipment, their logistical requirements increased as well. New weapons required new types of ammunition, often in vast quantities. Tanks, aircraft, and other machinery require spare parts and fuel. Not only must armies transport such materiel to the battlefield; they must also distribute the supplies to the precise points where their troops need them. If those troops are divided into small units, all of which are manoeuvring semi-independently across the battlefield, this process becomes more difficult than ever. Moreover, those units are likely to need much greater quantities of materiel at some times than others – if, for instance, they are making progress against the enemy, they will normally need large infusions of supplies and reinforcements to continue. All these facts further muddle the problem of using the new tactical system to achieve large-scale results.

For these reasons, the Soviet military thinker A.A. Svechin became acutely interested in the problem of reconnecting efforts to win tactical victories on the battlefield with efforts to achieve overall strategic war aims. In 1927, Svechin published a book known as *Strategy*, in which he popularised the concept of a third level of military planning between strategy and tactics.[16] Svechin called this middle level of planning operational art.

Unfortunately for the Soviet Union, Stalin had his country's most prominent theorists of operational planning killed in his purges of 1937–8. German military thinkers happened to have been working on similar ideas. The German armed forces went on to demonstrate the value of effective operational planning by crushing Poland in 1939, France in 1940, and, initially, the Soviet Union's own forces in 1941. Although Soviet commanders rediscovered operational planning as World War Two went on, later generations of strategic thinkers have tended to associate key operational concepts with German commanders and to refer to them using German words.

Since modern methods of war rely so heavily on adapting to local circumstances, operational success indeed depends more on art than science. The German armed forces of 1939–40 distinguished themselves for their success at encouraging commanders of smaller units the freedom to practise this art while maximising the chance that they would do so in ways that suited higher-level commanders' plans. Military thinkers commonly refer to this combination of low-level initiative and high-level direction using the German word *auftragstaktik*. English-speaking writers often translate *auftragstaktik* as 'mission-type orders'. A mission-type order explains what high-level commanders intend to achieve in general terms but leaves lower-ranking officers free to work out the best methods for making those intentions a reality.

The actual German commanders of World War Two did not use the term *auftragstaktik*, and their procedures for writing orders were not substantially different from the procedures in other armies.[17] Germany's success at fostering and exploiting low-level initiative appears to have had more to do with the attitudes that prevailed throughout the German armed forces than with any particular technique. German military culture encouraged boldness and accepted risk. German officers of all ranks practised making decisions as a routine part of training exercises.[18] Not only did these training techniques prepare individuals to make similar decisions on the battlefield, but it also gave commanders at all levels experience working together, helping all of them to understand how to interpret one another's messages and how to support one another's activities.

Other methods of improving performance at the operational level of war are easier to define. Although it is difficult and frequently unwise for senior officers to dictate what small units do in combat, high-level commanders still decide where to deploy their troops before battle. Commanders also decide when and how to send those troops towards the enemy. If commanders make these decisions effectively, they can maximise the chances that their units will be in useful places at useful times.

The basic principles of positioning troops at the operational level resemble the basic principles of positioning troops at the tactical level. For instance, a small-unit commander may send a point soldier ahead of their other troops to reduce the chances that the entire group will stumble into an ambush together. An operational-level commander will normally send reconnaissance units ahead of his main combat forces, for much the same reason. Commanders at all levels will try to ensure that the point units have enough firepower to overcome modest opposition on their own, so that their main forces will not have to waste time spreading out for combat unless absolutely necessary.

Commanders at all levels are wise to position their troops so that they can move and shoot in as many directions as possible. Commanders at all levels must try to keep their troops close enough together to come to each other's aid – while keeping them far enough apart to minimise the number that the enemy can catch in the blast radius of various area-effect weapons. Commanders at all levels must try to keep some of their forces temporarily out of combat as a reserve, so that those forces will be free to take advantage of opportunities that emerge during the battle – or, perhaps, to rescue friendly units that fall into trouble. Operational-level commanders will need to take similar issues into account as they allocate supplies, organise their communications networks, and decide where to position special types of weapons such as tanks and artillery.

One purpose of operational-level planning is to help small units fight their own small battles. Most small units will have similar needs – plentiful ammunition, for instance, and protection from enemy troops that may be attempting to get around them to attack them from behind. For this reason, one can reduce a great deal of the process of deploying forces at the operational level to routine procedures. Once, for instance, planners have worked out effective formations for positioning their units in common combat situations, they can train their troops to take up those formations as standard practice. Standardised operational procedures make up a considerable portion of most armed forces' military doctrine.

Some armies have chosen to base their operational planning more heavily on doctrine than others have. Soviet forces, for instance, used doctrine extensively. The German army of World War Two, by contrast, was famous for encouraging officers to improvise. Relying on doctrine forces commanders to sacrifice some of their ability to tailor plans to local circumstances, but it saves time, helps troops learn to carry out complex activities under stress, and helps friendly commanders anticipate each other's needs and actions, thus allowing them to cooperate more effectively.

There is, however, more to operational-level planning than providing general support to tactical-level units. As operational-level commanders position their troops and resources, they can concentrate forces in selected areas. This is the point at which operational planning connects with the higher levels of strategy. Just as commanders of small units attempt to find places at which the terrain, the state of the enemy forces, and other factors make it possible for them to carry out their missions, operational-level commanders may attempt to concentrate their forces at places which, due to similar considerations, allow them to make tangible progress towards achieving the larger aims of the war.

Clausewitz referred to the point at which an army focuses its main effort as the *schwerpunkt*. Contemporary military writers have adopted this term for the area on which commanders concentrate their forces in operational planning. Like so many things in warfare, forming a *schwerpunkt* is simple in theory but complicated in practice. The obvious way to concentrate one's forces is to mass the maximum possible number of troops, tanks, artillery pieces, and other military assets in the same place – but this is useful only if all of them can fight effectively together.

As earlier sections of this chapter have stressed, modern weapons make it suicidal for soldiers to cluster together in combat. Even when forces disperse sufficiently to fight on a modern battlefield, excessive numbers of troops operating in congested areas get in each other's way. A *schwerpunkt* can easily become a colossal traffic jam. Moreover, troops fighting in overcrowded areas of operations are at high risk of firing on their own comrades by mistake.

For these reasons, the art of forming an effective *schwerpunkt* relies on effective logistical planning. This art depends particularly heavily on commanders' ability to use roads and other transportation infrastructure efficiently. Nevertheless, even the most skilful logistical planners are likely to encounter limits on the number of troops and vehicles they can bring to bear at any given location. Therefore, commanders must develop ways to combine the combat power of their forces without physically placing all their units in the same area.

Thus, when operational-level commanders wish to maximise their combat power at a particular point, they seldom try to mass all their forces directly opposite the enemy. Instead, they feed their units into the battle in a series of waves (also known as echelons), so that the number of friendly troops attempting to move about the battlefield at any moment remains manageable. This has the added advantage of allowing commanders to direct units in the later waves to the areas of the battlefield where they can do the most good. Late-arriving units may, for instance, reinforce units from earlier echelons, block gaps where opposing forces have broken through or mop up enemy forces that earlier waves left behind.

When operational-level commanders prepare to fight this way, they must normally position the units designated to take part in the various waves one behind the other. Thus, the column of units waiting to join the battle may stretch back for as much as several hundred miles behind the nominal front. Military thinkers refer to the distance from the foremost wave to the one in the back as the depth of the formation. Aircraft, artillery, and other long-range weapons allow both sides to attack units scheduled to take part in the enemy's later waves before they ever have a chance to reach the so-called front line. Troops that smash or sneak their way through enemy's forward defences may attack units in rear echelons as well.

Success at the operational level of warfare often depends on success at winning the so-called deep battle by preserving one's own rearward echelons while disrupting those of the enemy. Soviet military thinkers have traditionally emphasised this concept. When both sides attack the other in depth, the idea that there is a front line where fighting takes place and a relatively safe rear area behind it frequently loses all relationship with reality. This is why contemporary military thinkers often refer to the area in which fighting takes place as a geographically broad 'battlespace' and to the band along which the foremost opposing echelons meet, not as a sharply defined 'front' but as the 'main line of resistance' or as the 'forward edge of the battle area'.

Depth is only one way to achieve a greater concentration of force. Not only may commanders concentrate their forces' efforts in space; they may also concentrate their forces' efforts in time. In other words, they may order units to attack the enemy in many places at once. Moreover, as armies field an increasing variety of long-range weapons, commanders increase in their ability to keep their units physically dispersed while having all of them shoot at the same selected targets, thus achieving concentration of fire. Operational-level commanders may also try to maximise the strength of their forces in the *schwerpunkt* through such methods as deceiving the enemy to gain surprise, striking too rapidly for the enemy to respond, targeting the enemy's weaker units, taking advantage of terrain, assigning their most brilliant tactical commanders to the most important missions, or any other means of gaining the upper hand.

Not only may commanders wish to concentrate combat power in the broad sense; they may also wish to concentrate specific types of forces. One of the best-known reasons why the German forces won such spectacular victories in the early years of World War Two is that they had the wisdom to keep their tanks together in dedicated Panzer (armoured) divisions, rather than spreading them out among the infantry. This made it possible for the tanks to attack in sufficient numbers to break through the enemy lines. Once they were through, they could take advantage of their speed to advance rapidly in behind the enemy, rather than waiting for soldiers on foot.

As one considers the variety of ways that commanders may concentrate combat power, one sees that the concept of a *schwerpunkt* can mean dramatically different things in different situations. Therefore, the concept is useful only for those who are prepared to apply it flexibly.

Moreover, commanders must take care to form their *schwerpunkts* in such a way that they can respond to the changing circumstances of war. At a minimum, commanders will wish to position their units so that the *schwerpunkt* can advance or withdraw in more than one direction.

Commanders will not be able to use any of the methods for forming a *schwerpunkt* unless they have trained, organised, and equipped their troops to perform them. To concentrate forces at the operational level of warfare, one must prepare extensively and act spontaneously – both. All too often, these demands prove incompatible. Little wonder that even the most famous commanders working within the most vaunted armies have so often failed to reconcile them. For all their victories of 1939–41, the Germans lost World War Two.

Still, for all its intangibles, the art of concentrating forces at the operational level of planning remains basic to the problem of achieving meaningful results in war. Concentration allows one to gain numerical superiority at critical times and places. A relatively small force that can use all of its strength in a single engagement is more powerful than a larger force that is too dispersed to bring its resources to bear. Moreover, by massing sufficient force to overcome the enemy at well-selected points, one gains the ability to injure the enemy in especially significant ways.

To begin with, concentrating one's forces maximises one's ability to drive deep into the enemy's system of defences. Generally, the deeper one manages to penetrate, the more seriously one can disrupt the enemy's ability to fight. One reason is that one practically always kills enemy soldiers and destroys enemy equipment in the process. The harder the enemy tries to resist, the more damage one will have the opportunity to inflict – and therefore it is often worth attacking otherwise unimportant territory simply because the enemy may try to defend it.

The farther ones' forces penetrate, the more they can interfere with the enemy's transportation and communications networks. Forces that manage to penetrate their opponents' defences can also strike airfields, headquarters, artillery positions, logistical depots, and other vulnerable enemy assets. Additionally, breaking through the enemy's defences is a particularly effective way of shocking, confusing, and disheartening the enemy's troops. Moreover, when one breaks through enemy forces in any location, the enemy units on either side must either retreat or take the risk that the breakthrough forces will turn to attack them from the flanks or the rear.

Victims of flank attacks and rear attacks commonly find themselves at a tactical disadvantage, particularly if they are simultaneously trying to engage enemies in front of them. Seldom is it possible for troops to position themselves so that they can fight at full effectiveness in all directions. (There are partial exceptions to this principle: airborne troops, for instance, must prepare to confront opponents on all sides when they parachute into the middle of an enemy position, and commanders who expect to be surrounded may form their units into 'hedgehogs' with soldiers in a ring facing outward.) Furthermore, troops who fear that they may be surrounded are particularly vulnerable to panic.

Since flank attacks and rear attacks are frequently more effective, operational-level commanders try to move their forces into positions from which they can carry them out. If that is impossible, operational commanders are still wise to move their forces to block or avoid flanking attacks by the enemy. This process may be as simple as locating one's *schwerpunkt* in an area where the terrain and the disposition of the enemy forces allow friendly troops to follow up a breakthrough by turning to 'roll up' opposing forces on one side or the other. Attackers may be able to inflict even greater damage by going through or around their opponents' defences in two places so as to surround the enemy troops in the middle.

Here, once again, mid-level war planning resembles tactics. Just as low-level commanders try to win small battles by moving their sections and platoons into positions that afford them better cover or a better shot at the enemy, mid-level commanders may try to put significant portions of their armies in advantageous positions through a process of operational manoeuvre. The two practices have so many things in common that it is worth noting the issues that make manoeuvre at the operational level special.

For starters, although armies may manoeuvre at the operational level, combat is – by definition – tactical. As earlier sections have noted, combat at the tactical level involves a complex mix of variably sized – and often small – units fighting variably sized – and often small – battles. The fact that a division of perhaps eight thousand troops has managed to attack an enemy division from the rear through a successful operational-level manoeuvre does not guarantee that its troops will be able to shoot their opponents in the back! In fact, many of those troops may learn that whatever cunning feats their commanders have accomplished at the operational level, the enemy soldiers they happen to be fighting have found tactical-level ways to outmanoeuvre them. Mid-level commanders must accept that their ability to influence these engagements will be limited at best. For this reason, operational-level manoeuvres must be exceptionally simple and exceptionally flexible. One of the few – and most important – things that mid-level commanders can do to influence the outcome of operational manoeuvres is to gather sufficient reserves to follow up tactical-level successes (or defeats) with further operations.

Another distinctive feature of operational manoeuvre is its scale. Modern industrial economies make it possible for even medium-size military powers to wage war over thousands of square miles using hundreds of thousands of troops. Earlier sections have noted that the problem of concentrating such an army is mainly one of logistics. The logistical challenges of shifting major portions of such armies about in search of a superior position are even more significant.

Here, operational planning intersects with strategy, grand strategy, and high politics. To supply ambitious operational manoeuvres, military commanders may need more fuel, motor vehicles, amphibious landing craft, and other material than their countries can easily provide. Either the operational commanders must modify their plans or the nation's political leadership must find a way to make sufficient resources available. If political leaders and operational commanders cannot work together effectively, the manoeuvres are likely to end in disaster.

Moreover, the space required for operational manoeuvres may be larger than the countries involved in the war. This may make the manoeuvres particularly effective – it may, for instance, allow attackers to overrun entire enemy states – but it may also mean that commanders are unable to put their plans into effect without violating the territory of neutral countries. This clearly has profound political implications. In a similar vein, small states may find that they cannot defend themselves without cooperation with their neighbours – and without accepting that they may lose most or all of their own territory, at least temporarily.

Operational manoeuvres make for dramatic chapters in history books, but wise commanders take care to be realistic about what such movements can accomplish. Situations in which armies can conquer entire countries merely by staging an offensive operation do arise, but they are rare. The rest of the time, it is less clear what operational manoeuvres can accomplish. Although troops that manage to attack the enemy from the flank or the rear can cause heavy casualties, this is not always the most promising way to inflict attrition on the enemy.

Enemy troops may, in fact, resist flank attacks and rear attacks as vigorously as they resist attacks from the front. Worse, troops that manoeuvre too rashly to get around the enemy flanks expose themselves to situations in which their enemies can do the same to them. Moreover, troops that manoeuvre without regard for the political consequences risk drawing new opponents into the war. Even when manoeuvres succeed, they may be too costly in terms of time and resources to justify the investment. One can often inflict attrition at lower cost and lower risk merely by concentrating one's forces and methodically pushing them forward.

Manoeuvre advocates would respond that there can also be many other ways to cripple opposing forces, if one is bold and perceptive enough to take advantage of them. Even if one cannot overrun the enemy country in its entirety, one may be able to manoeuvre for control of important bridges, road junctions, industrial regions, or other strategically useful objectives. One may be able to overwhelm one's enemies psychologically by the speed, audacity, and perhaps savagery of one's actions. One may be able to undermine enemy morale or influence enemy leaders by carrying out operations that have some sort of symbolic significance. In many countries, for instance, people are likely to perceive losing their national capital as a serious defeat, even if the city is unimportant in purely military terms. Military thinkers of the early twenty-first century encouraged commanders to seek ways of influencing enemy morale and decision-making in writings on so-called effects-based operations (EBO).

Carl von Clausewitz entertained the possibility that one might be able to achieve strategic war aims through some such master stroke in a chapter titled 'The Key to the Country' and later throughout his work in various passages on the concept he termed 'centre of gravity'.[19] Although Clausewitz believed that there were circumstances in which commanders might be able to achieve results by striking at vital points, he also warned readers that these circumstances were rare. 'The real key to the enemy's country is usually his army'.[20] The process of overcoming enemy armies remains slow, risky, and cruel.

Conclusion

Few of the problems in modern land warfare are new, and few of the solutions are completely new either. Entrenched defenders were almost impossible to overcome in the early years of World War One, but walled cities were almost impregnable in ancient Greece. British commanders at Cambrai achieved success by combining tanks with other types of forces, but Alexander the Great won victories by combining phalanxes of spear-wilding soldiers with cavalry. Books Three to Eight of Carl von Clausewitz's *On War* deal extensively with the issues that twentieth-century theorists encountered as they sought methods to use forces effectively at the operational level of warfare. British forces developed effective fire and movement tactics for use against the Boers in the war of 1899–1902.[21] The evolution of land warfare over the past two centuries also reminds us of more general truths about warfare, such as von Moltke the Elder's warning that no plan survives first contact with the main body of the enemy forces.

The story of modern tactics and operations is largely a story of how age-old principles of war manifest themselves under contemporary conditions. As a strategist, one must understand this story to assess what one might be able to do with one's own forces, what one might expect of one's opponents, and, if one is unhappy with what one finds, what steps one might take to rectify the situation. Sun Tzu suggests that such 'estimates' are the foundations of strategy.[22] When one reflects that during the Cold War, national leaders had to assess their armies' chances of winning a land battle for Europe to decide when it might become necessary to launch an all-out nuclear war, one sees how fateful such 'estimates' can be.

Since World War Two, military thinkers have repeatedly announced that technology was making so-called conventional land warfare obsolete. During the 1950s, for instance, both US and Soviet military manuals downplayed the concept of operational art.[23] Military planners in both countries assumed that future wars would begin with widespread exchanges of nuclear weapons. The side that prevailed in such a nuclear exchange would win the war without needing to stage a protracted land campaign, and the mass armies necessary to carry out land campaigns would not survive long enough to fight.

By the 1960s, however, Western and Communist strategic thinkers alike had concluded that it would be preferable – for reasons that should be obvious – to accomplish their strategic aims without nuclear war. Strategists also realised that unless they maintained the ability to fight in other ways, they might lose this option. Not only would that increase the chances of nuclear war, but it would also sabotage their respective countries' ability to influence political events through military threats, since opponents would know that their leaders would be reluctant to use force in any but the most extreme circumstances. For this reason, strategists on both sides of the Iron Curtain became interested in land warfare again. This, in turn, led them to rediscover operational art.

Meanwhile, improvements in electronics have made it possible to build increasingly accurate missiles, guided bombs, artillery shells, and other ordinance. Since smaller rounds that achieve direct hits can destroy enemy military assets as surely as more powerful but less accurate armaments, so-called precision-guided munitions (PGMs) have the potential to inflict nuclear levels of disruption on opposing forces' war-making potential while avoiding the fallout – both literal and figurative – associated with WMDs. In a war in which both sides used large numbers of PGMs, victory would presumably go to the side that managed to aim its weapons most effectively. Offensive power would come from successful targeting; defensive power would come from successful concealment; and although both swift victories and defensive stalemates would remain possible, the techniques of using and thwarting the new technology would displace the tactics of twentieth-century combined-arms warfare.

Chapter 4 provides more detail on the possibility that PGMs may contribute to a so-called revolution in military affairs. However, large-scale clashes between PGM-armed opponents remain hypothetical. Only the United States has invested in a substantial PGM arsenal.[24] Military author Barry Watts explores the implications of this, noting that although Russia and the PRC are developing highly accurate weapons, global trends in PGM procurement point towards a world in which the US's rivals try to threaten Washington's ability to move forces into their region of the world rather than trying to match the full range of US capabilities.[25]

The existence of highly accurate ordinance will affect the course of any future wars among these powers. The United States' PGMs would currently give it a significant advantage in any conflict. Nevertheless, until one of these countries radically changes its defence procurement policies, one cannot foresee a point when any two potential opponents will have enough precision weapons to render more traditional forces obsolete. This could change eventually, but by that time, other political and technological developments may have transformed the strategic environment yet again, forcing military thinkers to reassess both PGMs and traditional forces.

US Marine colonel Thomas Hammes, for instance, imagines a day when opposing forces will be able to engulf each other with swarms of cheap pilotless aircraft.[26] If these robot swarms perform as effectively as he predicts, they will neutralise traditional land forces in much the same way as PGMs, but less expensively and with less need for support from intelligence and command-control systems.[27] Hammes predicts that this will lead to wars of attrition analogous to World War One–era trench warfare, as opponents attempt to wear each other down by launching drones in the greatest possible numbers.[28] Whether or not Hammes's prediction comes true, it illustrates the point that by the time PGMs achieve their revolutionary potential, something even more disruptive may come along.

Meanwhile, late-twentieth-century strategists have debated the degree to which insurgency, guerrilla warfare, asymmetric warfare, low intensity conflict, and other variants of irregular warfare might serve as an alternative to so-called conventional land warfare. The fact that guerrillas who seem to lack the numbers, training, and equipment for conventional war have so often embarrassed the armies of powerful states appears to support this idea. Chapters 8 and 9 discuss irregular warfare in detail. For the purposes of this chapter, upon examination, irregular warfare consistently proves to have more in common with conventional war than many assume.

One of the main reasons why US forces found it so difficult to fight their Communist opponents in Vietnam, for instance, is that the Communists could combine guerrilla raids with extended operations in which thousands of troops attacked using an increasingly complete range of modern weapons systems, notably tanks and heavy artillery. Meanwhile, throughout its history, the Soviet Union faced continual uprisings by ethnic and political factions. The Soviet government found it expedient and useful to suppress these asymmetric enemies by maintaining an internal army of between 500,000 and 750,000 troops, again equipped with armour, artillery, combat aircraft, and the other instruments of contemporary combined-arms warfare.[29] Weapons function the same way in irregular warfare as they do in the regular kind. The side whose commanders succeed in sending their troops into battle equipped to use modern weapons most effectively is likely to win. The tactical and operational concepts that emerged from the world wars of the twentieth century remain the most straightforward guides to doing so.

This leaves open the question of whether there might be political circumstances in which actual combat plays a secondary role in determining the victor. One might, for instance, ask whether it has become possible to defeat Western liberal democracies by influencing their citizens through the news media. One might also wonder whether, just as modern firearms forced strategists to rethink their methods of waging land war in the twentieth century, other emerging technology might have a similar effect in the twenty first.

Key points

1   Modern weapons are so lethal that ground troops must adopt complex tactics to survive.
2   Those who wish to use ground troops to achieve strategic goals must ensure that their plans allow friendly soldiers to use those tactics effectively.
3   The tactics of modern land warfare feature small-unit manoeuvre, extensive use of fire and movement, and coordinated action by troops equipped with a wide variety of weapons systems (combined arms).
4   Since these tactics require small units to act semi-independently, they actually complicate the problem of higher-level commanders trying to achieve larger strategic goals.
5   Therefore, military thinkers have had to give renewed thought to the middle, or operational, level of war planning, which links tactics with strategy.
6   Effective operational planning requires preparing troops to implement their commanders' overall goals while responding flexibly to local circumstances, deploying troops so that they can bring the maximum possible force to bear at the place where it is likely to prove most effective and, perhaps, use large-scale manoeuvres.

Questions

1   What makes it useful to distinguish between operational planning and strategy?
2   How often can one win wars by striking at some sort of enemy 'centre of gravity'?
3   What forces would you want in order to block an enemy armoured offensive in a desert?
4   How differently would you answer question 3 if the offensive took place in a settled area?
5   To what degree can firepower compensate for inferior numbers of troops in contemporary war?

Notes

1   Joseph Wylie, *Military Strategy: A General Theory of Power Control* (Annapolis, Naval Institute Press, 1967), p. 72.
2   Paddy Griffith, *Battle Tactics of the Western Front: The British Army's Art of Attack, 1916–18* (New Haven, Yale University Press, 1994), p. 38.
3   Ibid., p. 115.
4   Stephen Biddle, 'The Past as Prologue: Assessing Theories of Future Warfare', *Security Studies* 8:1 (Autumn 1998), p. 15.
5   Griffith, *Battle Tactics*, p. 77.
6   Ibid., p. 78.
7   Ibid., p. 96.

8 Ibid., p. 95.

9 19. Jurgen Forster, 'Evolution and Development of German Doctrine 1914–45', in John Gooch (ed.), *The Origins of Contemporary Doctrine* (Camberley, Strategic and Combat Studies Institute, 1997), p. 19.

10 Griffith, *Battle Tactics*, p. 21.

11 Ibid., p. 79.

12 Ibid., p. 163.

13 Ibid., p. 164.

14 Heinz Guderian, *Achtung-Panzer: The Development of Tank Warfare*, trans. Christopher Duffy (London, Cassell, 1992), p. 11.

15 Ibid., pp. 178–88.

16 John English, 'The Operational Art: Developments in the Theories of War', in B.J.C. McKercher and Michael Hennessy (eds.), *The Operational Art: Developments in the Theories of War* (Westport, Greenwood, 1996), p. 13.

17 Franz Uhle-Wettler, '*Aufragstaktik*: Mission Orders and the German Experience', in Richard D. Hooker, Jr. (ed.), *Maneuver Warfare: An Anthology* (Novato, Presidio, 1993), pp. 238–9.

18 Ibid., p. 242.

19 Carl von Clausewitz, *On War*, trans. Michael Howard and Peter Paret (Princeton, Princeton University Press, 1976), pp. 456–9, 485–7.

20 Ibid., p. 458.

21 Griffith, *Battle Tactics*, p. 49.

22 Sun Tzu (Tao Hanzhang, commentator, Yuan Shibing, trans.), *Sun Tzu's Art of War: The Modern Chinese Interpretation* (New York, Sterling, 1987), pp. 94–6.

23 John Erickson, 'The Development of Soviet Military Doctrine', in John Gooch (ed.), *The Origins of Contemporary Doctrine* (Camberley, Strategic and Combat Studies Institute, 1997), p. 136.

24 Barry Watts, *The Evolution of Precision Strike* (Washington, DC, Center for Strategic and Budgetary Assessments, 2013), pp. 1–2, http://csbaonline.org/uploads/documents/Evolution-of-Precision-Strike-final-v15.pdf (accessed April 21, 2017).

25 Ibid., pp. 27, 31–2.

26 Thomas X. Hammes, 'Cheap Technology Will Challenge U.S. Tactical Dominance', *Joint Force Quarterly*, No. 81 (2nd Quarter 2016), pp. 76–85, http://ndupress.ndu.edu/Portals/68/Documents/jfq/jfq-81/jfq-81_76-85_Hammes.pdf (accessed April 21, 2016).

27 Ibid., pp. 76–85.

28 Ibid., p. 80.

29 Peter Deriabin and T.H. Bagley, *The KGB: Masters of the Soviet Union* (New York, Hippocrene Books, 1990), p. 25.

Further reading

Fuller, J.F.C., *Machine Warfare: An Enquiry into the Influences of Mechanics on the Art of War*, (London: Hutchinson and Co. Ltd., 1942).

Griffith, Paddy, *Battle Tactics of the Western Front: The British Army's Art of Attack, 1916–18*, (New Haven: Yale University Press, 1994).

Guderian, Heinz, *Achtung-Panzer: The Development of Tank Warfare*, trans. By Christopher Duffy, (London: Cassell, 1992).

McKercher, B.J.C. and Michael A. Hennessy (eds.), *The Operational Art: Developments in the Theories of War*, (Westport: Greenwood, 1996).

Hooker, Richard D. Jr. (ed.), *Maneuver Warfare: An Anthology*, (Novato: Presidio, 1993). http://ndupress.ndu.edu/Media/News/News-Article-View/Article/702039/cheap-technology-will-challenge-us-tactical-dominance/-Hammes says swarms return us to WWI

Sea power 8

Reader's guide

Defining sea power and the maritime environment; command or control of the sea; using sea power for strategic effect; maritime power versus continental power; contemporary sea power issues; the rise of peer competitors; good order at sea; technological developments (networks, unmanned systems, the littoral threat environment).

Introduction

As with so many other subjects in strategic studies, discussions on strategy at or from the sea are somewhat clouded by problems of definition. The three main terms as contenders for this form of strategic power are 'maritime', 'naval', and 'sea'. The subject is further complicated by the fact that, individually, these terms may mean substantially different things to different people. Essentially, the problem of definition comes down to scope. What capabilities, resources, and activities should be included in an analysis of strategy at or from the sea? The terms 'naval' and 'maritime' are perhaps the easiest to distinguish. It is generally accepted that the former refers to military capabilities. This includes platforms such as ships, aircraft, and submarines, as well as the people and infrastructure on which they rely. In contrast, maritime is a far more encompassing term, including as it does 'the full range of mankind's relationship to the seas and oceans'.[1] In addition to military assets, maritime includes such activities as merchant shipping and insurance. It also covers assets from the other geographical environments that may influence actions at sea, such as land-based airpower. The difficulties of definition really begin when one considers sea power. For Geoffrey Till, sea power is synonymous with the broad definition of maritime power.[2] In contrast, Eric Grove prefers to limit his discussion of sea power to military matters.[3] This chapter will adopt the latter, more-restrictive approach and thereby use the term 'sea power' to discuss the use of military power at or from the sea for the attainment of policy objectives.

While it is undoubtedly the case that non-military maritime assets play a role in power exercised at or from the sea, in strategic terms, this role is limited. For example, as a mode of transport, merchant shipping may play an important role in periods of peace and of war. Nonetheless, in relation to the projection of military power for policy effect, they are secondary to dedicated military capabilities. And when merchant shipping is used in wartime for the transportation of troops and material, it could be argued that they have effectively become military in character anyway. By restricting our definition of 'sea power' to military capabilities and activities, we avoid the problem of defining 'sea power' so broadly that it ceases to have a strong profile in strategic terms. Finally, when considering the relationship between mercantile and military assets, as Grove notes, the traditional idea that naval power is built on a strong merchant fleet is no longer valid.[4]

Even within the narrower definition, sea power remains a very flexible instrument of strategy. This chapter will discuss the many strategic options open to those who possess a form of sea power, as well as how to offset the sea power of others. As the air environment shapes the strengths and limitations of air power, so it is with sea power. Thus, the first task of this chapter is to outline the characteristics of the maritime environment.[5] Having outlined the environment and the characteristics of sea power (with the aid of important theorists), this work will address the most important questions in the discipline. In the first instance, we must address the issue of sea power's relative significance in the outcome of strategy. There is a school of thought that argues that states with a strong sea power dimension have an advantage over their continental enemies, in major conflicts.[6]

The second main area of discussion relates to modern sea power, in particular how it will develop in the near future. Through concepts such as network-centric warfare (NCW) and the works of people such as Admiral William Owens, sea power has been at the forefront of the RMA debate.[7] And although air power has led the drive for unmanned systems, crewless ships are beginning to emerge. In early 2019, the U.S. Navy's Sea Hunter unmanned surface vessel (USV), designed as an anti-submarine and electronic warfare platform, completed its first voyage between San Diego and Pearl Harbor.[8] One of the main advantages of unmanned vessels is their unit and running costs. Sea Hunter costs approximately $20,000/day to operate, compared to $700,000 for a crewed destroyer.[9] In the submarine environment, there is the Remus drone, which autonomously clears mines and provides ISR at the cost of $400,000 per unit.[10] With unmanned systems, cheaper unit costs enable mass and swarming. Of course, the development of future naval capabilities will be influenced not only by technological possibilities but also by mission requirements. Thus, the future maritime security environment must be understood. In this respect, piracy, counternarcotics, an increasingly hostile littoral environment, and the rise of potential peer competitors to the United States (i.e. China) currently occupy the minds of sea power theorists and practitioners.

The maritime environment

When discussing the maritime environment, a number of well-worn, but important, facts and figures enable us to understand both the significance of sea power and its inherent characteristics. The landmasses of the world are connected by a continuous ocean that covers

70% of the globe's surface. Unlike the land and air environments, which are dissected (to a greater or lesser degree) by political boundaries, the open sea is legally available to all. This gives the sea the attributes of a global highway for the transportation of civil and military vessels. Indeed, sea transportation dominates global trade, accounting for over 90% by weight and volume.[11] This reliance on the sea has significantly shaped the development of human societies. The majority of the world's great cities lie within 200 kilometres of a coastline. And as Till reminds us, the interaction of sea-based communities has had a significant impact on the exchange of cultures and ideas (including technology), in addition to promoting a rise in the global economy.[12]

Although the sea may appear to be rather empty and featureless, this is far from the truth. The world's oceans contain vast food and mineral resources. Of humanity's daily protein intake, 20% originates from the sea. In terms of mineral extraction, oil and gas deposits at sea have become increasingly economically viable and significant.[13] In terms of physical features, human usage of the sea is affected by a number of factors. This includes weather and its impact on sea conditions, varying sea depths, currents, and the influence of land masses. Coastlines (and how humans use them) can have a significant impact on sea power. The formation of harbours, inland seas, and the existence of choke points all shape sea power to a greater or lesser extent, depending on the context. In addition, humankind has the ability to shape the geographic context of sea power in rather dramatic ways. The building of the Suez and Panama Canals are extreme examples of how humankind can shape the maritime environment to our advantage. Also, technological developments have significantly altered how humankind is able to use the sea. Self-powered vessels (those not reliant on the wind) have given navies greater flexibility by breaking their dependence on prevailing winds. In addition, the development of submarines has enabled humankind to explore and use the submarine environment.

The characteristics of sea power

Box 8.1 The characteristics of sea power

Platform-centric.
Versatility.
Global access.
Manoeuvrability.
Poise.

The nature of the maritime environment endows sea power with some significant characteristics in the practice of strategy. First, and most obviously due to the inhospitable nature of the environment, sea power is platform-centric. This creates both advantages and disadvantages for those exercising sea power. Like most platform-centric forms of strategic power, sea power is relatively expensive. The platforms are costly, both to procure and operate. Such costs ensure that even the greatest navies have relatively few warships. The U.S. Navy, which is not surprisingly the largest in the world, has less than three hundred warships (including submarines). The Royal Navy has approximately 70 hulls. With such small numbers, warships tend to be highly prized assets, the loss of which is keenly felt. As the experience of the Royal Navy during the Falklands War indicates (almost), or indeed the Japanese experience in the Pacific War, losses can quickly accumulate to the point at which an effective maritime campaign becomes unsustainable. There is, however, a significant advantage to relying on large platforms; they tend to be fairly versatile. A warship is able to perform a number of different functions and roles. Among other things, it can house various forms of air power, engage in attacks against other ships or against the shore, act as an intelligence platform, move large numbers of people and supplies (both military and civilian), and provide substantial mobile medical and disaster-relief facilities.

The appearance of unmanned vessels, such as Sea Hunter, may lead to an increase in smaller but more numerous units. It is too early in the unmanned era to accurately predict the impact of unmanned systems on naval warfare. A reasonable guess, but only that, is to envision a hybrid force composed of large crewed mothership platforms that deploy swarms of smaller unmanned units. Such a hybrid approach would retain the benefits of versatile large platforms while gaining the advantages wrought by swarms of the small and many.

As a consequence of the world ocean, naval forces have the advantage (all things being equal) of global mobility and access. While historically certain landlocked areas have been beyond the reach of sea power, this is increasingly less the case in the modern environment. Sea power's successful adoption of air power ensures that there is nowhere on the surface of the Earth beyond the reach of naval forces. This is, of course, also true of air power. However, the limited lift capacity of air platforms limits what can be done at great distance. This is less an issue for sea-based air assets, because being based just offshore, they can operate with higher sortie rates.

As a direct result of operating in an essentially continuous ocean, sea power has great manoeuvrability. Within the confines of the physical features of the sea (including the shoreline) and enemy actions (e.g. the creation of a hostile littoral environment), naval forces can choose their axis of advance. This provides a number of advantages. As witnessed on D-Day, the enemy may be unsure of where an amphibious assault will occur, and thereby have to spread their defensive forces more thinly. A maritime force can completely outflank the enemy, as occurred successfully at Inchon during the Korean War. A maritime force can also engage and disengage more easily than land power can.

A crucial characteristic of sea power is poise. Partly due to the legal neutrality of the high seas and partly due to a ship's relative ability for self-sustenance, naval forces can stay on station for extended periods of time without having to commit themselves to action. In this manner, a naval force is able to exert leverage for long periods, without the political and military ramifications of violating someone else's territory or air space. The deployment of land forces along a border or into an ally's country, or even just their use in military exercises, can have a similar effect. Nonetheless, it is generally true that the deployment of land forces tends to be regarded as more threatening and/or more of a commitment. In this sense, sea power is a more flexible instrument for policymakers. By deploying naval forces, policymakers may be able to exert influence while retaining more finely tuned control over the military and political situation. Also, a modern warship, especially if it has air capability, brings with it considerable fire power for coercive purposes. Alternatively, its lift capacity may be vital if called upon (either to deliver supplies or evacuate nationals from a hostile area).

Command or control of the sea

An important prerequisite for taking full advantage of the aforementioned characteristics of sea power is to gain some form of command or control of the sea. Again, this is an area of the subject that suffers somewhat from problems of definition. As indicated in the title of this section, the issue of definition centres on two terms: 'command of the sea' and 'sea control'. The former, which is strongly associated with the American naval theorist Mahan, is often taken to denote a circumstance in which one protagonist has the ability to use the sea for their purposes while denying the same to the enemy.[14] In contrast, sea control normally refers to a less absolute imbalance in the strategic situation. As Admiral Stansfield Turner notes, sea control depicts a situation in which command of the sea environment is limited in both time and space.[15] The latter should not be taken necessarily as a watered-down, less-effective form of command. For most operations, command is required only in a certain area for a certain period of time – this is, arguably, a more efficient use of resources. In contrast, a force attempting to achieve total command of the sea may dedicate so many resources to the task that subsequent exploitation of said command may be impossible. At this juncture, note that command or control of the sea is not an end in itself. Rather, command establishes a situation in which the maritime environment can be exploited for strategic effect. Command, therefore, is required to enable sea-based operations without fear of significant interference from the enemy.

The level of sea control that can be established will be heavily dependent on one's ability to deal with enemy naval forces. When attempting to establish sea control, the enemy's naval forces may not be the only problem. As the Falklands War illustrates, the enemy may be able to interfere with one's operations by using land-based air assets. In the Falklands, the main task for the Royal Navy was to put ground forces ashore and then provide them with support. Although this was eventually achieved, the operation was less effective and more costly than planned. During the conflict, the Argentinian air force destroyed seven British ships, including two destroyers, two frigates, an amphibious craft, and a landing ship. Equally worrying for a force attempting to establish sea control are submarines, mines, and shore batteries.

Sea control can be pursued by a number of means and methods. The method that has attracted most contentious debate is decisive battle. For Mahan, this was the preferred means for achieving command of the sea. While this approach has been criticised for being overly simplistic and one-dimensional, there is merit in it. If the enemy fleet can be brought to battle and destroyed, then command of the sea can be potentially achieved in an afternoon. In addition, an enemy fleet at the bottom of the sea cannot challenge one's sea control for some time to come. A fleet can be rebuilt, but this is both time-consuming and expensive. Finally, and assuming that the victorious fleet is in a reasonable condition, the winning side is able to move directly to exploit the newly won sea control rather than having to expend more time and resources neutralising further enemy threats.

The important point to remember on this issue is that battle is not an end in itself. Rather, it is to be thought of largely as a means to achieve control of the sea. However, battle has other potential benefits. Engagement may be a means to coerce the enemy by inflicting losses and inducing pain. It is reasonable to assume that had the Argentineans sunk a few more British ships during the Falklands, the British may have felt compelled to withdraw due to the increasing costs of the conflict.

Despite the potential advantages to be gained from decisive battle, historically the occurrence of a genuinely decisive engagement is rare. Having identified Trafalgar (1805), Navarino (1827), Tsushima (1905), and Leyte Gulf (1944) as examples, Ian Speller correctly notes that more often than not the enemy fleet is destroyed in a series of encounters.[16] This does not undermine the potential significance of battle; rather, it presents a more realistic interpretation of its role in gaining sea control. Nonetheless, the emphasis on battle should not be underestimated. It is fashionable in modern strategic studies to downplay the role of battle in strategy and to lampoon those theorists who emphasise violent engagement (e.g. Mahan and Clausewitz). As an alternative to battle, some modern commentators proffer complex and/or subtle theories of control. In such visions, the security agenda grows ever wider, and the means become ever subtler. However, in such theories exists the real danger of overegging the pudding. Clausewitz is compelling when he writes that the enemy can change everything with a successful battle. In addition, his proclamation to the advantages of the simple over the complex is hard to ignore.[17]

Nonetheless, it is important to recognise that seeking a decisive battle is fraught with challenges and potential risks. It may be that the enemy cannot be brought to battle. In such a scenario, not only will sea control be unobtainable via battle, but also time and resources (which could have been used elsewhere for strategic effect) would have been wasted in the effort. There is also the real danger that the battle may be lost. As Admiral Jellicoe was aware during the First World War, the results of a lost battle can potentially be catastrophic for a maritime power. Thus, whether or not a decisive battle should be sought is entirely dependent on the context. Certain questions need to be asked when considering decisive battle. Will it achieve or contribute to the attainment of sea control? Can the enemy be brought to battle on favourable terms? How likely is success? Would failure be damaging? Taken together, these questions are asking the same thing: will decisive battle contribute to positive strategic effect?

Beyond battle, a further method for achieving sea control is blockade. In theory, enemy maritime activities (both civil and military) can be prevented via a close blockade of the enemy's ports. Such a blockade can be undertaken by various means, including surface vessels, submarines, and mines. However, close blockade is wearing on both the vessels and people conducting it. Blockade has also become increasingly dangerous as the littoral environment has become more hostile.[18] Thus, the blockading power may have to settle for distant blockade. This, however, brings with it a potential downgrading of the blockade's effectiveness. Some enemy vessels may be able to successfully run the blockade and gain access to the open sea; thereby reducing the totality of sea control. However, a distant blockade may still enable control of the sea in a limited space for a limited period of time. And as noted earlier, that may be enough to achieve one's operational and/or strategic objectives.

In the interactive and dynamic environment of war, the enemy has a role to play in one's quest for sea control. Rather than attempt to gain control of the sea for themselves, weaker maritime powers may opt for a campaign of sea denial: 'Here the objective is not to use the sea oneself, but to prevent the enemy from doing so'.[19] Or, as Hughes describes it, the object of sea denial is to 'deny safe movement'.[20] For a continental power such as Imperial Germany or Nazi Germany, whose wars were to be won and lost on the continent of Europe, attempting to gain command of the sea would have been both unrealistic and unnecessary. However, two of their main enemies, the United Kingdom and the United States, were heavily reliant on maritime communications. Thus, in both world wars, the objective of Germany's U-boat campaigns was to deny use of the sea to their maritime enemies. Sea denial, rather than sea control, was the focus of Germany's sea power operations. Denied use of the sea for substantive strategic effect, the ability of the United States and the United Kingdom to interfere with German control of Europe would have been severely curtailed. Most obviously, D-Day would have been impossible in the absence of sea control. Just as importantly, the Soviet war effort would have been substantially undermined without the sea transportation of vast quantities of equipment.

Sea denial can be achieved by various methods, and with varying degrees of efficacy. A state that has a heavy reliance on seaborne trade and supplies is vulnerable to a guerre de course, in which transportation shipping is attacked, normally by individual vessels or small groups of surface raiders or submarines. The German U-boat campaigns during the First World War and the Second World War are examples of relatively successful sea-denial operations. During the Second World War, German U-boats sank, destroyed, or captured 3476 Allied merchant ships.[21] Such a rate of attrition famously led Winston Churchill to declare the U-boat campaign one of the main threats to Allied victory.[22] As it was, the German guerre de course, although it interfered with Allied control of the sea, did not produce war-winning effects. This was partly due, once again, to the paradoxical logic of strategy. Just as a relatively weaker sea power can offset (to some degree) the level of control of a stronger opponent, so too can the latter offset the effects of a sea-denial campaign. Intelligence, convoys, and air cover all helped to reduce the impact of the U-boat campaigns.

However, to have strategic effect, a sea-denial campaign need not be a total success. The U-boat campaigns, conducted with relatively few vessels, not only reduced the amount of supplies that made the trip across the Atlantic but also tied up Allied resources that could have been used elsewhere. This effect can be seen to a greater degree during the sixteenth-century conflict between England and Spain. Despite the fact that English privateers intercepted only 2% of Spanish treasure crossing the Atlantic from the New World, the threat produced a disproportionate response from Imperial Spain. Again, this diverted both Spanish resources and attention away from other theatres.[23]

Sea denial does not have to be as active or aggressive as a guerre de course. The enemy's maritime operations can be impaired by a fleet in being. An inferior sea power can attempt to avoid enemy forces in order to maintain its fleet, either by remaining in a defendable harbour or by seeking security in the vastness of the ocean. Although not active in an aggressive sense, the mere existence of said fleet is likely to be a concern for the superior sea power. Thus, resources will have to be diverted to maintain a watch on the enemy fleet in being. As noted in relation to guerre de course, these diverted resources could have been used in exploitation of sea control.

Despite its appeal, a largely passive approach to fleet in being does not fully exploit the potential of this method of sea denial. A fleet-in-being campaign can be combined with raiding operations against shipping, coasts, and even port facilities. Not only does this have the advantage of depleting enemy resources via raids; it also increases the need for the enemy to divert substantial resources to deal with a real, as opposed to a potential, threat. It is even possible for a fleet-in-being campaign to morph into an attempt to gain sea control. This was very much the approach advocated by the French naval officer Raoul Castex, who theorised that an inferior fleet could exploit the manoeuvrist characteristics of sea power to manipulate the balance of forces. In Castex's theory, enemy resources could be diverted by raids and guerre de course. With the enemy dispersed, rapid manoeuvre would enable a concentration of force against a section of the enemy fleet. Over time, the balance of forces would begin to favour the initially inferior fleet.[24] Such an approach motivated the German *Kaiserliche Marine* during the First World War, as it sought opportunities to attack small enemy detachments in a process of gradual attrition. Of course, these more active and aggressive forms of fleet in being need to be carefully managed. Undue risk taking, leading to substantial losses, defeats the very purpose of a fleet in being.

Sea denial can be performed by those with few or no naval assets of any significance. Short-range fast attack craft, mines, shore-based batteries, and aircraft can all be used to create a hostile littoral environment and thereby deny control of the sea in a specific locale. Such an idea was developed, but eventually rejected, by the Soviet New School in the 1920s and 1930s.[25] It does not take much imagination to understand how differently D-Day could have ended had the Germans been able to create a more hostile littoral environment.

This discussion indicates that sea denial can have varying degrees of success and scope. A less-than-perfect sea-denial campaign may still achieve its strategic objectives. Depending on the circumstances, it may be enough to divert enemy naval resources, reduce the flow of transportation shipping, or deny free and safe access to a locale for a specific period of time. Taken together, this discussion of sea control and sea denial highlights a number of important points. The quest to gain control of the maritime environment, as with other strategic activities, is a dynamic one. Control cannot be taken for granted. Indeed, it normally requires constant action and vigilance. The intelligent enemy is just as prominent in the maritime environment as elsewhere. In addition to the enemy, context is also critical. How much control or denial is required will be dictated by strategic circumstances. Thus, the maritime commander must be guided not himself purely by doctrinal concepts but also by the specific circumstances in which he find themselves. Any discussion of sea power, whether it relates to the value of battle or a fleet in being, must be grounded in a specific context. That being said, Clausewitz was still persuasive when he wrote that destruction of the enemy's forces is normally the best place to start.[26] Finally, it is important to note that an important balance has to be struck between achieving sea control and exploiting it. As Corbett so clearly argued, command of the sea is nothing in itself. Rather, it has significance only insomuch as it can be exploited to exert leverage ashore.[27]

Exploiting sea control for strategic effect

Box 8.2 The uses of sea power

Raids.
Amphibious assault.
Naval fire support.
Coercion.
Nuclear deterrence.
Blockade.
Guerre de course.
Logistics.
Intelligence.
Humanitarian tasks.
Good order at sea.
Naval diplomacy.

Once some form of sea control has been achieved, there are many options open to the maritime commander, depending on the circumstances and the capabilities at their disposal. In a general sense, the exploitation of control of the sea can be divided into two categories: power projection ashore and transportation.[28] Of course, these are normally complementary, as the former will usually require use of the sea as a highway to transport forces and then sustain them once ashore. The word 'usually' is used as recognition that some forms of sea power projection require little or no transportation before deployment or use. The most obvious example of this would be a submarine-launched ballistic missile (SLBM), such as the current Trident II D-5, which has a range of approximately 4600 miles. With such a range, a Trident SSBN could theoretically project substantive levels of power as soon as it has left harbour (depending on where the target is based).

What forms of strategic power can be projected ashore? Since sea power has a degree of flexibility in axis of advance and place of attack, and also has the potential for rapid disengagement; it is an ideal instrument for *raids*. History is replete with coastal raids, from Drake's success at Cadiz in 1587 to the failure at Dieppe in August 1942. At Cadiz, Drake destroyed approximately 33 Spanish vessels, delaying the planned Spanish invasion of Britain for a year.[29] In contrast, although Dieppe was a tactical failure, with 60% casualties among the troops that landed ashore, many valuable lessons were learned for future amphibious operations, including D-Day.[30] These two examples not only show the range of success and failure that raids can produce but also the varying objectives that raids can serve. Drake's was a spoiling attack on enemy forces, whereas Dieppe was an experiment to test the feasibility of amphibious raids against defended ports. In a general sense, raids gain much of their strategic value from the effects they have on the mind of an opposing commander. The sense of vulnerability over a wide area (e.g. coastline) will likely compel an enemy commander to spread their forces more thinly and/or divert resources into coastal fortifications. In addition, enemy decision-making can be manipulated by the employment of small decoy raids, designed to divert focus from the real event.

Raids are identifiable by their lack of permanence. Forces engaged in a raid will at some point disengage having achieved their objectives (whether that be intelligence gathering or the destruction of a key target). In contrast, large *amphibious assaults*, although they have much in common with raids in the early stages of an operation, normally have much larger objectives. The greater ambition of an amphibious assault can be measured in time, by objectives, and by the forces engaged. Often, amphibious assaults seek to establish a permanent presence ashore and perhaps open up a new front entirely. D-Day and the Inchon landings in Korea both sought to establish new fronts and turn the tides of their respective wars. D-Day is notable not just because of its scale and success but also for the impressive levels of jointery in the face of a well-defended coastline.[31]

Box 8.3 The Inchon landings

In Korea, in September 1950, with United Nations troops barely holding on in the Pusan Perimeter, General Douglas McArthur proposed a risky and controversial amphibious attack on the defended port of Inchon. Despite the challenging geographic and tidal conditions, this bold manoeuvre turned the tide of the Korean War. Within 11 days of the assault, United Nations forces had captured the South Korean capital, Seoul, and cut the supply lines of Northern forces attacking the Pusan Perimeter.

Successfully landing troops ashore and establishing a secure beachhead in the face of a well-prepared enemy is challenging. However, the very nature of maritime power makes success a possibility. Not only, as at D-Day, is the point of attack open to dispute, but also naval forces can bring a range of capabilities to an operation. For example, during the Falklands War, British aircraft carriers were able to provide organic air cover for the amphibious landings. In addition to combat air cover, naval forces can also provide airmobile troops to sow confusion and seize key objectives behind enemy lines. However, even with such capabilities, amphibious assaults are risky affairs. Landing forces are in danger of being pushed back into the sea, and the amphibious ships themselves may be vulnerable to air attacks, submarines, mines, other surface vessels, and coastal batteries. Despite these risks, as the Inchon landings reveal, amphibious assaults can produce outstanding success. The modern form of amphibious assault is codified in the U.S. Marine Corps (USMC) concept of operational manoeuvre from the sea (OMFTS), which combines the traditional idea of amphibious with modern notions of manoeuvre, deep battle, and operational art.[32]

In addition to delivering land power ashore, and often in support of such operations, naval forces can also project power in a direct manner in the form of *naval firepower*. Historically, based as it was on naval artillery (naval gunfire support), naval firepower was largely limited to coastal areas. However, in the modern era, air and missile attack have provided maritime forces with even greater range and capabilities. Such firepower can be used in support of other operations or can be used in isolation. In the former category, naval firepower can play an essential role in preliminary and ongoing bombardments in support of an amphibious operation. By necessity, amphibious forces have limited firepower when operating ashore. Thus, naval forces can provide important support by destroying key enemy capabilities and defences or by limiting enemy resistance by the suppression of enemy forces. However, even with the levels of firepower available to navies, distant firepower can sometimes prove ineffective against well-prepared enemy positions, as the United States found during the Pacific War, when naval gunfire failed to neutralise Japanese bunkers.[33]

In isolation, naval firepower can be used to destroy important targets or to act as an instrument of coercion. In many recent conflicts, including Kosovo and the 1991 and 2003 Iraq wars, naval air and missile attacks have been used in support of coercive bombing campaigns. Indeed, in some circumstances, naval forces may be the only ones available. For the United Kingdom, with its lack of long-range bombers, carrier-borne air power or submarine-launched TLAMs are realistically the only option for global strike missions. Even for the United States, which has a long-range bomber capability, naval firepower could likewise be the only realistic option in certain contexts. Where in-theatre airfields are not available, carriers act as an offshore airbase that can provide high sortie rates and rapid response, something that long-range bombers may not be able to achieve.

Coercion, of course, is also about the threat of latent force. With the ability to loiter offshore in international waters with substantial firepower at hand, naval forces are able to exert coercive effect by their ability to poise or maintain presence in an area for extended periods of time. The deployment of a US carrier battle group may be enough to affect the decision-making of relevant actors. This can be achieved without the need for violence or any breach of sovereignty.

When one thinks of *deterrence*, one's mind immediately turns to nuclear weapons. For those who can afford and acquire such a capability, SLBMs have become a mainstay of nuclear force structures. Nuclear weapon submarines (SSBNs) are well suited to a second-strike role due to a combination of their technical features and the nature of the submarine environment. Taken together, these provide SSBNs with impressive stealth capability. They also complicate notions of sea control. Indeed, an SSBN arguably has control of the sea somewhat built in – at least in terms of being able to use the sea for one's own purposes. It is not impossible to track and target a modern SSBN, but it is certainly challenging. The sea control implications of this are interesting. For example, Country A may have a workable control of the sea on the surface, to the point that it is able to operate while the enemy is not. However, Country B may have an SSBN force that is able to operate with relative impunity in the submarine environment. Thus, assuming that neither the surface fleet or submarine fleet are able or willing to engage with each other, command of the sea can be shared by both countries, albeit operating at different depths.

Ideally, a country with nuclear weapons would have a range of different delivery methods (the nuclear triad). However, if this is not feasible and only one method has to be chosen for a global power, SLBMs are probably the best bet. Due to their relatively secure status and global manoeuvrability, an SSBN force provides a relatively reliable and flexible nuclear capability. This appears to be the thinking behind the United Kingdom's decision to base all of its nuclear weapons in its SSBN force.

Much of the *transportation* role of sea power is obvious and self-explanatory but crucial nonetheless. The movement of troops and the movement of supplies are important maritime tasks that normally require some form of sea control. However, there are tasks in this category that can be performed without needing to establish observable sea control first. For example, the insertion of special forces, either by surface vessel or submarine, may be achieved even in the face of substantive levels of enemy sea control. Similarly, 'sneaking' through an enemy blockade may enable the transportation of key resources, including the safe passage of people. Transportation tasks can also include the extraction of nationals from dangerous environments or indeed the mass evacuation of forces from hostile terrain. The most notable example of the latter was the successful evacuation of over 300,000 British and French troops from the beaches of Dunkirk in May/June 1940. On this occasion, maritime power provided the only route to safety for these troops.

Beyond power projection and transportation, maritime power can perform a range of *Miscellaneous* tasks in support of national policy. There are too many to examine them all in detail, but noteworthy among these roles are humanitarian tasks, good order at sea, and naval diplomacy. Clearly, not all of these roles require sea control in the face of an enemy, although they do require the ability to use the sea. Humanitarian operations, for example, are often undertaken with the support and aid of various countries, with no hint of sea denial. However, as the Bosnian War and US operations in Somalia (1990s) indicate, there are occasions when actors in a region may seek to interfere with humanitarian relief efforts. It is not implausible that future humanitarian efforts with a large maritime contingent may require the establishment and maintenance of sea control. Naval forces are well suited to humanitarian tasks. Among a wide range of roles that they can perform, maritime forces can transport large quantities of aid to affected areas, evacuate large numbers of civilians, and provide floating medical facilities. However, if they are not close to the affected areas, their relatively slow speed of travel may prevent maritime forces from making a crucial difference in the immediate aftermath of a disaster.

The world's oceans contain vast deposits of natural resources and act as essential arteries for global trade. Unsurprisingly, this same global highway is used for nefarious activities as well. As a result, maintaining *good order at sea* is an important task for modern maritime forces. The range of activities performed includes dealing with piracy and counternarcotics (both of which will be discussed in detail later) and protecting shipping in danger from regional conflicts. A significant example of the latter is the naval patrols to protect merchant shipping during the Iran/Iraq War in the 1980s. Indeed, at the time of writing, merchant shipping is once again coming under attack from Iranian forces in the Gulf of Oman. In June 2019, two oil tankers were attacked with limpet mines. The following month, the frigate HMS

Montrose prevented five Iranian attack boats from attacking a British oil tanker in the Strait of Hormuz. This came after Royal Marines had seized an Iranian tanker in breach of EU sanctions forbidding the delivery of oil to Syria.

As the Royal Marines example indicates, good order at sea also includes embargo enforcement. During a conflict, or in response to unacceptable actions and policies, international actors may seek to enforce an embargo against a state or group of states. Often, an important but challenging component of embargo enforcement is monitoring and intercepting shipping. This task is normally complicated by the fact that certain goods (humanitarian aid) are permitted into the target state, but others (weapons) are strictly prohibited. The challenges of this form of operation are well illustrated by the deaths of nine crewmembers on a Turkish aid ship that was intercepted and boarded by Israeli commandos in June 2010. At the time, Israel was enforcing a blockade against Hamas-controlled Gaza to prevent the delivery of weapons. In contrast to humanitarian operations, many of the good-order-at-sea activities have a strong sea control dimension. Counternarcotics, anti-piracy, and embargo enforcement operations are all concerned with controlling the use of the sea to promote 'our' positive uses (legitimate trade and others) and prevent the nefarious activities of 'others'.

Naval diplomacy is yet another subject fraught with definitional problems. The problems stem largely from confused notions about what constitutes war and how we understand and codify military activities short of all-out war. The most common mistake made is to overemphasise the difference between war, coercion, and deterrence. This creates a false dichotomy in which the direct use of force, most particularly warfighting, is disassociated from the threat of force. Such a misunderstanding has the potential to result in a disjointed, non-unified, and incoherent concept of strategy. The end result of this problematic approach is a rather unhelpfully broad concept of naval diplomacy, which encompasses acts of coercion and deterrence as well as intelligence-gathering activities.

Rather than focusing on the difference between war and so-called acts short of war, the theorist and practitioner should instead focus on strategy: the process of converting military force (including the threat of force) into policy effect. With strategy as the focus, all military activities that relate to the fighting potential of forces (including war, general displays of force, coercion, and deterrence) can be considered together along a spectrum. This is in tune with Clausewitz's theory that even when battle does not occur, the outcome is decided on an approximation of what would have occurred had battle taken place.[34]

By correctly reconnecting activities on the basis of the threat of force with the actual use of force (including war), this leaves us with a far narrower, but more credible, notion of naval diplomacy (one that does not include coercion). Thus, naval diplomacy is restricted to such activities as port visits and coalition-building actions. Naval diplomacy can therefore be defined as the use of naval assets to help grease the wheels of diplomacy, but in a manner that does not involve the use or threat of force. Of course, a port visit can fulfil multiple objectives simultaneously. A ship in port can be a demonstration of power, which at some level has a coercive or deterrent effect and which might at the same time be used merely as a venue to foster greater diplomatic ties. In this sense, naval diplomacy is certainly an aspect of grand strategy, but not strategy. Understanding the boundaries of naval diplomacy is important because naval diplomacy activities, as defined here, do not really have a sea control dimension. In contrast, the coercive use of naval force might.

Under this narrower definition, *intelligence* gathering would also not be included under the heading of naval diplomacy. If said intelligence activities were purely in support of military operations, they would come under the rubric of military strategy, as a support function. In contrast, if they were being used for general intelligence gathering, they would be fed into the central intelligence machinery and would therefore be most accurately described as intelligence operations. This conceptual delineation of intelligence tasks is supported by the structure of the intelligence communities in both the United States and the United Kingdom. In both cases, intelligence gathered by military assets can be fed into the central intelligence machinery or, if the intelligence is predominantly military in nature, can be processed within the remit of the Pentagon or Ministry of Defence.

This discussion clearly demonstrates that sea power is a flexible instrument of strategy and is most potent when used to project power and influence ashore. For many naval activities, some form of sea control is required. Most often, the extent of sea control required will be limited in both time and space. However, it has been demonstrated that certain actions, especially those that come under the heading of naval diplomacy and good order at sea, do not always rely on the establishment of sea control. Thus, we can conclude that sea control is still of central importance to sea power, but it is not always strictly necessary.

The leverage of sea power[35]

The utility of sea power has thus been established. But how important is it in the practice of strategy? Does sea power win wars and enable the achievement of policy objectives? These perfectly valid questions almost pose themselves in response to some of the great works of maritime theory. This is most obviously the case in relation to Mahan's *The Influence of Sea Power on History*. This subject also leads us into the interesting, but somewhat abstract, world of geopolitics. The contest between great continental powers and their maritime equivalents is the domain of great struggles in history and broad-brush strokes across maps. As with much in sea power, Mahan is our first port of call. Although Till is quite correct to note that Mahan understood that a nation's power was not based solely on maritime resources, the American theorist did attribute much influence to sea power.[36] For Mahan, maritime trade was the primary basis of a nation's power. As a consequence, control of the oceans (via naval forces) was the primary route to success or failure in world politics.

The notion that sea power has dominance in international politics has been challenged in the modern era (twentieth century) by writers such as the great geopolitical thinker Halford MacKinder, whose theories were later supported by the maritime historian Paul Kennedy. Writing in the early years of the twentieth century, MacKinder theorised that the period of maritime dominance, which he labelled the Columbian Era (c. 1500–1900), was coming to an end. The decline of sea power would be the result of new and developing transportation technology on land. MacKinder theorised that motorised land transport would facilitate a substantial increase in the ability of continental powers to exploit their mineral and industrial resources and hence enhance their power. In effect, one of the defining characteristics of sea power, efficient transportation, was being equalled or overtaken by developments in land power.[37]

MacKinder's position, although influential in some circles, is not universally accepted. In *The Leverage of Sea Power*, Gray argues that the Columbian Era has been indefinitely extended. To support this argument, Gray cites the examples of the Second World War, the Cold War, and to a lesser extent the First World War as proof that sea power is still a powerful enabler of victory in great conflicts. In each of these conflicts, maritime-based alliances were able to gather and exploit their global resources in order to outlast and overawe their continental foes. In such protracted conflicts, maritime-dependent resources could be translated into continental power, which was used to defeat continental foes on their own ground. Crucially, the continental powers were not able to emulate this and defeat their maritime opponents on the oceans. Importantly, though, Gray reminds us that sea power does not produce victory independently, in most cases; rather, it acts as a crucial enabler for the accumulation and expression of dispersed land power.[38]

An important aspect of Gray's explanation for the continued dominance of sea power is its ability to adapt to, and co-opt, new technology. Rather than being replaced by air power, nuclear weapons, or cyber power, sea power has often been at the forefront of integrating these new developments. This can be seen clearly by the development of aircraft carriers – the first of which appeared as early as 1913, when the light cruiser HMS Hermes was converted to launch and recover seaplanes.

The strategic utility of sea power is not just dependent on its ability to enable great conflicts to be won. Corbett reminds us that maritime power also has great utility in limited conflicts.[39] Because sea power is a more controllable, less escalatory instrument of strategy, it may give a policymaker the flexibility that they require while providing enough power to get the job done.

Most importantly, Corbett is noted for his logical claim that sea power must exert leverage ashore to be successful in strategy. This idea sits comfortably with Wylie's oft-quoted pronouncement that strategy is about control, and control is achieved ultimately by the man on the scene with a gun. Although sea power can coerce or deter without help from the other services, it is most potent when used in a joint environment. In the first instance, sea power makes an overall contribution through the medium of global maritime trade, which is instrumental in providing the economic basis for a state's military power. More specifically in support of a joint venture, naval assets can transport ground forces into theatre; sustain them with logistical support; provide firepower and cover with organic air and missile forces; and ultimately extract ground forces when the objectives have been achieved. In this sense, sea power may be the foundation on which a joint campaign is built.

Contemporary and future sea power

Although the logic of war never changes, its grammar is a constantly changing and evolving phenomena.[40] The twenty-first century is already shaping up to be a period of continuing and significant change. From a geostrategic perspective, although the War on Terror and fight against global Islamist insurgency continues, a resurgent Russia, empowered China, and nuclear-armed North Korea are significantly changing the focus of Western defence policy. Planning for large-scale conflict is very much back on the agenda. This is reflected in changes to US maritime strategy documents in recent years. In the 2007 *A Cooperative Strategy for 21st Century Seapower*, although maritime power projection was still given prominence, there was also considerable concentration on soft power, including a particular focus on coalition building, humanitarian operations, and disaster relief. In response, some theorists bemoaned the absence of explicit reference to more aggressive uses of maritime power, such as amphibious assault and strike operations.[41] This has changed significantly in more recent documents, including the 2015 *A Cooperative Strategy for 21st Century Seapower: Forward, Engaged, Ready*; the 2017 *Surface Force Strategy: Return to Sea Control*; and the 2018 *Design for Maintaining Maritime Superiority*.

As the titles of the latter two documents attest to, there has been a shift back to the exercise of hard power to ensure sea control. This reflects a growing realisation of the threat posed by China and Russia, specifically the need to counter increasingly aggressive Chinese behaviour in the South China Sea and the threat from increased anti-access, area denial (A2/AD) capabilities. For example, Russia is investing in advanced anti-ship missiles and its submarine force, while China launched its first indigenous aircraft carrier in 2017 and seeks to project maritime power to control the First and Second Island Chains and beyond into the Far Seas. To counter this, the United States Navy (USN) is investing in all-domain access and littoral operations in a contested environment (LOCE). This means the USN must work even more closely with the USMC and United States Air Force (USAF) on networked-enabled integrated operational concepts such as joint access and maneuverer in the global commons and ship-to-objective manoeuvre (STOM). In traditional terms, the USN is seeking the capability to defeat enemies and exert sea control in a limited area for the time required to fulfil its function in the joint campaign.[42] The most recent strategy documents also acknowledge the maritime environment as a complex contested space, in which enemies challenge established norms and operate across the spectrum of competitive relationships: a sort of maritime version of hybrid warfare.[43] Hence, the USN needs a range of capabilities and a more aggressive doctrinal approach to sea power.

Although sea control and warfighting are back centre stage, smaller-scale good-order-at-sea challenges continue to elicit attention – most notably piracy, terrorism, and trafficking of people and illicit goods. In this sense, the constabulary role of maritime forces is alive and well. Indeed, coordinated international efforts have helped mitigate the impact of piracy. This is especially evident in the Malacca Straits and off the Somali coast; two areas that in recent years were wracked by attacks on commercial shipping. In 2009, there were 217 attacks off the Horn of Africa, with pirates based on the Somali coast operating over 1000 miles from their bases.[44] In contrast, the International Chamber of Commerce's International Maritime Bureau reports that in 2018 there were only three incidents attributed to Somali pirates. Despite these successes, piracy remains a problem, with 201 reported incidents occurring in 2018, many of them in the Gulf of Guinea.[45]

Successful anti-piracy operations are costly and require a range of well-coordinated actions. In 2016, it is estimated that the cost of anti-piracy activities off the coast of East Africa amounted to $228 million.[46] Successful counter-piracy work includes naval patrols, seizing or freezing pirate finances, and developing increased defences for merchant ships. However, while these are all important and necessary, it is generally accepted that the problem can only really be solved on land. Social, economic, and political issues on land must be addressed to reduce the need for many to turn to piracy as a source of income. Therefore, we can conclude that maritime initiatives, many of which need to be international in nature, are important in containing the pirate problem. However, as always, it is the human (sociopolitical) dimension that must be addressed to achieve a long-term solution.

Trafficking demands a similar broad set of countermeasures, with much of the maritime work falling on coast guards or specially constituted naval forces. The challenges are substantial, not least because the sea represents a colossal space for illegal activities. The scale of the problem is represented by two sets of figures from drugs and human trafficking. In 2017, the U.S. Coast Guard seized 207 tonnes of cocaine, worth an estimated $6 billion. In the Mediterranean, by 2016 EU naval forces had rescued over 26,000 migrants.[47]

Terrorism at sea is quite rare but can be quite devastating nonetheless. Operating at sea represents a series of challenges that many terror groups are not well placed to meet. It is simply much easier for them to achieve their objectives on land. That being said, like aircraft, sea vessels represent big targets that if attacked successfully can create substantial casualties and/or economic damage and thereby promote the terrorists' cause. Many examples illustrate this point. In October 2000, the destroyer *USS Cole* was attacked by an al-Qaeda small suicide attack craft while in port at Aden. The attack killed 17 US sailors, wounded a further 39, and caused $250 million worth of damage to the ship. In February 2004, Islamist terrorists planted a bomb on the *SuperFerry 14*, travelling from Manila in the Philippines. The explosion eventually sank the ferry, killing 116. As with most phenomena in strategy, terrorism at sea is not new to the twenty-first century. British warships maintaining the Palestine Patrol in the 1940s were under threat from Jewish terrorists while in harbour at Haifa.[48] In 1979, the IRA killed Lord Mountbatten and two children when they planted a bomb on his boat off the Irish coast. The threat of terrorism at sea, then, is not a new challenge for maritime forces; but as the Hezbollah anti-ship missile attack on an Israeli corvette in 2006 illustrates, the threat continues to evolve. This merely adds to the considerable constabulary function of modern maritime forces.

From a technological standpoint, developments in information technology, robotics, and AI provide the wherewithal for new capabilities, while threats, both old (mines, submarines) and new (advanced hypersonic anti-ship missiles, high-speed swarming attack craft), continue to challenge maritime forces, especially in the littoral environment. Since 'navies are material services',[49] technology really matters, although it is still only one component of maritime power. Perhaps the most significant question for future navies in this respect is the fate of the great or capital ship. Certain periods in maritime history have been dominated by particular types of vessels. These were regarded as the most important and powerful vessels of their day, on which the fate of fleets and nations could rest. Examples of capital ships include First-Rate Ships of the Line during the age of sail, dreadnought battleships, and aircraft carriers in the contemporary setting. However, the continued prominence of large, powerful great ships is open to question. On the one hand, in general, warships are getting larger and more expensive and decreasing in number. This can be explained by a number of factors. Larger vessels can be made more resilient; they can be more flexible by virtue of being able to house a greater range of capabilities; and finally, with an emphasis on modular ship design, their primary role can change during the ship's operational lifespan.[50]

In contrast to the few large ships approach, is one enabled by the proliferation of information technology and unmanned systems. Specifically, the rise of networks and autonomous unmanned units suggests a future in which power is distributed rather than concentrated. There are different ways of achieving this distributed lethality. A more modest approach is to ensure that 'every ship is a shooter'. Such an approach would still be based on reasonably large platforms. Alternatively, maritime forces could adopt their own version of 'the small and the many', whereby the fleet is composed of hundreds, perhaps thousands of small unmanned units, employing swarming tactics. In a shared information environment, many smaller vessels could coordinate their capabilities, massing effect rather than massing force. One significant advantage of this approach is the ability to do away with the great ship, which is an extremely valuable but also vulnerable asset. However, one might argue that the network itself, on which the entire fleet would rely, is another potentially vulnerable target.

A possible compromise, which combines the advantages of both large vessels and small distributed units is the 'mothership' option. One possible option is to have a fleet comprising a few large crewed platforms, commanding many smaller uncrewed vessels. At the time of writing, it is not clear which direction naval forces will take. There are many possible futures. For example, the U.S. Navy is investing in medium and large uncrewed vessels. This includes $2.7 billion on a ghost fleet of ten corvette-sized uncrewed ships. In the submarine environment, the USN is developing the Orca extra large unmanned undersea vehicle (XLUUV). This 51-foot submersible has all of the advantages of a multirole platform, being able to engage in a variety of roles from ISR and Anti-submarine warfare (ASW) to strike missions. In terms of naval air power, the current trend seems to emphasise a hybrid mixture of manned and unmanned systems, but with the former still dominating. For example, the F-35C manned fighter is likely to benefit, in terms of increased range, from the unmanned carrier-based MQ-25A Stingray aerial refuelling platform. Interestingly, the USN cancelled the successful X-47B carrier-based Unmanned Combat Aerial Vehicle (UCAV).

In this uncertain technological and operational environment, it is probably wise, resources permitting, to follow Till's advice: invest in a number of different futures – not forgetting the core strategic missions of navies. Also, the new is not always as revolutionary as it first seems. Distributed lethality sounds very cyber age; but naval operations have, since at least the age of sail, always been about gathering information on the enemy fleet and coordinating distributed firepower. Indeed, the more radical approach to modern distributed lethality somewhat echoes the French *jeune ecole* of the nineteenth century. Questions over the viability of the capital ship are also not new. After the Second World War, the rise of air power and nuclear weapons inspired many commentators to signal the end of large vessels. This suggests that we should treat with caution radical statements about the demise of any particular maritime capability.

Likewise, despite the increased lethality of the littoral environment, amphibious operations will continue to be an important function for maritime forces. Indeed, amphibious capabilities are actually proliferating.[51] As Corbett so clearly indicated, maritime power gains its strategic utility from projecting power ashore. It may be that 'over the horizon' plays a bigger role in maritime power projection and/or that smaller uncrewed vessels undertake the riskier missions closer to shore. Despite coming technological changes, the basic functions of maritime forces will not change.

One overriding problem with arguments of a technological nature, whether based on hypersonic missiles, networks, and/or unmanned systems, is that they tend to focus on warfighting and the delivery of firepower. As noted earlier, the great strength of naval forces is their ability to perform a range of tasks, both in and out of conflict. Substantial amphibious operations, humanitarian work, and other good-order-at-sea operations are likely to require flexible large vessels capable of operating in a complex and often-dangerous environment. A great ship is arguably more capable of self-sustaining action in this respect. Networks are undoubtedly having an impact on the structure and composition of modern armed forces. However, the rise of the network does not fundamentally change the nature of maritime operations. Hence, large flexible vessels are likely to remain in operation, albeit supported by smaller uncrewed vessels and the advantages of operating high-tempo decision-making AI in support of ship defence.

Conclusion

Those involved in contemporary sea power face a range of developing challenges. At present, the maritime security environment is complex and contested, with threats and missions ranging from piracy and migrant flows to the growing potential for great naval battles for sea control. In addition, there is much uncertainty concerning the future development of naval technology and the operational implications thereof. Will the capital ship continue to exist in some form, or will networks lead to the distribution of power among many smaller uncrewed vessels? To deal with said complexity and the uncertain direction of future sea power, there is much to recommend holding onto established concepts and classic theoretical writings.

In this respect, although there is much value to be gained from an appreciation of the entire range of maritime activities, the narrower definition of sea power provides greater conceptual clarity. Restricting one's analysis to the use of military naval assets for the attainment of policy objectives ensures clear strategic focus. As important as merchant shipping and maritime insurance may be, the strategist needs to concentrate on naval forces and the contribution that they can make to national security policy. It is also important not to overthink or unnecessarily delineate the functions of sea power. The key variable in defining an act of strategy is violence. Military force, whether in actual use or merely threatened, is the basis for strategy. This includes acts of coercion or intelligence gathering in support of operations and constabulary operations such as anti-piracy and anti-trafficking operations. Humanitarian operations and naval diplomacy, although they make use of naval vessels, belong to a different category of missions, as they do not rely on the application of violence to achieve effect. They are still an expression of sea power and therefore must exert some influence on the design and procurement of ships; but they are not an act of strategy.

As an instrument of policy, sea power is characterised by a range of missions, global reach, and great flexibility. Often central to the success of sea power is sea control. Total command of the sea, however much desired, is neither realistically possible nor necessary. To achieve positive strategic effect, a maritime power need only attain control of the sea over a certain area for a certain period of time. Indeed, attempting to gain total command of the sea may be a waste of vital resources and may prevent proper exploitation of sea control. The latter is not an end in itself, but rather must be exploited to have value. As Corbett notes, in some way or another, that exploitation must affect change on the land environment. Sea power is useful only insomuch that it extends its influence to land, where humans dwell. In support of this core function, navies must contend with the increasingly dangerous littoral environment and developing A2/AD capabilities. Yet just as the competitive nature of strategy ensures that sea-denial options will develop, so too does it ensure that maritime powers will counter with their own capabilities. Hypersonic missiles and increasingly smart mines may be countered by swarms of uncrewed vessels and/or high-tempo AI-controlled ship defence. The paradoxical logic of strategy operates at sea just as it does in the other domains.

It should be clear from this analysis that sea power is an extremely useful instrument in strategy. But just how influential is it in world politics? The history of geopolitics suggests that nations and coalitions built around sea power have tended to prevail in large conflicts in the modern period. This is largely due to the ability of maritime power to gather together resources on a global scale. However, the outcome of wars depends on so many variables that it would be unwise to extrapolate too much from recent geopolitical history. What can be said with more confidence is that the role of sea power is primarily that of an enabler to land power. Nonetheless, with its ability to integrate new technology and adapt to changes in the grammar of war, sea power is likely to continue to play an important role in deciding the outcome of future security challenges.

Key points

1. Sea power provides a limited, but more viable definition of strategy at or from the sea.
2. Control of the sea denotes a more realistic, limited notion of command of the sea.
3. Defeat of the enemy will remain an important component of sea power.
4. Sea power is a flexible instrument of strategy.
5. In the modern era, maritime-based alliances have tended to succeed over continental enemies.
6. Despite the rise of networks and unmanned systems, sea power is likely to remain platform-centric in some form.

Questions

1. Is command of the sea possible?
2. How significant is battle in acquiring command or control of the sea?
3. What are the main advantages and limitations of sea power?
4. Will modern sea power change significantly from that which went before?

Notes

1 Ian Speller, 'Naval Warfare', in David Jordan et al. (eds.), *Understanding Modern Warfare* (Cambridge, Cambridge University Press, 2008), p. 125.

2 Geoffrey Till, *Seapower: A Guide for the Twenty-First Century*, 4th ed. (Abingdon, Routledge, 2018).

3 Eric Grove, *The Future of Sea Power* (Annapolis, Naval Institute Press, 1990), p. 3.

4 Ibid., pp. 3–4.

5 Although the term 'sea power' is used to describe strategic power at or from the sea, it is still legitimate to discuss sea power operating within the maritime environment. This is recognition of the fact that the sea environment is significantly shaped by the adjacent land and air environments. For example, how the sea is used depends largely on the physical and human geography of the land.

6 See, for example, Colin S. Gray, *The Leverage of Sea Power* (New York, The Free Press, 1992).

7 See Admiral William Owens (with Ed Offley), *Lifting the Fog of War* (Baltimore, John Hopkins University Press, 2001); Vice-Admiral Arthur K. Cebrowski, 'Network-Centric Warfare: An Emerging Military Response to the Information Age', Command and Control Research and Technology Symposium, June 29, 1999.

8 Joseph Trevithick, 'Navy's Sea Hunter Drone Ship Has Sailed Autonomously to Hawaii and Back Amid Talk of New Roles', *The Warzone*, February 4, 2019, www.thedrive.com/the-war-zone/26319/usns-sea-hunter-drone-ship-has-sailed-autonomously-to-hawaii-and-back-amid-talk-of-new-roles

9 'Sea Hunter: Inside the U.S. Navy's Autonomous Submarine Tracking Vessel', *Naval Technology*, May 3, 2018, www.naval-technology.com/features/sea-hunter-inside-us-navys-autonomous-submarine-tracking-vessel/

10 David B. Larter, 'Kongsberg's Hydroid Hoping REMUS Drone Will Help Marines Clear Mines in Shallow Water', *Defense News*, September 27, 2018, www.defensenews.com/digital-show-dailies/modern-day-marine/2018/09/27/kongsbergs-hydroid-hoping-remus-drone-to-help-marines-clear-mines-in-shallow-water/

11 Speller, pp. 126–7.

12 Till, p. 9.

13 Ibid., p. 8.

14 Alfred Thayer Mahan, *The Influence of Sea Power upon History* (Boston, Little Brown, 1890).

15 Quoted in Grove, p. 12.

16 Speller, p. 136.

17 Clausewitz, pp. 97, 271.

18 Speller, p. 137.

19 Till, p. 158.

20 Captain Wayne P. Hughes, 'Implementing the Sea Power Strategy', www.usnwc.edu/getattachment/cefca5c6-70e3-4f29-be10-80b571002793/Implementing-the-Seapower-Strategy-Hughes,-Wayne

21 www.uboat.net/allies/merchants/losses_year.html

22 Winston S. Churchill, *The Second World War, Vol. II: Their Finest Hour* (London, Penguin, 1985), p. 529.

23 Geoffrey Parker, *The Grand Strategy of Philip II* (New Haven, Yale University Press, 1998).

24 Speller, pp. 141–2.

25 Ibid., p. 139.

26 Clausewitz, p. 720.

27 Julian Corbett, *Some Principles of Maritime Strategy* (Annapolis, MD, Naval Institute Press, 1988).

28 Till, p. 193.

29 Colin Martin and Geoffrey Parker, *The Spanish Armada* (Manchester, Mandolin, 1999), p. 110.

30 Gerhard L. Weinberg, *A World at Arms: A Global History of World War II* (Cambridge, Cambridge University Press, 1994), p. 360.

31 Max Hastings, *The Korean War* (London, Guild Publishing, 1987).

32 Till, p. 71.

33 Ronald H. Spector, *Eagle against the Sun: The American War with Japan* (New York, Free Press, 1985), p. 262.

34 Clausewitz, p. 97.

35 For an excellent discussion of the issues covered in this section see Colin S. Gray, *The Leverage of Sea Power: The Strategic Advantage of Navies in War* (New York, Free Press, 1992).

36 Till, p. 40.

37 For an outstanding analysis of Mackinder's theories, see Geoffrey Sloan, 'Sir Halford J. Mackinder: The Heartland Theory Then and Now', in Colin S. Gray and Geoffrey Sloan (eds.), *Geopolitics: Geography and Strategy* (London, Frank Cass, 1999), pp. 15–38.

38 Gray, *The Leverage of Sea Power*.

39 Till, p. 47; Corbett, *Some Principles*.

40 Clausewitz, p. 606.

41 Geoffrey Till, '"A Cooperative Strategy for 21st Century Seapower" A View from Outside', www. usnwc.edu/getattachment/5ee8dc34-ad28-4817-b76c-8b453365ba61/-Cooperative-Strategy-for-21st-Century-Seapower,-A

42 Ian Speller, *Understanding Naval Warfare*, 2nd ed. (Abingdon, Routledge, 2019), pp. 163–5.

43 U.S. Navy, *A Design for Maintaining Maritime Superiority*, December 2018, www.navy.mil/navydata/people/cno/Richardson/Resource/Design_2.0.pdf

44 Lesley Anne Warner, 'Pieces of Eight: An Appraisal of US Counterpiracy Options in the Horn of Africa', p. 63, www.usnwc.edu/getattachment/7eaf3023-526f-4d34-ae81-5233dc8694b1/Pieces-of-Eight-An-Appraisal-of-U-S-Counterpirac.

45 ICC International Maritime Bureau, *Piracy Report 2018*, www.icc-ccs.org/index.php/1259-imb-piracy-report-2018-attacks-multiply-in-the-gulf-of-guinea

46 Speller, *Understanding Naval Warfare*, p. 180.

47 Ibid., pp. 178–9.

48 Till, p. 318.

49 Ibid., p. 120.

50 Ibid., p. 122.

51 Ibid., p. 276.

Further reading

Black, Jeremy, *Naval Power: A History of Warfare and the Sea from 1500 Onwards*, (Basingstoke: Palgrave Macmillan, 2009).

Bruns, S., *US Naval Strategy and National Security: The Evolution of American Maritime Power*, (Abingdon: Routledge, 2017).

Corbett, Julian, *Some Principles of Maritime Strategy*, (Annapolis, MD: Naval Institute Press, 1988).

Friedman, Norman, *Seapower as Strategy: Navies and National Interest*, (Annapolis, MD: Naval Institute Press, 2001).

Gray, Colin S., *The Leverage of Sea Power*, (New York: The Free Press, 1992).

Mahan, Alfred Thayer, *The Influence of Sea Power upon History*, (Boston: Little Brown, 1890).
Speller, Ian, *Understanding Naval Warfare*, 2nd Edition, (Abingdon: Routledge, 2019).
Tangredi, Sam J. (ed.), *Globalisation and Maritime Power*, (Washington, DC: NDU Press, 2002).
Till, Geoffrey, *Seapower: A Guide For The Twenty-First Century*, 4th Edition, (Abingdon: Routledge, 2018).
Vego, Milan, *Operational Warfare at Sea: Theory and Practice*, (Abingdon: Routledge, 2010).

Air power

9

Reader's guide

The strengths of air power; the limitations of air power; the historical development of air power: First World War, interwar theory, Second World War, modern air power; air power as a flexible strategic instrument, best used in support of surface forces.

Introduction

As far as military innovations go, air power must be regarded as one of the most genuine and significant. The exploitation of heavier-than-air aircraft in the twentieth century changed the character of warfare in a lasting fashion. Almost every conflict is now influenced, to a greater or lesser degree, by air power. Indeed, as Field Marshal Montgomery noted, the outcome of certain conflicts will be largely determined by who controls the skies: 'If we lose the war in the air, we lose the war and lose it quickly'.[1] Nonetheless, it would be a mistake to assume that air power has become the decisive instrument in modern strategy. As noted in the Introduction to this book, strategy is a complex, multidimensional activity. That being the case, to identify any one factor as being decisive would be an oversimplification. In light of this, the current chapter seeks to analyse the development of air power and its strengths and weaknesses and to determine its role in the current strategic environment.

Like every other domain of strategy, the air environment presents a unique set of opportunities and challenges. Like the sea, the air environment is hostile for human beings. Thus, to exploit the air environment for strategic effect, humans require vehicles to survive in, and traverse, the third dimension. Inevitably, this means that air strategy is platform-centric, although this may be changing somewhat with the further development of unmanned systems. The latter include largish platforms such as Global Hawk and Predator, which can carry a multitude of ISR and strike assets. However, the coming development of drone swarms suggests that there will also be a place for 'the small and the many' in the third dimension.

The coming of small drones is significant because air power has traditionally been based on moderate numbers of expensive platforms, which in turn produces warfare that is attritional in nature. This could mean going from manned air fleets in the tens and hundreds to uncrewed fleets in the tens of thousands. The tactical and operational implications of such a possibility are only now being actively discussed.

Regardless of whether the aircraft in question are manned or unmanned, air power is reliant on technology. Therefore, depending on the context, small differences in technical specifications can make a big difference at the tactical and operational levels. In air-to-air combat, for example, having more advanced avionics and weapons systems relative to the enemy will likely result in victory. Once decent platforms have been acquired, air power proves to be a surprisingly flexible instrument of strategy. Most obviously, aircraft can be used in combat, either to counter other aircraft or to attack surface targets (including military forces, infrastructure, and populations). They also have prominent roles in reconnaissance and logistics. These various uses of air power will be explored in greater detail as the chapter develops.

The strengths of air power

Box 9.1 The strengths and limitations of air power

Strengths
Speed of movement.
Multiple axis of attack.
Overhead flank.
Flexibility.
Strategic effect with limited commitment.
Cutting-edge technology.

Limitations
Inability to control ground.
Fleeting presence (except for drone loiter capability).
Expensive (reduced by unmanned systems).
Vulnerable to weather.
Tendency to alienate locals.

Operating in the third dimension has a number of advantages. Aircraft can usually reach their intended destination much more quickly than other forms of transport can. Thus, the use of air power may be critical for mission success in certain circumstances. The interdiction of an enemy convoy; urgent resupply or redeployment; and casualty evacuation are just three examples of when speed may be a crucial factor. Due to the lack of physical obstacles, air power also offers multiple axes of advance and attack. And with in-flight refuelling, aircraft potentially have global reach. This is unlike the land domain, where physical characteristics of the terrain shape operations significantly. Similarly, although less obviously, the maritime environment also contains features (such as land or depth of water) that may limit the geographic extent of operations. In contrast, the air environment is fairly uniform in nature. This is not to overlook the fact that certain climates are more favourable than others for aircraft. Nor can one overlook the fact that national airspace imposes an artificial limit on the extent of air travel. However, the latter consideration will often be ignored during military confrontations. Finally, it is worth noting that operations involving helicopters may be affected by undulations in the terrain below. Nonetheless, generally speaking, those conducting air operations have greater freedom when planning routes to target. This clearly creates significant problems for those on the receiving end of an air campaign.

Air power gives its user the advantage of operating on the overhead flank. Being able to bypass enemy forces on the ground (assuming that anti-air defences are not especially effective) enables air power to attack targets deep behind the enemy. Indeed, the promise of strategic bombing was based largely on the ability to attack enemy centres of population and industry without first defeating their ground forces. The overhead flank also acts as the ultimate high ground for intelligence reconnaissance and surveillance (ISR). The Duke of Wellington noted that a significant part of warfare was concerned with discovering what was over the hill.[2] Air power enables one to do that over a large area. However, as with most aspects of strategy, this is not a one-sided affair. Enemy forces can hide from air-based ISR assets. And as was amply demonstrated in Kosovo, even the most modern of air- and spaced-based ISR assets can be deceived by those on the ground.[3]

Although common perceptions of air power may be dominated by advanced fighters such as the F-35 and the Reaper attack UAV, air power is actually a flexible instrument of strategy, capable of much more than just destroying targets. However, in our haste to highlight said flexibility, we should not underestimate the significant contribution that air power makes in the projection of firepower. For example, a B-2 bomber has a 40,000-lb. payload, which can accommodate various configurations of weapons, including 80 500-lb. Joint Direct Attack Munition (JDAM) guided bombs.[4] As will be discussed in detail later in this chapter (in relation to the bombing campaigns during the Second World War), strategists can harness the enormous firepower offered by air power to weaken an enemy's will and capability to resist. This may involve targeting large areas of significant industrial or population centres or may be more focused for coercive effect. Modern air power in particular, due to advances in precision, is often regarded as an ideal coercive instrument. In theory, a modern air campaign can attack key targets (nodes) in the enemy system, thereby breaking their cohesion and will. The 1999 war in Kosovo is a controversial case of a coercive air power campaign. Some commentators and practitioners have claimed that air power alone compelled the Serbian government to accede to NATO's demands.[5]

Over the battlefield, fighter bombers and helicopters have the ability to inflict significant damage on infantry and armour, as witnessed from the Second World War to the ongoing conflict in Syria. Field Marshall Rommel's comment on the dominance of Allied air power in the former conflict still holds true today in many circumstances: 'In every battle to come the strength of the Anglo-American air force was to be the deciding factor'.

Beyond the delivery of firepower, aircraft play a significant role in logistics. Although limited in what they can carry relative to sea transport, aircraft are able to deploy or resupply more rapidly. There are circumstances when air transportation is the only viable option. The most striking example of this is the 1948–9 Berlin Airlift, when Allied aircraft supplied the city of Berlin, which was isolated in Soviet occupied East Germany, with approximately 13,000 tons of supplies a day.[6] Without the air corridor, it is likely that Berlin would have fallen to the Communists.

Aircraft not only transport equipment and supplies, they can also project military power through the use of airmobile and airborne forces. The former primarily refers to the movement of forces via helicopters. A fine example of the advantages of air mobility can be seen in the battle for Ia Drang Valley (November 1965) during the Vietnam War. In the densely wooded terrain of South Vietnam, air mobility enabled US air cavalry forces to engage the North Vietnamese forces at Ia Drang. Helicopters were used exclusively to deploy forces onto the battlefield, maintain them, and evacuate casualties.[7] Airborne forces, in the form of parachute troops, dropped from fixed-wing aircraft or landed via gliders, deploy via a one-way transport mission. Airborne forces had their heyday during the Second World War (in such operations as the capture of Eben Emel, Crete, and the crossing of the Rhine in Operation Varsity), although they are still occasionally used (as in the capture of airfields in Afghanistan and Iraq).

Aside from being flexible, air power benefits from being able to provide strategic effect without the need for presence on the ground. In certain circumstances, the deployment of ground troops could create substantial political problems. For example, the deployment of ground forces may stimulate public and international outcry at what is perceived as the 'invasion' of a sovereign state. In this sense, air power can reach targets that otherwise would be difficult to access. The US-led campaign against Islamist and Taliban forces in the Pakistan Tribal Areas is one such example. It would be politically difficult to deploy substantial US ground forces in Pakistan. Air power gives the United States the ability to project military power into the area.

Moreover, the deployment of ground troops normally increases the risk of friendly casualties. This too can have serious political ramifications at home. In contrast, theoretically at least, air power is able to deliver strategic results with a fleeting overhead presence, thereby reducing the political costs and minimising the chance of friendly losses. Unmanned air power further accentuates this characteristic. As Eliot Cohen notes, this makes modern air power a particularly attractive instrument for policymakers: 'Air power is an unusually seductive form of military strength, in part because, like modern courtship, it appears to offer gratification without commitment'.[8]

If it can be attained, control from the air is potentially a more efficient form of control, in contrast to the risks associated with intervention on the ground. During the interwar period, the United Kingdom relied on the newly formed RAF to control vast tracks of land in its imperial possessions (e.g. in modern-day Iraq).[9] Even if ground cannot be reliably controlled from the air, it may still be possible to deny it to the enemy. One of the advertised features for forthcoming loitering drone swarms is their ability to act as instruments of 'terrain denial'.[10]

Aircraft are often at the forefront of developments in military technology. Hence, air power may be perceived as a measure of a state's development, status, and power. This, allied to the aforementioned firepower, suggests that air power can be used as a display of military power in order to exert leverage. During the British involvement in Sierra

Leone, the mere presence of Harrier jets overhead could subdue militants for periods of time.[11] The deployment of an aircraft carrier can be a potent signal of intent. The strategic effect in such circumstances is strongly related to the latent power of carrier-borne aircraft.

Overall, air power appears to be an extremely useful instrument of strategy. It has many uses, is largely unrestrained by geography, is rapid in its execution, and is able to project substantial levels of firepower. In addition, it is potentially far less vulnerable than other forms of military power and less controversial as a result. However, the weaknesses of air power are just as noteworthy as these strengths.

The limitations of air power

Ironically, one of the more obvious weaknesses of air power relates to one of the aforementioned strengths: lack of physical presence on the ground. Reluctance by a state to deploy ground forces may be an indication of a lack of genuine commitment to a security issue. This is problematic because, as Clausewitz reminds us, war is essentially a battle of wills. In such circumstances, an enemy may be able to sit out an air campaign, working on the assumption that the (already questionable) will of the enemy may weaken further over time. This appears to have been Serbia's chosen strategy during the Kosovo conflict. However, as this example reveals, those conducting an air campaign may show surprising levels of commitment over a prolonged period.

Nonetheless, a lack of boots on the ground has other disadvantages. Air power, especially when conducted via loitering unmanned systems, may be effective at terrain denial; but control from the air is a poor substitute for the man on the scene with a gun. An enemy on the ground can conduct a deception campaign or adopt a form of warfare (irregular, small unit) that is difficult for air power to cope with. Once again, Kosovo presents us with a striking example of this truism. Although the NATO campaign was ultimately successful in forcing the withdrawal of Serbian forces, an estimated 10,000 Albanians died after the campaign had started. This was mainly because Serbia was able to conduct their ethnic cleansing campaign using small irregular units, which were difficult targets for NATO pilots.[12] Again, loitering high endurance unmanned ISR and strike assets potentially increase the potency of air power in small wars. Nonetheless, as evidenced by the continued stalemate in Afghanistan, where drones have been used extensively, complex irregular strategic issues cannot be resolved simply by an effective reconnaissance-strike operational approach.

This suggests that as flexible as air power may be, it lacks the versatility of ground forces. The latter can not only fight and provide physical security but also be used in support of development projects. In some operations, such as counterinsurgency, interaction with the local population is vital to build trust and garner intelligence. This is possible only with dismounted infantry. This speaks to the human, social, and cultural dimensions of strategy. Not only is air power distant and lacking in human interaction, but also the firepower it delivers may be an alienating factor. Put simply, the local population may regard those using air power as abstract bringers of death and destruction rather than as someone with whom they share a sense of humanity. Again, this is accentuated by unmanned systems. The ever-present but unseen drones in Afghanistan can have psychological effects on those beneath.

In defence of air power, aircraft may be a welcome presence when they bring vital supplies, such as food and medical aid. Also, although flexible, infantry forces can still alienate the local population with the misuse of deadly force or simply by showing cultural insensitivity. In the final analysis, as with any instrument of strategy, the use of air power must be carefully moulded to the specific needs of the situation. Context is everything in strategy.

Over time, air power has become an exceptionally expensive form of military power. This is especially the case with manned combat aircraft. The B-2 bomber costs approximately $2 billion per unit. Although this is an unusually high unit cost (partially due to the small numbers produced), the RAF's main fighter bomber, Typhoon, still costs approximately $58 million each. The F-35A costs approximately $80 million per plane. Air-launched munitions can also be expensive. The GBU-22 Paveway III air-ground bomb, used on Typhoon, has a production cost of approximately $50,000. Thus, air power is a very expensive means to deliver high explosives to a target. And as indicated by the Kosovo conflict, the efficacy of this expensive instrument can be seriously degraded by air defences and simple cost-effective acts of deception. However, political and military leaders may feel that the costs of air power are justified, since it can reduce the chances of friendly casualties relative to the deployment of ground forces.

However, air power is on the verge of becoming a significantly less expensive instrument. A significant proportion of an aircraft's cost relates to the presence of a human being in the cockpit. Keeping the pilot alive and in control of a modern aircraft is costly and restricts the performance of the platform. Since humans are limited in the amount of g-force they can withstand, the manoeuvrability and speed of a manned aircraft is similarly limited. The increasing use and development of unmanned aircraft is therefore reducing the cost of air power and will lead to more agile and capable aircraft. A Reaper UAV is still fairly expensive at a unit cost of $17 million. However, the new XQ-58A Valkyrie UCAV, designed to operate alongside the F-22 and F-35, has a unit cost of $2 million. Effective tactical ISR can be had with the Raven UAV for just $35,000.

Weather still has the potential to seriously disrupt an air power campaign. As is described later in this chapter, the flow of the Battle of the Bulge during the Second World War was substantially influenced by the weather. Although modern air power is better able to overcome the effects of the weather, the 1999 Kosovo conflict provides striking evidence of how significant this factor still is in the exercise of strategy in the third dimension.

As with any form of military power, air power has distinct advantages and limitations. It is capable of undertaking a range of different missions. However, its strategic efficacy will depend on a range of factors, including the nature of the enemy, the terrain over which it operates, and the objectives set. To accentuate the positives and minimise the negatives, air power is best used in coordination with other strategic instruments.

Historical development

> ## Box 9.2 The main uses of air power
>
> Close air support (CAS) and interdiction.
> Strategic bombing.
> Coercion.
> Nuclear deterrence.
> ISR.
> Airborne/airmobile forces.
> Logistics.
> Terrain denial.

The First World War

Although air power appears to be a modern instrument, typified by stealth fighters and unmanned systems, most of the roles we associate with it today were present (either in practice or in theory) during its first serious military outing in the First World War. Strategic bombing, ISR, interdiction, CAS, and aircraft carriers, to name but five roles, were all developed substantially between 1914 and 1918. During the First World War, the pioneers of air power were learning as they went along. Doctrine and technology developed at a rapid pace as military commanders began to understand what this new tool was capable of.[13]

The first notable use of air power during the war was ISR. This was not an entirely new use of air power, however. Balloons had been used for this purpose since at least the Napoleonic Wars. Nonetheless, the invention of heavier-than-air flight gave air reconnaissance assets much greater flexibility, control, and range. The static character of trench warfare ensured that tethered balloons could still provide useful coverage of the enemy's positions. Nonetheless, aircraft considerably enhanced ISR. Typically, balloons could reconnoitre 15 miles; the French Breguet XIV aircraft provided photographs up to 100 miles behind enemy lines.

In the early stages of the war, the air ISR assets of each side did not interfere with their opposite numbers. However, this soon changed, and dedicated fighter aircraft were developed to intercept enemy reconnaissance aircraft. In turn, these fighters began to engage one another in order to gain control of the skies, and thus was the concept of air superiority born. In these early days, we witness the beginnings of the rapid race for technological advantage. It soon became apparent that fighter aircraft needed advantage in the characteristics of speed, manoeuvrability, vision, and firepower. The speed of development was fantastic. In 1903, the Wright Brothers Flyer had 15 bhp; only 15 years later, the Rolls Royce Condor v12 engine was pushing out over 600 bhp. As power increased, so did the airframes of fighters, making them more agile in flight. Armaments also evolved. At first, air-to-air combat was limited to pilots firing revolvers from their cockpits. However, it was not long before armaments were attached to the aircraft themselves. Eventually, the Fokker Eindekker went into battle with a sophisticated timing firing mechanism that enabled a front-mounted machine gun to fire through the propellers.[14]

CAS was also introduced during the First World War. Casualties among the air units engaged tended to be high. For example, the Royal Flying Corps No. 80 Squadron suffered 75% casualties in the final ten months of the war, primarily from ground attack missions.[15] As with air-to-air combat operations, so-called trench-strafing missions led to more specialist development of aircraft. By the end of the war, the most advanced CAS aircraft in the British Royal Flying Corps, the Sopwith Salamander, had an armour-plated fuselage, two Vickers machine guns and carried four light bombs. The Germans developed the Junkers J 1 aircraft for ground attack missions, which is notable for being the first aircraft with an all-metal fuselage. Although the ground attack role was clearly an important development in air power, it made little impact on the outcome of battles during the First World War. Victory or defeat, especially in the final stages of the war, was generally decided by ground operations involving artillery and combined-arms units. That being said, aircraft played an important role in 'spotting' for artillery.

In relation to the interwar development of doctrine and air power theory, the most significant role for air power in the First World War was strategic bombing. The scale of operations, and the associated damage from aerial bombardment of urban areas, was minimal during the war. In turn, strategic bombing had little, if any, strategic impact on the outcome of the conflict. However, the little bombing that did occur fired the imagination of theorists and practitioners. Theorists extrapolated from the limited experiences of the war and theorised what would occur if large numbers of bombers were used against industrial targets and civilian populations. During the war, both sides experimented with strategic bombing. The Germans, using both zeppelins and Gotha G IVs (the latter had a 1000 lb. bombload), bombed the urban areas of Southern England, causing over 1300 fatalities and £7 million in property damage. In turn, the British tended to focus on military-related targets, launching 675 raids against airfields, railways, and military-industrial sites, causing over 700 fatalities.

Perhaps the most surprising innovation during these early days of air power was the development of naval aviation. The British Admiralty had been studying the use of aircraft since before the war. By the outbreak of the conflict, the Royal Naval Air Service had been established, with 93 aircraft and six airships under its command. However, it was a private citizen, Eugene Ely, who made the first takeoff from a naval vessel, in 1910. Indeed, the general public was quite involved in the early development of air power. In the buildup to the war in Europe, it was reasonably common practice for members of the public to raise funds (crowdfunding) to buy military aircraft for their region or nation. Once the war began, the primary role for naval aviation was ISR. Naval aircraft were involved in anti-submarine warfare operations, spotting for naval gunfire, and conducting raids against German naval forces in their bases, such as the Cuxhaven raid in December 1914. The latter involved carrier-borne aircraft.

All told, the First World War was critical for the development of air power. Although military innovation is also pursued during peacetime, developments during wartime are afforded the opportunity of being tested in the cauldron of battle. With all sides looking for a crucial breakthrough in the war, the various roles of air power were tried and developed. Thus, by coming in the early stages of heavier-than-air flight, the 1914–18 conflict gave air power an accelerated start to its strategic career. However, for the same reasons, air power was not able to mature sufficiently during the war and thus had little impact on the final outcome. Importantly, though, the pioneers of air power learned many valuable lessons that could be refined and applied in the future.

The development of interwar theory

The type of air power that each country developed during the interwar period was influenced by their respective strategic cultures and current strategic challenges. This can be seen, for example, in how the United Kingdom and Germany developed different approaches to air power during this period. Due to their physical separation from the continent of Europe, the British saw air power as a means of long-range attack. A bomber fleet could perform a similar function to that of gunboat diplomacy, by striking directly at perceived centres of gravity for strategic effect. However, in contrast to the American approach, which focused on military-industrial targets, the British opted for morale bombing against civilian populations. For their part, the Germans, who had a land-based strategic culture, focused their development efforts on CAS. The primary objective of German air power was to support the army in the quick defeat of their neighbours. These distinct approaches to the development of air power led to significant differences in design and procurement. The British eventually developed heavy four-engine bombers such the Halifax and Lancaster. In contrast, Germany focused its attention on battlefield support aircraft, such as the Stuka. The Germans did develop long-range bombers, but only lighter variants with two engines, which consequently had smaller payloads. At one stage during the interwar period, the British gave too much prominence to their bomber fleet, giving insufficient support to fighter development. Thankfully, Sir Thomas Inskip, in his role as Minister for the Coordination of Defence, noted the dangers of such an approach, and the United Kingdom consequently entered the war with a workable fighter force, which proved critical in the Battle of Britain.[16]

In light of the experiences of the First World War, the interwar period saw air power theory develop in a number of different directions. Strategic bombing was of interest to all of the great powers, but their differing strategic cultures led them to develop slightly different approaches. Although not mutually exclusive or entirely distinct, two different theoretical approaches to strategic bombing developed: morale bombing and industrial web theory. Both of these approaches focused on the destruction of the enemy's will and capability to resist. However, they each focused on different target sets and routes to victory. At the forefront of morale bombing theory was Italian pilot Giulio Douhet. The industrial web theory was developed primarily in the United States, with Captain Billy Mitchell being the leading exponent.

Douhet's main work of theory, *The Command of the Air*, contains two main steps to successfully exploit air power. The first step, as the title of the book implies, is to gain command of the air. Douhet defines this condition as being able to fly against the enemy while denying them the same. Command of the air is to be gained by offensive action against the enemy's airbases, destroying their aircraft on the ground.[17] During the Second World War, the German Luftwaffe almost achieved this when attacking RAF bases. However, a shift to attacks against urban areas took pressure off the RAF and enabled it to recover sufficiently. In contrast, later in the war, the Luftwaffe was largely destroyed in the air while defending Germany from aerial bombardment. Thus, it is clear from the experience of the Second World War that command of the air can be achieved by destroying the enemy either on the ground or in the air. The war in Europe also suggests that strict command of the air is not necessary in order to achieve significant results from an air campaign. In 1944–5, the Allied air forces were still taking heavy losses over Germany but were in turn destroying large areas of Germany's main cities.

The experiences of the Second World War suggest that Douhet may have been slightly in error on the methods to establish command of the air. Additionally, history suggests that with the use of the term 'command', he also demanded too benign a situation for offensive air operations. As shown earlier, a substantial bombing campaign could be conducted in the face of significant enemy opposition. However, the Italian theorist was correct to advocate a position in which the enemy was unable to mount offensive operations. In particular, the absence of an enemy offensive capability enables one to concentrate one's own aggressive efforts against them rather than diverting resources into defence. It may be prudent, therefore, to conclude that the term 'command of the air' suggests an absolute position. As with sea power, it may be more appropriate to talk in terms of 'control of the air'. This term refers to a more limited condition, in which successful air operations may be mounted in a specific area for a period of time. 'Control' denotes a situation in which the enemy may still be able to reduce the efficacy of one's operations to some extent, which may in turn lead to some losses. However, for control to exist, the main mission must still be able to be undertaken with relative operational success. In modern doctrine parlance, Douhet's command of the air is akin to air supremacy, whereas control is referred to as air superiority.

Once command of the air has been established, the second phase of Douhet's theory of air power can be undertaken: bombardment of urban areas. For Douhet, the great strategic promise of air power was its ability to literally fly over the enemy's surface forces and strike at vulnerable centres of gravity, especially the civilian population. Having lived through the costly stalemate of the First World War, Douhet saw air power as a means to revive quick and decisive victories. Douhet argued that the untrained civilian population would not be able to withstand aerial bombardment and would quickly pressure their political leaders into compromise or surrender. In this way, air attack could rapidly destroy the will of the enemy to resist. To achieve this, Douhet proposed using three types of munitions: high explosives, incendiary, and gas. The latter, aside from acting as a terror weapon, would be used to complicate the recovery efforts of the emergency services in the bombed cities. When one considers the panic caused by the limited air raids of the First World War, Douhet's theory, based as it was on significantly greater numbers of bombers and more diverse munitions, appears plausible. It is a theory built on experience, with the addition of modern technology applied in greater numbers.

However, as will be discussed shortly, Douhet's theory did not survive the test of the Second World War. Both in Europe and in Japan, gas was never used during air raids. Thus, in one aspect, Douhet's theory was never *fully* put to the test. However, as valid as this defence of the theory may appear, the addition of gas may not have increased the levels of terror and devastation much beyond than that achieved with the fire-storms in Hamburg, Cologne, and Tokyo. The supporters of Douhet have another moment in the Second World War that may verify the theory: the atomic attacks on Japan and the empire's subsequent surrender. This debate will be addressed shortly.

In contrast to Douhet's area bombing of civilian districts, industrial web theory, pioneered by the U.S. Army Air Corps, sought to destroy the enemy's ability to resist by attacking key nodes in the socioeconomic infrastructure. Invariably, this approach to strategic bombing required good – one might say impossibly good – intelligence on how the enemy's system functioned. It also demanded the capability to perform precision bombing. The latter could be partially met by technological advancements such as the Norden Bombsight. However, the quest for precision also led to the doctrinal development of high-altitude precision daylight bombing (HAPDB). In practice, the latter, even when conducted with the B-17 Flying Fortress, proved to be an extremely costly approach in terms of men and equipment lost.

The Second World War

The Second World War provided an extensive test for the theory of strategic bombing. It was evident from the early years of the war that the practice of bombing from altitude was far more difficult than the theory assumed. Navigating over central Europe and hitting the designated targets proved to be a significant challenge. With the technology available at the time, bomber crews occasionally bombed the wrong city and would often miss their target by five miles or more. If they did reach their intended target, defences proved to be far more robust than the mantra of 'the bomber will always get through' assumed. Aircraft losses were substantial, and in response, the RAF's Bomber Command had to shift to nighttime bombing raids. Although it took a few years for the instrument to mature, eventually Allied air power was capable on inflicting terrifying levels of destruction on Germany and Japan. In total, against Germany, the Allied bombing campaign destroyed 40% of the urban areas of its 70 largest cities and killed approximately 305,000 of its civilians.[18] Despite the massive increase in efficacy, the bombing raids did not lead to a collapse in morale. The German raids on the United Kingdom fared no better. Although there is some evidence that the V-2 rocket attacks on London caused considerable panic at the time, it did not come close to knocking the United Kingdom out of the war.

In addition to the disappointing results of morale bombing, the economic effects were also less than hoped for. Despite substantially increased levels of bombing, by March 1945, German armament production was 50% higher than in January 1942.[19] This places a considerable question mark over the ability of strategic bombing to affect the will and capability of the enemy to resist. However, while air power may have fallen short of Douhet's predictions, strategic bombing did make a considerable contribution to the war effort. To defend the Reich from the air, Germany had to divert considerable resources to the effort. It has been estimated that two million Germans were involved in defence against the air raids, as well as 60,000 valuable 88 mm anti-aircraft guns.[20] The latter is significant because the 88 mm was a notoriously effective anti-tank weapon. It is interesting to speculate what would have occurred had these guns been available on the Eastern Front, along with the aircraft and pilots fighting the bombing fleets in the air above the Reich.

Moreover, although industrial production rose during the bombing campaign, it is reasonable to suggest that it would have been much higher without the destruction and disorder wrought by the bombers. In addition, for much of the war, the air campaign was the primary means by which the Western allies could attack German interests. This not only improved morale at home but also kept (just) the Soviet leadership satisfied that it did not have to bear the burden of fighting alone.

There is an important postscript to this debate: Hiroshima and Nagasaki. The atomic attacks on Japan in August 1945 are significant in the morale bombing debate. This is because the Japanese government surrendered not long after the attacks and without the need for an invasion of the home islands by US forces. Indeed, some within the Japanese government, such as Prince Konoye and Premier Suzuki, explicitly make reference to the atomic attacks as one of the main reasons for the decision to surrender.[21] It is therefore plausible that Douhet's theory was finally vindicated, albeit with a technology that he did not originally envisage. There is some evidence that the prospect of further city devastation by a lone B-29 bomber did play a part in the Japanese decision to surrender. However, it is disingenuous to assess the atomic attacks in isolation. As with the Transportation Plan in the campaign against Germany (discussed later), the atomic attacks came at the end of a war that was becoming increasingly costly for Japan, without much prospect for success. The homeland was already suffering from the effects of a devastating conventional area-bombing campaign. Just as importantly, the Japanese economy had been severely curtailed by a maritime blockade. Finally, all of these depravations were in support of a war that was obviously being lost. This final point had been made clear by the defeat of the main Japanese Kwantung army in Manchuria. Thus, as in Germany, the bombing campaign against Japan did make a significant contribution to the war effort, but its effects must be considered in conjunction with the surface campaigns.

While the British had been developing area morale bombing, the Americans had been constructing a different form of strategic bombing for the war in Europe: industrial web theory. This approach was based on the idea that a modern industrial economy was constructed of various key industries and services. Key nodes in the system included the railway network and coal and steel production. It was hoped that precision attacks against such target sets would severely disrupt the war-making potential of an enemy. Indeed, industrial targets could be narrowed down to even a handful of factories or dams. Although the Dambusters Raid was a British operation, it owed much to the American industrial web theory. Those who planned and approved the raid hoped that the destruction of three key dams would severely retard German industrial production by interfering with the supply of electricity and flooding parts of the Ruhr region, Germany's industrial heartland. In a similar vein, in October 1943, the United States 8th Air Force attacked three ball bearing factories at Schweinfurt in Germany. Ball bearings were a crucial component of the German war machine, and as such, the planners hoped they had identified a key node in Germany's industrial web. In reality, both raids failed to achieve significant results, both at a high cost. Of the 19 aircraft involved in the

Dambusters Raid, eight were lost. At Schweinfurt, 291 B-17 bombers were used, and 77 failed to return.

The experiences of the Second World War reveal that precision bombing campaigns face some severe operational challenges. It also reveals that modern industrial economies are far more robust than imagined by the theorists. However, modern research suggests that the industrial web theory had some significant success late in the war when the bombing campaign made a concerted effort to attack the German railway network. The Transportation Plan made it extremely difficult for Germany to move around the fruits of its industrial output.[22] However, while successful, the campaign against the railway network came towards the end of a long and costly war. Also, without the pressure being applied by ground forces, the impact on Germany's industrial and supply system would have been minimal. Even when the correct target set was identified, the results of air power still relied on synergistic action with ground forces. Without surface action, German logistical demands would have been far smaller, and thus the impact of air raids against industry and transportation would have been less keenly felt. As will be discussed later, the industrial web theory has continued to develop, and in recent years, it has been extremely influential in shaping modern air campaigns.

The overall impact of strategic bombing in the Second World War may be open to question, but the debate is less contentious concerning CAS. As mentioned, General Rommel and General Montgomery recognised the importance of gaining command of the air for ground operations. In the relatively short time since the First World War, air power's role over the battlefield had matured substantially, making significant contributions in a number of campaigns. However, as with strategic bombing, some of the limits of air power were still evident. For example, the weather could all but neutralise the effects of CAS.

The Battle of the Bulge (December 1944–January 1944) provides us with a telling example of these strengths and weaknesses. It also provides an excellent indication of the requirements for a successful air-land battle and what happens when these are ignored. In all, over 8000 aircraft were used during the battle. The Germans contributed 2400 aircraft, which was more than what they had committed to the Battle of France in 1940. In response, the Allies was able to deploy 6000 tactical aircraft and heavy bombers into the theatre. Already outnumbered, the Germans suffered further because during the planning phase, the Luftwaffe were kept in the dark about the real nature of their mission. To minimise the chances of their Ardennes offensive being uncovered before the assault, the German high command limited knowledge of it within their own armed services. Thus, the Luftwaffe had been ordered to prepare for a concentrated defensive operation against the Allied bombing campaign over Germany. On this basis, they planned and designed their forces in isolation from the ground commanders, ready for air-to-air combat rather than air-to-ground operations. German hopes relied on poor weather to reduce the significance of the Allies' numerical air advantage. Despite the cloudy weather, the Allied Ninth Air Force made 136 kills in the first three days of the battle. However, on the 19th of December (the offensive began on the 16th) the weather deteriorated to the point that aircraft were grounded until the 23rd. It was during this period that the German advance reached its deepest penetration.

In contrast to the Luftwaffe, whose primary objective was direct support for the ground forces, Allied aircraft first concentrated on achieving air supremacy. Beyond this, Allied air forces were ordered to attack German ground spearhead forces and to conduct an interdiction campaign. The Allied air campaign in Europe enjoyed central command and control under General Eisenhower and his deputy Air Chief Marshal Tedder. Once the weather cleared on the 23rd of December, Allied aircraft focused their attention on the Luftwaffe. They constructed a layered defence over the battlefield, engaging German fighters in the air, and also attacked the German air force at its bases. Such was the success of the air supremacy campaign that the Luftwaffe failed to make any impression on Allied ground operations during the entire battle.

To make matters worse for the Germans, as the battle progressed, the Luftwaffe lost focus. They split their sorties between ground support missions and defensive air operations. The result was a failure to concentrate their efforts in either direction. However, even when the Luftwaffe did mass their forces, they suffered a near-fatal blow. On January 1, 1945, the Luftwaffe launched a dawn raid on Allied airbases. For the loss of 127 Allied aircraft (which were replaced in a day), the Luftwaffe lost 300 aircraft and many of their experienced leaders and unit commanders. As an aside, the Allied aircrews attacking German airfields benefited enormously from good intelligence operations. Thanks to radar and radio intercepts, Allied aircraft were able to time their attacks to coincide with the return of Luftwaffe forces to their bases. In this way, they engaged the Luftwaffe when they were low on fuel and ammunition.

In contrast to the ineffectiveness of the German air effort, once air supremacy had been achieved, Allied air forces were able to launch devastating attacks on German forces and their supply routes. In a battle in which the Germans needed to maintain a good operational tempo, Allied air supremacy restricted the enemy to nighttime manoeuvre. In support of this ground attack element, the interdiction campaign further stymied German operations. Hundreds of German vehicles (including tanks) were abandoned due to a lack of fuel. Overall, during the Battle of the Bulge, the Allies conducted an effective air-ground campaign, within which, as noted by the commander of German Army Group B Field Marshal Model, air power blunted the German advance and then starved German forces of its essential supplies. The success of the CAS operations was made possible by an effective initial air supremacy campaign. Thus, it appears that Douhet's focus on achieving command or control of the air received important validation over Europe. In addition, Allied air forces undertook some significant resupply operations. Most notably, before the siege of Bastogne was lifted on the 26th of December, 962 air sorties were flown in to deliver 850 tons of supplies to the Allied forces defending the town.

Beyond the Battle of the Bulge, the Second World War bore witness to numerous examples, both good and bad, of CAS. From the experiences of 1939–45, a number of principles for success can be constructed. CAS is a role that has to be developed over time. As the Germans discovered at the Battle of the Bulge, it is not something that can be simply bolted on existing arrangements. The equipment, doctrine, procedures, and personnel have to be prepared in advance for the CAS mission. This refers to those on the ground as well as those in the air. Such issues as friend and foe identification require diligent work. At the Battle of the Bulge, German pilots paid a heavy price for failures in this aspect of CAS. Over 100 German fighters were brought down by their own ground forces when returning from one particular mission. To ensure smooth and effective coordination, central command and control is essential. The air and ground assets must be perceived as an organic whole. This is further facilitated by the embedding of forward air controllers among the ground units and the co-location of headquarters. As in any military operation, the personnel are crucial. An understanding must be developed among the air and ground staff. Once established, a good working relationship must be maintained.

In terms of air logistics, there is no better example than the campaign in Burma. The geography of Burma, allied to the initial success of the Japanese in the theatre (in particular the capture of Rangoon and its important transportation links), made movement and resupply a significant problem for Field Marshal Slim's Fourteenth Army. Much of Burma was covered by thick forest, with mountains that split the country into three enclaves and funnelled the main transport links along a north–south axis. Thus, for Slim, who was often moving either east or west, this presented a severe challenge. Air-based logistics provided Slim with much-improved ability for resupply and deployment. This was particularly important and impressive at the Battle of Imphal, where 155,000 British troops were surrounded. During the battle, 540 tons of supplies were air lifted into Imphal every day, casualties were evacuated, and an entire division (5th) was moved 260 miles to reinforce the beleaguered troops.

Beyond resupply, air power gave Slim the ability to conduct offensive operations deep in behind the enemy. Up to this point in the campaign, the Japanese had enjoyed a significant advantage in manoeuvring, often flanking the more cumbersome British forces. To complicate Japanese operations and to retake the initiative, Orde Wingate and his Chindits were deployed and supplied by air to operate behind the enemy. Particularly noteworthy was Operation Thursday, which included three brigades, two of which were deployed by air, along with 2000 mules.[23]

Wingate's operations in Burma provide us with a glimpse of what some considered to be air power's greatest potential contribution. Alongside strategic bombing, airmobile and airborne forces appear to offer a genuinely new capability in warfare. The prospect of deploying troops by air has been under discussion since at least the eighteenth century. However, inevitably, it was not until the invention of heavier-than-air flight that the theory could become reality. To this end, Billy Mitchell devised an ambitious plan for an airborne operation during the First World War, involving the deployment of 19,000 troops. However, the conflict ended before the plan could be fully realised. Thus, as with other innovations in air power, it was only during the Second World War that airborne forces came of age. However, unlike strategic bombing, which has continued to develop and prosper in many respects, airborne operations experienced both their zenith and fall during the Second World War. Although airborne forces enjoyed some notable successes, success was often unpredictable and came at too high a price.

Examples of success for airborne forces include the capture of the Belgium fort Eban Emel during the invasion of the Low Countries in 1940. This seemingly impenetrable fortification was captured by German glider-borne troops, who were able to bypass the main defences by landing directly on top of the fort. Another successful operation was the rescue, by German forces, of the Italian fascist leader Mussolini from a mountain top hotel in the Appenine mountains. Again, glider-borne forces were used, and they completed their mission without firing a single shot. Ironically, from a German perspective, the greatest airborne raid of the Second World War, the capture of Crete, was the operation that signalled the end of large-scale airborne operations for them.

> ## Box 9.3 Airborne operations: lessons from the Second World War
>
> ### Crete, May 1941
>
> 10,000 airborne troops enabled the German capture of Crete, including the key airport at Maleme, although at a high price (7,000 casualties).
>
> ### Sicily, July/August 1943
>
> Operation Huskey, a tactically chaotic airborne operation in support of the invasion of Sicily, resulting in many losses; it achieved some of its objectives, but ultimately, 130,000 German and Italian troops escaped from the island.
>
> ### Normandy, June 1944
>
> Three airborne divisions provided important support to the D-Day landings. Despite a rather chaotic drop, the scattered paratroopers still managed to help protect the beach landings, capture or blow key bridges, and disable the Merville Gun Battery.
>
> ### Market Garden, September 1944
>
> An overly ambitious plan to push into Germany through the Netherlands failed when three airborne divisions met heavier-than-expected German resistance. Key bridges were not captured, delaying the advance of Allied ground forces.
>
> ### Varsity, March 1945
>
> This was a well-coordinated combined-arms operation, in which the 18th Airborne Corps captured 14 key bridges and protected the bridgehead over the Rhine.

The German capture of Crete in May 1941 was led by 10,000 airborne troops. The invasion plan centred on the capture of four key points, with Maleme airfield being the most significant. The airborne forces were split between four objectives so as to maximise surprise and confusion among the defenders. However, the lack of concentration of force hindered German progress, and by the end of the first day, none of their objectives had been captured. It took the unnecessary withdrawal of New Zealand troops from Hill 107, which overlooked Maleme airfield, to enable the capture of this key point. With the airfield secure, German reinforcements could be flown in, and the fate of Crete was sealed. However, the Germans paid a heavy price for the capture of Crete, taking approximately 7000 casualties.[24]

Despite the successful capture of Crete, the German high command perceived the costs of the operation to be too high. Hitler's judgement on the implications of the mission for the future of airborne forces was stark: 'The day of the parachutist is over'. This negative assessment was not, however, shared by the Allies. The British and Americans, who had been developing their airborne component since before the war, put faith in divisional-scale drops during the Normandy landings and in Operation Market Garden that followed. In support of the Normandy landings, generally speaking, Allied airborne forces (containing both para-troopers and glider-borne forces) achieved their primary objective, which was to protect the beach landings from German counterattack. This was achieved by capturing or destroying key bridges, neutralising enemy capabilities (such as the artillery battery at Merville), and generally sowing confusion in the German ranks. Although successful, the operation did highlight some of the key deficiencies of airborne operations. Poor weather and inadequate navigation meant that the forces often missed their landing zones and were dispersed over a wide area. Thus, without sufficient mass, the units tended to suffer higher rates of casualties in the coming battles than anticipated. It is to the credit of the troops involved that their objectives were met.

Even more problematic than Operation Tonga (airborne operations in support of the Normandy landings) was Operation Market Garden in September 1944. Field Marshal Mont-gomery was looking for a quick end to the conflict in the West, so he put together a plan for an audacious thrust through the Netherlands into the Reich. Central to the mission was the rapid capture of a series of road bridges. This was essential to maintain the momentum of the Allied armoured forces advancing from the Belgium border. The task of capturing the key bridges was given to the US 101st (around Eindhoven) and 82nd (Nijmegen) Airborne Divisions, alongside the British 1st Airborne Division (Arnhem), supported by the Polish 1st Independent Parachute Brigade.

There were a number of significant problems with the operation. In the first instance, it was extremely ambitious. The airborne (Market) and ground (Garden) components were entirely reliant on each other. So that the latter could advance to the German bor-der, the former had to seize and hold bridges in the face of growing German opposi-tion. However, the airborne forces, which were inevitably lightly armed, needed rapid support from XXX Corps. Unfortunately, the 50,000 troops and 20,000 vehicles of XXX Corps were tasked with covering 64 miles (to Arnhem) in 48–72 hours along a narrow road, Hell's Highway, which crossed approximately (depending on the exact route) seven canals or major rivers.

Other problems included the geography of the landing zones, poor intelligence, and insuf-ficient planning. At Arnhem, as a result of the terrain and German flak guns, the 1st Para-chute Division had to land approximately 8 miles from their objective, losing the element of surprise in their attempt to quickly seize the bridges. Poor intelligence, or rather the poor use that was made of the available intelligence, failed to note that elements of the 9th and 10th Panzer divisions were in the area at the time. And because the advance of XXX Corps inevita-bly took longer than anticipated, 1st Parachute at Arnhem was decimated by heavy German forces. All of these issues were compounded by the fact that the operation was planned in just five days. As a consequence of these failings and difficulties, Operation Market Garden failed to achieve its objectives, and it did so at a heavy cost. The 1st Parachute Division lost three-quarters of its troops (killed and captured).[25]

In contrast to Market Garden, Operation Varsity (the airborne component in support of the crossing of the Rhine) was a textbook example of large airborne operations. The objec-tives for Varsity were to secure the bridgehead over the Rhine; capture bridges over the next river, the Ijssel; and support the breakout of Allied forces. During the operation, the 18th Air-borne Corps coordinated closely and effectively with ground and air forces, receiving quick support from artillery and CAS aircraft. All objectives were rapidly captured, including 14 river bridges, and the breakout towards the River Elbe was achieved.

In light of the experiences of the Second World War, although airborne forces are still maintained in many armies, they have seldom been used in their primary role and certainly not in significant numbers. Notable operations include the Korean War, Suez (1956), and the French disaster at Dien Bien Phu (1954). In the latter, 10,000 French paratroopers were insufficient to save the ill-planned and isolated French stand against the Viet Minh. There have been a few successful operations in the post-war environment, including largely unopposed drops in Afghanistan and Iraq.[26] However, it seems that Hitler's assessment has proven correct, and the airborne revolution, which could have been one of air power's great contributions to warfare, suffered near-fatal wounds on the island of Crete and around the bridges of Arnhem and then breathed its last in a waterlogged valley in Northern Vietnam.

While fixed-wing airborne operations have failed to meet early expectations, rotary-wing air power has flourished as a strategic instrument. Air mobility provides forces with increased manoeuvrability and higher operational tempo. This may be especially valuable in hostile terrain against elusive irregular foes waging a guerrilla campaign, in which hit-and-run tactics are used to evade prolonged enemy contact. As will be discussed in more detail in Chapter 14, helicopters afforded the United States significant and safer manoeuvrability in Vietnam. Indeed, although they may be vulnerable to ground fire in certain situations, helicopters can offer significantly increased levels of force protection in other circumstances. During British Army operations in Northern Ireland, helicopters were used to reduce the exposure of forces to IRA roadside explosive devices. More recently, there has been much criticism of the British government concerning the lack of helicopters for operations in Afghanistan. The vast majority of British casualties in Afghanistan were caused by Improvised Explosive Device (IED) aimed at mounted or dismounted infantry forces. The increased use of helicopters reduces the threat from IEDs while forces are in transit. However, as noted in the section on the limitations of air power, the forces engaged in counterinsurgency operations at some point have to patrol on foot among the population. Thus, helicopters cannot provide the entire answer to this problem, but they do give a commander greater flexibility when balancing operational efficacy with force protection.

As an asset of air power, helicopters have utility in many contexts. In the maritime environment, they play a significant role in anti-submarine warfare and airborne early warning. In support of ground forces, attack helicopters are potent offensive instruments. Due to their low profile, they are also ideal for insertion and extraction operations. In many respects, the varied roles that helicopters perform are indicative of air power in general, in that they have significant utility and influence in most aspects of modern warfare. However, as with air power in general, their role is normally supportive rather than decisive.

Modern air power

Air power theory in the modern period has tended to focus on the coercive use of air power, and in particular, it highlights the potential advantages to be gained from attacking the cohesion and function of the enemy system.[27] These air missions have been supposedly enhanced by the use of precision attacks against key nodes. In essence, the aforementioned industrial web theory has evolved to take account of changing technological parameters and the changing cultural perceptions on the use of force. Morale bombing, certainly in its area-bombing guise, has all but disappeared. From an operational perspective, precision munitions appear to bring the industrial web theory to fruition. However, as will be revealed, even the addition of precision weapons, guided by advanced ISR assets, has failed to deliver decisive strategic effects.

The first true post-war test of air power as a coercive instrument came during the Vietnam War. Rolling Thunder (1965–8) was a campaign of graduated response, designed to force the North Vietnamese to halt their support of the Communist insurgency in South Vietnam. During the bombing campaign, 643,000 tons of munitions were dropped. This represents a considerable military effort and is actually greater than the tonnage dropped by the combined bomber offensive against Germany in the Second World War.[28] Despite such effort, Rolling Thunder failed to achieve its objectives. This failure was due to a wide range of factors.

Graduated response is a flawed strategy for the application of air power for coercive effect. As the name suggests, it works by slowly increasing the intensity of a bombing campaign. In theory, the target actor, having suffered a small amount of pain, should be coerced by the fear of greater levels of punishment. However, in reality, the gradual increase in activity merely enables the target state to become accustomed to the pain and adapt accordingly. To facilitate peace negotiations, Rolling Thunder included a number of bombing pauses. This is clearly problematic as it gives the enemy respite and the chance to recover in both physical and morale terms. The limited nature (certainly in the early stages) of graduated response was also inappropriate for the circumstances of the Vietnam War. For the North Vietnamese leadership, the war was very much a total effort. As a consequence, the infliction of limited amounts of pain had little impact on their decision-making. The American campaign was also ill-suited to the context of Vietnam, because it focused on industrial and logistics targets. Although North Vietnam did have some industrial assets, and the conventional operations of the NVA relied on regular supplies, the insurgency could be maintained with minimal logistical support. Moreover, against a predominately agricultural society (such as North Vietnam), the destruction of industrial targets had little sustained impact. The one target set that may have had a more substantial impact, irrigation dams, were not bombed due to concerns about the impact on the rural population. Finally, Rolling Thunder also suffered from a range of other restrictions. Most of North Vietnam was off-limits for the bomber crews. This included the main urban and industrial centres of Hanoi and Haiphong. These, and other potential targets, were avoided so as not to antagonise the Soviet Union and China and thereby to avoid an escalation of the conflict.

Many of the shortcomings of Rolling Thunder were rectified during the Linebacker raids in December 1972. The Linebacker campaign had the similar objective of coercing North Vietnam to the negotiating table. On this occasion, the campaign was intense and short-lived and included targets in the North such as Hanoi and Haiphong. In the short term, the Linebacker raids appeared to be successful, as the North's leadership returned to negotiations that eventually led to the Paris Peace Accords. However, a closer examination of those accords reveals a less-than-satisfactory outcome for the United States and South Vietnam. Under the terms of the accords, the North Vietnamese were allowed to maintain forces in South Vietnam (under certain conditions). In reality, the accords were really a means to withdraw

American forces from South Vietnam. This was the objective of the Nixon administration and also that of North Vietnam. Indeed, the North soon restarted its operations in the South and eventually captured Saigon in April 1975.

It can be concluded that although the Linebacker raids undoubtedly did inflict pain on North Vietnam, they did not coerce the North's leadership into giving up its goal of conquering South Vietnam. The bombing raids may have accelerated the negotiation process, but it was a process that the North Vietnamese were happy to engage in so as to facilitate the withdrawal of American forces from the conflict.[29] Vietnam is a telling example of the significance of context in strategy. American air power was a potent tactical instrument, but in the context of Vietnam, it was unable to produce significant strategic effect.

At the forefront of modern air power theory is the work of Colonel John Warden III. Warden's theory is built on the premise that an enemy should be perceived as a system, represented by concentric circles. Each circle represents an enemy asset. The inner ring is leadership, with energy conversion, infrastructure, population, and military forces making up the four outer rings. Within each ring are strategic aim points that represent key nodes to be targeted. Warden's theory is very much in the mould of Clausewitz's theory of centre of gravity. Although Warden believes that leadership is the key asset, because ultimately the decision makers can bring an end to the war, attacks should be conducted throughout the circles simultaneously. By conducting this form of 'parallel warfare', the enemy's system will be overloaded, its cohesion undermined, and it will be unable to respond effectively. The leadership's ability to conduct an effective campaign will be damaged, and it will be subjected to pressure from many directions. In tune with Douhet's classical approach, Warden identifies achieving air supremacy as the initial priority for air forces.[30]

Warden's work is yet another attempt to codify an independently decisive strategic role for air power, with information-age technology providing new levels of potency. This advanced form of strategic air power was put to the test at the beginning of the 1991 Gulf War and the conflict in Kosovo in 1999. (Although the latter was not an example of parallel warfare, it did benefit from more advanced weapon systems than in 1991.) Both of these conflicts provide plenty of scope for debate. The 1991 Gulf War had to be concluded with a ground campaign. However, the short duration of the land phase (a hundred hours) is seen by some as evidence of the maturation of air power as a decisive instrument. Upon initial investigation, air power in the Kosovo conflict appears to have been even more decisive. Unlike the Gulf War, NATO achieved its objectives without an offensive ground campaign. Indeed, respected military commentators such as John Keegan have argued that the success of the coercive air campaign in Kosovo is proof that air power is now able to win wars independently.

However, when these two conflicts are examined more closely, the evidence in favour of independent strategic effect is less compelling. Statistics for the 1991 air campaign are certainly impressive. Within the first three days of the air campaign, 70% of Iraq's 'strategic' targets were hit. The electrical power grid was virtually destroyed, and within ten days, Iraq's refined oil production was totally eliminated.[31] In addition to attacking the inner rings of Iraq's system in and around Baghdad, air power assets were also engaged in interdiction operations and direct attacks against fielded Iraqi forces. These direct attacks severely damaged the Iraqi army's logistics and morale. One has to conclude that the rapid disintegration of the Iraqi army in Kuwait once the ground campaign began was largely a result of the cumulative effects of the air campaign. However, there are a number of factors specific to the Gulf War that, once taken into account, begin to question whether the success of the air campaign could be applied elsewhere. That being the case, 1991 may not be the turning point in the development of air power that it is often claimed to be.

In 1991, Iraq was almost the perfect enemy for Coalition forces. The Iraqi military used largely Soviet equipment and doctrine – precisely the type of enemy that the United States had been training to fight against for 45 years. In addition, the war was fought in open desert terrain, which, due to the absence of cover, suits air power perfectly. Many of the Iraqi front-line units that crumbled in the face of the ground assault were made up of conscripts. Argu-ably, the effects of the air power campaign would have been more pronounced on these units than professional forces. Also, the nature of the Iraqi withdrawal, especially the escape of the Republican Guard units, suggests that Iraqi command and control was still functioning despite the air attacks launched against it. Also, the fact that a ground campaign had to be fought at all is a clear indication that air power, as an instrument of decision, still suffers from an inability to physically control ground. Finally, the coercive campaign against the inner rings of the Iraqi system failed to exert sufficient pressure on the leadership. However, none of these factors can hide the fact that air power played a major role in bringing about a successful end to the Coalition campaign. Air power may not have been independently decisive, but it was certainly an indispensable component of Coalition strategy.

In the absence of a ground campaign, Kosovo provides an even more contentious case study in modern air power. In contrast to the Gulf War's high intensity Instant Thunder cam-paign, air operations in Kosovo took a more graduated-response approach. However, the use of graduated response does not seem to have been planned. Rather, it happened by default as naïve pre-war assumptions by the Clinton administration, concerning how little bombing would be required to coerce the Milošević government, had to be re-evaluated.[32]

The air campaign in Kosovo had two main components. Targets associated with the leadership were attacked in Serbia (including attacks on communications infrastructure), to coerce Milošević to cease his campaign of ethnic cleansing in Kosovo. The second element of the campaign was directed at Serbian forces in Kosovo and the logistics infrastructure sup-porting them. This part of the campaign was designed to degrade the Serbian forces' ability to continue their operations. Post-war analysis has revealed that the air campaign in Kosovo was remarkably unsuccessful. Few Serbian forces were hit, and approximately 10,000 Kosovo Albanians died during the period of the campaign. The failure of the campaign was largely due to a combination of effective deception operations by the Serbs and overly cautious oper-ational procedures on the part of NATO. In particular, the latter included instructions for NATO pilots to fly above 15,000 feet in order to reduce their vulnerability to Serbian air defences.

Despite the failings of the air campaign in Kosovo, Milošević did accede to NATO demands. Therefore, it seems plausible to suggest that the coercive campaign against Serbia was successful. Attacks later in the war targeted against the business interests of Milošević's close allies appear to have made the difference. In addition, despite the many shortcomings of the campaign, NATO did not relent. It seems to have become increasingly clear to the Serbian leadership that NATO would continue to inflict increasing levels of pain, with no end in sight. Towards the end of the conflict, the Serbian forces in Kosovo also began to feel the pain. As the Kosovo Liberation Army (KLA) increased its operations on the ground, Serb units had to concentrate in greater numbers and thus became increasingly vulnerable to NATO air power.

However, there were a number of factors not directly related to the air campaign that also appear to have had an impact on Serbian decision-making. As the intensity of the air campaign increased, NATO leaders also began to openly discuss and prepare for a ground campaign. Thus, although NATO ground forces did not engage their Serbian counterparts, they may still have had a coercive effect. Serbia also became increasingly politically isolated, especially after one its closest allies, Russia, called on Serbia to accept the terms of the Ramboulliet agreement to end the conflict. Finally, it is important to note that one of NATO's primary objectives, the return of Kosovo Albanian refugees, could be completed only with the deployment of NATO ground forces into Kosovo. Without the physical security provided by NATO ground forces, many of the refugees would not have returned home. This again reveals serious shortcomings in the concept of control from the air.

All told, the Kosovo campaign provides an intriguing and controversial case study in air power at the turn of the century. Clearly, factors other than air power played a part in convincing the Serbs to accede to NATO demands. In this sense, air power appears to have once again failed to achieve independent strategic effect. However, it would be churlish to downplay the prominent role played by air power. The exercise of power in the third dimension provided NATO with the ability to coerce Serbia, over a prolonged period of time and at minimum cost, in contentious political circumstances. And although other factors were clearly in play, air power was the dominant instrument of strategy. If anything, air power may have proven to be even more potent had NATO not displayed such poor strategic judgement in the early stages of the campaign. NATO proved to be an overly large, cumbersome alliance when it came to offensive operations. Although it is undoubtedly true that the air campaign could have been waged in a more potent manner, Serbia was an incompetent strategic foe. By intensifying the campaign of ethnic cleansing, Milošević played into the hands of those in the West who were calling for increased NATO effort. In conclusion, it seems that air power was the most suitable instrument to lead NATO's campaign against Serbia. And generally speaking, it did the job required of it despite the shortcomings of NATO. Finally, though, the strategic impact of air power was complemented by other factors.

Two years after the apparent triumph in Kosovo, the strategic environment changed dramatically on September 11, 2001, presenting modern air power with a new set of challenges. The War on Terror period began with a crude but tactically effective use of air power by al-Qaeda. Terrorists had used airliners before to pursue their objectives, either via hijackings or by sabotaging aircraft in flight. However, 9/11 was the first instance of a non-state actor commandeering civilian air assets and transforming them into devastating weapons. The post-9/11 world presented the West with a set of strategic challenges. Most significantly, the enemy was irregular, dispersed on a global scale, and often based in difficult-to-reach places. Air power plays an important role in this security environment, often categorised as the Afghan Model. Under the latter, air power provides ISR and firepower support to small numbers of Western forces on the ground (often special operations forces) working in conjunction with larger local forces. Sometimes this results in CAS missions, but it can also manifest in independent signature and personality strikes against difficult-to-reach targets.

The results of this approach have been mixed, and they once again speak to the relationships among the levels of strategy and the significance of context. In Afghanistan, it is estimated that tens of thousands of Taliban fighters have been killed or captured. And yet 18 years after the US-led war began, against an enemy with no air power or air defence system and with US aid to the Afghan government standing at over $100 billion, the situation is currently best described as a stalemate, with fortunes moving slightly in favour of the Taliban. Afghanistan is proof that air power–enabled tactical proficiency does not automatically translate into decisive strategic effect in unpromising sociopolitical circumstances. Neither the Afghan government nor their security forces have been able to exert authority over much of the country.

The situation in Iraq and Syria has proved more positive, with air power playing a leading role in the defeat of territorially defined ISIS. As described in Chapter 14, the latter had a meteoric rise to power in 2014, eventually controlling over 88,000 km^2 and approximately eight million people. However, in March 2019 the last territory controlled by ISIS was liberated. Air power, both manned and unmanned, including precision strikes in important urban areas, such as Mosul and Raqqa, provided essential ISR and CAS to Iraqi, Syrian, and Kurdish ground forces. In Syria, coalition aircraft conducted over 30,000 sorties, killing thousands of ISIS soldiers. Moreover, it is no exaggeration to claim that Russian air power, alongside equipping and training Syrian ground forces, helped save the Assad regime. In 2015, when Russian forces deployed into the region, the Assad government controlled approximately 17% of the country. When Russian operations ended, this had risen to over 50%. Russian air power helped stabilise the military situation on the ground with CAS, interdiction, ISR, logistics, and attacks against rebel C^2. At the time of writing, ISIS still poses a terrorist threat, and the war in Syria is far from over. Nonetheless, modern air power has undoubtedly contributed significantly to a shift in the strategic situation in the region. Against air power–deficient forces, and in support of competent ground forces, modern air power has proven to be tactically decisive and strategically important, but only in joint operations. In these complex irregular campaigns, the man on the scene with a gun is essential, albeit empowered by modern air assets.

Perhaps the most impressive use of air power in the modern period is the aerial intervention in Libya in 2011. With no losses, a NATO-led coalition was able to affect the overthrow of the Qaddafi regime during the Libyan civil war. Acting with remarkable speed and planning, coalition air power stopped the Qaddafi regime's forces as they advanced to crush the Benghazi-centred opposition movement. This was achieved by enforcing a no-fly zone to prevent Libyan government air attacks on the rebels, in addition to conducting CAS and interdiction strikes against advancing Qaddafi forces. Once the rebel position had been stabilised, NATO-led air power provided essential aerial support, including ISR and air-based logistics, as the rebels went on the offensive. NATO-led air power contributed to the defeat of Qaddafi loyalist forces via attrition and by giving the rebels time to arm and train. All of this was achieved with limited effort. During the campaign, daily sortie rates never went above the 200 mark and were often much lower.[33]

Conclusion

Soon after the invention of heavier-than-air flight, it became clear that air power was a surprisingly flexible instrument with a range of military uses. Most of these were tested and developed during the First World War. However, the rudimentary nature of the technology at the time ensured that the third dimension had little impact on the outcome of the Great War. The experiences of 1914–18 did, however, initiate a period of rapid technological and doctrinal development. The Second World War saw most of these developments tested on a grand scale, although not all of them escaped with their reputation intact. Despite high levels of operational performance and a significant contribution to the war effort, area bombing was not tried again in any real sense. Perhaps even more perplexing is the demise of airborne operations. Paratroopers and glider-borne troops had some notable successes during the war, including at Eban Emel, Crete, and Varsity. However, the high casualty rates and unpredictability of operations make them high-risk operations, certainly when conducted on a divisional scale.

In contrast to the demise of these types of operations, CAS has arguably become air power's greatest contribution to warfare. The sentiments of Rommel and Montgomery concerning the necessity of controlling the air over a battlefield are perhaps even truer today given the development of precision munitions. Air mobility has also developed into a valuable capability. In recent years, this is most obvious in irregular forms of warfare in difficult and hostile terrain.

The version of air power that still appears to command the most attention, especially in a theoretical sense, is precision strategic bombing. Warden's theories are merely the search for ever-more-critical targets but still with the aim of destroying the enemy's will and ability to fight. The ideas and capabilities that have developed from the industrial web theory have been applied in many conflicts, including Vietnam, the Gulf War, and Kosovo, to name just three. Although Kosovo and the 1991 Gulf War appear to signal an advance in the potency of air power, the instrument has yet to convincingly display an independent war-winning ability. This failure to fulfil the ultimate promise of Douhet's theory is largely due to the innate shortcomings of air power. In particular, air power's inability to control ground, due to its lack of physical presence, will always stymie it as an instrument of decision. However, this should not blind us to the many strengths that air power has in the field of strategy. Its rapid exploitation of the overhead flank, allied to modern navigation and precision munitions, endow it with substantial military potency. In this sense, Douhet was correct to promote the acquisition of command or control of the air. However, because warfare has a polymorphous character and because strategy is so complex, a range of military capabilities is usually required to prevail. Air power is but one of those capabilities. And as evidenced by the mixed fortunes in Afghanistan, Syria/Iraq, and Libya, context is essential to understanding the role that air power can play. Unmanned systems have given air power a new permanence and terrain denial ability, but they have not solved the problem of control.

Key points

1 Air power is a surprisingly flexible instrument of strategy, but it is limited by its inability to hold ground.
2 Most modern uses of air power were first developed during the First World War.
3 The Second World War revealed that CAS was air power's greatest contribution.
4 The Second World War also showed that strategic bombing and airborne operations, while useful, failed to fulfil their promise.
5 Modern air power focuses on ISR, close air support. and coercive missions.

Questions

1 What are the characteristics that make air power a distinctive tool of strategy?
2 Can air power achieve independent and decisive strategic outcomes?
3 Is air power best thought of as a support to surface forces?
4 Has air power become the leading edge in modern warfare?
5 Do loitering unmanned systems give air power increased strategic utility?

Notes

1 Quoted in Andrew Lambert and Arthur C. Williamson (eds.), *The Dynamics of Air Power* (Bracknell, Joint Services Staff and Command College, 1996), p. xxi.
2 Basil H. Liddel Hart, *The Other Side of the Hill* (London, Papermac, 1993), p. 7.
3 Benjamin S. Lambeth, *NATO's Air War for Kosovo: A Strategic and Operational Assessment* (Santa Monica, RAND, 2001).
4 For details on the B-2, see www.airforce-technology.com/projects/b2/
5 This was the position taken by the military historian and commentator John Keegan. See John Keegan, 'Please Mr Blair, Never Take Such a Risk Again', *Sunday Telegraph*, June 6, 1999, www.telegraph.co.uk
6 Jeremy Isaacs and Taylor Downing, *Cold War* (London, Bantam Press, 1998), p. 70.
7 This is vividly described in Lt. Gen Harold G. Moore and Joseph L. Galloway, *We Were Soldiers Once . . . and Young* (London, Corgi, 2002).
8 Eliot Cohen, 'The Mystique of US Air Power', *Foreign Affairs*, January/February 1994, www.foreign affairs.com/articles/49442/eliot-a-cohen/the-mystique-of-us-air-power
9 See David E. Omissi, *Air Power and Colonial Control: The Royal Air Force 1919–1939* (Manchester, Manchester University Press, 1990).
10 David Hambling, *Swarm Troopers: How Small Drones Will Conquer the World* (Archangel Ink, 2015), p. 234.
11 Tim Butcher, 'RAF Harriers Left Guns behind in Jungle Action', *The Telegraph*, August 1, 2000, www.telegraph.co.uk/news/uknews/1366856/RAF-Harriers-left-guns-behind-in-jungle-action.html

12 Lambeth, p. 225.

13 For details, see Lee Kennett, *The First Air War* (New York, Free Press, 1991).

14 David Jordan, 'Air and Space Warfare', in David Jordan et al. (eds.), *Understanding Modern Warfare* (Cambridge, Cambridge University Press, 2008).

15 For details on CAS during the First World War, see Brereton Greenhous, 'Evolution of a Close Ground-Support Role for Aircraft in World War I', *Military Affairs* 39:1 (February 1975), pp. 22–8; Tami Biddle, 'Learning in Real Time: The Development and Implementation of Air Power in the First World War', in Sebastian Cox and Peter Gray (eds.), *Air Power History: Turning Points from Kitty Hawk to Kosovo* (Abingdon, Frank Cass, 2002), pp. 3–20.

16 Max Hastings, *Bomber Command* (London, Michael Joseph, 1979), p. 49.

17 Giulio Douhet, *The Command of the Air* (Washington, DC, Office of Air Force History, 1983). For further analysis of Douhet's theory see David MacIsaac, 'Voices from the Central Blue', in Peter Paret (ed.), *Makers of Modern Strategy: From Machiavelli to the Nuclear Age* (Oxford, Oxford University Press, 1986), pp. 624–47.

18 Robert Pape, *Bombing to Win: Air Power and Coercion in War* (Ithaca, NY, Cornell University Press, 1996), pp. 254–5.

19 John Terraine, *The Right of the Line: The Royal Air Force in the European War 1939–1945* (London, Sceptre, 1988), p. 281.

20 Richard Overy, *Why the Allies Won* (London, Pimlico, 1996), p. 131.

21 James Lea Cate and Wesley Frank Craven, 'Victory', in James Lea Cate and Wesley Frank Craven (eds.), *The Army Air Forces in World War II, Vol. Five, The Pacific: Matterhorn to Nagasaki June 1944 to August 1945* (Chicago, IL, University of Chicago Press, 1953), p. 756.

22 Alfred C. Mierzejewski, *The Collapse of the German War Economy 1944–45: Allied Air Power and the German National Railway* (Chapel Hill, NC, University of North Carolina, 1988).

23 Thomas M. Kane, *Military Logistics and Strategic Performance* (London, Frank Cass, 2001).

24 Ian McDougal Guthrie Stewart, *The struggle for Crete, 20 May–1 June 1941* (London, Oxford University Press, 1966).

25 For an outstanding analysis of British airborne operations during the Second World War, see Brian Stevenson, *Training Airborne Forces in the Second World War* (Unpublished MPhil thesis, Hull, University of Hull).

26 Airborne Operations in the 21st Century, www.globalsecurity.org/military/ops/airborne4.htm

27 Col John A. Warden, III, 'The Enemy as a System', *Airpower Journal* (Spring 1995), www.airpower. maxwell.af.mil/airchronicles/apj/apj95/spr95_files/warden.htm

28 Mark Clodfelter, *The Limits of Air Power: The American Bombing of North Vietnam* (New York, Free Press, 1989), p. 134.

29 William R. Hawkins, 'Imposing Peace: Total vs. Limited Wars, and the Need to Put Boots on the Ground', *Parameters* 30:2 (2000), p. 78.

30 Warden, 'The Enemy as a System'.

31 Richard Hallion, *Storm Over Iraq: Air Power and the Gulf War* (Washington, DC, Smithsonian Institution Press, 1992), p. 193.

32 Ivo H. Daalder and Michael E. O'Hanlon, *Winning Ugly: NATO's War to Save Kosovo* (Washington, DC, Brookings Institution Press, 2001), p. 91.

33 Karl P. Mueller (ed.), *Precision and Purpose: Airpower in the Libyan Civil War* (Santa Monica, RAND, 2015), www.rand.org/pubs/research_reports/RR676.html; Erica D. Borghard and Constantino Pischedda, *Allies and Airpower in Libya*, 2012, https://ssi.armywarcollege.edu/pubs/parameters/articles/2012spring/Borghard_Pischedda.pdf

Further reading

Biddle, Tami Davis, *Air Power and Warfare: A Century of Theory and History*, (Carlise: SSI & U.S. Army War College Press, 2019).

Clodfelter, Mark, *The Limits of Air Power: The American Bombing of North Vietnam*, (New York: Free Press, 1989).

Corum, James and Wray Johnson, *Airpower in Small Wars: Fighting Insurgents and Terrorists*, (Lawrence: University Press of Kansas, 2003).

Cox, Sebastian and Peter Gray (eds.), *Air Power History: Turning Points from Kitty Hawk to Kosovo*, (Abingdon: Frank Cass, 2002).

Gray, Colin S., *Airpower for Strategic Effect*, (Maxwell: Air University Press, 2012).

Hallion, Richard, *Storm Over Iraq: Air Power and the Gulf War*, (Washington, DC: Smithsonian Institution Press, 1992).

Lambeth, Benjamin S., *NATO's Air War for Kosovo: A Strategic and Operational Assessment*, (Santa Monica: RAND, 2001).

Olsen, J.A. and D.A. Deptula, *Routledge Handbook of Air Power*, (Abingdon: Routledge, 2018).

Pape, Robert, *Bombing to Win: Air Power and Coercion in War*, (Ithaca, NY: Cornell University Press, 1996).

Terraine, John, *The Right of the Line: The Royal Air Force in the European War 1939–1945*, (London: Sceptre, 1988).

Space power

10

> **Reader's guide**
>
> Strategic thinkers have only begun to consider space; use of spacecraft in strategy; capabilities and limitations of communications satellites; capabilities and limitations of navigation satellites; capabilities and limitations of surveillance satellites; capabilities and limitations of space weapons; problems of developing theories to explain the role of space power in strategy.

Introduction

Battles beyond the atmosphere remain science fiction – for natives of this planet, at any rate. Nevertheless, spacecraft already play a critical role in Earth's wars. Much of the most important new military technology of recent decades depends on satellites. Many of the most promising approaches to conducting military operations that have developed since that time depend on satellites as well. Thus, twenty-first-century strategists must consider how to use space-based systems and how to complicate the enemy's attempts to do so.

The United States and Russia have been conducting military activities in space since the late 1950s. Emerging powers such as India and the PRC are expanding their fleets of satellites and, in China's case, testing anti-satellite weapons. Insurgents in the least-developed parts of the world take full advantage of satellite telephones. Nevertheless, military thinkers have only begun to develop theories about how to incorporate space technology into strategic planning. Like space itself, the significance of space technology for twenty-first-century strategy remains largely unexplored, and this introduces an element of the unknown into all discussions of contemporary politics and contemporary military technology.

This chapter summarises how space technology affects strategic thought in the early twenty-first century. The first four sections introduce the spacecraft and related technology that have proven most useful in military operations and other strategic activities. These sections outline what currently existing space systems can and cannot do. A concluding section discusses issues space technology raises for strategists. These range from theoretical questions about whether strategists should treat space strategy any differently from any other form of strategy to more-immediate debates concerning which branches of the armed forces should control space operations.

Space systems and what they do

Anyone who uses a mobile telephone, drives a car with a satellite navigation system, or watches weather reports featuring satellite photographs knows the basic functions that spacecraft can perform. The limits to what spacecraft can do are less obvious. Nevertheless, most space vehicles perform only a few specific tasks. The way they perform these tasks is often predictable. Moreover, building and launching such vehicles is extraordinarily expensive, and even the richest space powers must content themselves with relatively small satellite fleets. Those who lose even a few of their satellites may find themselves deprived of important capabilities.

For these reasons, strategists have often found space systems insufficiently reliable and insufficiently flexible. Armed forces that lack satellites of their own remain capable of besting space powers in war. Prudent commanders are reluctant to become dependent on space systems, and yet these systems offer unique capabilities that armed forces cannot afford to ignore. The following sections explore both the capabilities and the limits of early-twenty-first-century communications satellites, navigation satellites, surveillance satellites, and space weapons, in that order.

Communications satellites

Wireless radios were a fabulous improvement over earlier forms of military communication, but they have significant limitations. The farther one wishes for a radio system to broadcast messages, the larger and heavier both the transmitter and its power source must be. Moreover, radio emissions travel in straight lines. Solid obstacles such as hills and trees can block them. Furthermore, since the Earth's surface is curved, this means that it is difficult to send radio signals to earthbound recipients beyond the horizon; instead of curving with the Earth, the signals go straight into space.

Even without spacecraft, there are ways to overcome these problems. Radio energy takes the form of a series of waves, and when the waves come relatively slowly – in other words, when the transmitter emits them at a lower *frequency* – they tend to warp and scatter in the atmosphere. Low-frequency waves are also more likely to reflect from solid objects. This allows them to bend and bounce their way around large obstacles, including the Earth itself. One can even aim relatively low-frequency radio transmissions at the level of the upper atmosphere, called the ionosphere, so that they bounce back to points far beyond the horizon.

Lower-frequency transmissions are, however, more susceptible to interference of all types, including intentional jamming. Conditions in the ionosphere change constantly, making ionospheric communications particularly unreliable. Low-frequency transmitters also require greater amounts of energy to broadcast a signal over a given range. This limits the number of data a low-frequency transmitter can send over any period. The fact that low-energy transmissions spread in all directions is a boon to enemies who may wish to listen in.

If one can transmit one's messages in a straight line up to a satellite overhead and have it relay them in a straight line down to a recipient on the ground, one can use higher frequencies. This makes it possible to transmit more data more reliably with more security while using more compact equipment over longer ranges. If one has access to a network of well-positioned satellites and ground stations, it becomes relatively easy to relay messages back and forth between any points on Earth. For a strategist, this means that military personnel have gained an unprecedented capability to exchange information with comrades throughout the world. This also means that commanders have gained an unprecedented degree of control over their forces, even when those forces are far away, widely dispersed, or both. Armed forces have found a mind-boggling variety of uses for these improved capabilities.

The path a communications satellite follows as it orbits the Earth determines the times and places at which people on the ground will be able to use it. For most countries most of the time, the most useful position for a communications satellite is in a nearly circular orbit 36,000 kilometres above the Earth's equator. In this position, the satellite circles the Earth at the same speed that the planet revolves around its own axis, so that it remains fixed above the same point on the Earth's surface. This is known as a geosynchronous orbit.

For those on the Earth's surface and within range, a geosynchronous communications satellite is available 24 hours a day. Moreover, one can keep surface-based antennas pointed at the satellite without the need for complex and bulky tracking equipment. A satellite at 36,000 kilometres can look down on nearly one-third of the planet's surface, so three of them working together can relay communications to and from almost any part of the world. There is, however, an exception – due to the curvature of the planet: latitudes above 70 degrees north latitude and below 70 degrees south latitude are invisible to geosynchronous satellites.

Since substantial parts of Russian territory are above 70 degrees, the Soviet Union placed one of its main constellations of communications satellites in what has become known as the *molniya* orbit. This orbit traces out a highly elliptical path at 63 degrees latitude. The *molniya* path rises from a low point (perigee) of approximately 450 kilometres to a high point (apogee) of approximately 40,000 kilometres. During the approximately six hours that the satellite spends on each rise and descent, it appears almost stationary to ground-based observers. Thus, the *molniya* orbit makes some of the convenience of geosynchronous communications satellites available at the poles.

One disadvantage of geosynchronous and *molniya* orbits is that since they are so high, satellites following this path must broadcast their messages down over a substantial portion of the Earth's surface. This makes it relatively easy for enemies to intercept them. Advanced communications systems can focus their transmissions sufficiently to overcome this problem (occasionally using laser beams rather than radio waves), but those who lack this technology may find communications satellites in lower orbits more secure. Placing objects in geosynchronous orbit also requires approximately 60% more launch energy, making satellites that operate at lower altitudes more economical. For these reasons, armed forces continue to supplement geosynchronous communications satellites with platforms in lower orbits despite the difficulties of tracking them and despite the danger that they will be out of range at critical moments.

Navigation satellites

Like communications satellites, satellite navigation systems improve on capabilities that armed forces already possessed. Maps, compasses, and sextants help military personnel figure out where they are and how to get where they need to be. Radar allows one to locate ones' position relative to fixed geographical features such as mountains. Since the mid twentieth century, navigators have also been able to determine their position to within yards of a radio transmitter by using direction-finding equipment. Nations have set up networks of ground-based radio beacons allowing those equipped with suitable receivers to locate themselves. Although the procedures for using signals from radio beacons to find one's position on a map can be complex, advances in electronics have made it possible to produce cheap, compact receivers that perform the necessary calculations automatically. Missiles and other crewless vehicles equipped with appropriate sensors and data-processing devices can also navigate by using these methods.

Nevertheless, for human beings, these methods require training, skill, and concentrated effort. For crewless vehicles, these methods require expensive, complex, and potentially unreliable technology. Most of these techniques also depend on favourable weather. Radio navigation using ground-based transmissions has the potential to be easier to use, but it suffers from all the drawbacks of ground-based radio communications systems. Moreover, beacon networks are expensive to maintain.

Just as a small number of communications satellites can relay messages to any point on the Earth's surface, a small number of orbiting transmitters can serve as radio navigation beacons for the entire planet. As of 2019, the best-known, most-accurate, and most widely accessible constellation of navigation satellites is the US's Global Positioning System (GPS). The European Union has begun to deploy a comparable system known as Galileo. Meanwhile, the PRC operates the Beidou system, and Russia maintains the Glonass constellation.

Modern satellite navigation systems perform even better than their designers originally hoped. The original specifications for the GPS called for a system that would allow military users to determine their position on the globe to within a 16-metre radius. In 1988, the U.S. Air Force revealed that the system was actually accurate to within 10 metres.[1] If one can receive signals from a GPS receiver at a well-surveyed position on the Earth's surface, one can use a technique known as differential GPS to achieve accuracy of 4 metres or better.[2]

Since the GPS system works by timing radio signals as they travel from navigation satellites to receivers on the ground, it offers users the additional feature of access to atomic clocks accurate to within a hundred nanoseconds. Whereas users of more primitive space navigation systems often had to wait for satellites to line up in favourable orbital positions before taking a reading, GPS allows users to update their position as often as once per second. The GPS system can encrypt its transmissions and modulate them over a wide range of radio frequencies. This gives users protection against enemy attempts to jam GPS signals or to override them with fake ones.

GPS is so much more convenient and reliable than earlier methods of navigation that it has allowed armed forces to carry out operations that would previously have been impossible. A spectacular example of this took place in the 1990–1 Gulf War. In that war, the coalition of forces fighting under UN authorisation defeated the numerically superior Iraqi army by sending a force of 200,000 troops on a 320-mile march through the desert to attack Iraq's forces from the flank.[3] This manoeuvre took the Iraqi commanders by surprise, at least partially because the Iraqis had assumed that it was impossible. Iraq's own troops, despite their superior experience with desert conditions, would have found the wastelands the UN troops travelled through unnavigable.[4] The GPS-equipped coalition forces were able to sweep through the region in large numbers at high speed in operations that continued throughout the hours of darkness with minimal casualties and no significant mishaps.

The following bullet points summarise a few of the ways GPS gives armed forces new or substantially improved capabilities.

- GPS simplifies the procedures that FOs use to direct airstrikes and artillery fire against enemy positions. This allows aircraft and artillery to hit targets faster and more accurately, with less waste of ammunition. This also reduces the risk that the airstrikes or artillery will hit civilians, friendly troops, or other unintended targets. All this is true even when the aircraft and artillery use 'dumb' weapons systems. Aircraft firing PGMs – which may also rely on GPS – can achieve even greater accuracy while involving even fewer risks.

- As the previous point notes, bombs, missiles, and other forms of ordinance can carry their own GPS receivers to guide them towards targets. GPS is more accurate than many methods for guiding munitions in flight. One can improve the accuracy of a projectile yet further by combining GPS with other guidance systems, so that the weapon continues to home in on its target even if it loses radio contact with the navigation satellites. Unlike many forms of precision weapons, GPS-guided munitions function in all types of weather, at all ranges, and under all conditions of visibility. GPS also helps commanders target long-range weapons, such as cruise missiles, faster. In a similar fashion, GPS improves commanders' ability to retarget such weapons in flight. These facts make it easier for commanders to use such weapons against the most important targets in rapidly developing situations.

- When armed forces attack high-priority targets, they normally fire multiple shells, missiles, and other types of ordinance to be sure that at least one will hit. Because GPS makes munitions more accurate, commanders can use fewer of them. This reduces collateral damage, allows commanders to use scarce precision weapons against more targets, and saves armed forces money. When one considers the fact that a single missile may cost over US$1 million dollars, one sees that the savings may be considerable.

- GPS guidance offers nuclear weapons the same conveniences that it offers conventional ones. By making nuclear warheads more accurate, GPS allows armed forces to use lower-yield weapons to destroy targets that would otherwise have required larger and more destructive blasts.

- GPS simplifies the process of refuelling an aircraft in flight, allowing commanders to plan and execute long-range air missions faster with fewer chances of mishap.
- GPS offers similar benefits to commanders who wish to airdrop supplies to forces or civilians on the ground.
- GPS is a special boon for airborne troops, special forces, and all others who must operate in remote locations behind enemy positions. Among other things, GPS allows multiple teams operating in different areas to coordinate their actions with a historically unprecedented chance that they will all be in the right places at the right times.
- In a similar vein, GPS makes it easier for commanders to manoeuvre major forces with formerly unattainable confidence that their tanks, aircraft, artillery detachments, infantry units, and other military assets will move and fight together as planned, with a minimum number of traffic jams. GPS also reduces the need for large units to mark their routes in advance. This means that, by historical standards, commanders of large forces can better change their plans on short notice, even when operating around minefields or in difficult terrain.
- The combination of GPS and night vision equipment allows military forces to operate with unprecedented efficiency after dark.
- GPS simplifies the task of rescuing downed pilots, marooned sailors, and other lost personnel. This is good for morale, allows commanders to plan a greater number of daring missions with lower risk, and maximises the chance that these highly trained fighters will return to battle.
- GPS simplifies the task of drawing accurate maps.
- Troops, vehicles, and other military assets equipped with GPS receivers and suitable communications equipment can send commanders continuous up-to-date information on their location. This allows commanders to use data-processing systems such as the U.S. Military's Blue Force Tracker to follow their forces' movements. Such systems can integrate information on friendly units with data on the location of opposing forces. (This data will also normally come from devices that use GPS technology.)
- GPS helps logistical units deliver the right supplies to the right places at the right times faster and with less waste. This in turn allows forces of all types to carry out more ambitious operations more effectively on shorter notice and at lower cost.

Box 10.1 Selective availability

The US's GPS originally included a feature allowing US government authorities to degrade the system's accuracy for users of standard GPS receivers while continuing to broadcast accurate signals in encrypted form. This feature, known as selective availability, was supposed to allow the United States to deny GPS access to its opponents. U.S. Military GPS receivers incorporated equipment allowing them to decrypt the signals and go on using the system at full accuracy. In the 1990–1 Gulf War, however, GPS proved so useful that US forces supplemented their officially issued receivers with large numbers of commercial models. Therefore, the US government chose to make fully accurate signals available to all users even though it was in the middle of a war.

Since 1991, the United States has increased its stockpiles of military GPS receivers to the point at which it could use selective availability without harming its own troops. Nevertheless, selective availability reduced the GPS's value to commercial users. Since satellite navigation benefits such major industries as the airlines, US policy of limiting access to the GPS retarded US economic growth. Meanwhile, the European Union announced that its Galileo satellite navigation system would always be fully available.

In 2000, US President Bill Clinton made fully accurate GPS signals available to everyone. In 2007, US authorities announced that the next generation of GPS satellites would lack the selective availability feature, so that future presidents would not be able to reverse Clinton's decision even if they might wish to. Meanwhile, the European Union has made China a partner in the Galileo Project. China transmits signals from its independent Beidou satellite navigation system on the same frequencies used by Galileo. This could permit Chinese authorities to mingle Galileo signals and Beidou signals in a confusing manner, giving Beijing the power to limit other users' access to both systems in much the same way that the United States once limited access to GPS by using selective availability.[5]

Nevertheless, a variety of factors complicate the problems of developing and maintaining space-based positioning systems. Many of the most significant stem from the fact that that such systems do not work unless users can figure out exactly where the navigation satellites are. The laws of physics dictate that satellites must drift out of their original orbits over time, making their location gradually less certain. Factors ranging from collisions with micrometeorites to irregularities in the Earth's gravitational field introduce further randomness into this process.

Satellites may use engines to help maintain their original positions. Such engines, however, require fuel. When this fuel runs out, there is no practical way to replace it. Fuel supplies also make satellites heavier, increasing the cost of launching them. For this reason, navigation satellites have relatively short lifespans. The designers of the GPS system planned for satellites to last seven and a half years.[6] (Actual satellite lifespan varies, and often exceeds these specifications.) Less-sophisticated navigation satellites may cease to function in a matter of months.

One way to keep navigation satellites more accurate for longer is to place them in relatively stable orbital paths. The Earth bulges slightly at the equator, creating a corresponding perturbation in the planet's gravity. Since the geosynchronous orbital path passes directly above this bulge, it is comparatively unstable. For this reason, GPS, Glonass, and Galileo use circular orbits inclined at approximately 63 degrees and at an altitude of approximately 10,800 nautical miles above the Earth's surface. Satellites at this altitude appear to move through the sky, so these systems require constellations of approximately two dozen satellites to provide 24-hour access at full accuracy to all points on the Earth's surface.

The PRC, by contrast, based the first generation of its Beidou navigation system on geo-synchronous satellites and a network of ground stations. This allowed it to achieve basic space navigation capabilities within China by using only two satellites. China, however, has had to deploy more satellites to improve the accuracy, coverage, and lifespan of the system. When complete, the Beidou system will require a similar number of satellites to GPS, Glonass, and Galileo, and these satellites will follow a variety of orbits.

The original version of Beidou was completely dependent on ground stations. GPS, Glonass, and Galileo require support from Earth-based monitoring facilities as well. These installations track the location of the satellites and the performance of their internal clocks. Ground controllers use this information to recalibrate the satellites' signalling equipment to keep the navigation system functioning at maximum accuracy.

Those who wish to interfere with their opponents' satellite navigation systems may attack such Earth stations. This will not, however, bring instant results. Even if the United States' enemies succeeded at physically destroying the GPS ground network, GPS satellites would continue to provide accurate readings for approximately six months.[7] Such an attack would also require successful strikes on multiple well-defended installations and is unlikely to be feasible except in such extreme scenarios as nuclear war.

Under most circumstances, the most practical way to stop opponents from using space-based positioning systems is to jam transmissions from satellites. GPS incorporates counter-measures against jamming. One may safely assume that any other satellite navigation system designed with military purposes in mind will do the same. Nevertheless, no countermeasures are foolproof, and none can prevent a powerful electromagnetic pulse from disrupting all types of radio communication. Nuclear weapons generate such pulses, but there are non-nuclear devices for producing them as well.

Moreover, civilian satellite navigation equipment is not equipped to use anti-jamming countermeasures. This is an obstacle for those who wish to save money by adapting cheaper civilian systems to military use. Even the U.S. Armed Forces found it necessary to use civilian systems during the 1990–1 Gulf War. The fact that commercially available satellite naviga-tion equipment is vulnerable to jamming is also an obstacle for terrorists and other non-state actors, who may not be able to obtain purpose-built military hardware.

Since one cannot rely on uninterrupted access to satellite transmissions in combat, most armed forces continue to train personnel to navigate in older ways. Satellite-guided weapons frequently carry backup guidance systems based on other forms of technology. For missiles and other guided weapons, the combination of two types of guidance technology can be more accurate than either system would have been on its own. For humans, the need to learn and practise traditional methods of navigation often seems like a burden. Military personnel face a continual temptation to become overreliant on space-based systems.

Surveillance satellites

When the United States and the Soviet Union began their respective space programmes in the late 1950s, both placed projects to develop orbiting surveillance platforms among their first priorities. The U.S. Air Force launched its first operational observation satellite in 1961.[8]

Strategists almost always find it useful to look down on rivals – or whatever else happens to interest them – from above. The fact that Western military planners of that period had few reliable sources of information within the hostile Soviet Union made space-based surveillance particularly valuable to them at that time.

Reconnaissance satellites permitted Western strategists to find Soviet airfields, missile silos, military bases, industrial complexes, and other assets. This allowed Western strategists to choose targets for their nuclear forces. Satellites also allowed Western strategists to map even the most remote portions of Soviet territory. This would have made it possible for Western forces to guide bombers and missiles to those targets with great precision.

Space-based systems can also detect enemy missile launches sooner than ground-based radar can, giving friendly strategists extra minutes in which to respond – probably by launching missiles of their own – before the incoming warheads strike their targets. Without such early warning systems, all nations would be highly vulnerable to a nuclear surprise attack. On a more benevolent note, surveillance satellites made it easier for the Cold War rivals to negotiate arms control treaties. Space-based observation helps all parties assure themselves that their opponents are abiding by such agreements without requiring any country to accept visits from human inspectors or overflights by air-breathing aircraft.

Contemporary reconnaissance satellites can photograph objects on the Earth's surface to a resolution of a few centimetres. This means that they can distinguish among objects no more than centimetres apart. By using ultraviolet and infrared imaging systems, satellites can detect details that may not be apparent in visible light. Certain types of infrared photography, for instance, can identify heat sources against cold backgrounds – such as the wake of a ship at sea, or the plume of exhaust from a missile in flight.

Satellites can also use imaging systems known as synthetic aperture radars (SARs). Technologically advanced SARs can achieve resolutions of between 1 metre and 2 metres. In other words, such systems can pick out objects as small as a ground vehicle, but they may not be able to determine whether the vehicle is a tank or a truck. SAR satellites require a great deal of electricity and must often rely on nuclear generators.

Satellites can also intercept radio transmissions. As wireless communication becomes more common for a wider range of applications, space-based ELINT platforms become capable of eavesdropping on an increasing variety of transmissions. Additionally, ocean surveillance satellites intercept emissions from electronic equipment on board ships to find and track vessels at sea. In the 1980s, ocean surveillance systems based on emissions interception could locate ships to within 2 kilometres.[9] One can achieve higher levels of accuracy by combining data from multiple satellites and by supplementing passive electronic interception systems with SAR. Not only do ocean surveillance satellites have obvious applications in large-scale naval warfare, but they also help detect vessels operated by pirates, smugglers, and terrorists.

Small wonder that, during the Cold War, approximately 40% of all satellites launched were observation platforms of one type or another.[10] Despite all the surveillance equipment that the United States and its allies placed in orbit, the Soviet Union apparently managed to build and deploy over 12,000 nuclear weapons in secret.[11] Western analysts did not learn of these weapons until the head of Russia's Ministry of Atomic Energy revealed it in 1993. Almost a decade later, surveillance and information processing technology of all types had improved dramatically, but Serbia still managed to embarrass the combined efforts of the United States, the United Kingdom, France, Germany, and the other Western powers to find and destroy its military hardware in the Kosovo War of 1999. Media sources suggest that Western forces fired over 3000 precision-guided weapons but destroyed fewer than 50 Serbian tanks.[12] Several reports place the number of tanks destroyed at fewer than 13.[13]

The same measures that help armed forces deceive observers operating within the Earth's atmosphere work against spacecraft. Serbia concealed its armoured vehicles from Western satellites by using much the same combination of camouflage, decoy equipment, electronic warfare, secret agents, and artfully leaked falsehoods that the United Kingdom and the United States used to deceive Nazi Germany about their plans to invade Normandy in 1944. Surveillance satellites cannot see through solid objects. Satellites that photograph the Earth's surface using visible light cannot see through clouds either, nor can they function at night. Although infrared sensors and SAR are somewhat more versatile, they produce lower-quality images at lower resolutions.

Resolution and image quality are critical, since even the clearest satellite images can be difficult to interpret. Computers running pattern recognition software can help – but they can also lead users astray. When images are poor and the situation under observation is complex, even the most skilled analysts will make mistakes. This is as true for satellites that intercept electronic emissions as it is for those that produce visual pictures. Smugglers and pirates, for instance, can evade maritime surveillance satellites by operating near islands, complex coastal features, and crowded shipping lanes.

Moreover, imaging satellites can survey only a miniscule portion of the Earth's surface at a time. Surveillance satellites suffer from a problem familiar to anyone who has used binoculars or a telescope: the more one magnifies an image to make out details, the smaller one's field of vision. Even after a satellite has collected information, it must transmit that data to Earth. Because satellites scan large areas at high resolutions, the number of data outstrips the capabilities of most radio transmitters. For this reason, early surveillance satellites took pictures on photographic film and dropped the exposed film back to Earth in specially designed capsules. Both the United States and the Soviet Union continued to use this method until the 1980s, if not longer.

Communications technology has improved enough to allow satellites to transmit high-resolution photographs by radio. Nations have enhanced their ability to receive radio information from orbiting surveillance devices by launching dedicated communications platforms, known as relay satellites, to assist with the process. Nevertheless, transmitting images from space still consumes bandwidth, computer processing power, and time. Even after one has the images, one still needs to interpret them. This is also a time-consuming task – to examine a complete picture of North America or the Soviet Union at 10-centimetre resolution would, according to one estimate, require between 10,000 and 100,000 person years.[14] Also, as noted earlier, photo interpretation requires a high degree of skill, and trained analysts are practically always in short supply.

The laws of physics further limit the capabilities of space-based surveillance systems. Like other types of satellites, reconnaissance platforms can operate in a variety of orbital paths. Different paths offer different combinations of capabilities and drawbacks. A satellite designed to produce high-resolution images, for instance, needs to get as close to its target as possible. To get the highest-quality pictures, one would normally launch such a satellite into an elliptical orbit that brings it as low as 150 kilometres over the areas one wishes to photograph.[15] One can also time the satellite's orbit to increase the frequency with which it arrives over its target during daylight.

Such an orbit, however, makes it relatively easy for enemies – or anyone else – to identify the satellite as an observation platform and determine what targets it is observing. Since satellites in this orbit go around the Earth at a fixed rate of approximately once every 90 minutes, anyone who knows about the satellite will also be able to figure out when it will be overhead.[16] In 1999, this fact allowed the Serbs to hide their armoured vehicles from NATO air strikes by displaying the vehicles prominently in certain locations while they knew that US satellites were watching and then moving the vehicles to safety elsewhere after they knew that the satellites had passed.[17] Also, each time the satellite descends over its target, it encounters drag from the Earth's upper atmosphere. This will eventually slow it enough to degrade its orbit. When that happens, the satellite falls into the Earth's atmosphere and burns or, if large enough, crashes.

If one can accept lower-quality images, one can place one's surveillance satellites in more circular orbits at higher altitudes. These satellites are easier to disguise, although all spacecraft have distinctive characteristics that will allow someone who is aware of those characteristics to identify them. For this reason, intelligence agencies prize data on the technical specifications and operating procedures of other countries' surveillance satellites. If one can afford to operate at much higher altitudes, one can place surveillance satellites in a geosynchronous orbit, ensuring that it has a perpetual view of specific parts of the Earth's surface, or in a sun-synchronous orbit, ensuring that it will always be over areas illuminated by daylight.

Since geosynchronous orbits are too high for most surveillance purposes, those who wish to gather strategically useful information from space must normally resign themselves to the fact that no individual satellite can be present over the areas that interest them for more than a brief period. As noted earlier, most surveillance satellites go around the Earth at a rate of once every 90 minutes. To complicate matters further, as the satellite goes around the Earth, the Earth rotates beneath the satellite. Therefore, a satellite will be available to observe a chosen location on the planet's surface only when its orbit and the Earth's rotation coincide. For satellites in most suitable intelligence-gathering orbits, this will take place at fixed times twice in a 24-hour period, once in daylight and once in darkness.[18]

The fact that satellites visit their targets only intermittently makes it difficult to use them to obtain timely information about rapidly developing situations. Moreover, unless one has positioned a satellite to pass over the area one happens to be interested in, one cannot observe it from space at all. Although it is technically possible to equip a satellite with engines so that it may move from one orbital path to another, this takes time and (generally) irreplaceable fuel. If a crisis breaks out in an unexpected area, satellites may prove at least temporarily unavailable.

One can partially solve these problems by launching large numbers of surveillance satellites, to cover as many areas as much of the time as possible. The most reliable way to get satellites where one wants them when one wants them there is to launch new ones into the orbits that will be most useful at the moment. This is one reason why the Soviet Union went on using surveillance satellites with relatively short lifespans even after it developed the technical ability to build platforms that would function for longer. By continually launching new spacecraft, the Soviet Union could maximise its chances of having satellites available to view whatever areas interested its strategists the most at any given time. Iraqi dictator Saddam Hussein took much of the world by surprise when he invaded Kuwait in 1990, but Soviet analysts, who had possessed the foresight to launch the reconnaissance satellite Cosmos 2089 into an orbit suitable for imaging the Persian Gulf region only ten days before the invasion, were well equipped to monitor the unfolding Gulf War.[19]

In the twenty-first century, Western space power advocates have become interested in developing so-called tactical satellites that they could launch or reposition rapidly to maximise their coverage of fluid situations. Twenty-first-century electronic technology would make it possible for such spacecraft to be cheaper than earlier generations of surveillance satellites. Contemporary technology also allows them to be smaller, making them easier to launch on short notice, possibly from ships or aircraft. Nevertheless, even the smallest, cheapest tactical satellites are likely to remain too costly for any power to deploy in large numbers, and the ability to use spacecraft to track battles in real time remains out of reach.

Space weapons

For as long as people have had space programmes, people have experimented with weapons designed to destroy enemy spacecraft. The United States began to research anti-satellite (ASAT) devices in 1956 – almost a year before anyone possessed any satellites to shoot down.[20] The United States went on to place token numbers of Thor and Nike-Zeus anti-ballistic missiles in readiness for anti-satellite missions between 1964 and 1976. Moscow deployed rockets carrying anti-satellite satellites at launch sites throughout the Soviet Union in 1971 and may have used a laser to blind American surveillance satellites on select occasions.[21] The United States countered in the 1980s by testing a device known as the Miniature Homing Vehicle (MHV). Fired from an aircraft, this weapon could navigate into an enemy satellite's path and destroy it in a collision. The PRC tested an anti-satellite missile in 2007 and may be experimenting with coorbital anti-satellite satellites as well. (For a definition of 'coorbital anti-satellite weapons', see Box 10.2.) In 2008, the United States destroyed one of its own satellites with a ship-based weapon adapted from its missile defence programme, officially to prevent the defunct satellite from crashing with its load of toxic hydrazine fuel but quite possibly to remind potential opponents that it can match China's ASAT capabilities. Media sources reported that the U.S. Military was monitoring a series of Russian ASAT experiments in 2016, although the same sources acknowledged that US officials were unwilling to confirm this assertion.[22] India, meanwhile, tested an ASAT in 2019.

Box 10.2 Types of ASATs

There are a variety of ways to destroy enemy satellites. The three that weapons designers have researched most extensively are known as coorbital satellites, direct-ascent weapons, and directed-energy weapons. All are more useful if they are small enough to base on mobile platforms such as ships or aircraft. If an ASAT system is mobile, one can move it to whatever location offers the best shot. Those who rely on static ASAT systems may have to wait longer until the satellites they wish to attack reach a vulnerable point in their orbit.

A brief description of each type of ASAT follows:

- A coorbital weapon is a vehicle designed to approach an enemy spacecraft, orbit alongside it for a specified period, and then take some action to destroy it. In the 1950s and 1960s, the U.S. Air Force developed plans for a coorbital weapons platform that would have shot at its targets using a rocket launcher. The Soviet Union used coorbital satellites in its operational ASAT system. Rather than relying on rocket launchers, Soviet coorbital vehicles merely drew close to their targets and exploded.

- Direct-ascent weapons are missiles or other projectiles that fly right to their targets, in a straight or parabolic path. The anti-satellite missiles that the United States deployed in the 1960s and early 1970s were direct-ascent weapons. Since they were not accurate, they carried nuclear warheads. When the United States tested these warheads, it discovered that nuclear explosions at high altitudes generate an electromagnetic pulse that can damage all satellites and Earth-based electronic equipment throughout a wide area, friendly and enemy alike.

  For this reason and many others, all countries have abandoned nuclear ASATS. Contemporary direct-ascent weapons are accurate enough not to need such warheads. The United States' later ASAT weapon, the MHV, was a direct-ascent device, as was the Standard Missile it used against a satellite in 2008. The ASAT that China tested in 2007 was a direct-ascent weapon as well.

  Weapons designers have considered the possibility of using magnetic devices known as railguns to accelerate small pieces of metal to high speeds and fire them at satellites. This would be a direct-ascent weapon of a sort. Such weapons, however, would require extraordinary amounts of energy, and practical anti-satellite railguns remain to be developed.

- Directed-energy weapons fire lasers or beams of subatomic particles at their targets. Both types of directed-energy can burn enemy hardware, and particle beams can disrupt electronic equipment even if they fail to destroy it. Directed-energy weapons can also strike at the speed of light. Other forms of ASAT, by contrast, may take hours to reach their targets.[23] During this time, the ASAT weapon itself is vulnerable to attacks by enemy ASATs.

  Although the technology to build directed-energy weapons exists, it remains difficult to generate enough energy to allow these weapons to damage distant targets. Clouds and other weather phenomena may also interfere with such weapons' performance – which is one reason why the Soviet Union considered deploying them above the atmosphere on orbiting battle stations. One may also equip satellites with protective shields to help them resist this type of weapon. For these reasons, directed-energy weapons have been more useful for dazzling sensors on surveillance platforms than for physically destroying satellites.

Despite all the interest in anti-satellite warfare, the Soviet Union is the only country to have maintained an operational ASAT system of any size. The Union of Concerned Scientists believes that Russia continues to have at least part of that system in the twenty-first century.[24] Therefore, any discussion of how strategists might use ASAT systems to achieve long-term political goals remains abstract. The fact that only one power has chosen to develop a significant anti-satellite arsenal hints at the limitations of space weapons as an instrument of strategy.

One reason why nations have not exploited ASAT technology more extensively is that space warfare is politically controversial. Even in 1960, with Cold War antagonism at its height, the U.S. Department of Defense ordered the U.S. Air Force to stop publicly mentioning the possibility of equipping its proposed interceptor satellite with a 'kill capability'.[25] Arms control advocates have persistently sought treaties prohibiting weapons and military activities in space.

This squeamishness might seem strange, since space combat would normally be casualty-free. Those who resist the so-called weaponisation of space would counter that wars that begin in space could easily develop into far bloodier wars on Earth. Space weapons may also make accidental war more likely. Satellites often break down for unknown reasons, and when rival powers possess arsenals of space weapons, it becomes be easier for their leaders to mistake such mishaps for enemy action. If, for instance, national leaders lost contact with satellites designed to warn of incoming enemy missiles, they might overreact.

Moreover, although there are few advantages to using orbital platforms to bombard enemies on the Earth's surface – ballistic missiles can hit the same targets more reliably – arms control advocates would prefer to ban space weapons before anyone is tempted to develop a real-life version of George Lucas's Death Star. There are also mundane reasons to oppose space weapons. Each time one tests or uses such devices, one leaves debris in orbit. This debris can damage or destroy unintended satellites. The area around the Earth is already polluted with such space junk, and everyone who launches satellites has a common interest in minimising the amount of it.

Box 10.3 Fractional Orbital Bombardment Systems

Military thinkers of the 1960s discussed the possibility of placing nuclear weapons in orbit, for use against Earth-based targets. Soviet Premier Nikita Khrushchev repeatedly threatened to do this. Nevertheless, as the text notes, there are drawbacks to basing nuclear delivery systems in space. This method of deploying weapons would be expensive, the consequences of any accident could be extreme, and since space-based platforms would pass over enemy positions only at certain points along their orbital paths, ballistic missiles are normally able to hit a wider range of targets on shorter notice. This may help explain why the United States and Soviet Union were willing to sign the 1967 Outer Space Treaty, which banned WMDs from space.

There is, however, a partial exception to these points. In 1969, the Soviet Union equipped intercontinental ballistic missiles at 18 locations to launch a nuclear delivery vehicle known as the OGCh Fractional Orbital Bombardment System (FOBS). Instead of going directly to its target, the FOBS was to pass part way around the Earth, and then, having completed a fraction of an orbit, descend on its victims from a presumably unexpected direction. In the late 1960s, the FOBS could possibly have avoided detection by US early warning radars, allowing the Soviet Union to carry out a successful surprise attack.

As the United States and the Soviet Union deployed surveillance satellites capable of detecting each other's missile launches, it became unlikely that either side could fire a FOBS without being noticed. Nevertheless, the victim of a FOBS attack would still find it difficult to predict what targets the incoming warheads were about to strike. This would complicate any attempts to plan a response or to block incoming FOBS warheads with anti-ballistic missile defences. The Soviet Union maintained its fractional orbital bombardment capability until 1983, when it dismantled the system to comply with the second Strategic Arms Limitation Treaty (SALT II). Moscow did, however, keep six former FOBS silos to launch permitted varieties of spacecraft.

Hypothetically, a country might improve on the FOBS by secretly placing weapons in orbit disguised as less-threatening types of satellites. The orbiting weapons could then descend on their targets at some later time without attracting attention from satellites designed to detect new missile launches. Although orbital weapons of this type would be less efficient than intercontinental ballistic missiles in most ways, they might take their victims by surprise. There is, however, no evidence that any country has developed orbiting weapons of this type. Moreover, if such weapons used nuclear warheads, they would violate the Outer Space Treaty.

Another reason why most nations have refrained from deploying large-scale ASAT systems may be that while the cost of developing space weapons is high, the benefits of possessing them can easily seem remote. No anti-satellite weapons known to exist in 2017 can hit targets higher than a few thousand kilometres. This leaves communications and early warning satellites in geosynchronous orbits far out of reach. Twenty-first-century navigation satellites – including those of the GPS – also typically orbit beyond ASAT range. In December 2016, popular media sources reported that Russia was developing a projectile capable of reaching higher orbits, but Moscow claims that the weapon in question is for use against incoming ballistic missiles, not satellites.[26] Since launching a weapon into a high orbit would be a slow process that would leave the victims time to retaliate, missile defence would probably be a more useful role for the experimental Russian missile.

Most surveillance satellites are vulnerable to low-orbit ASATs. Some communications satellites operate at low altitudes as well. Unfortunately for those who wish to wage space warfare, developed space powers such as China, Russia, and the United States have more satellites of these types than currently feasible ASAT systems would be able to shoot down. (Emerging space powers, which depend on smaller numbers of less technologically advanced satellites, might be more vulnerable – China's ASAT tests present only a modest challenge to the United States, but Indian defence planners may find them of greater concern.)

There are still moments at which strategists might wish to blind selected surveillance satellites before they observe some particularly sensitive activity. The Soviet Union may have used its anti-satellite laser for this purpose. Strategists might also wish to combine strikes against satellites with attacks on other targets to disrupt enemy operations as much as possible in an all-out war. If the war involved maritime operations, ocean surveillance satellites would be particularly tempting targets. Objects in *molniya* orbits are vulnerable to ASATs as they swing towards the Earth – which may be another reason why the Soviet Union based its military space programme on launching large numbers of relatively expendable satellites. Nevertheless, under the technological and political conditions of the early twenty-first century, there are unlikely to be many occasions in which shooting down modest numbers of low-orbiting satellites would, by itself, achieve significant advantages.

As technology improves, ASATs may become more useful, and countermeasures to protect spacecraft from enemy ASATs may become more necessary. There is no reason why one could not develop a weapon to attack platforms in higher orbits. The Soviet Union made progress towards developing a missile capable of reaching geosynchronous satellites in the 1980s.[27] Soviet researchers also explored the idea of attacking high-altitude spacecraft by firing laser beams from orbiting battle stations.[28] US government sources allege that the PRC tested a high-altitude ASAT in 2013.

Since early-twenty-first-century navigation, early warning, and communications systems depend on small numbers of platforms in widely known orbital paths, a high-altitude ASAT with even rudimentary capabilities could have devastating effects.

Advances in so-called smallsat technology could also make space warfare more feasible. Smallsats are miniature versions of larger satellites, based wherever possible on existing technology. The fact that they are physically small makes them cheaper and easier to launch. The fact that they make greater use of commercially available hardware makes them cheaper to build.

As noted earlier, satellite designers have considered using smallsat technology to develop so-called tactical satellites, which armed forces would launch to support particular operations. Most proposed tactical satellites would operate in low orbit, and no nation would be likely to deploy more than a few at a time. Therefore, enemy forces could realistically hope to neutralise the tactical satellites by shooting them down. Moreover, smallsat technology could make coorbital anti-satellite devices cheaper and easier to launch in larger numbers, further reducing the barriers to space warfare. The PRC appears to be working on miniaturising coorbital ASATs, and the U.S. Air Force's experimental smallsat XSS-11, among others, could serve as a prototype for a weapon.

Meanwhile, if one is to take any countermeasures against enemy space capabilities at all, one needs to know what satellites one's potential opponents possess. The 1975 Convention on Registration of Objects Launched into Outer Space requires nations to report all space launches to the United Nations. Historically, however, nations have interpreted this convention loosely. As of 1990, neither the United States nor the Soviet Union had reported launching a single satellite for military purposes.[29] Therefore, most spacefaring nations have deployed extensive networks of land- and ship-based sensor systems to find and track space objects as thoroughly as possible. One may safely assume that most nations supplement these networks by using surveillance satellites to monitor each other's launch sites and by practising more traditional forms of espionage. As space operations assume an increasing role in warfare, these monitoring systems are likely to prove even more critical than ASATs.

Conclusion: lost in space?

Up until this point, this chapter has focused on the specific ways in which strategists use specific types of satellites. Space technology also raises more general issues for strategic theorists. The broadest of these issues may be the question whether strategists need a distinct theory of space power at all. For all their importance, satellites do practically nothing on their own. Military satellites exist to support forces operating within the atmosphere, and the functions they perform for those forces may not appear to have enough in common to sustain a coherent theory of space power as separate from power in its more familiar forms.

Nevertheless, military and political leaders must craft distinctive policies that will affect their ability to use space assets of all types. Such leaders must, for instance, decide what proportion of their resources to invest in space programmes and which programmes to invest in. Some of these decisions will have particularly far-reaching consequences. Political leaders' choice of a launch system, for instance, will affect their ability to deploy satellites of all types, as will their decisions about where to site launching facilities. Choices about which forms of emerging technology to invest in may also have far-reaching effects.

Just as political leaders must decide what space capabilities to invest in, military leaders must decide how to allocate those capabilities during operations. This gives urgency to the theoretical question about whether space power is a distinct branch of warfare requiring distinct strategic concepts. If one believes that satellites are merely new tools for the ground, sea, and air forces, one may wish to divide responsibility for one's satellites among army, navy, and air force commanders. If, however, one believes that space operations raise unique problems and reward a unique approach, one may wish to place all of one's satellites under the control of a unified space command structure.

If one plans to use ASATs in a systematic effort to destroy enemy space capabilities, a centralised space command becomes almost essential. A centralised command structure may be almost equally important if one needs to implement comprehensive defensive measures against hostile ASATs. Thus, in 1948, U.S. Air Force General Hoyt S. Vandenberg called for a unified space command under the ultimate control of the Air Force.[30] The United States has indeed adopted such a system. More recently, US President Donald Trump has proposed making the space force fully independent, and in 2019, France established a so-called Space Command.

As of the early twenty-first century, the results of the US system have been mixed. ASAT duels demanding a centrally coordinated space strategy remain hypothetical. Commanders from other branches of the U.S. Armed Forces continue to complain that they have difficulty getting support from satellite assets when they need it. Meanwhile, the armed services of emerging space powers have begun to debate similar issues. India, for instance, recently placed its military space assets under the control of an Integrated Space Cell, and Indian leaders have contemplated merging both air and space assets into an Aerospace Command.

Another reason why strategists may need to develop a unique theory of space power is that different countries experience different advantages and disadvantages when using satellites. Northerly countries, for instance, find it more expensive to launch satellites into equatorial orbits, and as noted earlier, they may not be able to use geosynchronous communications platforms as effectively. Moreover, certain regions of space have particularly great significance; the zone in which a satellite can maintain a geosynchronous orbit is an obvious example.

These critical regions of space are already crowded with satellites and space junk. Space powers may soon come into conflict over the right to launch new satellites into them. By the same token, one must assume that any space power that uses ASATs will try to deploy them in such a way as to gain maximum influence over these critical regions. Plans for space warfare – like more familiar forms of strategic planning – must take geography into account.

Since launching and maintaining space systems is expensive, space strategy must also take economics into account. Space strategy may have to take a government's ability to form and sustain long-term policies on such matters into account as well. To develop a successful space programme, a country must foster skilled scientists and technicians, and thus, space strategy may involve basic questions about how a society views science and how it educates its young people. This in turn raises the question whether certain countries with certain cultures and certain political institutions are natural space powers – and, if so, how others might wish to respond.

In the nineteenth century, Alfred Thayer Mahan noted similar points about strategy at sea. Thus, space power theorists often look to sea power theorists for inspiration. Since Mahan's ideas remain controversial after more than a century, one must give space power theorists credit for making as much progress as they have over a few decades. Although space power theory remains in its infancy, political leaders must make strategic decisions about space power now. Moreover, our theories about how strategists might take advantage of twenty-first-century information technology can be only as good as our ability to maintain access to the space resources that make so much of that technology possible.

Key points

1   Satellites allow people to transmit unprecedented amounts of information to and from almost any locations on Earth with unprecedented reliability. Nevertheless, no one type of communications satellite is fully satisfactory. There are different kinds of communications satellites that follow different orbital paths, and each one has special advantages and disadvantages.

2   Contemporary satellite navigation systems, of which the United States' GPS is the most developed example, simplify a wide range of critical problems for those who must mount military operations.

3   Indeed, satellite navigation systems are so valuable that one of the main drawbacks of these systems is that they tempt users to become excessively dependent on

them. Since these require maintenance and are vulnerable to radio interference, it is unwise to assume that they will always be available at full accuracy.

4　Surveillance satellites performed indispensable functions for the Western countries during the Cold War and remain invaluable today. Nevertheless, they remain vulnerable to countermeasures, and they are not always available at the times and places where one might want them.

5　Although various countries have developed functioning anti-satellite weapons, few have invested in deploying them on a large scale. One reason may be that, as of 2009, such weapons remain unable to strike many of the most important satellites. Another reason may be that these weapons are both expensive and politically controversial.

6　Military thinkers continue to debate the question of who should be responsible for allocating access to space assets to commanders of atmosphere-based forces.

7　The factors that help nations develop space power appear to parallel the factors that help nations develop sea power.

Questions

1　How actively should countries seek a treaty banning all space weapons?
2　How useful are anti-satellite weapons under early-twenty-first-century conditions?
3　Who is most likely to find anti-satellite weapons useful?
4　What role can space assets play in attempts to suppress terrorism?

Notes

1　Lyn Dutton, Davie de Garis, Richard Winterton, and Richard Harding, *Military Space* (London, Brasseys, 1990), p. 78.

2　Ibid., pp. 79–80.

3　Michael Rip and David Lusch, 'The Precision Revolution: The Navstar Global Positioning System in the Second Gulf War', *Intelligence and National Security* 9:2 (April 1994), p. 175.

4　Ibid., p. 206.

5　Taylor Dinerman, 'Galileo and the Chinese: One Thing after Another', *The Space Review* (February 9, 2009), www.thespacereview.com/article/1307/1 (accessed April 15, 2009).

6　Dutton, de Garis, Winterton, and Harding, p. 83.

7　Ibid., pp. 80–1.

8　Michael Muolo, *Space Handbook: A War Fighter's Guide to Space* (Maxwell AFB, Air University Press, 1993), http://jya.com/sh/shall.htm#sh5 (accessed April 5, 2009).

9　Dutton, de Garis, Winterton, and Harding, p. 111.

10　Ibid., p. 95.

11　William Broad, 'Russian Says Soviet Atom Arsenal Was Larger Than West Estimated', *New York Times*, September 26, 1993, www.nytimes.com/1993/09/26/world/russian-says-soviet-atom-arsenal-was-larger-than-west-estimated.html?n=Top/News/World/Countries%20and%20Territories/Russia& pagewanted=all&pagewanted=print (accessed May 10, 2009).

12 Timothy Thomas, 'Kosovo and the Current Myth of Information Superiority', *Parameters* 30:1 (Spring 2000), p. 20.

13 Ibid., p. 21.

14 H. York, 'Reconnaissance Satellites and the Arms Race', in David Carlton and Carlo Schaerf (eds.), *Arms Control and Technological Innovation* (London, Croom Helm, 1997), p. 229.

15 Dutton, de Garis, Winterton, and Harding, p. 97.

16 Ibid.

17 Thomas, 'Kosovo and the Current Myth of Information Superiority', p. 24.

18 Dutton, de Garis, Winterton, and Harding, pp. 97–8.

19 Harold Rood, 'The War for Iraq: A Study in World Politics', *Claremont, The Claremont Institute*, 2003, www.claremont.org/writings/030320rood.html (accessed November 13, 2003).

20 Muolo, *Space Handbook*.

21 Harold Rood, *Kingdoms of the Blind: How the Great Democracies Have Resumed the Follies That So Nearly Cost Them Their Life* (Durham, NC, Carolina Academic Press, 1980), pp. 257–8; Dutton, de Garis, Winterton, and Harding, p. 157.

22 Jim Sciutto, Barbara Starr, and Ryan Browne, 'Sources: Russia Tests Anti-Satellite Weapon', *CNN Politics*, www.cnn.com/2016/12/21/politics/russia-satellite-weapon-test/ (accessed April 23, 2017).

23 Paul Stares, *Space and National Security* (Washington, Brookings Instition, 1987), p. 88.

24 Laura Grego, 'A History of Anti-Satellite (ASAT) Programs', *Nuclear Weapons and Global Security, Union of Concerned Scientists*, 2003, www.ucsusa.org/nuclear_weapons_and_global_security/space_weapons/technical_issues/a-history-of-anti-satellite.html#russmain (accessed April 8, 2009).

25 Muolo, *Space Handbook*.

26 Kyle Mizokami, 'Russia Tests a New Missile That Can Destroy Satellites', *Popular Mechanics*, December 21, 2016, www.popularmechanics.com/military/research/news/a24455/russia-anti-satellite-weapon/ (accessed April 23, 2017).

27 Muolo, *Space Handbook*.

28 Ibid.

29 Dutton, de Garis, Winterton, and Harding, p. 56.

30 Muolo, *Space Handbook*.

Further reading

Dutton, Lyn, David de Garis, Richard Winterton and Richard Harding, *Military Space*, (London: Brasseys, 1990).

Muolo, Michael J., *Space Handbook: A War Fighter's Guide to Space*, (Maxwell: AFB, Air University Press, 1993), online at http://jya.com/sh/shall.htm#sh5, (accessed 05/04/2009).

Rip, Michael R. and David P. Lusch, 'The Precision Revolution: The Navstar Global Positioning System in the Second Gulf War', *Intelligence and National Security*, Vol. 9, No. 2 (April 1994), pp. 167–241.

States, Paul B., *Space and National Security*, (Washington: Brookings Instition, 1987).

Thomas, Timothy L., 'Kosovo and the Current Myth of Information Superiority', *Parameters*, Vol. 30, No. 1 (Spring 2000), pp. 13–29. www.defenseindustrydaily.com/Small-Is-Beautiful-US-Military-Explores-Use-of-Microsatellites-06720/

Cyber power   11

Reader's guide

The rise of cyber power; how cyber strategy works (defence, espionage, information manipulation, cyberterror, widespread disruptive acts [WDA], raids, deterrence, joint operations); challenges for cyber strategy (reductionism; control and geography; intelligence; the enemy; the polymorphous character of war; ethics; lack of commitment; friction); a comprehensive cyber strategy.

Introduction

The twentieth century arguably witnessed the most dramatic set of changes to the strategic landscape. Before 1903, warfare had been largely limited to two domains: land and sea. As discussed in Chapters 9 and 12, the first half of the twentieth century brought the arrival of air power and nuclear weapons, both of which have had significant impact on the theory and practice of strategy. Yet in the final decades of the century, the picture became even more complicated with the appearance of cyberspace as a new domain for strategic activity. The antecedents of cyberspace can be traced to at least 1969, when four university computers across the United States were connected – the first message being sent from UCLA to Stanford on October 29, 1969. This Advanced Research Projects Agency Network (ARPANET) was the forerunner of the modern Internet. 1971 saw the first email sent, but it was not until 1991 that the first website went online at CERN.

As use of the Internet spread rapidly, it was not long before the strategic implications began to be explored. In the mid 1990s, as modern society's dependence on the virtual domain increased, discussion of a potential 'electronic Pearl Harbor' surfaced in the strategic discourse. Thus, as with the arrival of air power, the new technology was understood in the threat/opportunity paradigm. Moreover, akin to the early years of the nuclear revolution, technology was developing more quickly than our ability to fully comprehend its strategic implications. As we enter the third decade of the twenty-first century, this is still arguably the case. As humanity stands on the threshold of the 'Internet of everything' and 'next billion users', the great powers have yet to produce comprehensive cyber strategies. The *US National Cyber Strategy, DoD Cyber Strategy* (both 2018), and the United Kingdom's *National Cyber Security Strategy 2016–2021* represent important developments in this field, but they still fall someway short in their strategic analysis.

As a subject in strategic studies, cyber power suffers from much hype and misunderstanding. Despite the strong threat-based discourse that has surrounded cyber power since its inception, the reality falls well short of the apocalyptic commentary. For example, Richard Clarke, a former White House staffer in the fields of counterterrorism and cybersecurity, predicted that cyberwar could cause such disruption as to lead to social breakdown. Even more dramatic are the views of Mike McConnell, the former Director of National Intelligence, who compared the effects of a substantial cyberwar to those of a nuclear attack.[1] In contrast to these dire warnings, although there is ample activity in cyberspace, the strategic effects of cyber power have been rather limited, though not without import. This is not to say that national security does not now have a strong cyber dimension. There is ample evidence that critical national infrastructure (CNI) is vulnerable to cyberattack. The cyberattacks Bronze Soldier (2007), Stuxnet (2010), Shamoon (2012), and BlackEnergy (2015), to name just four, all bear witness to that fact. However, that such incidents exist merely represents a tactical and, at best, an operational level of analysis. It is the objective of this chapter to provide a comprehensive strategic analysis of cyber power.[2] Methodologically, strategic studies provides a series of conceptual tools that enable us to appreciate an instrument's efficacy in building the bridge between policy and military/cyber power.[3]

This chapter posits that cyber power provides the strategist with a flexible tool that can make a limited, but potentially important, contribution to strategy. However, its potential is inhibited by a number of factors that impinge on its strategic efficacy. We identify eight such factors: reductionism; geography; intelligence; the enemy; the polymorphous character of war; ethics; lack of commitment; and friction. The chapter is divided into four sections. First, the existential threat posed by cyberattack is discussed. Second, the chapter presents the various elements of cyber strategy. Third, it looks into how cyber power actually functions as an instrument of policy. Finally, the limitations of cyber power are examined. The chapter concludes with a call for a unified, comprehensive approach to cyber strategy. This means embracing the destructive and non-destructive forms of cyber strategy and fully integrating them with the other instruments of policy.

The rise of cyber power

Box 11.1 Significant cyberattacks and their targets

Bronze Soldier (2007) – Estonian CNI.
Georgia (2008) – Georgian government services and websites.
Stuxnet (2010) – Iranian nuclear programme.
Shamoon (2012) – Saudi Aramco (oil company).
BlackEnergy (2015) – Ukrainian electricity grid.

It is safe to say that cybersecurity is now firmly established on the security agenda. It continues to attract substantial academic comment, government resources, and has spawned a global industry estimated to be worth somewhere between $80 billion and $150 billion annually.[4] Indeed, cyberspace has become a major domain for sociopolitical action, with claims of significant, but questionable, implications for the distribution of power in the international system.[5] The following definition of cyberspace, by Joseph Nye, is useful in that it alerts us to the physical underpinnings of this new domain and the political implications thereof. However, out of this physicality, a virtual reality has appeared, to such a point that the virtual (informational) now has social, economic, cultural, and political significance.

> 'The Internet of networked computers . . . intranets, cellular technologies, fiber-optic cables, and space-based communications. Cyberspace has a physical infrastructure layer that follows the economic laws of rival resources and the political laws of sovereign justification and control'.[6]

The spectre of the great powers being crippled by an unseen virtual enemy holds a firm grip on security discourse: 'Individuals can now thwart authority and conduct asymmetrical attacks that can paralyze an entire infrastructure and stall communications, and the weakest systems can now threaten the security of the greatest of nations'.[7] These concerns have been echoed in the highest policy circles. For example, President Obama reflected this view: 'It's now clear this cyber threat is one of the most serious economic and national security challenges we face as a nation'.[8]

Interestingly, and perhaps signalling a more considered appreciation of the empirical evidence, in testimony to the Senate Armed Services Committee, then–Director of National Intelligence James Clapper talked down the possibility of an 'electronic Pearl Harbor'. Instead, he focused attention on ongoing 'low-to-moderate' threats.[9] Although the more extravagant claims are receding somewhat, there is considerable empirical evidence to support the notion that cyber power is a strategic reality. From the 1994 Rome Labs incident (the hacking of a USAF research facility) to reports of a US attack on Iran in June 2019, cyberattack continues to develop as a tool of policy.

From a general security perspective, the statistics concerning cyberattacks are compelling and make sober reading for information-age societies. It is now well understood that socioeconomic wellbeing for a modern state depends on a functioning CNI. Most critical services rely on computer networks; CNI SCADA control systems are notoriously vulnerable to cyberattack; and E-commerce totals over 10 trillion dollars in annual sales.[10] In the face of such evidence it has to be of great concern that by 2013 McAfee were discovering one new malware (malicious software) every second.[11] On the defence front, it is reported that U.S. Military networks are probed and scanned millions of times each day.[12] In terms of the damage that can be inflicted, the Love Bug virus presents a telling example. Developed by a lone hacker in the Philippines, Love Bug caused an estimated $15 billion of damage worldwide.[13] Similarly, the Shamoon attack on Saudi Aramco is estimated to have caused billions of dollars of losses for the oil producer. In the first of its kind, the BlackEnergy attack on Ukraine in December 2015 disconnected 27 electricity substations from the grid, affecting

225,000 customers. This was part of a 'digital blitzkrieg' against the country that witnessed 6500 cyberattacks in a two-month period.

In response, governments are investing substantial resources and creating new organisations to exert cyber power and protect the nation's cyber infrastructure. In the United States, the Pentagon has designated cyberspace as a 'warfighting domain', established Cyber Command as a fully independent command, and created cyber mission forces for offensive and defensive operations. The financial costs are substantial. US major executive branch agencies spend approximately $17 billion annually on cybersecurity.[14] In 2016, the United Kingdom established the National Cyber Security Centre to coordinate all government activity under the leadership of Government Communications Headquarters (GCHQ). This is backed by £1.9 billion over five years, with £250 million dedicated to the National Offensive Cyber Programme.[15]

Although states for many years publicly discussed only *defensive* measures, there is now increasing acknowledgement of the development of *offensive* capabilities. The latest US DoD cyber strategy discusses the need to continuously engage adversaries and fight to win in cyberspace.[16] Similarly, 'Britain will build a dedicated capability to counter-attack in cyberspace and, if necessary, to strike in cyberspace'.[17] It has also been reported that the United Kingdom is developing an information manipulation capability to operate within and through social media, or what is more traditionally referred to as covert propaganda and psychological warfare.[18] Clearly, then, something of strategic import is occurring in cyberspace. What is now required is a clearer understanding of the strategic function of cyber power.

How cyber strategy works

> ### Box 11.2 Forms of cyber power
>
> Defence (cybersecurity).
> Espionage.
> Information manipulation.
> Cyberterror.
> Widespread disruptive acts (WDAs).
> Raids.
> Deterrence.
> Joint operations.

To understand the process of cyber strategy, it is first necessary to construct a viable definition. To do that, we must return to our definition of military strategy: 'the process that converts military power into policy effect'. This definition identifies the core relationship in strategy: the one between military power and the policy objective. It also describes strategy as a dynamic process. Strategy in cyberspace works no differently from this. And so, we can define 'cyber strategy' as *the process that converts cyber power into policy effect.*

To be effective, cyber strategy must be holistic and fully incorporate both the destructive (in informational and physical terms) and non-destructive components of cyber power. In this way, it makes sense to use both Sun Tzu and Clausewitz. The former has a somewhat broader conceptual outlook, incorporating the strategic utility of information (central to operating in cyberspace). In contrast, Clausewitz provides a focus on the instrumentality of military power and its dialectical and trinitarian nature. Cyber strategy must also be conscious of the close, overlapping relationships among the various actions in cyberspace and the potential implications thereof. It matters that an espionage mission is tactically almost identical to an attack aimed at shutting down critical infrastructure. Espionage is not usually regarded as an act of war. However, in the nebulous, complex world of cyberspace, such actions have the appearance of an attack. Indeed, both espionage and disruptive attacks may coincide, as they did in the Stuxnet Olympic Games campaign. This could have unintended policy consequences: an act of cyber espionage could be perceived as the early stages of a cyberattack. Those responsible for cyber strategy must be cognisant of these issues and plan accordingly – hence the need for a comprehensive cyber strategy.

What follows is an analysis of cyber strategy. It will provide a more complete understanding of the various elements of cyber power and how they can contribute to the pursuit of policy objectives. It is, in essence, an exploration of the process of cyber strategy, and it incorporates defence, espionage, information manipulation, cyberterror, WDAs, raids, deterrence, and joint operations.

Defence

Cybersecurity (defence) is perhaps the best-understood component of cyber strategy. Low-level cyberattacks and cyber intrusions are an everyday occurrence. As a consequence, in the public and the private sectors, cyber defences have been developing out of necessity over many years. Good cybersecurity is based on a number of different, mutually reinforcing components: maintaining the security of key networks that underpin the CNI and core services (governance, security); raising awareness and good cyber-hygiene practices; improving cyber-skills; building resilience into the socioeconomic system; establishing norms and standards of security; and establishing organisations (such as the National Cyber Security Centre (NCSC) and computer emergency response teams, or Computer Emergency Response Teams (CERTs)) to coordinate cybersecurity and information sharing. Interestingly, the United Kingdom had previously hoped that the private sector (which owns much of the CNI infrastructure, including power generation, banking, transportation, etc.) would regulate itself and establish effective standards of security. However, the 2016 strategy acknowledges that this approach has failed, and thus the government must take a more active, leading role.[19]

The initial defensive focus of cyber strategy contrasts somewhat with air power, which was dominated in the early years by an offensive outlook. Does this suggest that cyber defence, already reasonably well developed, will eventually hold the upper hand in the competitive world of cyber strategy? There is certainly optimism is some quarters. Referencing the Battle of the Atlantic, Jon Lindsay speculates that the 'happy time' for offensive cyber warriors may be passing.[20] Among other things, this optimism is based on technological developments in encryption, identity management, and the increasing use of AI in cybersecurity. Cyber defence can now be conducted at the speed of light. However, strategic theory and history alerts us to the ever-present paradoxical logic of strategy, which suggests that offence/defence relationships are dynamic.

Indeed, the balance between offence and defence is quite complex in cyber strategy. On the one hand, defence potentially holds the upper hand because good cyber-hygiene equals 'no forced entry' in cyberspace.[21] In this sense, the technology exists to make cyber-security robust. However, strategic capabilities can never be reduced to technology only; we have to think in terms of systems. Thus, an analysis of cyber defence must factor in the complexity of modern networks and information systems, management and coordination issues between the public and private sectors, resource concerns, and the inevitability of human error. On the latter, IBM's Cyber Security Intelligence Index makes for sober reading. According to IBM's report, 95% of security breaches are due to human error (e.g. responding to phishing emails). Thus, although the technological dimension suggests that defence should have the upper hand, when the other dimensions are factored in, 'malware often gets through'.

Seemingly good defences can be overcome by determined, well-resourced attackers. Stuxnet is a classic example of this theory in practice. Backed by $300 million and the skills of the US and Israeli intelligence services; making use of four or five rare zero-day exploits; and containing a staggering 650,000 lines of code, Stuxnet was able to penetrate an air-gapped network and attack an underground uranium enrichment facility that had been especially designed to prevent attack and sabotage.[22] Moreover, given the future of automation in cyber-security, attackers can also make use of AI. Thus, although cybersecurity is a problem that can be solved in theory, good defence requires constant, almost impossible levels of vigilance in practice. Nonetheless, for the most part, and on a day-to-day basis, our CNI and cyber networks function perfectly well. As online banking and retail prove, trust is maintained. Whether that would be the case in a period of conflict is more open to question, as the Black-Energy example reveals.

In conclusion, because perfect defence is impossible to attain, 'resilience' has increasingly come to the fore.[23] Thus, the defensive element of cyber strategy is based on both trying to keep the attacker out and being able to function in the face of an attack, should one get through.

Cyber espionage

It should come as no surprise that in the information age, access to information has strategic significance (as it always has). This relates to many aspects of security, including defence industrial secrets, economic policy, operational plans, and so on. It is to be expected, then, that cyber espionage is on the rise. In contrast to Clausewitz's dismissal of intelligence, cyber espionage fits well with Sun Tzu's promotion of knowledge as the key to the successful pursuit of policy.[24] Nonetheless, conceptually, espionage is generally regarded as a separate activity to strategy. Espionage is, after all, used to support policy rather than pursue it (with some forms of covert operations being the exception). However, the tactical and operational overlap between cyber espionage and cyberattack means that those developing and executing cyber strategy must be cognisant of cyber espionage operations and their potential implications.

As a consequence of said overlap, cyber espionage may be considered more aggressive and more intrusive than traditional forms of espionage. This is evident, at least to some degree, in the rising tensions between the United States and China over the latter's aggressive use of cyber espionage. This includes Shady Rat, a five-year data-theft operation that targeted over 70 organisations around the world, including governments, international organisations, and defence contractors. In addition, Chinese hackers have targeted F-35 contractors in the United States and Australia, with some commentators claiming that, as a consequence, China's J-20 stealth fighter bears a striking resemblance to the US aircraft.[25]

Thus far, these 'continuous and sophisticated intelligence contests' have not escalated to physical conflict.[26] However, this could change as the security profile of cyber intrusion grows. Both the United States and the United Kingdom have publicly declared that cyberattack is considered to be the equivalent of kinetic attack. In that case, and with the aforementioned overlap in mind, cyber espionage risks breaking down the distinction between intelligence operations and war. This possibility is noted in *The Tallinn Manual*, a leading authority on cyber legal issues: 'A cyber operation by a state directed against cyber infrastructure located in another state may violate the latter's sovereignty'.[27] In light of this, a unified and coherent cyber strategy must monitor cyber espionage operations and exert control over all government activities in cyberspace.

Indeed, in the ambiguous security domain of cyberspace, aggressive forms of cyber espionage may represent a low-level means to offset the more powerful actors in the international system.[28] And as a consequence of the anonymity of cyberattack, the attribution problem, cyber power is potentially an effective means to pursue policy through covert operations. This is evidenced in alleged Russian interference in elections through social media and hacking the emails of political parties (including the Democratic National Committee before the 2016 Presidential Election).

Thus, it is clear that cyber espionage (with associated covert operations) is a rapidly growing area of state activity.[29] This is true, both as a means to support policy (more traditional intelligence gathering) and in the pursuit of policy (covert operations and aggressive forms of industrial and military espionage). With this in mind, allied to the tactical overlap between espionage and attack operations, we are left to conclude that cyber espionage impinges on the realm of strategy. Thus, cyber espionage must be incorporated into a unified cyber strategy, one that carefully coordinates and manages all of the state's actions in cyberspace.

Information manipulation

Feeding out of our discussion of covert operations is information manipulation. Various terms and activities fit under this category of cyber power. Sun Tzu discusses 'cultural warfare' and deception.[30] Alternatively, we might use the terms 'propaganda', 'subversion', 'psychological operations', or 'active measures' or the rather unhelpful phrase 'political warfare'. Whatever nomenclature is used, the essence is the same: an attempt to pursue policy by manipulating the information environment to influence perceptions and behaviour. Both state and non-state actors are actively involved in information manipulation. This includes the use of social media by terrorists to enhance 'propaganda of the deed' and states' covert use of trolls and bloggers to promote their national narratives.[31]

Of course, aside from the technological means, there is nothing new here. Information manipulation is as old as politics. Throughout the Cold War, both superpowers were engaged in election interference. One of the most successful examples was the CIA's support for non-communist parties in Italy's post-war elections. However, cyber-means do provide especially efficient global reach and multiple forms of media to impact the target audience. The term 'Netwar' was coined to describe this new means of empowerment, this new form of strategy: 'Adversaries are learning to emphasize "information operations" and "perception management" – that is, media-orientated measures that aim to attract or disorient'.[32]

The objectives for such campaigns are numerous, and in addition to the aforementioned may include the publicising of acts and threats for deterrence or coercion; terror/insurgent recruitment; destabilising sociopolitical relations; and so on. The key to all such actions is shaping and manipulating the information environment. An especially aggressive form of cyber information manipulation was evident in the Distributed Denial of Service (DDoS) attacks against Georgia in 2008 during the conflict with Russia. With their websites disabled, the Georgian government saw a degradation of its ability to communicate with the outside world. As a result, their presence and perspective in the global information environment was diminished.

While clearly of import, it is impossible to gauge with any degree of accuracy the strategic impact of information manipulation. Despite claims of a long and distinguished history, accurately identifying direct policy casual effect for information manipulation is difficult.[33] The information environment is dynamic and extremely competitive, and the target (psychology and decision-making) is ethereal. Thus, the results of a campaign are uncertain and cannot be relied on to directly achieve most policy objectives. In the case of Georgia, for example, assessments of the campaign's efficacy are mixed. On the one hand, Rid argues that the impact in this particular case was minimal, lasting only four days.[34] In contrast, Lucas Kello takes a somewhat broader perspective of the Russian cyber campaign and concludes that the cyberattacks significantly impacted Georgia's ability to communicate with the outside world and its own forces and affected military procurement at a crucial time.[35]

As with cyber espionage, the most important point to note in relation to any information campaign is that it must be integrated into a unified and comprehensive cyber strategy, which itself must be guided by a comprehensive grand strategy.[36] We are left with something of a strategic paradox. Due to its importance, the information environment cannot be left to the mercy of one's enemies. At the same time, as an instrument of strategy information manipulation lacks palpability and therefore struggles to assert control. Thus, it is wise to attach the unquantifiable results of an information campaign to the more measurable and tangible effects of other cyber and kinetic operations.

Cyberterror

Evidently, cyber power is not restricted to state actors. This is important, and for the most part, it distinguishes cyber from many of the other forms of strategic power (land, sea, air, and nuclear). From the earliest days of the information age, fears about the use of cyber-means by non-state actors have been expressed.[37] We see in recent remarks that the threat of cyber-terror continues to hold sway in policymaking circles. Announcing the United Kingdom's cyber plan in November 2015, Chancellor George Osborne spoke of ISIS's desire to harness the potential of cyberattack against critical infrastructure.[38] However, it is not clear how substantial the threat actually is. For example, Erik Gartzke states that 'cyberwar is arguably especially poorly suited to the task of fomenting terror'.[39] It is undoubtedly true that cyber disruption cannot compete with the terror generated by extreme acts of violence targeted at our cities, holiday resorts, and transportation networks. In this sense, terror groups have generally continued to prefer physical acts of violence to pursue their policy objectives.

Nonetheless, as a form of strategy, terrorism does not rely solely on the formation of terror. Yes, a terror attack seeks to coerce through the use and threat of violence. However, it can also serve two further functions. First, a terrorist attack may have the primary goal of advertising the cause. This is often referred to as 'propaganda of the deed', a notion that originated with the early anarchist movement.[40] In this way, a cyberattack may serve to announce a cause or maintain its position on the security agenda. Something as novel and potentially far-reaching as a cyberattack against CNI could achieve significant propaganda effect. Second, terrorists and insurgents normally seek to undermine the functioning of the state. By sowing chaos, an irregular force can undermine confidence in political authorities. A series of cyber-attacks that shut down banking or electrical power for a few days, for example, could sow a degree of chaos, raising questions about the state's ability to secure the nation.

As an instrument of strategy, then, for a terror or insurgent group, a cyber campaign is unlikely to achieve a policy objective on its own. Yet it may act as a potent component of an overall campaign that includes violence. In this way, violent acts and cyber actions become mutually reinforcing. One can easily envisage a terror campaign in which information manipulation and cyberattack supplement traditional acts of violence. It must be borne in mind, however, that terror groups are unlikely to possess the substantial resources required to launch a sustained and effective campaign of cyberterror.

Widespread disruptive attacks

Although officially, cyber policies are still dominated by defensive discourse, states are gradually becoming more open about their offensive cyber capabilities. As previously discussed, both the United States and the United Kingdom have publicly incorporated an offensive element into their respective cyber strategies. This is an important development, as Aaron Metha notes: 'That is a major change from how the Pentagon has discussed cyberattacks in the past, when using the term "offensive cyber" would provoke denials'.[41] Although Russia and China are less forthcoming about their offensive cyber forces, details of their respective capabilities are becoming increasingly evident.[42] Russia has an equivalent of cyber command, which according to senior Russian military officials can conduct offensive cyber operations.[43] Echoing our call for a holistic cyber strategy, Russia perceives cyberattack within the broader concepts of information warfare and informationisation. This more unified approach to cyber operations taps into Soviet Cold War thinking on controlling the information environment and is evidenced in the campaigns against Estonia, Georgia, and Ukraine.[44] Meanwhile, China has shown great interest in information and network warfare, and the 2013 White Paper *The Diversified Employment of China's Armed Forces* hinted at offensive cyber operations in cyberspace: 'We will not attack unless we are attacked; but we will surely counterattack if attacked',[45] Indeed, the People's Liberation Army (PLA) has spent much time discussing what they term 'informationisation', 'acupuncture war', and 'computer network attack'. For China, cyber warfare is seen as a great asymmetric leveller against the conventional might of the United States.[46] However, the 2019 Defence White Paper claims that China still needs to urgently improve its informationisation.[47]

Thus, although the great powers may use different nomenclature and may have differing doctrinal frameworks, the end result is the same: cyberattack is now an instrument of strategy for them all. From a strategic perspective, the question is, what are the offensive options available, and how effective are they in pursuing policy – the very essence of strategy? One option that has attracted much attention since the mid 1990s is large-scale independent attacks against critical infrastructure, or what used to be called strategic information warfare (SIW). 'WDAs', to use another appropriate term, bolster fears of an electronic Pearl Harbor. In theory, the will and/or capability of a state can be destroyed by shutting down its critical infrastructure. In essence, this is the cyber variant of strategic bombing with air power. The technical means may be different, but the objectives and targets are similar.

There are two problems with WDA as an instrument of strategy. First, it has little empirical basis as an effective strategy of choice. Attacks of any scale on CNI are few and far between. In a search for case studies, we are largely restricted to Estonia, Georgia, Iran (Wiper), Saudi Arabia, and Ukraine. In all of these cases, the attacks were fairly limited in both targets and effects. Properly assessing the strategic efficacy of WDA is therefore problematic. One should certainly avoid the mistake of air power theorists in the interwar period, when the limited attacks of the First World War were used to unjustly extrapolate the forthcoming impact of strategic bombing on both morale and industrial 'centres of gravity'.

Indeed, rather than being a forerunner of larger, more-devastating attacks, the limited nature of strikes against CNI may be symptomatic of problems with the instrument. As Valariano and Maness note, the perpetrators of those attacks (Russia, the United States, and possibly Iran) have tended to be restrained in their cyber offensives. The evident restraint is likely due to a combination of factors, including fear of blowback, collateral damage, mutual vulnerability, and breaching developing norms.[48] However, it is also plausible that those responsible for offensive cyber operations have been unimpressed by the strategic efficacy of the instrument. In all of the cases mentioned, it is difficult to identify what objectives were achieved.

This leads to the second problem with WDA. It is, like its air power cousin, potentially hamstrung as an instrument of strategy. Specifically, both strategic bombing (historically) and WDA (theoretically) suffer from difficulties in strategic application (context is everything); operational difficulties (getting at the target can be challenging); enemy reaction and resilience; intelligence shortfalls; organisational problems (war is waged by bureaucracies); and poor doctrine (service culture).[49] All of these can be individually offset to some degree. However, taken together, they retard the strategic efficacy of 'strategic' instruments and their independent theories of victory. Taking strategic bombing as the basis for a comparative analysis, we are left to conclude that widespread cyberattack is likely to fail as an independent means to achieve decisive strategic effect. Furthermore, in the absence of violence, WDA will likely be even less effective as an instrument of coercion. A WDA campaign could no doubt contribute to a wider war effort in a similar manner to air power (see Chapter 9), but it is unlikely to prove decisive in most contexts.

Raids

Perhaps WDA sets the bar too high for cyberattack. Conceivably, limited raids represent a more suitable approach to cyber strategy. In contrast to WDA, raids at least have some empirical basis on which to build strategic analysis and doctrine. Wiper, Shamoon, and Stuxnet provide actual evidence of methods and results of this more limited form of cyberattack.

Wiper and Shamoon may be related. These so-called data-destruction attacks involved wiping the hard drives of oil production companies. Wiper, the first incident, attacked the Iranian Oil Ministry and the National Iranian Oil Company. Shamoon, an attack on Saudi Aramco, may have been a retribution attack by Iran.[50] Shamoon wiped the data from 30,000 hard drives, resulting in a massive loss of data and considerable financial losses. The raid appears to have had a specific target and goal. According to some observers, it may have been an Iranian attack designed to reduce Saudi production in order to raise the price of oil.[51] There was certainly a substantial cost to Aramco. Some estimates put the cost at billions of dollars. However, Aramco has daily revenue of $1 billion, and the US intelligence community concludes that the attack did not compromise oil production.[52] Here we have another example of a cyberattack of technical and tactical significance but somewhat lacking in strategic import. From a strategic perspective, no substantive policy gains appear to have been achieved by either Wiper or Shamoon. Rather, their significance stems from the fact that they illustrate that limited precision cyberattacks are tactically viable. While important, tactical efficacy on its own does not warrant a substantive reassessment of the strategic landscape.

Box 11.3 Stuxnet: a new form of warfare?

Stuxnet was a joint US–Israeli attack on the Iranian uranium enrichment facility at Natanz. The campaign began with a sophisticated intelligence operation, Duqu, to identify cyber vulnerabilities at the well-defended air-gapped Natanz site. Once launched, the Stuxnet malware covertly damaged centrifuges (by causing them to spin erratically) and released precious uranium gases by opening and closing valves. Although limited in its long-term effects, Stuxnet did complicate and delay the Iranian nuclear programme. Importantly, it did so without having to launch a kinetic military strike.

Stuxnet, described as an 'absolute game changer' and 'a potent new form of warfare', may be the cyber raid par excellence.[53] It was designed to take out a particular target (Iranian uranium enrichment) in a precision attack. From a technical and tactical perspective, it is undoubtedly impressive and appears to represent something new. Stuxnet proved that certain targets can now be physically affected via a cyberattack. Specifically, Stuxnet malware reprogrammed the control of the Iranian uranium enrichment process, destroying centrifuges by causing them to spin erratically. The attack also manipulated the opening and closing of valves in the system to waste precious uranium gas.

Without Stuxnet, the United States and Israel would have been left to choose between an airstrike or a special forces mission, with all the attendant risks and political implications. Instead, they could deploy malware in a covert raid. In this sense, capabilities such as Stuxnet increase the range of strategic options. Not only was Stuxnet less risky and less politically controversial; it also represented a further development in weapon precision. As military ethicist George R. Lucas states, 'Unless you happen to be running a large array of . . . Siemens centrifuges simultaneously, you have nothing to fear from this worm'.[54]

However, before we welcome this new strategic dawn, some alarms of caution must be sounded. Stuxnet may have been technically sophisticated, but the target network was air-gapped, meaning that the malware had to be delivered by hand, probably on a USB stick. Moreover, strategically, the results were somewhat muted. According to one assessment, Stuxnet destroyed 984 centrifuges (11.5% of the capacity at the facility in Natanz). That sounds impressive until one understands that the IAEA estimates a normal failure rate of 10%. The International Atomic Energy Agency (IAEA) also reports that the slack was taken up elsewhere in the system, thereby minimising the impact on the Iranian nuclear programme.[55] Stuxnet was not cheap either. Reportedly, it cost approximately $300 million to develop. This is significant, especially given that it was 'quickly and effectively disarmed'.[56] Nonetheless, Stuxnet certainly complicated Iranian enrichment efforts and may have delayed the progress of the Iranian nuclear programme.

Thus, given the empirical evidence, we can conclude that cyber raids work at a tactical level. They are possible. The fact that Wiper, Stuxnet, and Shamoon had little policy impact should not lead us to dismiss cyber raids per se as a strategic instrument. Like all forms of power, the strategic impact depends largely on the context and the strategic competency of those wielding the instrument. If the target is vulnerable, a cyber raid may be able to sabotage a specific target. In the right context, that could be strategically significant. Importantly, this could be achieved with less danger of collateral damage and political fallout than would be the case with conventional arms. However, cyber raids are still subject to some basic limitations of cyber strategy, which are discussed later in the chapter.

Deterrence

As with kinetic forms of power, deterrence has found a place in cyber strategy. With a growing dependence on cyberspace, the major powers hope to deter significant attacks on their cyber-enabled CNI. The chosen postures rely on both punishment and denial forms of deterrence. Yet as discussed later, cyber deterrence has both strengths and limitations. And like all forms of strategy, the efficacy of cyber deterrence depends on context, our conceptual understanding of how the instrument functions, and the competency of those waging it.

In terms of punishment, it matters that cyber retaliation is largely nonviolent and non-physical. This has positive and negative effects. The ability to project power in the absence of physical force, with the likelihood of zero casualties, makes cyber retaliation (to a cyber-attack) a more valid strategic option. This increases the credibility of response and thus the potency of the deterrent threat. Put simply, the threat is more credible because the costs of enacting it are lower. However, there is a flip side to the low-cost attribute. Decision makers, and indeed whole societies, have proven remarkably resilient in the face of the violent application of force. It seems implausible, then, to claim that potential attackers will be deterred by the threat of power outages (BlackEnergy) or a collapse of online services (Bronze Soldier).

As a consequence, with punishment forms of cyber deterrence, there may be an inverse relationship between the credibility and the potency of threat. This may partially explain why the great powers are linking cyberattack to physical (and even nuclear) forms of retaliation. Thus, akin to flexible response in nuclear deterrence, cyber retaliation increases the likelihood of response; but the threat of escalation to kinetic forms of power increases the potency of the threat.

Cyber deterrence may also suffer due to the complexity of information systems. Unless cyber deterrence is based on some form of mutually assured disruption, intended to take down large portions of the global Internet, the threat has to possess a degree of precision and containment. It needs to be able to target and damage that which the enemy values. Yet modern information systems and networks are so complex that the effects of an attack may be difficult to predict and control. As witnessed with Stuxnet, a carefully crafted precision attack can inadvertently spread to over 100,000 other systems in over 100 countries. As a consequence, the fear of unintended escalation may harm the credibility of the threat. However, in turn, and to cite Schelling's 'threat that leaves something to chance', the potential for unintended escalation may actually increase the potency of deterrence. States may be more conservative in their cyber actions if they fear rapid and uncontrolled escalation in cyber conflict.

A further problem is that cyber retaliation often represents a one-shot weapon. Once malware is used, targeted vulnerabilities can be patched and removed.[57] As a consequence, cyber deterrent threats have a short shelf life. There is some validity in this position; cyberattack does have certain tactical characteristics that limit its deterrent potency. However, it is good to remind ourselves that all forms of strategic power have to deal with the paradoxical logic of strategy. Retaliatory intercontinental ballistic missiles (ICBMs) and SLBMs are just a good ballistic missile defence (BMD) system away from obsolescence. Moreover, to address the one-shot nature of cyber weapons, a retaliatory-based cyber deterrent threat would have to be comprehensive and adaptive. A series of vulnerabilities and targets would have to be identified in advance. Additionally, new malware variants would have to be available to overcome adaptive defences.

We are left to conclude that cyber deterrence by punishment faces some substantial challenges as a consequence of its unique character. However, those unique characteristics also endow cyberattack with some strategic advantage – especially in the area of credibility. Cyber retaliation certainly increases the response options for modern strategic actors. As a consequence, the flexibility of deterrence is enhanced. Yet as with the other forms of cyber strategy, how effective it is will depend on the strategist conducting the campaign and the context in which it is being conducted. The enemy's vulnerabilities need to be identified; their pain threshold has to be estimated; and a sustainable cyber campaign needs to be in place that is able to target or threaten those vulnerabilities.

The other form of deterrence, denial, has a strong presence in the United Kingdom's cybersecurity strategy. The 2016 strategy seeks to make the United Kingdom a difficult target for those bent on cyber maleficence. This includes obvious defensive cybersecurity measures, network and economic resilience, and enhanced cyber forensic capabilities. Moreover, more offensive security measures are emerging. Search and destroy and offensive security seek to identify, track, disrupt, and neutralise cyberattacks before they reach their targets.

A robust defence may prove especially effective as a deterrent given the effort required for a large cyberattack and the limited gains to be made (see Stuxnet). Indeed, due to the challenges of retaliatory action in the cyber domain, which include attribution and the limited efficacy of cyberattack, denial may arguably be given a degree of priority in cyber deterrence. Bronze Soldier provides some empirical basis for this position. In 2007, Estonia was able to resist the cyberattack (coercion failed) with a series of defensive measures rather than resorting to punishment forms of retaliation. Arguably, resorting to the latter was unlikely – first because Russian state involvement could not be verified and second because Estonia lacked the capabilities to retaliate against Russia, which possessed cross-domain escalation dominance.

Moreover, denial and punishment can function together to provide more robust cyber deterrence. Effective cybersecurity may enhance the credibility of punitive attack response. A state with more effective cyber defences is better positioned to wage and survive a cyberwar, further enhancing credibility via a 'warfighting for deterrence' model.[58] A state that is better positioned to wage cyberwar possesses a more credible threat.

Although it is sensible to extol the virtues of deterrence by denial, even in the cyber domain, we should heed Clausewitz's warning about the strategic limits of a defensive posture:[59] if deterrence fails, cross-domain offensive options are needed. Specifically, they are required for damage limitation (attacking enemy capability), enhanced intra-war deterrence (through coercion), and the pursuit of victory (policy objectives). Of course, denial also functions in support of intra-war deterrence and damage limitation, thus further enhancing its utility.

This analysis of cyber deterrence leads to the following conclusion. Strategic logic demands a flexible and comprehensive approach that uses both offensive and defensive options to enhance deterrence against cyberattack. Additionally, a deterrence posture must be based on capabilities that enable a rational and flexible pursuit of policy in the event of deterrence failure. In this way, as in the nuclear and conventional realms, cyber capabilities attached to deterrence must always have a warfighting function – both to enhance deterrence and to enable the pursuit of policy if deterrence fails. In this sense, the US DoD Cyber Strategy is right to emphasise the need to fight and win in cyberspace.

Joint operations

We have seen how cyber operations as an independent tool offer some viable, if limited, strategic options. However, cyber power can also provide support to the joint commander, as a force multiplier to kinetic forces. In this sense, cyber power contributes to overall strategic effect but does not redefine the entire strategic landscape. The force multiplier effect can come in many forms. The 2007 Israeli attack on the Syrian nuclear facility at Kibar presents an interesting case. Before the air assault, the Syrian air defence network was hacked, giving Israeli jets a free run to their targets.[60]

In another incident, insurgents in Iraq hacked a US drone feed to confer tactical advantage.[61] In Ukraine, 'Russian cyberattacks had collapsed the communication systems of almost all Ukrainian forces that could pose a danger to the invading Russian troops'. As one intelligence analyst put it, Russia thus gained complete information dominance in Ukraine.[62]

Conscious of the advantages to be gained, the United Kingdom is rapidly adding a cyber dimension to its operational planning and capabilities. In addition to contributing to a new 2000-strong offensive cyber force with GCHQ, the Ministry of Defence has two principle cyber roles: defend its own networks and develop cyber capabilities to enhance military operations.[63] As part of Joint Forces Command, Defence Cyber Operations Group (DCOG) is responsible for delivering military effect through cyber operations. With intelligence support from GCHQ, DCOG prosecutes its cyber missions through the Joint Cyber Unit, which became fully operational in March 2015.[64] General Shaw, then–assistant chief of defence staff, signposts the need to go on the offensive and to manoeuvre in cyberspace and to break down the distinction between cyber and other forces. The emphasis, he argues, should be placed on the effect, not the means of delivery: '[cyber] is merely the latest medium though which to achieve effect'. Thus, in the United Kingdom, all operational planning now includes a cyber dimension.[65]

Such joint use of cyber power enhances operations and fulfils some of the promises of the earlier information warfare literature. In this way, cyber operations are used to dominate the operational information environment, help shape the battlespace, and thereby provide a force multiplier effect for friendly forces. There are striking similarities to air and sea power, both of which are most effective in support of land forces in the joint environment.

Conclusion – a unified cyber strategy

Cyber strategy is surprisingly broad and flexible. It includes espionage, information manipulation, defence, offensive operations of varying scale, coercion, deterrence, and joint operations. Indeed, one might conclude that due to the significance of information in the cyber age and the overlap between offensive techniques, activities such as espionage can no longer be decoupled from other strategic activities. This, however, places an even greater demand on the need for a unified, comprehensive strategic approach. Such a strategy must be based on an understanding of how the different expressions of cyber power interact among themselves and with the other instruments of strategy.

Some questions that may help in forming a cohesive strategy include the following. Are there cyber 'centres of gravity' that can be exploited? How does cyber warfighting function? Is cyberspace a separate domain for warfare? If so, what are its characteristics? Where does cyberattack sit on the ladder of escalation? Is cyberattack primarily a joint instrument, or does it have independent strategic effect? Is cyber espionage a form of attack? When does cyber information manipulation constitute an aggressive action? These are a selection of the questions that may help stimulate strategic discourse on cyber power and in turn help us to develop cyber strategy into an effective component of national policy.

The challenges of cyber strategy

The different forms that cyber strategy can take have been discussed individually, and their strengths and weaknesses have been identified. However, there are some general points about cyber power that must be considered. These pose substantial challenges to those conducting cyber strategy campaigns and may significantly affect the strategic efficacy of the overall instrument. Only by taking a holistic perspective, identifying the whole gamut of issues affecting cyber strategy, can we hope to provide a useful discussion of this new form of power.

Box 11.4 The challenges of cyber strategy

Reductionism.
Control and geography.
Intelligence.
The enemy
Polymorphous character of war.
Ethics.
Lack of commitment.
Friction.

Reductionism

Although distinct strategies are required for each form of warfare or new strategic instrument, there is an attendant danger that these individual strategies may begin to usurp the place of overall strategy. To put it another way, proponents often seek to translate a geographically constrained strategy into a general theory of victory. This form of reductionism has the aim of simplifying strategy, reducing it to success in just one environment or one form of warfare. Strategy in both theory and practice must be unified and inclusive in scope. Successful strategic performance is always the result of numerous dimensions at work. To expect any one instrument to dominate strategy is to commit the error of reductionism. Even in relation to the dominant role of infantry (man on the scene with a gun),[66] it is improper to overlook the many elements that get him there, sustain him, and support him.

Cyber strategy is most susceptible to reductionism in relation to its independent form, especially as it relates to WDAs and raids. This can be seen in the aforementioned comments regarding the potential catastrophic outcome of cyberattack on a modern society. As will be discussed later, Armageddon levels of disruption are unlikely to be realised, for a number of reasons. Nonetheless, even if we accept the vision offered by Clarke and McConnell, in which cyberattack is able to create substantial levels of social disruption, there is still no guarantee that policy outcomes will be achieved via this route.

In this sense, this analysis takes issue with Kristin M. Lord and Travis Sharp's comment regarding the coercive potential of cyberattack: 'The magnitude and intensity of cyberattacks make them ideal instruments of coercion'.[67] Like all instruments of strategy, cyberattack can be used for coercive effect. However, its potential is far from 'ideal'. Strategic actors have shown remarkable resilience in the face of coercive air campaigns. Important examples of this can be found in Vietnam and Kosovo. North Vietnam withstood the three-year onslaught of Rolling Thunder. And although the communist North did eventually acquiesce to US demands for a peace agreement, partly in response to the Linebacker air campaigns, the strategic outcome generally worked in the North's favour. The Paris Peace Accords, signed in 1973, paved the way for the US withdrawal from Vietnam and left the South vulnerable to eventual conquest from the North. In Kosovo, NATO's original anticipation of a four-day coercive air campaign proved woefully optimistic. Operation Allied Force actually lasted 78 days. And in the final analysis, it is clear that factors other than the air campaign played a significant role in Milošević's decision to submit (see Chapter 9).

These examples from air power coercive campaigns suggest that the disruption caused by WDA is far from guaranteed to produce decisive coercive effect. Indeed, both examples illustrate that coercive effect often emanates from a complex series of actions working together over time. The Linebacker campaigns came after at least seven years of sustained US action in Vietnam. Likewise, the coercive effect of NATO's air campaign against Serbia was supported by diplomatic pressure from Russia and the increasing likelihood of a NATO ground campaign.

Control and geography

As independent instruments of decision, cyber, air, sea, and space power all stumble when faced with the geographic dimension of strategy. Although no solider is an island, their role in 'control' does leave the other instruments somewhat in their strategic shadow. Politics, and therefore strategy, is about people. It is concerned with the ability to influence human behaviour. It is undoubtedly true that human behaviour can be affected psychologically without reference to geography. Nonetheless, geography is central to a valid understanding of human political behaviour. Geography is the stage on which human affairs are conducted. This is not just the case in the most obvious of ways, in relation to the territorial delineation of people and resources. The significance of geography also functions at an emotional level, both for the individual and for the group. It is axiomatic to claim that people often form an emotional attachment to the land on which they dwell.[68] The conclusion from this brief discussion of geography is that because physical terrain matters in politics, the control of it matters as well. And because control can be reliably exercised only by the physical presence of people, the physical expressions of force play the leading role in the drama of politics.

This discussion should not be mistaken for a rejection of cyberspace as geography. Clearly, there is a geographic reality to cyberspace. Many forms of human interaction occur within and through cyberspace. These include cultural, social, political, economic, and strategic forms of interaction. Additionally, important resources (information) reside within cyberspace or can be manipulated by actions through it. This point merely emphasises the important relationship between the physical and the virtual worlds. Indeed, as noted earlier, cyberspace itself is constructed of physical objects: computers, servers, fibre optics, and so on.

Despite cyberspace being a geographic reality with sociopolitical significance, basic human needs and desires are to be found on the territory under our feet. In light of this, activities in cyberspace can have only minimal, indirect strategic effect. Cyber power has only limited opportunity to shape the physical environment. In this sense, Kenneth Geers is persuasive when he argues that '[b]asically, tactical victories amount to a successful reshuffling of the bits – the ones and zeroes – inside a computer. Then the attacker must wait to see if anything happens in the real world'.[69] In this, we are reminded of Sir Julian Corbett's theory of sea power: events at sea have significance only in how they affect events on land. Indeed, Valeriano and Maness convincingly argue that disputes in cyberspace actually map traditional geopolitical disputes. In this sense, cyber conflict has not redefined the geopolitical landscape; rather, it echoes that landscape.[70]

Intelligence

When the proponents of a particular military instrument or form of war seek to sell their vision of future operations, they often underestimate the intelligence challenge involved. Not only is there an assumption that 'the virus will always get through'; there is also naïve optimism regarding the ability of the attacker to understand the nature of the enemy's system. There is a sense that those conducting the attack will be able to identify key targets, destroy or disrupt said targets, and then enjoy the predictable results. In contrast, strategic history teaches us that all of these steps to victory are fraught with difficulties. This is especially the case regarding the intelligence challenge of such a mission. Take, for example, the history of strategic bombing. Enemy industrial systems have proven far more complex and unpredictable than assumed. It took until late in the Second World War to fully appreciate that the railway network was one of the key vulnerabilities of the Nazi war economy.[71]

It is often argued that the arrival of cyberspace has brought with it a redistribution of power within the international system. Specifically, the low entry costs for cyber power provide many non-state actors with new opportunities to offset the conventional dominance of the great powers.[72] However, a substantial cyber campaign requires significant investment in intelligence capabilities to understand the nature of the target system and the likely outcome of attacks.[73] This is evidenced in Stuxnet and the necessary substantive intelligence component of the attack, Duqu. The latter was a substantial and sophisticated intelligence campaign, and this was only for a specific, contained target. The intelligence challenge of attacking the entire CNI of a nation can only be imagined.

In the intelligence challenge of cyber strategy, strategic effect is not limited to the physical or virtual domains. In this sense, a plan of victory cannot be reduced to an empirical analysis of physical or virtual systems, their vulnerabilities, and the potential outcomes from attacking them. As Clausewitz teaches us, war is predominately a battle of wills, carried out through the interaction of physical (or virtual) forces.[74] Thus, political outcomes are often the result of impact on intangible forces such as will or morale. These factors are difficult to quantify with any significant degree of certainty.

These intelligence challenges clearly have resonance for cyber power, especially in its independent form. As a coercive instrument, it is essential that those conducting an independent cyber campaign have a reasonably accurate understanding of the enemy, in relation to both tangible and intangible factors. Even when operating in the joint environment, cyber actions must be based on a sound understanding of how the enemy functions as a fighting force. How does the enemy's command and control system function? How robust is it? How quickly can it recover from an attack? Another substantial challenge relates to battle damage assessment (BDA). Attacking a target is one thing; accurately assessing the effect of said attack is quite another. Again, the history of strategic bombing is illustrative here. The results of attacking German industrial production were at times predicted on the percentage of roofing destroyed. However, it was often the case that machine tools survived even when the buildings around them did not.[75]

Even in light of these intelligence challenges, the attacks against Iran, Estonia, Georgia, Saudi Arabia, and Ukraine suggest that intelligence does not pose an insurmountable difficulty in all cases. Thus, this section of the analysis is not designed to imply that the intelligence challenges associated with cyber strategy are uniquely difficult. Rather, it is merely designed to tone down the enthusiasm of the cyberattack theorists, by noting the many intelligence questions that have to be addressed when conducting a campaign. Clausewitz may have overplayed his hand when he denigrated the value of intelligence in war, but his comments on the potency of uncertainty should be borne in mind.[76]

The enemy

The tendency to underplay the role of the enemy in war is perfectly illustrated by the following statement from Confederate General George Picket. When asked why the Confederacy had lost the battle of Gettysburg, Picket replied, 'I think the Union Army had something to do with it'.[77] Libicki performs an important service in his paper *Cyberdeterrence and Cyberwar*, by noting that the target of a cyberattack has the ability to respond.[78] Indeed, as noted earlier, there is a reasonable sense of optimism concerning the future of cyber defences.

A country under attack can take many steps to reduce its vulnerability to cyber power. As illustrated by the Estonian case, a target can limit access to its systems by isolating itself from the Internet, to prevent further disruption.[79] As previously noted, despite Stuxnet's tactical sophistication, once discovered, it was quickly disarmed. Moreover, as we have seen, states are investing considerably (money, time, and effort) in defensive measures, including developing cybersecurity skills and awareness and generally enhancing the resilience of their socioeconomic functions.

Indeed, information-age economies and systems may be far more robust than is often assumed in the cyberattack literature. Adam Smith's comment that 'there is a lot of ruin in a country' is as applicable to an information-centred state as it was to the industrial variant that Smith had in mind. Robert Anderson, Greg Rattray, and Winn Schwartau all highlight the robust nature of modern socioeconomic structures. Indeed, Rattray notes that the complex nature of information infrastructures provides them with a sort of built-in robustness.[80]

With limited evidence available on substantive cyberattack, we can turn once again to the history of air power to provide empirical evidence of the range of responses available to those under attack. During the Combined Bomber Offensive against Germany, ball bearing production was identified as a key and vulnerable target, concentrated as it was in the city of Schweinfurt. The U.S. Army Air Force attacked the city on August 17, 1943. Once this vulnerability had been highlighted by the attack, the Germans responded by dispersing ball bearing production and redesigning equipment to be less reliant on this particular component. Similarly, during the Korean War, the North Koreans reduced the water levels behind irrigation dams to make them less vulnerable to air attack.[81]

The role of the enemy goes beyond robustness and operational responses. The very nature of the enemy can significantly decide the fate of a cyber campaign. For example, sub-state actors may be largely immune to the effects of some forms of cyber power. Both their systems and style of warfare may be far less reliant on information-age principles than is the case for most modern states. This merely emphasises the point that in the multilevel world of strategy, the enemy is not restricted to responding at the same level as the attacker's actions. When facing a competent tactical cyber opponent, a strategic actor can choose to negate the tactical effects by responding effectively at higher levels. For example, a state on the receiving end of an effective cyberattack may shift its stance to one that relies more heavily on irregular forms of warfare, taking advantage of a less-information-reliant form of strategy. Alternatively, facing cyber-defeat, an actor may seek to escalate into the kinetic realms of force, perhaps seeking to break the will of a casualty-averse cyber-savvy foe. For much of the Pacific War, Japan knew it could not hold back the US onslaught. With tactical and operational setbacks inevitable, Japan's strategy increasingly relied on breaking the will of its opponent. In this way, Japan sought to inflict substantial losses on the United States to force the latter to some form of negotiated peace.

As with our discussion of earlier restrictions, these comments regarding the role of the enemy should not be taken as a blanket negation of cyber power as a strategic instrument. In the dynamic relationship of strategy, even a robust and resourceful enemy can be overcome by clever strategies or cumulative effects over time. However, the nature of cyber power, especially its inability to exert physical control or inflict much destruction, suggests that it may be even more difficult to wield strategically than other forms of warfare in the face of enemy response.

The polymorphous character of war

Feeding directly out of this discussion of the enemy is the self-evident comment that war has a polymorphous character. Put simply, war can take many forms. Again, this is not fatal to cyber power as a form of strategy, but it does complicate the ability of cyber-actors to exert significant strategic effect. The polymorphous character of war is the result of a number of factors, including the nature of the belligerents; the technology available; the geography of the theatre of operations; the policy objectives sought; and the length of the conflict. Taken together, these characteristics ensure that each war is unique.

Cyber strategy exists within this complex polymorphous reality. It does not take much imagination to conclude that cyber power is better suited to some situations than to others. Some policy objectives will demand physical control or the destruction of the enemy; some enemies will be less vulnerable to cyber coercion; some enemies will have more advanced cyber defences; some conflicts will be too short for information manipulation to influence perception; and so on. It is tempting to suggest that, as a general rule, the more regular the belligerents and their form of warfare, the more effective cyber power will be. And yet we can also conclude that a regular, well-resourced state has more potential (resources) to withstand a cyber campaign. All forms of strategy, including cyber, must face the polymorphous character of each unique war, and it is a character that can evolve over the course of a conflict.

Ethics

The relationship between cyber power and ethics is complex and underexplored.[82] On the one hand, as a virtual form of conflict cyberattack has an advantage over physical instruments of power. The almost complete lack of violence means cyberattack is immune from many ethical dilemmas: 'many cyberattacks will not be lethal and will not even result in permanent damage to physical objects'.[83] In this way, cyber power provides extra options for the ethically minded strategist. Policy can be pursued with minimal physical risk to either the attacker or the victim. Geers is convincing in his analysis of the ethical and political advantages of the Stuxnet attack: 'Stuxnet may have been more effective than a conventional military attack and may have avoided a major international crisis over collateral damage'.[84] Moreover, the effects of certain cyberattacks (e.g. DDoS and ransomware) are instantly reversible, leaving no residual damage to the target. This potentially changes the moral calculus of using force. Finally, as witnessed with Stuxnet, a cyberattack can be designed to be incredibly discriminating.

On the other hand, cyberattack runs into a host of ethical problems. Most obviously, a WDA would likely breach the discrimination criteria of just war doctrine. Attacking CNI is likely to have considerable impact on civilians. Indeed, like its air power equivalent, the efficacy of independent cyberattack may partially depend on destroying the will of the population so as to exert leverage against policymakers. Even a carefully orchestrated attack, aimed solely at government infrastructure and targets, could have effects that impact the civilian population. This is especially plausible in cyberattack because of the interconnectedness of networks and information infrastructure. The effects of attacking infrastructure can be difficult to predict with certainty. Even if the intention of attackers is not to cause widespread disruption, a cyber campaign may cause unforeseen escalation via 'deleterious side effects that cannot adequately be anticipated'.[85] In this sense, both discrimination and proportionality may be difficult to ensure with a cyberattack. Moreover, as society becomes ever-more cyber dependent, ethicists have raised the thorny issue of cyberharm. Under this developing concept, strategic actors may have to employ a new form of moral reasoning to account for the moral implications of cyberattack on informational/virtual objects and services.[86] What moral value should be ascribed to digital cultural artefacts or social media? Should they be classed as civilian objects and protected under IHL?

In the face of these ethical dilemmas, we are left with the real possibility that states respectful of the norms-based international order will be restricted in their use of cyber power.

Again, this may be another contributory factor to the restraint identified in the exercise of cyber power. Thus, in order to fully exploit the potential of WDA, or perhaps even a substantive coercive attack, a state would have to risk breaching well-established norms of behaviour.

Lack of commitment

One of the main attractions of cyber power for policymakers is that it offers the opportunity for strategic engagement, but with minimal risks. The following quote by Eliot Cohen was written with air power in mind but is arguably even better suited to cyber power: 'Air power is an unusually seductive form of military strength, in part because, like modern courtship, it appears to offer gratification without commitment'.[87] In comparison to air power, which still risks the lives of pilots (in its manned guise) and civilians, cyber power looks almost risk-free (aside from the ethical issues raised earlier) and is reasonably cost-effective. The prospect for global intervention without any physical presence on or over the target seems ideally made for our post-heroic societies.[88]

However, the promise of zero footprint comes with some serious strategic shortcomings. Committing oneself to a conflict without physically committing shows a distinct lack of commitment. The very fact that a state is not prepared to deploy physical forces suggests that its commitment to the cause is lukewarm at best. That being the case, the target of a cyberattack can merely wait out the campaign until the aggressor loses interest. In fact, this may be far easier to achieve under cyberattack than against an air power campaign. Whereas a bombing campaign can become more effective over time through escalation and the cumulative effect of pain (Kosovo), cyberattack is most likely to have its greatest impact in the opening stages of a conflict.

An alternative to weathering a cyber-storm is for the opposing side to escalate the conflict into the physical realm and thereby test the resolve of the cyber-actor. Whether this is a sensible move depends partly on the relative balance of forces, in particular whether the side escalating the conflict has an advantage in the physical realm. This is why having an integrated strategy, one that merges both cyber and kinetic capabilities, is preferable. It is also why escalation dominance has a role to play all forms of strategy, cyber included. In May 2019, the Israeli Defence Forces (IDF) launched an airstrike against a building housing Hamas hackers. Arguably, this is the first instance in history when a state has deliberately escalated a conflict from the virtual to the physical in order to play to its strengths.

The issue of commitment is well illustrated by the Kosovo conflict. For much of the NATO coercive campaign against Serbia, the alliance explicitly relied solely on air power. A ground campaign was publicly ruled out. Thus, Serbia, with limited potential for retaliation, decided to wait out the attacks until divisions within NATO proved fatal to the campaign. Post-conflict analysis proved that for much of the campaign, NATO had little success in hurting Serbia and certainly could not prevent the ethnic cleansing of Kosovo Albanians. The fact that NATO ultimately succeeded can be attributed to a number of factors. The intensity of the air campaign was increased considerably, and the cumulative effect began to produce coercive results. This was in addition to increasing preparations for a ground campaign and the loss of political support for Serbia in the international community. Finally, Serbia made the mistake of escalating the ethnic cleansing, which only strengthened NATO's resolve and unity. Despite the ultimate success of the NATO campaign, evidenced by the fact that Serbia withdrew its forces from Kosovo, 10,000 Kosovo Albanians died during the period of the air assault. This final point is a sober warning to those who promote coercive campaigns with no ground (or physical presence in the case of cyber power) presence. In certain contingencies, there is no workable alternative to committing physical ground forces.

Friction

Friction, which limits performance at all levels of strategy, applies to all forms of warfare, cyber power included. The originator of this strategic concept, Clausewitz, describes friction as 'the only concept that more or less corresponds to the factors that distinguish real war from war on paper'.[89] Friction has almost limitless causes. Thus, to make our analysis manageable, we shall make use of a Barry D. Watts's taxonomy, which he in turn extracted from a study of Clausewitz's *On War*. Watts's taxonomy is constructed of eight broad categories that constitute the unified concept of general friction: danger; physical exertion; uncertainties and imperfections in information; resistance within one's own forces; chance events; physical and political limits on the use of force; unpredictability emanating from interaction with the enemy; and disconnects between means and ends.[90] This chapter will now assess cyber power in light of each of these causes of friction, and it will thereby provide a greater understanding of how it is likely to function in the real world of strategy.

Cyber power fares well against the first two categories. As a source of friction, physical exertion can be almost entirely ruled out. Likewise, danger is almost entirely absent from warfare in cyberspace. Resistance within one's own forces is another area where cyber power has an advantage. Although the notion of a single cyberwarrior wreaking havoc is somewhat fanciful, it is still true to argue that operations in cyberspace require substantially fewer personnel than most physical expressions of military power. By definition, the fewer 'moving parts' there are, the less chance for friction. People still need to be managed and led effectively in the exercise of cyber power, but the challenge is still substantially lower than in traditional expressions of military force, with its workforce running into the tens and hundreds of thousands. Thus, in reference to these categories of friction, the strategic performance of cyber power should be substantially less affected.

It has already been noted that cyber power will face challenges in intelligence. This is important because shortfalls in information can have an impact on the ability of a campaign, virtual or physical, to fulfil its goals. Without good information on the enemy system, a cyber power campaign may not act as a significant force multiplier or lead to sufficient coercive effect. In reference to chance events, cyber power is as susceptible as any other mode of warfare: servers and networks can go down. The worst case scenario for a cyberwarrior is to be cut off from the Internet. Without access to the Internet, a cyberwarrior will find it difficult to function. An electrical power cut would have a similarly disabling effect on cyber strategy. Of course, just as in the other forms of warfare, cyberwarriors can take protective measures to minimise the impact of chance events. However, as is true elsewhere, by definition, the full range of chance events cannot be foreseen in advance.

In terms of physical and political limits on the use of force, it has already been established that ethical concerns are likely to retard the operational freedom of cyber power. As an instrument of policy, operating within the framework of the unequal dialogue, cyber strategy cannot operate within a vacuum.[91] Rather, it is always likely to be on a short political rein. As previously noted, empirical evidence suggests that restraint is already apparent in cyberspace. There are two important qualifications to this. First, non-state cyber-actors may operate with less political inhibitions, in which case cyberattack can operate more closely to its absolute form (resources permitting). Second, the more total the policy objective, the more total the means become. That being the case, in a large-scale war, cyberattack may be let loose in a similar way to how air power was released during the Second World War. However, the history of the latter suggests that even in such permissive conditions, decisive strategic performance is not guaranteed.

The influence of the enemy has already been discussed. Thus, at this stage, we need only remind ourselves that the presence of an intelligent foe, and how one responds to that presence, introduces further complexity and unpredictability into strategy. Disconnects between ends and means strikes right to the heart of strategy. An instrument that performs well at the tactical and operational level will count for little if it is ill-suited to the strategic task at hand or if the policy objective is unobtainable. It is true that tactical and operational efficacy can compensate for ineptitude at the strategic level, to some degree. This is evidenced most clearly by Nazi Germany, which fought competently for years in the service of flawed and unrealistic strategic goals. Nonetheless, generally speaking, a lack of harmony among the levels of strategy will neuter the impact of tactical and operational greatness. As efficient as cyber strategy may be, it still needs to be used correctly in the service of achievable policy objectives.

This section on the play of friction in cyberspace has produced mixed results. In some important areas cyber strategy possesses significant advantages. Indeed, some causes of friction either do not apply to cyber power, or are severely muted in their effects. However, friction is so ubiquitous that no form of warfare can escape its grasp. That being the case, the strategic potential of cyber power will be degraded by friction. This does not mean that cyber power cannot contribute to strategy. However, it does mean that it is unlikely to fulfil its potential as a decisive means to pursue policy objectives.

Conclusion

As an umbrella concept, cybersecurity deserves its place in contemporary security discourse and on the policy agendas of modern states. The empirical evidence is too strong to conclude otherwise. Various forms of cyberattack (including crime and espionage) threaten the wellbeing of modern information-age societies. In this sense, then-secretary-general of the International Telecommunication Union Hamadoun I. Touré is undoubtedly correct in his assessment that 'protecting critical information infrastructures are now essential elements of each nation's security and economic well-being'.[92]

What is less clear is what contribution cyber power can make to achieving policy objectives. Much of the extant literature tends to be based on a technical and tactical assessment of cyber power. As a result, the strategic potential of cyber power may have been exaggerated. This chapter has sought to rectify that problem. By basing the analysis within the conceptual framework of strategic studies, allied to reference to historical strategic practice, we have sought to provide a more balanced appraisal of the strategic worth of cyber power. In particular, it has been argued that cyber strategy must be unified and comprehensive, composed of the destructive and non-destructive components of cyber power, and fully integrated with the other traditional instruments of strategy.

In this way, we are able to appreciate the flexible nature of cyber strategy. It has been noted that cyber power can operate in a defensive form; has a deterrence role; can be used to pursue espionage; or can engage in manipulating the information environment. More aggressively, it can be used for widespread disruptive attacks, although limited raids are likely to prove more strategically useful. Finally, it can contribute to the joint battlespace, acting as a force multiplier for physical expressions of force.

One of the primary characteristics of cyber power is the overlap between the various activities. Many of the different forms of cyber action share technical and tactical characteristics. Intrusion into an enemy system and/or the insertion of malware potentially signal many forms of intent, from a low-level form of industrial espionage to the prelude for a massive WDA. As a result of this overlap, the various expressions of cyber power must be at the behest of a unified strategy, guided by clear policy objectives and integrated into the other instruments of strategy. This is especially important because of the potential for blowback and loss of control in cyberspace. The increasing use of AI in cybersecurity raises some interesting challenges in this respect.

So cyber power is a flexible tool of strategy. However, it has been shown that its strategic potential is somewhat retarded by a number of factors. The analysis identified eight limiting factors: reductionism; geography; intelligence; the enemy; the polymorphous character of war; ethics; lack of commitment; and friction. Although all of these can be individually mitigated to a greater or lesser degree, when taken together, they stymie cyber power when acting in the service of policy. In particular, it has been shown that choosing cyber power as the strategy of choice may reveal a distinct lack of commitment. In war, which is essentially a battle of wills, displaying weak commitment often proves to be fatal.[93] Ironically, the independent form of cyberattack, which gets most of the headlines, is the least likely to produce significant strategic effect. Modern societies have proven extremely robust in the face of strategic bombing and terror campaigns. It is unlikely that a virtual coercive campaign will prove independently decisive in strategy. In this sense, cyber power is likely to be most productive when contributing to a joint campaign. In this way, the future of cyberattack may come in the form of skirmishing before kinetic combat begins, followed by an ongoing disruption of the enemy system.[94]

To summarise, cyber strategy is an emerging reality for all the great powers. However, at present, it is underdeveloped and poorly articulated. To be effective, cyber strategy must be comprehensive and coordinated. In the first instance, the different components of cyber strategy must be used in a complementary manner. In addition, cyber strategy must be harmonised with the other forms of state power. Cyber power does not change the basic rules of strategy. Like all forms of strategy, its efficacy will depend on context and be at the behest of a strategist who has taken into consideration both the strengths and weaknesses of this new form of power.

Key points

1 Modern societies, including their CNI, depend on cyberspace.
2 Cyber power is a flexible (normally nonviolent) instrument of policy.
3 Cyberattack has limited strategic utility and is better suited to raids and joint ops.
4 Cyber strategy needs to be comprehensive and linked to physical expressions of power.

Questions

1 Is cyberspace a warfighting domain?
2 Has cyberattack been overhyped as an instrument of strategy?
3 How does deterrence function in cyberspace?
4 Is cyber power an effective instrument of strategy?

Notes

1 'War in the Fifth Domain: Are the Mouse and Keyboard the New Weapons of Conflict?', *The Economist*, July 1, 2010, www.economist.com/node/16478792. Following years of dire warnings about the threat from cyberattack, an increasing raft of literature has appeared questioning its potency and even the existential reality of cyberwar. Some of the more sceptical writings include Erik Gartzke, 'The Myth of Cyberwar', *International Security* 38:2 (Fall 2013), pp. 41–73; Thomas Rid, 'Cyber War Will Not Take Place', *Journal of Strategic Studies* 35:1 (2012), pp. 5–32; Colin S. Gray, *Strategy for Chaos: Revolutions in Military Affairs and the Evidence of History* (London, Routledge, 2004); and David J. Lonsdale, *The Nature of War in the Information Age: Clausewitzian Future* (London, Frank Cass, 2004).
2 For a broader appreciation of cyber power, see Brandon Valeriano and Ryan C. Maness, *Cyber War Versus Cyber Realities* (Oxford, Oxford University Press, 2015); Lucas Kello, 'The Meaning of the Cyber Revolution: Perils to Theory and Statecraft', *International Security* 38:2 (Fall 2013), pp. 7–40; and Kristin M. Lord and Travis Sharp (eds.), *America's Cyber Future: Security and Prosperity in the Information Age*, Vols. 1 & 2 (Washington, DC, Center for a New American Security, 2011).
3 Colin S. Gray, *The Strategy Bridge: Theory for Practice* (Oxford, Oxford University Press, 2010).
4 Peter W. Singer and Allan Friedman, *Cybersecurity and Cyberwar: What Everyone Needs to Know* (Oxford, Oxford University Press, 2014), p. 163.
5 One of the earlier arguments in favour of a redistribution of power is Jessica T. Matthews, 'Power Shift', *Foreign Affairs* 76:1 (1997).

6 Joseph S. Nye, Jr., 'Power and National Security in Cyberspace', in Kristin M. Lord and Travis Sharp (eds.), *America's Cyber Future: Security and Prosperity in the Information Age*, Vol. 2 (Washington, DC, Center for a New American Security, 2011).

7 Jody R. Westby, 'Introduction', in Hamadoun I. Touré and the Permanent Monitoring Panel on Information Security (eds.), *The Quest for Cyber Peace* (Geneva, International Telecommunication Union & World Federation of Scientists, 2011), p. 1.

8 The White House, *Remarks by the President on Securing Our Nation's Cyber Infrastructure*, The White House, May 29, 2009, www.whitehouse.gov/the-press-office/remarks-president-securing-our-nations-cyber-infrastructure

9 James R. Clapper, *Statement for the Record US Cybersecurity and Policy, Senate Armed Services Committee*, Senate Armed Services Committee, September 29, 2015, p. 2.

10 Singer and Friedman, p. 15.

11 Ibid., p. 60.

12 Deputy Secretary of Defense Robert O. Work, *Opening Statement before the Senate Armed Services Committee*, September 29, 2015, p. 1.

13 Nye, p. 13.

14 www.statista.com/statistics/675399/us-government-spending-cyber-security/

15 Cabinet Office, *Progress of the 2016–2021 National Cyber Security Programme*, March 15, 2019, www.nao.org.uk/wp-content/uploads/2019/03/Progress-of-the-2016-2021-National-Cyber-Security-Programme.pdf

16 *Department of Defense Cyber Strategy*, 2018, https://media.defense.gov/2018/Sep/18/2002041658/-1/-1/1/CYBER_STRATEGY_SUMMARY_FINAL.PDF

17 Ministry of Defence, 'New Cyber Reserve Unit Created', September 29, 2013, www.gov.uk/government/news/reserves-head-up-new-cyber-unit

18 Ben Quinn, 'Revealed: The MoD's Secret Cyberwarfare Programme', *The Guardian*, March 16, 2014, www.theguardian.com/uk-news/2014/mar/16/mod-secret-cyberwarfare-programme

19 HM Government, *National Cyber Security Strategy 2016–2021*, https://assets.publishing.service.gov.uk/government/uploads/system/uploads/attachment_data/file/567242/national_cyber_security_strategy_2016.pdf

20 Jon R. Lindsay, 'The Impact of China on Cybersecurity: Fiction and Friction', *International Security* 39:3 (Winter 2014/15), pp. 7–47, 24.

21 Martin C. Libicki, *Cyberdeterrence and Cyberwar* (Santa Monica, RAND, 2009), p. xiv.

22 Kim Zetter, *Countdown to Zero Day* (New York, Broadway Books, 2014).

23 Singer and Friedman, pp. 169–73.

24 Sun Tzu, *The Art of War*, trans. Samuel B. Griffith (London, Oxford University Press, 1971).

25 'China's J-20 Stealth Fighter Might Have Some F-35 "DNA" after All', *The National Interest*, March 31, 2019, https://nationalinterest.org/blog/buzz/chinas-j-20-stealth-fighter-might-have-some-f-35-dna-after-all-50017

26 Lindsay, p. 45.

27 Schmitt, p. 16.

28 Valeriano and Maness, p. 74.

29 For example, MI5 officially regards cyber espionage as an extension of traditional espionage techniques. www.mi5.gov.uk/home/about-us/what-we-do/the-threats/cyber.html. Furthermore, the reports of the *Intelligence and Security Committee*, although subject to redaction in this area, acknowledge an increasing cyber dimension in intelligence work. Intelligence and Security Committee, *Annual Report 2011–2012* (Norwich, The Stationary Office, 2012); Intelligence and Security Committee, *Annual Report 2012–2013* (Norwich, The Stationary Office, 2013).

30 Sun Tzu.

31 Shaun Walker, 'Salutin' Putin: Inside a Russian Troll House', *The Guardian*, April 2, 2015, www.theguardian.com/world/2015/apr/02/putin-kremlin-inside-russian-troll-house. Also, DDoS can be used as a more aggressive form of information manipulation. See Thomas Rid, 'Cyberwar and Peace', *Foreign Affairs*, November/December 2013.

32 John Arquilla and David Ronfeldt, 'The Advent of Netwar (Revisited)', in John Arquilla and David Ronfeldt (eds.), *Networks and Netwars: The Future of Terror, Crime, and Militancy* (Santa Monica, CA, RAND, 2001), p. 2.

33 For a generally positive analysis of the strategic worth of information manipulation, see Frank R. Barnett and Carnes Lord (eds.), *Political Warfare and Psychological Operations* (Washington, DC, National Defense University Press, 1989).

34 Rid, *Cyberwar and Peace*.

35 Lucas Kello, 'The meaning of the Cyber Revolution: Perils to Theory and Statecraft', *International Security* 38:2 (Fall 2013), pp. 24–5.

36 This apes earlier calls for unified and comprehensive political warfare campaigns, using all elements of grand strategy. See Fred C. Ikle, 'The Modern Context', in Frank R. Barnett and Carnes Lord (eds.), *Political Warfare and Psychological Operations* (Washington, DC, National Defense University Press, 1989), p. 6.

37 See, for example, John Arquilla and David Ronfeldt (eds.), *Networks and Netwars: The Future of Terror, Crime, and Militancy* (Santa Monica, CA, RAND, 2001), pp. 239–88.

38 HM Treasury, 'Chancellor's Speech to GCHQ on Cyber Security', November 17, 2015, www.gov.uk/government/speeches/chancellors-speech-to-gchq-on-cyber-security

39 Gartzke, p. 69.

40 The term was officially adopted at an 1881 international conference of anarchists. See Richard Jensen, 'Daggers, Rifles and Dynamite: Anarchist Terrorism in Nineteenth Century Europe', *Terrorism and Political Violence* 16:1 (2004).

41 Aaron Metha, 'Cyber Strategy Relies on Deterrence, Industry', *Defense News*, April 26, 2015, www.defensenews.com/story/defense/policy-budget/budget/2015/04/26/pentagon-new-cyber-strategy-deterrence-industry/26298913/

42 Eugene Gerden, 'Russia Revamps Its Infosec Strategy', *SC Magazine*, January 1, 2015, www.scmagazineuk.com/russia-revamps-its-infosec-strategy/article/390175/; Amy Chang, *Warring State: China's Cybersecurity Strategy*, Center for a New American Security, December 2014, www.cnas.org/sites/default/files/publications-pdf/CNAS_WarringState_Chang_report_010615.pdf

43 James R. Clapper, 'Statement for the Record: Worldwide Threat Assessment of the US Intelligence Community', *Senate Armed Services Committee*, Feburary 26, 2015, p. 2, http://cdn.arstechnica.net/wp-content/uploads/2015/02/Clapper_02-26-15.pdf.

44 Michael Connell and Sarah Vogler, *Russia's Approach to Cyber Warfare*, CAN Occasional Paper, September 2016, https://apps.dtic.mil/dtic/tr/fulltext/u2/1019062.pdf; Kenneth Geers (ed.), *Cyber War in Perspective: Russian Aggression against Ukraine* (Tallinn, NATO CCDCOE, 2015), https://ccdcoe.org/uploads/2018/10/CyberWarinPerspective_full_book.pdf

45 Chang, p. 20.

46 Gurmeet Kanwal, 'Acupuncture Warfare: China's Cyberwar Doctrine and Implications for India', *Indian Defence Review*, July 11, 2019, www.indiandefencereview.com/spotlights/acupuncture-warfare-chinas-cyberwar-doctrine-and-implications-for-india/; Nicholas Lyall, 'China's Cyber Militias', *The Diplomat*, March 1, 2018, https://thediplomat.com/2018/03/chinas-cyber-militias/

47 Dennis J. Blasko, 'Steady as She Goes: China's New Defense White Paper', *War on the Rocks*, Texas National Security Review, August 12, 2019, https://warontherocks.com/2019/08/steady-as-she-goes-chinas-new-defense-white-paper/

48 Valeriano and Maness, p. 67.

49 For a more detailed analysis, see Lonsdale, *The Nature of War*, Chapter 4.

50 Kim Zetter, 'The NSA Acknowledges What We All Feared: Iran Learns From US Cyberattacks', *Wired*, February 10, 2015, www.wired.com/2015/02/nsa-acknowledges-feared-iran-learns-us-cyberattacks/

51 Valeriano and Maness, p. 157.

52 Ibid., p. 159.

53 Quoted in Singer and Friedman, p. 118; Lindsay in Valeriano, p. 149.

54 Quoted in Singer and Friedman, p. 119.

55 Valeriano and Maness, pp. 153–4.

56 James P. Farwell and Rafal Rohozinski, 'Stuxnet and the Future of Cyber War', *Survival* 53:1 (2011), p. 27.

57 Libicki, *Cyberdeterrence*, p. xv.

58 Colin S. Gray, 'Warfighting for Deterrence', *Journal of Strategic Studies* 1:1 (1984); David J. Lonsdale, 'Warfighting for Cyber Deterrence: A Strategic and Moral Imperative', *Philosophy and Technology* 31:3 (September 2018).

59 Clausewitz, p. 358.

60 Singer and Friedman, p. 127.

61 Noah Shachtman, 'Insurgents Intercept Drone Video in King-Size Security Breach', *Wired*, December 17, 2009, www.wired.com/2009/12/insurgents-intercept-drone-video-in-king-sized-security-breach/

62 James J. Coyle, 'Russia Has Complete Information Dominance in Ukraine', *Atlantic Council*, May 12, 2015, www.atlanticcouncil.org/blogs/new-atlanticist/russia-has-complete-informational-dominance-in-ukraine

63 House of Commons Defence Committee, *Defence and Cyber Security, Sixth Report of Session 2012–13*, December 2012, p. 11, www.publications.parliament.uk/pa/cm201213/cmselect/cmdfence/106/106.pdf.

64 See House of Commons Defence Committee and Cabinet Office, p. 26.

65 House of Commons Defence Committee, p. 21 and Ev. 9–12 & 22.

66 Vegetius, *Epitome of Military Science*, trans. N.P. Milner (Liverpool, Liverpool University Press, 1993).

67 Lord and Sharp, p. 25.

68 Colin S. Gray, *Perspectives on Strategy* (Oxford, Oxford University Press, 2013).

69 Kenneth Geers, *Strategic Cyber Security* (Tallinn, NATO Cooperative Cyber Defence Centre of Excellence, 2011), p. 10.

70 Valeriano and Maness, p. 9.

71 Alfred C. Mierzejewski, *The Collapse of the German War Economy 1944–45: Allied Air Power and the German National Railway* (Chapel Hill, NC, University of North Carolina Press, 1988).

72 David J. Betz and T. Stevens, *Cyberspace and the State: Toward a Strategy for Cyber-Power* (New York, Routledge, 2011).

73 Gregory Rattray and Jason Healey, 'Non-State Actors and Cyber Conflict', in Kristin M. Lord and Travis Sharp (eds.), *America's Cyber Future: Security and Prosperity in the Information Age*, Vol. 2 (Washington, DC, Center for a New American Security, 2011), p. 67.

74 Clausewitz, p. 97.

75 This and other difficulties are discussed in detail in Charles Webster and Noble Frankland, *The Strategic Air Offensive Against Germany 1939–45* (London, HMSO, 1961); Wesley Frank Craven and James Lea Cate (eds.), *The Army Air Forces in World War Two* (Chicago, IL, University of Chicago Press, 1951).

76 Clausewitz, pp. 117–18.

77 Quoted in R.L. DiNardo and Daniel J. Hughes, 'Some Cautionary Thoughts on Information Warfare', *Airpower Journal* 9:4 (1995), p. 76.

78 Libicki, *Cyberdeterrence*.

79 Although the attack on the Iranian facility at Natanz, against a closed air-gapped system, somewhat qualifies this statement.

80 Robert H. Anderson, *Securing the US Defense Information Infrastructure: A Proposed Approach* (Santa Monica, CA, RAND, 1999); Rattray and Schwartau.

81 Robert A. Pape, *Bombing to Win: Air Power and Coercion in War* (Ithaca, NY, Cornell University Press, 1996), p. 274.

82 John Arquilla, 'Ethics and Information Warfare', in Z. Khalizad, J. White, and A. Marshall (eds.), *Strategic Appraisal: The Changing Role of Information in Warfare* (Santa Monica, CA, RAND, 1999), p. 379.

83 Randall R. Dipert, 'The Ethics of Cyberwarfare', *Journal of Military Ethics* 9:4 (2010), p. 385.

84 Geers, p. 13.

85 Dipert, p. 385.

86 Ibid., pp. 397, 405.

87 Eliot Cohen, 'The Mystique of US Air Power', *Foreign Affairs*, January / February 1994, www.foreign affairs.com / articles / 49442 / eliot-a-cohen / the-mystique-of-us-air-power

88 Edward N. Luttwak, 'Towards Post-Heroic Warfare', *Foreign Affairs* 74:3 (1995).

89 Clausewitz, p. 119.

90 Barry D. Watts, *Clausewitzian Friction and Future War*, McNair Paper 52 (Washington, DC, Institute for National Strategic Studies, National Defense University, 1996).

91 The unequal dialogue between policy and the military is described by Eliot Cohen, *Supreme Command: Soldiers, Statesmen, and Leadership in Wartime* (New York, Free Press, 2002).

92 Hamadoun I. Touré, 'Cyberspace and the Threat of Cyberwar', in Hamadoun I. Touré and the Permanent Monitoring Panel on Information Security (eds.), *The Quest for Cyber Peace* (Geneva, International Telecommunication Union & World Federation of Scientists, 2011), p. 8.

93 For a discussion on the importance of commitment and perception in conflict, see Schelling, *Arms and Influence*.

94 Dipert, p. 403.

Further reading

Betz, David J. and T. Stevens, *Cyberspace and the State: Toward a Strategy for Cyber-Power* (New York: Routledge, 2011).

Dipert, Randall R., 'The Ethics of Cyberwarfare', *Journal of Military Ethics*, Vol. 9, No. 4 (2010).

Kaplan, Fred, *Dark Territory: The Secret History of Cyber War*, (New York: Simon & Schuster, 2016).

Libicki, Martin C., *Cyberdeterrence and Cyberwar*, (Santa Monica: RAND, 2009).

Lindsay, Jon R., Tai Ming Cheung and Derek S. Reveron, *China and Cybersecurity: Espionage, Strategy, and Politics in the Digital Domain*, (Oxford: Oxford University Press, 2015).

Lord, Kristin M. and Travis Sharp (eds.), *America's Cyber Future: Security and Prosperity in the Information Age, Volumes I & II*, (Washington, DC: Center for a New American Security, 2011).

Singer, Peter W. and Allan Friedman, *Cybersecurity and Cyberwar: What Everyone Needs to Know*, (Oxford: Oxford University Press, 2014).

Taddeo, Mariarosaria (ed.), 'Landscaping Cyber Deterrence', Special Issue, *Philosophy and Technology*, Vol. 31, No. 3 (September 2018).

Valeriano, Brandon and Ryan C. Maness, *Cyber War Versus Cyber Realities*, (Oxford: Oxford University Press, 2015).

Zetter, Kim, *Countdown to Zero Day*, (New York: Broadway Books, 2014).

Contemporary strategic challenges

PART III

Nuclear strategy   12

Reader's guide

The technology of nuclear weapons; nuclear strategy during the golden age (Cold War); nuclear strategy with limited warheads; BMD, arms control, and stability; contemporary nuclear strategy; nuclear strategy for the twenty-first century.

Introduction

Since nuclear weapons were first used in 1945, they have arguably posed the greatest challenge to modern strategy. The scale of the challenge is directly related to the enormous destructive power of these weapons. When nuclear warheads were placed atop ballistic missiles with flight times measured in minutes, the challenge was magnified. In an age of thermonuclear ballistic missiles, global devastation is potentially only minutes away. The challenge for strategists is how to harness such awesome power for strategic effect. This was made even more problematic by the security environment of the Cold War, into which nuclear weapons were born, in which fear of surprise attack was prevalent. In response to these challenges, the intellectual endeavour devoted to nuclear strategy gave rise to the modern academic subject of strategic studies. It may not be too far-fetched to say that this very book (written by two civilian academic authors) would not have been written were it not for the invention of nuclear weapons.[1]

This chapter will begin by outlining the basic characteristics of nuclear weapons and their delivery systems. The essence of nuclear strategy cannot be understood without some sense of the weapons themselves. This is one occasion in strategy when the technology of the weapons systems has a direct impact on the formation of strategy. After providing this technological backdrop, the chapter will analyse the rich history of Cold War nuclear strategy. This so-called golden age of strategic thought witnessed the development of most of the core concepts in nuclear strategy. Indeed, strategy in general benefited from the intellectual endeavours of the period. To cite one example, Thomas Schelling's work on the strategy of conflict has relevance well beyond the Cold War nuclear context.[2] The focus of the chapter is predominately on the United States. This is mainly for methodological reasons. In particular, it is because the United States has produced the most developed and open forms of nuclear strategy. However, reference is also made to Soviet/Russian, British, French, and Pakistani nuclear strategies. The chapter will conclude with an assessment of contemporary strategic thought and practice on nuclear weapons. After a fallow period following the end of the Cold War, nuclear weapons are rising on the agendas of the great powers. The chapter will assess the current state of nuclear strategy, before concluding with a modest attempt to formulate a theory of nuclear strategy for the modern age.

The technology of nuclear weapons

Nuclear weapons first came to public attention with the atomic attacks on the Japanese cities of Hiroshima and Nagasaki in August 1945. These two attacks involved the use of just one bomb and still represent the only use of nuclear weapons in anger against an opposing power. The attack on Hiroshima used a fission device with a yield of approximately 13 kilotons.[3] It was delivered to its target by a single B-29 bomber, which took approximately six and a half hours to reach its target from its base at Tinian Island. The devastation caused by the attack was substantial, destroying most of the city and killing at least 80,000 people. The challenge of Cold War nuclear strategy is clear, then, when one considers that the Minuteman I and II ICBM, which saw service from 1963 to 1993, had a warhead (the W-56) with a yield almost 100 times as powerful as that used at Hiroshima and a flight time of approximately 25 minutes. The challenge was further intensified by the vertical proliferation of nuclear weapons. The United States' nuclear arsenal peaked in 1966, with 31,700 warheads, and by 1986, the Soviet Union had 40,723.[4] The means of delivery also proliferated and eventually included mortars, artillery shells, bombers, SLBMs, and their land-based ICBM cousins.

The destructive power of a nuclear warhead is quantified in the equivalent tonnage of TNT explosive. Thus, the bomb that destroyed Hiroshima had a yield that was the equivalent of 13,000 tons of TNT. The yield of the Minuteman W-56 warhead was the equivalent of 1.2 million tons of TNT. The energy released when a nuclear weapon is detonated comes in three different forms: blast, heat, and radiation. The percentage of each of these outputs depends on the manufacture of the weapon. For example, the enhanced radiation weapon (neutron bomb) was designed to produce a high proportion of its energy as neutron radiation. Although such a weapon has a reduced yield in terms of destructive power (blast and heat), it was intended to be most useful as an anti-armour weapon, with radiation penetrating a vehicle's armour to kill the troops inside. There is one additional effect created when a nuclear device detonates, an electromagnetic pulse (EMP). The main attribute of an EMP is its ability to destroy electrical circuits.[5] Thus, among other effects, an EMP has serious implications for command and control infrastructure.

There are various means of delivering a nuclear warhead to its target. On the battlefield, smaller yield nuclear weapons can be delivered by mortars, artillery shells, short-range missiles, and air-delivered bombs. Intermediate range systems are composed primarily of ballistic and cruise missiles. The delivery means for longer ranges typically come under the umbrella term 'the nuclear triad', which is comprised of aircraft, SLBMs, and ICBMs. By varying the means of delivery, the nuclear triad was designed to ensure a response in the aftermath of a surprise enemy attack. If, for example, the enemy found a way to destroy one's bomber force and land-based ICBMs, the SLBMs would hopefully provide a means of retaliation. SLBMs deployed in modern nuclear-powered submarines (SSBNs) are particularly suited to this task because SSBNs are difficult to locate and track. In the other two arms of the triad, various methods were developed to increase survivability of the forces. For example, during the Cold War, the United States operated a policy of airborne alert, whereby a number of bombers were kept constantly in the air, thereby reducing their vulnerability to a surprise attack. In an attempt to protect the ICBM force, ICBM silos were hardened and dispersed, and eventually mobile ICBMs (such as the Soviet SS-20) were developed. Finally, nuclear weapons can be delivered by less technologically sophisticated means, such as in the back of a car or by various other methods that employ the infamous 'suitcase nuke'. Such rudimentary means of delivery would be ideally suited for use by either special forces or terrorists.

An area that received much attention during the Cold War was the offence–defence dynamic. Various anti-ballistic missile (ABM) programmes were developed, and some were even deployed in limited numbers. However, despite such efforts, operational advantage always lay with offensive forces. The number of warheads involved, their destructive power, and the short flight times of the missiles ensured that constructing a sufficiently reliable defensive system (one that was almost leak-proof) was essentially impossible. The basic challenge of BMD in the Cold War was made more difficult by technological developments in offensive systems. Offensive capabilities were enhanced with the introduction of multiple independently targeted reentry vehicles (MIRV). This system refers to a ballistic missile that has multiple warheads (perhaps as many as ten), each of which can be assigned to a distinct target. In addition to warheads, a missile can also carry penetration aids, such as chaff and decoy warheads to further complicate the defensive mission. Finally, with improved guidance systems, nuclear weapons became increasingly accurate, thus improving the chances of destroying the intended target with fewer warheads. The overwhelming challenge of the defensive mission is evidenced in the colossally expensive and complex multilayered Strategic Defence Initiative (SDI), first announced by the Reagan administration in 1983. SDI envisaged both Earth-based and space-based components and was designed to include exotic directed-energy technologies.[6] Even if such technologies could have been developed within a reasonable timeframe and at reasonable cost, the command and control issues in the face of a large Soviet attack may have presented insurmountable problems. The United States and Israel both now deploy limited BMD systems. However, the offence–defence dynamic continues, as evidenced by Russian development of hypersonic glide vehicles (HGV), which act as MIRVed warheads on an ICBM and which can manoeuvre vertically and horizontally at high speed to evade BMD.

Once a warhead reaches its target there are a number of attack options available. The warhead can be airburst or ground burst or can even penetrate into the earth. Airburst weapons are better suited against area targets, such as urban areas. In contrast, the ground-burst option is advisable against hardened point targets such as enemy missile silos. The latter, however, does produce more fallout since it drags up material from the ground, which is then irradiated in the mushroom cloud before falling back to Earth, often at great distances from the actual explosion. Finally, penetrating warheads are designed to destroy buried targets, such as underground facilities.

A critical component of any nuclear force is its command and control. Due to the marriage of destructive power and rapid delivery, the command and control system of nuclear forces must be robust and responsive. In the face of an actual or imminent enemy attack, it is vital that attack orders for retaliatory forces get through to the respective launch crews in time. However, responsiveness must be balanced with control and restraint. When dealing with such high stakes and short timelines, the accidental launch of nuclear weapons is a real danger.[7] This particular challenge raises questions about when one should actually launch a nuclear retaliatory strike. Does one pre-empt the enemy's attack? Does one launch on warning (when the early warning systems detect a possible enemy attack in its early stages)? Alternatively, does one launch under attack (only respond when the enemy's warheads have begun detonating on one's territory)? Responding to these, and other questions that arise from the technical characteristics of nuclear weapons, dominated strategic studies for much of the Cold War. This chapter now turns its attention to the details of those responses.

US nuclear strategy during the Cold War

Whatever form nuclear strategy took, the central challenge was always the same and can be summarised by the title of Henry Kissinger's work *Nuclear Weapons and Foreign Policy*.[8] In essence, the story of nuclear strategy is about harnessing the enormous destructive power of nuclear weapons in the service of rational policy objectives. It is an attempt to apply Clausewitz in a context where some believe Clausewitzian rules are inapplicable. Lawrence Freedman, for example, raises the question of whether nuclear strategy is a contradiction in terms.[9] Similarly, in one of his later works, Colin Gray concludes that in use (with the attendant risk of escalation), 'nuclear weapons would be most likely too powerful to serve political purposes'.[10]

Although nuclear weapons were first used for strategic effect in an offensive manner, the initial intellectual engagement with the subject established deterrence as the concept that would dominate the subject of nuclear strategy. The American strategic theorist Bernard Brodie set the tone for the next 45 years in the immediate aftermath of Hiroshima:

> Thus far the chief purpose of our military establishment has been to win wars. From now on its chief purpose must be to avert them. It can have almost no other useful purpose.[11]

The strategic theory and practice that followed on from Brodie's work, with some notable exceptions, is best regarded as the development of ever-more-sophisticated forms of deterrence.

Box 12.1 Nuclear deterrence

Two forms of deterrence
Punishment – threaten to impose costs on the enemy that outweigh any gains they would
make from their actions.
Denial – threaten to prevent the enemy from achieving their objectives.

Credible deterrence requires
Capability – the military capability to punish or deny.
Commitment – the will to enact a deterrent threat.
Communication – the enemy clearly understanding that one possesses capability and
commitment.
Context – tailoring these to the relevant context.

The following analysis will show that initial positions on nuclear strategy (massive retaliation and MAD) were too basic. In particular, they lacked flexibility and credibility and ruled out any real prospects for fighting and winning a nuclear conflict. In response, theorists and practitioners endeavoured to construct more credible limited options for nuclear strategy. In this pursuit, they contemplated nuclear strategy as a form of bargaining. They went further and developed warfighting options to increase the chances of surviving a nuclear conflict (damage limitation) and perhaps even the chances of emerging as victorious (prevailing). Despite this shift towards warfighting in the later stages of the Cold War, deterrence never lost its primacy.

A key question concerning nuclear deterrence is whether the details matter. Minimum and/or existential deterrence theories deny that the details matter much, suggesting instead that the enormous destructive power of nuclear weapons markedly simplifies the deterrence challenge.[12] From these perspectives, simply having the weapons in sufficient numbers is enough to deter potential aggressors. Why would anyone risk military adventure in the face of such overwhelming destructive power? Or so the argument goes. In this sense, nuclear weapons appear to be the perfect instruments of deterrence. However, a 1959 RAND study, the results of which were published in Albert Wohlstetter's article 'The Delicate Balance of Terror', made it clear that the details really did matter. Wohlstetter's group discovered that the United States' retaliatory forces were vulnerable to a surprise enemy first strike. Owning the weapons was not enough to ensure that a deterrent response would be automatic.[13] Nuclear weapons, it seemed, were akin to conventional weapons in that tactical and operational issues were essential for positive strategic effect. Questions began to be asked on such important topics as basing, defence, and penetration. A concept central to tactical and operational issues in nuclear strategy is second-strike capability. This refers to the ability to launch a devastating attack on the enemy even after absorbing an enemy first strike. To best ensure second-strike capability, one's forces have to be robust and numerous and have a diversified means of delivery.

Massive retaliation and mutually assured destruction

In some respects, the first declaratory nuclear strategy of the United States, massive retaliation, is indicative of the existential approach. In January 1954, Secretary of State John Foster Dulles of the Eisenhower administration announced that the United States would deter future communist aggression by depending 'primarily upon a great capacity to retaliate, instantly, by means and at places of our own choosing'.[14] Massive retaliation was not as simple as it is often portrayed (threatening massive nuclear response to any communist gains, however limited). Nonetheless, the administration did little to dispel this caricature, even though Dulles intended the policy to have short-term political leverage rather than have it be the basis for the development of long-term nuclear strategy. In addition, it seems that the military had little guidance from the administration on how and when to use nuclear weapons.[15] Thus, even if administration officials were privately of the opinion that the details mattered, at least in the short term, they were happy to opt for a simple declaratory deterrence policy, without worrying too much about tactical and operational matters. This simple reliance on nuclear weapons was influenced in part by the potential cost savings of nuclear deterrence relative to a substantial conventional buildup. Whatever the motivation for massive retaliation, it left too many questions unanswered and crucially failed the deterrence credibility test. In many respects, the strategic theory that emerged during the Cold War was a response to the issues raised by massive retaliation.

In deterrence, credibility is crucial. Those whom one wishes to deter must believe that one's threats are credible; otherwise, they may call one's bluff. Deterrence essentially comes in two, not mutually exclusive, forms: punishment and denial. The former seeks to deter an opposing power by threatening to impose punishing costs on them that outweigh any gains they may hope to achieve by their actions. Denial deters by persuading the opposing actor that they will be prevented from achieving their aims. To achieve credibility, a strategy of deterrence must fulfil the requirements of the 4 Cs: capability, commitment, communication, and context. Those wishing to deter must have the forces available to inflict the threatened punishment or deny the enemy their objectives. The enemy must also believe that one will use said forces when it comes down to the crunch. Additionally, the first two conditions must be effectively communicated to the enemy, through words and/or deeds. Finally, a deterrence posture must be appropriate to the context at hand. This relates to both general and immediate deterrence, although it is more obviously pertinent to the latter. General deterrence works in the background of a security relationship, deterring actions without the expressed intention of doing so. Immediate deterrence is more focused, designed to deal with a specific threat.[16]

Whatever form deterrence takes, it has one major weakness as a strategy: its success or failure resides with the enemy. They will choose whether or not to be deterred. In this respect, building a security policy on a foundation of deterrence is tantamount to relinquishing a degree of control.

The credibility of massive retaliation was most obviously open to question in relation to Soviet challenges of a limited nature. Certain plausible Cold War scenarios demonstrate his point. For example, would the United States respond with a massive nuclear attack in esponse to communist gains in Korea? Alternatively, was the United States prepared to kill nillions in response to Soviet-backed communist electoral gains somewhere in Europe, perıaps Italy? The most likely answers to these questions were probably not and almost certainly ıot, respectively. That being the case, the United States and its allies faced the danger of being ıibbled to death by communist encroachment, while NATO's nuclear weapons sat impotent ın the sidelines.

The credibility challenge was less problematic in relation to a Soviet attack on the United ¡tates.[17] However, as the leader of the free world, the United States had global interests and hus had to 'extend' its nuclear deterrence to its allies. The credibility problems associated vith extended deterrence quickly came to the fore when the Soviets tested their own nuclear veapon in 1949. By the 1960s, when both sides had the ability to inflict massive amounts ıf destruction, the question of credibility became acute. It was at least questionable, if not ınlikely, that the United States would risk suicide over West Germany or Japan, to cite just wo examples of extended deterrence from the period. Herman Kahn was correct in his ıssessment that deterrence is neither easy nor automatic; it must operate successfully in a ·ange of contexts.[18] Kahn referred to different 'types' of deterrence to cope with different ₃orms of threat. In the modern nomenclature of the 'fourth wave' of deterrence theory, we ¡peak of 'tailoring deterrence' to specific contexts.[19]

As the Soviet and American nuclear arsenals increased, a point was reached in the ₃960s when MAD became an accepted reality. Although often regarded as a strategy, MAD vas actually more an acceptance of a state of affairs brought about as a consequence ıf the arms buildup.[20] However, intended or not, to its supporters, MAD appeared to ıffer a near-perfect stable deterrence relationship between the two superpowers. With a ıuclear triad force structure in place on both sides and second-strike capabilities seemingly ıssured, it looked as though a stable condition had been reached. Stability was based on he premise that neither of the superpowers would risk a first strike in the knowledge that hey would be destroyed in response. Attempts were made to cement the MAD state of ₃ffairs. The most notable of these attempts was the 1972 ABM Treaty, which ensured the .ominance of retaliatory systems by severely restricting the development and deployment ıf BMD.

However, MAD was potentially flawed. Conceptually, there was little agreement between he superpowers over what constituted 'stability'. Without an agreed definition of stability, ₃ would be difficult to maintain. For many, especially those engaged in arms control negoıations, stability was often defined in technological terms. In this respect, weapon systems, ·oth in qualitative and quantitative terms, could be graded as either stabilising or destabilisıg. Unfortunately, this somewhat narrow approach to the question of stability underplayed he vital political component of a stable relationship.[21] Put under pressure by severe political ıntagonism, stability may have crumbled. MAD also seemed to offer a narrow approach to ıuclear strategy. Although it appeared to work well as the basis for deterring attack against he superpower homelands, it offered little else to the nuclear strategist. This was particularly ·roubling for the United States, which had global interests in defending against communist ıncroachment.

Beyond MAD: limited and flexible options

Thus, although MAD seemed fairly plausible as a basis for deterrence vis-à-vis an attack on the US homeland, it caused untold problems for the United States' extended deterrence posture. None of the NATO powers, including the United States, was prepared to spend the vast amounts of money required to offset Soviet conventional supremacy in Europe. Therefore, the security of Western Europe would have to rely on successfully extending the US nuclear umbrella over the continent. There were essentially three options available to the United States to achieve this. The least credible of these options relied on persuading the Soviet Union that the United States was prepared to accept assured destruction of its homeland to save its European allies. Alternatively, smaller battlefield nuclear weapons could be deployed to neutralise Soviet conventional dominance. This second option proved problematic when it became apparent how difficult it would be to limit nuclear conflict. Once the nuclear threshold had been crossed in Europe, there was a strong possibility that a conflict would rapidly escalate to central nuclear war involving attacks against the superpowers. Therefore, the second option clearly had a direct relationship with the first and suffered from the same credibility shortfalls. However, the third option, which is best described as a merger of the first two, actually relied on the possibility of escalation to MAD as a means to manipulate the enemy's decision-making.[22] This last option (detailed later on) produced some of the most sophisticated nuclear strategy of the period. Nonetheless, it too had potential shortfalls.

To enhance the credibility of extended deterrence, from the early 1960s, the United States began to develop a more flexible strategy. In particular, it required more limited options. Such an approach became official policy when flexible response was formally adopted by NATO in 1967. In theory, this gave the alliance the capability of responding to Soviet actions at an appropriate level. The options available included purely conventional responses, limited nuclear options, and finally large-scale central nuclear war. However, there was a fine balancing act to be performed within such a strategy. Although it was intended that a conventional Soviet attack could be met in kind (thereby increasing the likelihood and credibility of response), it was important to keep nuclear forces in the equation. With their conventional superiority, the Soviets may have been tempted to chance their arm in central Europe. Indeed, even limited nuclear options (with the damage restricted to Central and Western Europe) may have been regarded by the Soviets as a price worth paying for certain territorial gains. Therefore, it was important to maintain the possibility of escalation to central nuclear war, with its attendant devastation of the superpower homelands. In this sense, the threat of MAD did support the United States' extended deterrence posture, but only via the route of limited options. As a direct threat, MAD lacked credibility as the basis for extended deterrence. However, it could be threatened indirectly as a byproduct of limited response options.

The theorist Thomas Schelling codified this idea as 'the threat that leaves something to chance'. While demonstrating to a foe that one is able and willing to limit one's response, thereby increasing the likelihood and credibility of that response, one also willingly accepts that the conflict may escalate beyond one's control. In a sense, Schelling was advocating that policymakers should sacrifice some level of control and thereby limit their freedom of action. Being aware of this, an enemy would hopefully limit their own actions for fear of a general loss of control over an escalating conflict.[23] This is clearly a high-risk strategy, which is intended to place the onus of compromise on the enemy. These ideas led to the development of two interesting subsections of the debate. The first of these regards nuclear strategy as a form of negotiation or bargaining. The second subsection concerns the question of whether nuclear war could ever remain limited.

The discussion of nuclear strategy as a form of bargaining produced more-sophisticated forms of deterrence and perceived nuclear weapons as more-nuanced and more-flexible tools of strategy. For Schelling, the process of nuclear bargaining was all about risk manipulation. To demonstrate this process, the game of chicken is often used as an analogy. Chicken is a high-risk game of nerves in which two cars drive straight towards each other at high speed. The game is lost by the driver who is the first to swerve out of harm's way. The winner, therefore, appears more willing to run the risk for longer than their opponent. One way to increase one's chances of winning is to project an image of irrationality. If the opponent believes they are dealing with someone incapable of rational choice, they may feel compelled to act in a more controlled manner and initiate de-escalation. For example, in the game of chicken, acts of apparent irrationality could include drinking alcohol before the game, driving blindfolded, or even removing the car's steering wheel. In a nuclear standoff, irrationality could be displayed via public statements or by the deployment of forces that are more liable to accidental launch. Aside from an image of irrationality, bargaining reputation, much of which is based on previous actions, is also important.[24] This latter aspect of nuclear strategy is particularly pertinent in the contemporary period. In recent years, some Western leaders (notably President Obama) promoted a sole-use, abolitionist agenda for nuclear weapons. In doing so, they may have seriously harmed their bargaining position in future standoffs involving nuclear weapons.

Herman Kahn produced what is probably the most detailed attempt to understand how nuclear weapons can be used as a form of negotiation to pressure an adversary. In its complete form, Kahn developed the 44-rung ladder of escalation. Each rung of the ladder represents an increase in activity between two opponents. The object for each side in this relationship is to gain escalation dominance at the next rung of the ladder and thereby put the onus on the opponent to back down.[25] Kahn's ladder is based on the premise that the threat or use of nuclear weapons can be carefully controlled for the purposes of manipulating the will and decisions of an enemy. Put simply, if one side can demonstrate dominance on the next rung of the ladder, the other may be forced to prevent further escalation and compromise their position.

Box 12.2 Key rungs on Kahn's ladder of escalation

Rung 5 – Show of force.
Rung 16 – Nuclear ultimatums.
Rung 23 – Limited nuclear war.
Rung 34 – Slow-motion counterforce war.
Rung 39 – Slow-motion countercity war.
Rung 44 – Spasm or insensate war.

Although Kahn's work is an impressive attempt to construct a mature theory of nuclear strategy, it has been subjected to some fairly damning criticisms. Most obviously, it presupposes that both sides in a conflict will share the same ladder or at least understand how each other's ladder is constructed. In contrast, it seems at least plausible that culturally distinct actors will hold different views on what constitutes an act of escalation relative to other possible acts. That being the case, it is to be expected that one side may misinterpret the actions of the other. In a nuclear environment, such misunderstanding could prove fatal on a global scale. However, although easy to criticise, Kahn was at least attempting to understand how the threat of nuclear use could be used for positive strategic effect. At the very least, Kahn's work raises important questions concerning the feasibility of controlling war in a nuclear environment.

The prospect of being able to wage limited nuclear war motivated much strategic thought during the Cold War. Indeed, it was a central component of Henry Kissinger's aforementioned work, *Nuclear Weapons and Foreign Policy*. For many, including Kissinger and Halperin, limited nuclear war was a possible means to harness the enormous destructive power of the weapons in support of policy.[26] At the very least, controlling the use of nuclear weapons seemed imperative as a means of escaping Armageddon should war occur. There had to be an alternative to surrender or destruction.

War can be limited in four main ways: weapons, geography, targets, and objectives. In the case of nuclear weapons, a war may be limited by using warheads up to a certain yield. Kissinger suggested a rather large maximum yield of 500 kt.[27] In the context of the Cold War, a nuclear conflict could be limited geographically by maintaining the superpower homelands as sanctuaries, free from the effects of nuclear warheads. Even if the Soviet Union and the United States came under attack, limits could still be applied by avoiding civilian targets. Finally, limited objectives, which did not include subjugation or the complete collapse of the enemy system, may have been a method to limit the means used in wartime.

Efforts to construct a theory of limited nuclear war appear rational and worthwhile. However, there are a number of key difficulties with each of the methods just described. As with Kahn's ladder of escalation, limited nuclear war requires a degree of mutual understanding and respect. However, this could be easily undermined if there were disagreement over the nature of an objective. For example, a small territorial gain for one may be the loss of a culturally or politically vital area for another. If we examine the four means of limitation in more detail, we see an ever-expanding list of difficulties, which become more complicated when nuclear weapons are involved. If we take Kissinger's idea of capping the warhead yield, how can this be accurately judged in wartime? Does a 500 kt detonation appear significantly different from a 550 kt detonation? What should one side do if they believe the other has breached this limit?

Geographically limiting the conflict is also complicated when nuclear weapons are involved. The effects of nuclear weapons, particularly fallout, are influenced by the weather. Thus, the size of the area affected by nuclear fallout will be somewhat random. Does fallout landing in the Soviet Union represent a breach of pre-war agreed limits? What if a key enemy target lies on the border of the geographical limits of the theatre of operations? The effects of nuclear weapons also make it difficult to avoid civilian casualties. How does one distinguish between military and civilian targets in and around urban areas? Would US decision makers realise that an attack on Washington, which killed millions of Americans, was actually an attack on the Pentagon? Would it matter even if they did realise this? Finally, what about the prospects for limiting war via restricted objectives? Is it possible to have limited gains and losses in the intensely competitive atmosphere of the Cold War? This may be possible on the fringes of the superpower confrontation, in places such as Vietnam, Angola, or Afghanistan. However, limited objectives seem less viable if conflict occurs in Central Europe or the Americas. Again, context is crucial.

As this discussion reveals, there are many challenges involved in limiting nuclear conflict. And this still presupposes that limits can be agreed on. Perhaps agreed limits could be established through arms control and confidence-building measures. However, these processes are themselves fraught with difficulties, misunderstanding, and suspicions (especially in the context of the Cold War). Finally, even if agreed limits are established, universally understood, and physically possible, the effects of nuclear weapons (including EMP) may still destroy the whole enterprise by degrading command and control infrastructure. If forces cannot be adequately commanded, the notion of controlled exchanges of nuclear weapons is fanciful. Indeed, later versions of the US nuclear war plan, the Single Integrated Operational Plan (SIOP), included options to avoid targeting enemy command and control infrastructures, precisely to enable intra-war negotiation, war limitation, and termination.[28] This brief analysis has revealed that although noble, rational, and perhaps even necessary, theoretical attempts to construct a strategy of limited nuclear war face a host of serious practical obstacles.

Warfighting: damage limitation, countervailing, and prevailing

Perhaps the most strident attempts to exert control over nuclear conflict belong to the warfighting school of thought. 'Warfighting' is here defined as 'engagement with enemy forces to attain military objectives in the pursuit of policy goals'. For conventional forces, such a statement would be self-evident and non-controversial. Yet mention of warfighting in a nuclear context is often regarded as inappropriate and even dangerous.[29] A warfighting posture seeks to develop capabilities and plans to wage nuclear war in a controlled way and perhaps even in a protracted way. Although warfighting can be an important part of a credible deterrence posture, it can also be seen as a means to go beyond deterrence, to deny the enemy their objectives, or even to seek victory in a nuclear conflict. Although nuclear weapons certainly have unique characteristics, warfighting treats them as any other weapon. Military instruments must be perceived as rational means to achieve policy objectives. To achieve this, tactical and operational components must be developed in the quest for military goals in support of a policy objective. In this sense, warfighting categorically rejects existential deterrence and argues strongly that the details do matter. It can also be seen as a responsible approach to nuclear strategy by developing options other than surrender or Armageddon. Perhaps most importantly, warfighting is concerned with answering the question, what happens if deterrence fails?

Box 12.3 Nuclear warfighting

Five drivers for nuclear warfighting:

Enhance credibility.
Damage limitation.
Countervailing.
Victory.
Just war.

There are essentially five drivers for warfighting. The first is to enhance the credibility of one's deterrence posture. Clearly, credibility is at least open to question if one's only option is the initiation of global devastation. However, if one possesses the ability to wage limited nuclear war, perhaps even with the possibility of winning, one's nuclear threats look more plausible. The second driver is damage limitation. Should war occur, the state has a moral and political duty to limit damage to the nation. In this sense, we must escape from the mindset that sees Armageddon as the only possible outcome of nuclear conflict. Indeed, the scale of destruction suffered will partially depend on one's pre-war preparation.[30] Aside from a robust defensive capability (both passive and active), the surest way to blunt an enemy's attack is by destroying their offensive nuclear forces. Related to the objective of damage limitation is the third driver, 'countervailing', which seeks to prevent the enemy from achieving their strategic objectives. This strategy finds expression in President Carter's Presidential Directive NSC-59 (1980): 'if deterrence fails initially, we must be capable of fighting successfully so that the adversary would not achieve his war aims'.[31] Finally, a warfighting option can seek to prevail against the enemy – that is, achieve military objectives that promote policy goals. From a policy perspective, this approach was most clearly evident during Reagan's first administration; although it was somewhat sidelined after the 1983 Proud Prophet war game raised further concerns about the controllability of nuclear war.[32]

Finally, warfighting may actually be required under the terms of just war doctrine. As noted in Chapter 3, one of the criteria for a just war is that there must be a reasonable prospect for success. In the absence of warfighting, nuclear conflict has little chance of presenting a victor, and therefore one of the precepts for jus ad bellum will go unfulfilled.[33]

How does one translate the theory of warfighting into reality without the benefit of past experience of waging nuclear war? During the Cold War, the United States introduced the SIOP (now OPLAN), which consisted of a range of contingencies or attack options from which the president could choose. Within the context of rapid nuclear exchanges, a ready-made-plans approach is sensible enough. However, although the SIOP has never been tested in anger, evidence suggests that it may have suffered from some serious defects. Even after the Schlesinger Doctrine (1974), which called for the creation of a greater range of limited options for the National Command Authority, the SIOP was always restricted in its range of options. For example, when President Nixon and Secretary of State Henry Kissinger were briefed on SIOP 4 in 1969, they were horrified to discover that there were only five options available to the president, all of which involved the launch of massive numbers of warheads. SIOP 5, approved in 1976, was little better. President Carter complained that the options were rigid, and there was a distinct lack of limited options. Indeed, there appears to have been a running battle between administrations and the military. The administrations were constantly striving for greater flexibility in nuclear targeting, whereas the military seemed to prefer playing it safe and going big in their nuclear attack options. To protect this preferred approach, the military constantly baulked at or delayed studies and reform designed to promote limited options.[34] As Peter Feaver explains, via the secrecy of targeting policy, the military hid 'serious errors or deviations from national strategy'.[35] A final indicator of how ill-formulated the SIOP was is the fact that Jimmy Carter was the first president to undertake a full test of the system.

From a warfighting perspective, for much of the Cold War the SIOP was clearly inadequate. Many of the failings of the system appear to emanate from tensions and differing perceptions within the political–military relationship. However, a poor interface between the political and military worlds is not unique to nuclear strategy. As noted in the introductory chapter, one of the complicating factors in strategy is bringing together these culturally distinct groups in a successful manner. What makes nuclear strategy different is the compressed time for decision-making and the pace at which total disaster can unfold. Put simply, in a nuclear conflict, there may be little, if any, time to rectify initial mistakes. That being the case, it is imperative that nuclear strategy be discussed candidly in detail during peacetime. An existential or minimal deterrence head-in-the-sand approach is not only strategically negligent but also dangerous.

When one begins to discuss prevailing strategies in nuclear war, there is a distinct need to establish a definition of victory. What exactly would victory look like in a nuclear conflict? Do we need to redefine the concept? This is another area where Herman Kahn's work stands out, but it is also heavily criticised. In the early 1960s, Kahn broke new ground when he discussed in detail, and in public, what nuclear war might mean for the United States and how it could plan for such an eventuality. What is clear from Kahn's work is that prevailing in a nuclear war would require a new mindset – not least in relation to casualties and the period required for post-war recovery. Nonetheless, Kahn argues that with preparation the United States could survive a devastating nuclear conflict and eventually re-emerge as a functioning society. Nuclear war certainly presented new challenges. One particular challenge discussed in Kahn's *On Thermonuclear War* is the effect of radiation on the population. Kahn's litmus test for whether nuclear war was a survivable phenomenon is the question, 'will the survivors envy the dead?' Much of Kahn's work is devoted to ensuring that the answer to this question is in the negative. In terms of preparation, aside from offensive actions to degrade enemy offensive capabilities, Kahn put much emphasis on passive defensive measures.[36]

Taken together, the many challenges involved in waging nuclear war in a rational, controlled manner suggest that in all likelihood, victory in a superpower confrontation would have been pyrrhic. The propensity for escalation, whether intentional or not, would likely have led to unimaginable levels of devastation. However, we must resist the temptation to speak purely in absolutes when discussing the 'Absolute Weapon'.[37] Bernard Brodie, the noted deterrence theorist, is persuasive when he writes that 'So long as there is a finite chance of war, we have to be interested in outcomes; and although all outcomes would be bad, some would be very much worse than others'.[38] As problematic as this all seems, having the intention and the capabilities to control nuclear war is preferable to having Armageddon as the only option. Nuclear weapons have to be regarded as just another instrument of strategy. They cannot be left in some strategic and military operational limbo. If nothing else, warfighting options enhance the credibility of deterrence (assuming that they do not make the enemy so nervous as to pre-empt). And with capable forces, robust command and control, good planning, strong leadership, and a bit of luck, large-scale nuclear war may be survivable (in the long term) for the sociopolitical community. It should also be borne in mind, no matter how unpleasant, that survival does not have to be the ultimate, overriding objective. 'Better dead than red' is a catchy way of stating that denying the enemy conquest may be the ultimate objective and that the destruction of the state in the process may be a price worth paying for freedom.

Soviet nuclear strategy

The Soviet Union took a significantly different approach to nuclear strategy. Ironically, as sections in the United States defence community moved from existential deterrence to warfighting, Soviet thinkers moved in the opposite direction. Initially, the Soviet Union regarded nuclear weapons predominately as instruments of use and thereby as complements to existing conventional forces. In particular, it was envisaged that nuclear weapons would be used to achieve a breakthrough on the battlefield, which could then be exploited by conventional forces. Deterrence was not formally adopted until 1969. Prior to this, the Soviets understood nuclear strategy on the basis of pre-emption. Due to a history of suffering invasions to the Russian homeland (including the 1941 invasion by Nazi Germany), the Soviet Union sought to minimise its vulnerability in any future war by pre-empting an attack. On this basis, Soviet war plans envisaged two phases for nuclear operations. The first phase would be a massive nuclear salvo against the United States. The second phase involved the use of nuclear weapons in support of conventional forces, as noted earlier. In this early stage of Soviet nuclear strategy, the Soviets did not develop a second-strike capability. This was partly a result of the emphasis on pre-emption but also due to technical limitations in the forces and command and control infrastructure.

Over time, pre-emption was rejected due to an increasing fear of US second-strike capabilities. In its place, the Soviet Union developed its own second-strike capability but also gradually began to de-emphasise nuclear weapons in its military strategy. To this end, the Soviets hoped to deter the use of US nuclear weapons while playing to their strengths in conventional forces. To enable this, the Soviets pursued theories of escalation dominance, and in support of this, they deployed such systems as the SS-20 mobile IRBM. Although, for a while, they toyed with notions of limited nuclear options, by the end of the Cold War, the Soviets had rejected the idea that nuclear war could be won or controlled. With conventional superiority, it made sense for the Soviets to focus on deterring NATO's nuclear forces. Thus, a second-strike capability became central to their strategy, with damage limitation the objective should nuclear usage occur.

Nuclear strategy with limited numbers of warheads

The United States and Soviet Union both had the luxury (and associated problems) of substantial numbers of warheads and delivery systems. How different is nuclear strategy with limited numbers of warheads? In answering this question, the cases of the United Kingdom, France and Pakistan provide valuable insights. As smaller independent powers, neither the United Kingdom or France opted for a warfighting strategy. Facing the massive Soviet nuclear arsenal, it made no sense to engage in counterforce attacks. Such an approach would neither deter the Soviet Union nor lead to significant damage limitation in the event of a conflict. The one qualification to this position relates to British nuclear forces acting in support of US nuclear strategy. Under plans to operate in combined operations with the United Kingdom's transatlantic ally, its nuclear forces would have had some counterforce roles, including attacks against Soviet airbases.

Nonetheless, for the most part, British and French nuclear strategy was focused on deterring the Soviet Union via threats against countervalue targets. Despite overwhelming Soviet superiority, British and French deterrence rested on the threat of punishment metered out against Soviet cities (especially Moscow). The French described this strategy as 'deterrence by the weak of the strong' and spoke of the 'equalising power of the atom'. Over time, in order to enhance credibility (or perhaps to make the strategy more acceptable to their domestic population), both powers shifted from deliberately targeting population centres to political and industrial targets. In reality, of course, this shift still threatened massive civilian casualties.

As with the superpowers, this approach to deterrence rested on a secure second-strike capability. At varying stages of the Cold War, both the United Kingdom and France developed and/or deployed all aspects of the nuclear triad. However, towards the end of this period, they both increasingly relied on SLBMs, which are regarded as the most secure retaliatory capability. As a final point, the French did explore flexible options in their nuclear strategy. They wanted to avoid an all-or-nothing approach, so they explored a range of responses, which included single-warning salvos against military targets, intra-war deterrence, and nuclear bargaining.

Pakistan exists in a different security environment. Rather than facing a nuclear superpower, Pakistan's main threat comes from its neighbour, India. The latter enjoys a substantial conventional superiority over Pakistan, and it is this that has most heavily influenced Pakistani nuclear strategy. Until it became an official nuclear weapons state in 1998, Pakistan had what might be termed a 'catalytic' posture. Pakistan first developed the technical wherewithal to test nuclear weapons in the mid 1980s. With this technological foundation in place, and in the event of potential invasion and/or state collapse, Pakistan could threaten to rapidly develop and deploy nuclear forces. This would, it was hoped, act as a catalyst to force the United States to intervene on Pakistan's behalf to prevent escalation to the nuclear threshold on the subcontinent. In essence, this was an indirect form of deterrence. It was designed to deter Indian aggression, albeit via the intervention of a third power.

As US support ebbed away after the end of the Cold War, Pakistani nuclear strategy had to become more self-reliant. Facing a nuclear-armed (from 1998), conventionally superior India, Pakistan adopted a strategy of asymmetric escalation. In a posture not dissimilar to NATO's flexible response, nuclear weapons were fully integrated into Pakistan's conventional forces. Based on a range of nuclear capabilities, including battlefield weapons, cruise missiles, and mobile medium range ballistic missiles, Pakistan aimed to deter Indian aggression at any level. In the face of conventional defeat, Pakistan can threaten to escalate to the nuclear level, with second-strike weapons hopefully deterring India from going over the nuclear threshold. This is not dissimilar to Russia's new escalate-to-deescalate posture, and it allows a conventionally inferior state to deter a more powerful enemy.[39]

Stability: ballistic missile defence and arms control

An interesting and important addition to Cold War development of nuclear strategy is the debate surrounding BMD and the potential impact on stability. The paradoxical logic of strategy ensured that once ballistic missiles became a viable delivery option, countermeasures would be developed.[40] BMD development began early in the missile age. Both superpowers developed a number of systems. However, the ballistic missile, whether land based or launched from a submarine, maintained its position as the delivery system most likely to penetrate enemy defences. This dominance can be attributed to two main reasons. The first concerns the enormous technical difficulties of intercepting a ballistic missile. Successfully tracking and destroying a missile and/or its payload in flight, though not impossible, is a tough technological challenge. Even if that challenge can be individually overcome, leak-proof defence is far from guaranteed when one is dealing with multiple missiles, warheads, and decoys. One of the main problems is concerned with the command and control of a BMD system in the face of an overwhelming number of targets. Tracking, targeting, and then retargeting thousands of objects represents an enormous software challenge.

The technical aspects of BMD were only part of the problem during the Cold War. As previously mentioned, since MAD was perceived as a stable security relationship, the development of any system that could undermine MAD was discouraged. This reached its climax during the arms control agreements of 1972. The ABM Treaty restricted each superpower to the deployment of 100 interceptor launchers at one site. To all intents and purposes, this made BMD a none-starter in the Cold War. The argument against BMD focused on its potential efficacy against a degraded enemy second strike. Although BMD looked defensive in nature, it would be most effective in support of a first strike. In this manner, an enemy might fear the deployment of a BMD system because it undermines their retaliatory capability and may indeed be the prelude to a surprise attack.

The quest for technological stability was further promoted by SALT, which limited the numbers of offensive MIRVed warheads. MIRVed warheads were looked upon as a threat to stability because they were perceived as effective counterforce weapons. Again, this seemed to threaten the potential efficacy of retaliatory forces. However well intentioned, both the ABM Treaty and SALT were based on an approach that largely ignored the political dimension of stability and focused on the technical aspects. Therefore, these efforts to sure up stability may have been barking up the wrong tree.

Following the arms control agreements of 1972, BMD largely disappeared from the agenda, only to reappear in 1983 with President Reagan's announcement of SDI. The SDI programme was an extremely ambitious attempt to escape from MAD, and it envisaged the deployment of a layered defensive system that included space-based assets and directed-energy weapons. As it was, SDI never appeared in its original guise. However, the research and development projects that began under the auspices of SDI are now beginning to bear fruit with current missile defence deployments.

Whether or not SDI was ever a realistic attempt to deploy a workable ABM system, it certainly had an impact on the course of the Cold War. In conjunction with other defence projects (i.e. the B1-B bomber and MX Peacekeeper ICBM) SDI helped to precipitate a change in the superpower relationship. By the early 1980s, the Soviet leadership was increasingly concerned about the state of the Soviet economy. The Soviet Union simply could not match the defence modernisation being undertaken by the United States. As a consequence, the Soviets sought to improve the superpower relationship and reduce their defence commitments via a series of arms control agreements. The most notable of these was the Intermediate-Range Nuclear Forces (INF) Treaty in 1987, which scrapped an entire class of nuclear weapons from the superpower arsenals. To some, this was a welcome move in the direction of greater stability, since INF were potent first-strike assets, given their short flight times. To others, the INF Treaty blew a large hole in NATO's flexible response force structure.[41]

Arms control played an important cameo role in nuclear strategy during the Cold War. From the outset of the nuclear age, there were attempts to restrain the development of nuclear weapons and/or enhance the stability of the superpower nuclear relationship through arms control agreements. As the examples already given indicate, the arms control regime either placed ceilings on certain categories of weapons or removed them completely from the security environment. In addition, attempts were made to control the pace of weapons development with test-ban treaties. However, despite the enormous levels of effort expended on arms control, the superpowers continued to build up and modernise their forces. If there existed stability in the superpower relationship, it had little to do with arms control. Rather, stability was more likely due to a realisation of mutual vulnerability and the absence of a sufficient political cause to risk global devastation.

Arms control has often, and correctly, been criticised for ignoring the political dimension of the security environment. Ironically, it is the political dimension that dictates the fate of arms control talks and helps to explain the arms control paradox. The paradox states that when one really needs arms control (when the political situation is dire), it cannot be achieved; and when one does not need it (during a period of détente), it is easier to achieve. States embroiled in a tense security relationship are unlikely to sign away their key military capabilities. Events at the time of writing appear to confirm this position. As the US–Russian relationship has soured, some of the key arms control treaties of the Cold War (in particular the ABM and INF treaties) have fallen by the wayside. Indeed, there is now concern that the New START treaty, which limits deployed strategic nuclear weapons, may not be renewed in 2021.

From a strategic perspective, the main concern with arms control is that must not undermine strategic efficacy. Unfortunately, it seems that arms control negotiations are often conducted in a strategic vacuum, as evidenced by the INF Treaty. In this way, President Reagan's desire to reduce the threat of nuclear war may have overridden his strategic sense. Similar concerns can be raised about the Obama administration and the emphasis it placed on nuclear abolition, with little apparent concern for the effects on its nuclear strategy. Although the Trump administration is formally still committing itself to the general goal of nuclear disarmament, through its actions, it appears to be basing US security on force modernisation rather than the hope of arms control.

Contemporary nuclear strategy

Since the end of the Cold War, the most noticeable feature of nuclear strategy in the West has been a lack of development, both in policy and academic circles. To give some indication of the dearth of thinking on nuclear strategy, one can look to the level of coverage in the main academic journals. As an example, between 2000 and 2012, there were four articles in *International Security* that could be considered as works of nuclear strategy. Over the same period, *Survival* had only two articles that could properly be considered works on the subject. In stark contrast, from its founding in 1976 until 1988 (mirroring the 12 years of 2000–2012), *International Security* published approximately 91 articles on nuclear strategy. This figure excludes many of the nuclear non-proliferation articles, many on the subject of arms control. Happily, the scarcity of thinking on nuclear strategy may be changing somewhat. Since the publication of the first edition of this book – or, between 2012 and 2018 – *International Security* published nine articles on nuclear strategy; it is an improvement but still well short of the heyday of the subject.

In the years immediately following the end of the Cold War, strategic studies was dominated by civil conflict and the subject of peacekeeping (in response to the conflicts in Bosnia and Somalia). Following the 1991 Gulf War, defence professionals also became fixated on the RMA and on military transformation (see Chapter 4). The RMA school of thought focused distinctly on the development of conventional capabilities and in parts suggested that conventional arms were becoming so potent that they could replace nuclear weapons for certain missions. In particular, increased levels of precision gave conventional munitions an assured kill capability that previously had been limited to nuclear weapons. As strategic studies moved into the twenty-first century, the events of 9/11 and the wars in Iraq and Afghanistan refocused much intellectual activity into the fields of terrorism and counterinsurgency.

As far as nuclear strategy is concerned, the negative trend in academia has been mirrored in many Western polities. Some progress was made with the Bush administration's 2002 Nuclear Posture Review (NPR), which emphasised the need for flexibility in response, a closer connection between conventional and nuclear weapons, and the need to develop lower-yield warheads to support said flexibility. Unfortunately, much of the progress of the Bush years was lost during the Obama administrations. Although Obama reluctantly concluded that substantial investment was required to maintain the viability of US nuclear capability and eventually shied away from an explicit policy of sole use (that nuclear weapons exist only to deter nuclear attack) and no first use, his administration heavily de-emphasised nuclear weapons in US security policy.[42] This was a deliberate policy choice to push forward the goal of global nuclear abolition. As a senior State Department official commented, 'the NPR's "first step" involved "develop[ing] a nuclear force structure and posture for use in the negotiations" of the successor agreement to START I'.[43]

Across the Atlantic, successive UK governments' rationale for replacing the United Kingdom's Trident SSBN force reveals a paucity of thought on nuclear strategy. Although recent British governments have presented a strong case for why the United Kingdom requires a nuclear deterrent (their preferred term for the United Kingdom's nuclear weapons, linking them inexorably to a deterrence role), the lack of detail and engagement with warfighting is telling. The 2015 *National Security Strategy and Strategic Defence and Security Review* once again highlights the ambiguity of the United Kingdom's deterrence posture while also displaying the United Kingdom's commitment to minimum deterrence and the ultimate goal of nuclear disarmament.[44] This stance, considered alongside the fact that UK policymakers chose the easiest option for replacing Trident (a like-for-like capability, with no serious consideration of diversifying delivery options), suggests that the United Kingdom is a reluctant nuclear power with little interest in developing warfighting options or using nuclear weapons to exert leverage in international politics.

A lack of engagement with nuclear strategy, in both academia and policy circles, is problematic because the second nuclear age poses a series of challenges to strategists that must be met with intellectual rigour, sound policy, and robust capabilities.[45] One of the tasks facing strategists is to establish how much of Cold War nuclear strategy can be adapted to the contemporary environment and whether we need to develop new forms of thinking for the challenges ahead. One feature of the new nuclear environment that may demand change is the significant reduction in numbers of warheads possessed by the major nuclear powers. Under the terms of the 2011 New START Treaty, the United States and Russia are each able to deploy 1550 strategic warheads on 700 ICBMs, SLBMs and heavy bombers.[46] Both states also have approximately 6500 additional warheads in storage or retired. This is clearly a significant reduction from the 30,000–40,000 warheads during the Cold War. Beyond the United States and Russia, France has approximately 300 warheads, China 280, UK 215, India 145, Pakistan 135, Israel 80, and North Korea 15.[47]

Thus, although the arms control community may have celebrated the reversal of vertical proliferation in the United States and Russia, these gains are increasingly being offset by horizontal proliferation to other states, the death of the INF Treaty, concerns over the future of New START (due to expire in 2021), and the significant modernisation of nuclear forces. Nuclear weapons have spread to potentially unstable states such as Pakistan and North Korea, and in the near future, they could well be in the possession of a revolutionary state in the form of Iran. And as indicated in both the 2010 and 2018 NPRs, there is also the looming risk of nuclear weapons falling into the hands of terrorist organisations. An increase in the ownership of nuclear weapons, especially when unstable powers or terrorist organisations are involved, may increase the potential for accidental or even deliberate use of the weapons.[48]

Box 12.4 Nuclear weapons modernisation

US
Ground-based strategic deterrent (GBSD).
B-21 Raider stealth bomber.
Long-Range Standoff (LRSO) weapon.
Columbia-class SSBN.
Low-yield SLBM/nuclear-armed SLCM.

Russia
RS 28 SARMAT superheavy ICBM.
PAK DA stealth bomber.
Status-6 nuclear torpedo.
Avangard hypersonic glide vehicle.
Nuclear-powered ground-launched cruise missile.

China
DF-41 MIRVed mobile ICBM.
MIRVed version of DF-5 silo-based ICBM.
Type 096 SSBN (armed with the new JL-3 SLBM).
H-20 long-range stealth bomber.

In terms of modernisation, all of the major powers are now engaged in substantial efforts. Russia is pushing forward with the RS 28 SARMAT superheavy ICBM, PAK DA stealth bomber, Status-6 nuclear torpedo, Avangard hypersonic glide vehicle, and a nuclear-powered ground-launched cruise missile that places it in breach of the INF Treaty. As Colin S. Gray notes, this leaves the West 'perilously behind Russia in the development and deployment of . . . strategic forces'.[49] Moreover, Russia's force modernisation is linked to a more aggressive nuclear doctrine. This is exemplified by the doctrine of escalate-to-deescalate, in which non-strategic nuclear weapons could be used to control a conflict that is getting beyond Russian conventional capabilities.[50] For its part, China has developed the MIRVed DF-41 mobile ICBM, a MIRVed version of the DF-5 silo-based ICBM; is reportedly soon to begin constructing the type 096 SSBN (armed with the new JL-3 SLBM); and is developing the H-20 long-range stealth bomber.

It is clear from the evidence of horizontal proliferation and force modernisation that Obama's goal of nuclear abolition is dead and buried. The future strategic environment is, at least in part, nuclear. In response, Western powers are also modernising their forces and, at least in relation to the Trump administration, producing more robust nuclear weapons policies. As already noted, the United Kingdom will replace its Trident SSBN force with a like-for-like system. France is upgrading its M51 SLBM and is shortly due to begin development of the new SNLE-3G SSBN to replace the Triomphant-class vessels. France is also in the early stages of designing a new stealthier, extended-range air-launched cruise missile (ASN4G), to replace the existing ASMPA.

As outlined in the 2018 NPR, the Trump administration will continue, and in some cases accelerate and add to, existing US force modernisation programmes. Specifically, the Minuteman III ICBM will be replaced by the GBSD in 2029. Disappointingly, there are no plans to increase the number of warheads on Minuteman III, which were reduced from three to one under Obama. However, the 2018 NPR notes that the ICBM force can be uploaded (increased warheads per missile) as part of its hedging strategy. The B-52H and B-2A long-range bombers are to be replaced by the B-21 Raider, due to enter service in 2025. The air-launched cruise missile (ALCM) will be replaced by the Long-Range Standoff (LRSO) weapon, and the B61–12 (due for deployment in 2021) Life Extension Programme (LEP) will provide the United States with a precision-strike gravity bomb for its air-based nuclear forces. Beginning in 2031, the Columbia-class SSBN will replace the Ohio-class force. Finally, to increase flexibility and perhaps to match Russian tactical nuclear capability, the 2018 NPR initiated a programme for the near-term deployment of a low-yield SLBM and a new nuclear-armed SLCM.[51]

As impressive as these modernisation efforts are, strategic efficacy is built on more than just hardware. Just as important are doctrine and weapons policy. After the relative hiatus of the Obama years, the 2018 NPR presents a more robust, and strategic, nuclear weapons policy. In direct contrast to Obama's hopes for nuclear abolition, the 2018 NPR is quick to refute the viability of such efforts: 'the Nuclear Weapons Ban Treaty, opened for signature at the U.N. in 2017, is fuelled by wholly unrealistic expectations of the elimination of nuclear arsenals without the prerequisite transformation of the international security environment'.[52] As a consequence, and again in direct contrast to Obama, the Trump administration declared that for the United States, 'there is no higher priority for national defense' than modernising its nuclear forces.[53] From this robust position, the NPR paints a picture of US nuclear strategy that is more flexible in support of tailored deterrence.

Perhaps of even greater significance is the fact that the NPR explicitly states that 'deterring nuclear attack is not the sole purpose of nuclear weapons'.[54] Other roles for the US nuclear arsenal include deterrence of non-nuclear strategic attack (substantial attacks against US or Allied population, infrastructure, nuclear forces, nuclear command and control, and early warning systems); to assure allies (extended deterrence) in the face of nuclear or non-nuclear threats; to hedge against an uncertain future; and to achieve US objectives if deterrence fails.[55] The latter is especially significant, because it takes contemporary US nuclear strategy into the post-deterrence setting.

But what objectives does the Trump administration envisage for nuclear operations? One aim, perhaps with Russia's escalate-to-deescalate posture in mind, is to prevent enemy nuclear escalation from reaching its objectives.[56] This would be a countervailing strategy. Further detail on this is provided by the 2019 *Joint Publication No. 3–72 Nuclear Operations*, which outlines US thinking on the impact of nuclear weapons on the future battlefield. Interestingly, and one assumes in the context of a large conflict with a nuclear-armed power, it is reported that *3–72* considers nuclear use as '"essential" to mission success'.[57] This appears to be further evidence that nuclear weapons are being meaningfully reintegrated into US defence policy.

Beyond countervailing, the main objectives seem to be damage limitation and the re-establishing deterrence. Although the method has not been explicitly stated, these objectives would likely be pursued through counterforce strikes against key enemy capabilities. Indeed, it has been suggested that increases in accuracy and remote sensing have enhanced the potency of counterforce options, so that low casualty counterforce options are now possible.[58] In many respects, then, the 2018 NPR is something of a return to the later Cold War, with flexibility and warfighting options informing strategy. Certainly, the latest review seeks to enhance both the flexibility and credibility of the US nuclear posture. However, it still eschews the adoption of an unrestrained theory of victory and thereby cannot be considered as the basis for a full warfighting strategy. Indeed, the 2018 NPR is at pains to declare that the review 'is not intended to enable, nor does it enable, "nuclear war-fighting"'.[59] We are left to conclude, then, that as the world enters a new age of nuclear competition, the West (in both academic and policy circles) is taking some positive steps in the right direction but has not yet developed a comprehensive approach to nuclear strategy.

Nuclear strategy for the twenty-first century

What follows is a tentative attempt to construct a new US nuclear strategy for the twenty-first century. It will quickly become apparent that many of the concepts from the Cold War retain their validity in the second nuclear age. When one examines the security environment of the twenty-first century, it becomes readily apparent that flexible options must remain central to US nuclear strategy. To the credit of the Trump administration, the 2018 NPR seeks to increase flexibility in its nuclear posture. This is to be achieved via the comprehensive modernisation plans encompassing each leg of the triad: low-yield weapons, a more robust and responsive command and control infrastructure, and increased investment in BMD. As noted by Keith Payne, this is essential in the face of a changing security environment and the resultant increased number of deterrence variables.[60]

With such capabilities in place, a flexible deterrence posture could be constructed. Although deterrence can never provide an absolute guarantee of security, it should still provide the cornerstone of US nuclear strategy. In fact, deterrence of WMDs may be more important now for the United States since it enjoys conventional superiority. Preventing a conflict from crossing the WMD threshold plays to the strengths of the U.S. Military, at least in regular war. For this new deterrence posture, both forms of deterrence should be pursued. In the case of deterrence by denial, BMD and robust passive defences may be enough to prevent a smaller enemy (although probably not Russia) from achieving its goals in any WMD attack on the US homeland or deployed forces. Of course, BMD would have no role to play in a WMD terrorist attack using rudimentary means of delivery. However, passive civil defence could help to limit the number of casualties from such an attack (the WMD terrorist threat is discussed in more detail later on), and thereby deny a terrorist organisation its goal of creating massive casualties.

Low-yield precision nuclear weapons for counterforce missions may also play a deterrence-by-denial role against a foreign power's conventional capabilities and battlefield nuclear weapons. In the near term, US conventional superiority should be enough to deter regular forms of aggression against the United States and key allies. Nonetheless, the further ability to escalate to the use of low-yield precision weapons would all but guarantee that an enemy's offensive ambitions would be thwarted.

The punishment form of deterrence presents a slightly more challenging task for future nuclear strategists. This is particularly the case in relation to the issue of credibility. As simple as it would be to threaten the destruction of an enemy's homeland with city-busting warheads (as during periods in the Cold War), the West would now struggle to credibly threaten such an indiscriminate response. Thus, punishment forms of deterrence must be more discriminate and tailored more precisely to what the enemy leadership values. The most promising target sets in this respect are those associated with leadership, infrastructure, and the security forces on which political leadership often relies to maintain power. Narrowing possible target sets in this way does not, however, instantly solve the credibility problem, since many of these targets are in populated areas. This is where the mix of conventional and nuclear strike forces becomes especially useful. Precision conventional weapons can be used to attack targets in areas where collateral damage would be significant from nuclear usage. However, nuclear weapons, especially those of a lower yield, could conceivably be used against targets (especially those military in nature and hardened) away from population centres. Indeed, the use of nuclear weapons would be a significant signal of intent and a willingness and ability to escalate a conflict. In turn, this could be a useful coercive technique and could also fulfil the function of signalling for intra-war deterrence.

Despite the moral and strategic requirement for more limited and precise nuclear capabilities, a punishment role should be retained for the larger nuclear weapon systems. Although it is unlikely that large-scale devastation of an enemy's homeland would ever be seriously contemplated, the future is uncertain. As history teaches us, it is not beyond the realms of possibility that some form of total war will re-emerge in the future. As unlikely as this may seem, the reader should consider that the Second World War seemed impossible to many after the slaughter of the First World War. Similarly, a US-led invasion of Afghanistan was not on the agenda before the events of 9/11. Thus, retaining a large nuclear capability can be regarded as the equivalent of a car airbag. It is unlikely that it will ever be deployed in anger, but it would be crucial if needed. In this respect, having the capability to escalate and assuredly destroy the enemy is the ultimate threat that underwrites all others.

The prospect of retaining larger nuclear weapons for retaliatory punishment leads us once again into the subject of escalation dominance. Although the finer details of Kahn's theories on escalation may have been heavily criticised, the concept of escalation dominance has an undeniable logic behind it. For the purposes of deterrence, both pre-war and intra-war, the United States must ensure that it can dominate any level of conflict that involves nuclear weapons. This includes having the capability to prevail at the upper end of the nuclear weapons spectrum. At present, the United States already has such a capability vis-à-vis states such as Pakistan and North Korea. However, it must also seek to retain this capability in relation to any potential peer competitors, particularly Russia and an empowered China. If the United States forgoes the capabilities required for escalation dominance, it must accept a weakened bargaining position in any future conflict with a major nuclear power.

Retaining sufficient numbers of accurate, modern nuclear forces is also required for warfighting. Although some Western governments may prefer to regard their nuclear forces as weapons of nonuse, it is essential to retain both the capability and will to wage nuclear war. A warfighting capability is important for counterforce missions. In particular, future US admin-istrations must be able to degrade an enemy's offensive nuclear forces for damage limitation. This mission would be enhanced with the full deployment of BMD and a robust civil defence programme. In this way, a combination of modern offensive and defensive systems should provide the United States with the most advanced nuclear warfighting capability in the inter-national system. In turn, this should enhance deterrence, and should deterrence fail, it would give the United States a reasonable chance of limiting the amount of damage inflicted on its population.[61]

Alongside the adoption of an escalation dominance force structure, a warfighting capa-bility would provide the United States with considerable bargaining power during a future crisis. Inevitably, fears will be expressed concerning the stability implications of such a force structure. However, as ever, such fears are groundless if they are based purely on technical and operational concerns rather than on politics.

Much of this discussion may seem as if it has been lifted straight from the Cold War and is therefore of little relevance for today and certainly out of step with much current thinking. However, the similarity with previous strategy is so vivid because the fundamental principles of nuclear strategy have changed little since the first nuclear age. What has changed is that with fewer operational warheads, smaller, more precise counterforce options, and the deploy-ment of a robust missile defence system, nuclear weapons have been freed somewhat from the straightjacket of Armageddon. The increased ability to 'use' nuclear weapons (whether they are actually fired in anger or merely threatened) strengthens the credibility of deter-rence and also makes nuclear war potentially more survivable. If political leaders have the required courage, nuclear weapons could once again become viable instruments in interna-tional politics, in extremis. However, this reawakening of nuclear strategy is possible only if the required forces, doctrine, and will are acquired to construct a flexible force structure with warfighting and escalation dominance built in. This approach is in stark contrast to that which was followed during the Obama administration. Rather, by pursuing an abolitionist agenda that placed arms control and disarmament at the centre of US policy on nuclear weapons, the Obama administration neglected and undermined nuclear strategy. The 2018 NPR has repaired some of the damage done during the Obama years. Nonetheless, Trump's failure to embrace an unrestrained theory of victory means the United States cannot fully exploit the strategic and credibility advantages of a warfighting posture.

Although nuclear competition among great powers is back on the security agenda, the threat of WMD terrorism cannot be ignored. Indeed, the 2018 NPR notes that nuclear ter-rorism 'remains among the most significant threats to the security of the United States, allies, and partners'.[62] Without an easily identifiable 'return address', retaliatory deterrence threats appear to be impotent against irregular foes. However, further analysis suggests that many of the recognised elements of nuclear strategy do have a role to play, if only the strategist works that bit harder.[63] As already noted, punishment must threaten those assets or capabilities that an enemy values. Although terrorist organisations do not have such readily identifiable assets as nation-states, they do have some that may be targeted. Financial assets, logistical and training infrastructures, and leadership all appear to be plausible candidates for valued target sets. Clearly, some of these targets are not well suited to nuclear threats. However, should terrorists escalate to the threat and/or use of WMDs, the rules of the game would have changed. Lower-yield nuclear weapons may become the weapon of choice to provide an assured kill capability against terrorist WMD stocks or facilities. Attacks against such targets could be regarded as counterforce, damage-limitation missions. Furthermore, if they are actively deploying WMDs, terrorist leadership would become valid targets if they can be located. Moreover, while sensibly acknowledging the limited role of US nuclear weapons in this area, the NPR 2018 section on nuclear terrorism ends with an explicit threat of potential retaliation against terror groups and/or their state sponsors (deterrence by punishment).[64]

Finally, deterrence by denial has a role against a WMD terrorist threat. As discussed in the 2018 NPR, the detection and the interdiction of nuclear devices, alongside civil defence, have roles in preventing and mitigating the effects of nuclear terrorism. In this way, the NPR is communicating deterrence by denial. Similarly, the prospect of pre-emptive strikes (nuclear and/or conventional) against terrorist WMD assets, if they can be located, may compel a terrorist enemy to abandon any offensive plans. As with all deterrence postures, there are no guarantees that WMD-armed terrorists would be deterred. Nonetheless, a flexible force structure, which includes a range of nuclear and conventional capabilities, in addition to a viable civil defence element, improves the chances of constructing a workable deterrence stance against such a threat. And in the event of a deterrence failure, the same capabilities could support damage limitation.

The reader may conclude that this discussion of WMD terrorism is fanciful, given that we are discussing the possible, although not likely, use of nuclear weapons to kill a handful of individuals and their limited military assets. However, as the title of Herman Kahn's 1962 book indicates, when considering nuclear weapons and WMDs, we must be prepared to 'think about the unthinkable'. If states refuse to do so, they may be seriously unprepared if and when these weapons are used against them. Indeed, being unprepared may actually encourage others to use such weapons.

Conclusion

Although initially appearing to be the perfect instrument for existential deterrence, and thereby a positive force for stability, nuclear weapons proved to be somewhat of a headache for the practitioners of strategy. The basic technical characteristics of a nuclear weapon seem to reduce its credibility as a useful tool of strategy. It is a challenge to harness such enormous destructive power for the pursuit of rational policy objectives. The scale of the challenge was magnified substantially when thousands of warheads, only minutes from their targets, were deployed in the tense atmosphere of the Cold War. However, in response, the intellectual community produced extraordinary works of theory and, in the process, helped to create the distinct academic discipline of strategic studies.

Despite being used initially in an offensive manner against Japan, nuclear weapons became dominated by the theory of deterrence. In response to the shortcomings of massive retaliation and existential deterrence, the nuclear strategy community quickly understood that tactical and operational details mattered where nuclear deterrence was concerned. The maintenance of credible second-strike capabilities, on which MAD was based, required constant vigilance and developments. The details mattered even more in the field of extended deterrence. The theorists worked hard to produce a posture that would credibly persuade an adversary that the United States would respond with nuclear weapons in support of an ally, even in the face of assured destruction.

Various theories were developed in support of extended deterrence, but they all amounted to the same thing: how to control the dynamic of a nuclear relationship to gain advantage. Escalation dominance or 'the threat that leaves something to chance' were both concerned with establishing an advantageous position in nuclear bargaining and risk manipulation. The goal was to place the onus of compromise on the enemy. Should war occur, efforts were also made to construct workable theories of limited nuclear war. An attempt to control nuclear war to an even greater degree was developed in the warfighting school of thought. However, the further the theorists delved into limited war theory, the more difficult the whole enterprise appeared. The prospects for escalation seemed overwhelming. Nonetheless, there had to be an alternative to surrender or Armageddon. Thus, the search for warfighting options is the only responsible approach to nuclear strategy. Through warfighting, deterrence receives a credibility boost. And should war occur, warfighting would at least present the possibility for damage limitation, countervailing, and perhaps even victory (prevailing).

Unfortunately, much of the valuable work done on nuclear strategy during the Cold War has been neglected in the contemporary period. The push for nuclear abolition resulted in the neglect of nuclear strategy and a decline in capabilities. And yet in the face of increasing horizontal proliferation, countries like the United States require flexible nuclear strategy, which is based on modern, robust nuclear forces. Just as in the Cold War, a range of capabilities is required to ensure escalation dominance and a warfighting stance. If one accepts the obvious reality that nuclear weapons are here to stay, nuclear supremacy must be the goal for nuclear strategists. Without this, a state will leave itself in a weakened position vis-à-vis other developing nuclear powers. In this case, nuclear weapons will cease to be viable instruments of strategy. And as much as the civilised world may correctly despise nuclear weapons, they are part of our strategic reality and therefore must be incorporated into strategy in the most advantageous way possible. The logic of strategy does not cease to operate just because humankind has awoken the power of the atom.

Key points

1   Nuclear weapons pose a substantial challenge for the theorist and practitioner.
2   The challenge of nuclear strategy emanates from the destructive force of nuclear weapons allied to their means of delivery.
3   Deterrence lies at the heart of nuclear strategy.
4   The details matter in nuclear strategy.
5   Warfighting enhances deterrence, aids damage limitation, and promotes a theory of victory.
6   Contemporary nuclear strategy should not abandon the concepts developed during the Cold War.

Questions

1   Is nuclear strategy an oxymoron?
2   Is nuclear deterrence reliable?
3   Do the details matter in nuclear strategy?
4   Is victory possible in nuclear conflict?

Notes

1   For a discussion on the origins of the academic discipline of strategic studies, see David J. Lonsdale, 'Strategy', in David Jordan et al. (eds.), *Understanding Modern Warfare*, 2nd ed. (Cambridge, Cambridge University Press, 2016).

2   Thomas C. Schelling, *The Strategy of Conflict* (Cambridge, MA, Harvard University, 1980).

3   Nuclear weapons come in two variants: fission and fusion. For details on the difference between them, see Charles C. Grace and Charles Bridgman, *Nuclear Weapons: Principles, Effects and Survivability* (London, Brassey's, 1994).

4   These figures were taken from National Resource Defense Council, *Table of Global Nuclear Weapons Stockpiles, 1945–2002*, www.nrdc.org/nuclear/nudb/datab19.asp

5   One of the most detailed reports on the effects of nuclear weapons is Samuel Glasstone and Philip J. Dolan, *The Effects of Nuclear Weapons* (Washington, DC, Department of Defense and Energy Research and Development Administration, 1977).

6   Zbigniew Brzezinski (ed.), *Promise and Peril: The Strategic Defence Initiative* (Washington, DC, Ethics and Public Policy Center, 1986).

7   Bruce Blair, *The Logic of Accidental Nuclear War* (Washington, DC, Brooking's Institution, 1991).

8   Kissinger's 1957 book brought together the findings of the Council on Foreign Relations' Study Group on Nuclear Weapons. Henry Kissinger, *Nuclear Weapons and Foreign Policy* (New York, Harper and Brothers, 1957).

9   Lawrence Freedman, *The Evolution of Nuclear Strategy* (London, MacMillan Press, 1989), p. xxi

10   Colin S. Gray, *Theory of Strategy* (Oxford, Oxford University Press, 2018), p. 123.

11   Bernard Brodie, *The Absolute Weapon* (New York, Harcourt Brace, 1946), p. 31.

12   For a critical description and analysis of these ideas, see Herman Kahn, *On Thermonuclear War* (Princeton, Princeton University Press, 1960), pp. 8–9.

13   Albert J. Wohlstetter, 'The Delicate Balance of Terror', *Foreign Affairs* 37 (1959), pp. 211–34.

14   Freedman, *The Evolution of Nuclear Strategy*, p. 740.

15   Ibid., pp. 740–1.

16   Lawrence Freedman, *Deterrence* (Cambridge, Polity Press, 2004), pp. 40–2.

17   However, one may still question whether a president would kill millions of Soviet citizens in an act of revenge.

18   Kahn discusses deterrence at length in Herman Kahn, *Thinking about the Unthinkable* (London, Weidenfeld and Nicolson, 1962).

19   J.W. Knopf, 'The Fourth Wave in Deterrence Research', *Contemporary Security Policy* 31:1 (2010), pp. 1–33.

20   Gray, *Modern Strategy*, p. 306.

21   Colin S. Gray, *Strategy and History: Essays on Theory and Practice* (Abingdon, Routledge, 2006), pp. 127–8.

22 The development of these various options is discussed in some detail in Lawrence Freedman, 'The First Two Generations of Nuclear Strategists', in Peter Paret (ed.), *Makers of Modern Strategy: From Machiavelli to the Nuclear Age* (Oxford, Clarendon Press, 1986), pp. 735–78.

23 Thomas C. Schelling, *The Strategy of Conflict* (Cambridge, Harvard University Press, 1980), especially Chapter 8.

24 The chicken analogy is used effectively in Kahn, *Thinking About the Unthinkable*, pp. 45–6.

25 Herman Kahn, *On Escalation: Methaphors and Scenarios* (London, Pall Mall Press, 1965).

26 Morton H. Halperin, *Limited War in the Nuclear Age* (New York, John Wiley & Sons, 1963).

27 Kissinger, p. 228.

28 For discussions on the development of the SIOP, see David Alan Rosenberg, 'U.S. Nuclear War Planning, 1945–1960', in Desmond Ball and Jeffrey Richelson (eds.), *Strategic Nuclear Targeting* (Ithaca, Cornell University Press, 1986), pp. 35–56; Desmond Ball, 'The Development of the SIOP, 1960–1983', in Desmond Ball and Jeffrey Richelson (eds.), *Strategic Nuclear Targeting* (Ithaca, Cornell University Press, 1986), pp. 57–83.

29 See, for example, Gower, *The Dangerous Illogic*; Geoff Wilson and Will Saetren, 'Quite Possibly the Dumbest Military Concept Ever: A "Limited" Nuclear War', *The National Interest*, https://nationalinterest.org/blog/the-buzz/quite-possibly-the-dumbest-military-concept-ever-limited-16394?page=0%2C1 (accessed May 27, 2016). In the latter, the authors starkly declare: 'The notion that nuclear weapons can be used for anything "beyond deterrence" is reckless and dangerous thinking'.

30 Kahn, *On Thermonuclear War*, pp. 10–11; Gray, *Modern Strategy*, p. 307.

31 Presidential Directive NSC-59, www.fas.org/irp/offdocs/pd/pd59.pdf

32 Paul Bracken, *The Second Nuclear Age* (New York, St. Martin's Griffin, 2012), p. 89.

33 Colin S. Gray and Keith B. Payne, 'Victory is Possible', *Foreign Policy* 39 (Summer 1980), pp. 14–27. Of course, nuclear conflict would seem a prime candidate to fail many of the other criteria of jus in bello, to cite discrimination as just one example.

34 Ball, 'Development of the SIOP'.

35 Quoted in William Burr, 'Reagan's Nuclear War Briefing Declassified', *National Security Archive*, December 22, 2016, https://nsarchive.gwu.edu/briefing-book/nuclear-vault/2016-12-22/reagans-nuclear-war-briefing-declassified#_edn5

36 Herman Kahn, *Thinking about the Unthinkable* (London, Weidenfeld & Nicolson, 1962), Chapter 3.

37 This is a reference to Brodie's 1946 work, Bernard Brodie (ed.), *The Absolute Weapon: Atomic Power and World Order* (New York, Harcourt, Brace and Company, 1946).

38 Bernard Brodie, *Strategy in the Missile Age* (Princeton, Princeton University Press, 1959), p. 278.

39 See Vipin Narang, *Nuclear Strategy in the Modern Era: Regional Powers and International Conflict* (Princeton, Princeton University Press, 2014).

40 The paradoxical logic of strategy is a concept developed in Edward Luttwak, *Strategy: The Logic of War and Peace* (Cambridge, MA, The Belknap Press, 1987).

41 Gray, *Strategy and History*, p. 43.

42 Hans M. Kristensen, 'Remarks on Nuclear Modernization', www.fas.org/programs/ssp/nukes/publications1/2012BASICmodernization111312.pdf

43 Quoted in Anna Loukianova, *The Nuclear Posture Review Debate*, NTI, August 2009, www.nti.org/e_research/e3_nuclear_posture_review_debate.html

44 HM Government, *National Security Strategy and Strategic Defence and Security Review 2015*, https://assets.publishing.service.gov.uk/government/uploads/system/uploads/attachment_data/file/555607/2015_Strategic_Defence_and_Security_Review.pdf

45 The term 'second nuclear age' was coined by Colin Gray. See Colin S. Gray, *The Second Nuclear Age* (London, Lynne Rienner Publishers, 1999).

46 There is some concern that, due to counting methods in the treaty, numbers of deployed warheads could actually increase. David J. Trachtenberg, *Six Myths About the New START Treaty*, www.defense studies.org/?p=2093

47 Kelsey Davenport & Kingston Reif, 'Nuclear Weapons: Who has What at a Glance', *Arms Control Association*, www.armscontrol.org/factsheets/Nuclearweaponswhohaswhat

48 Importantly, not everyone subscribes to the notion that nuclear proliferation is inherently dangerous. Most famously, Kenneth Waltz has argued that nuclear proliferation creates stability among powers, mainly because, when nuclear armed, they have to be more cautious in their dealings with one another. The absence of major war between India and Pakistan since they both became declared nuclear powers may be evidence of Waltz's hypothesis. Kenneth Waltz, 'The Spread of Nuclear Weapons: More May Better', *Adelphi Papers*, Number 171 (London, International Institute for Strategic Studies, 1981).

49 Colin S. Gray, *Strategic Sense and Nuclear Weapons Today*, Information Series, National Institute for Public Policy, December 2017, www.nipp.org/2017/12/11/gray-colin-s-strategic-sense-and-nuclear-weapons-today/

50 Joshua Stowell, 'The Problem with Russia's Nuclear Weapons Doctrine', *Global Security Review* (April 24, 2018), https://globalsecurityreview.com/nuclear-de-escalation-russias-deter rence-strategy/. The existence of the escalate-to-deescalate posture has been questioned. Specifically, this concept does not appear in any Russian doctrine, which is discussed in Miller, 'Nuclear Battleground', p. 5. See also Olga Oliker and Andrey Baklitskiy, 'The Nuclear Posture Review and Russian De-Escalation: A Dangerous Solution to a Nonexistent Problem', *War on the Rocks*, February 20, 2018, https://warontherocks.com/2018/02/nuclear-posture-review-russian-de-escalation-dangerous-solution-nonexistent-problem/; Kristin Ven Bruusgaard, 'The Russian Rogue in the New Nuclear Posture Review, Policy Roundtable: The Trump Administration's Nuclear Posture Review', *Texas National Security Review*, February 13, 2018, https://tnsr.org/roundtable/policy-roundtable-trump-administrations-nuclear-posture-review/#_ftn108

51 Nuclear Posture Review, pp. 44–55.

52 Office of the Secretary of Defense, *Nuclear Posture Review*, February 2018, p. 72, https://media. defense.gov/2018/Feb/02/2001872886/-1/-1/1/2018-NUCLEAR-POSTURE-REVIEW-FINAL-REPORT.PDF

53 Nuclear Posture Review, p. 48. This reading of the change in emphasis on nuclear weapons is also noted by Michael E. O'Hanlon, *Trump's Nuclear Plan Mostly Makes Sense, Brookings Institute*, www. brookings.edu/blog/order-from-chaos/2018/02/06/trumps-nuclear-plan-mostly-makes-sense/ (accessed February 6, 2018).

54 Nuclear Posture Review, p. 20.

55 Ibid.

56 Ibid., p. 21.

57 Todd South, Stephen Losey, and Kristine Froeba, 'Blast from the Past: The Pentagon's Updated War Plan for Tactical Nukes', *Military Times*, July 10, 2019, www.militarytimes.com/news/your-military/2019/07/10/blast-from-the-past-the-pentagons-updated-war-plan-for-tactical-nukes/

58 Keir A. Lieber and Daryl G. Press, 'The New Era of Counterforce: Technological Change and the Future of Nuclear Deterrence', *International Security* 41:4 (Spring 2017), pp. 9–49.

59 Nuclear Posture Review, p. 12.

60 Keith B. Payne, 'Nuclear Deterrence in a New Age', *Comparative Strategy* 37:1 (2018), pp. 1–8. See also Keith B. Payne and John S. Foster, Jr., Chairman, 'Nuclear Force Adaptability for Deterrence and Assurance: A Prudent Alternative to Minimum Deterrence', *Comparative Strategy* 34:3 (2015), pp. 247–309, in which the authors call for an adaptable nuclear force built on flexibility and resilience.

61 These ideas are developed in Colin S. Gray, 'War-Fighting for Deterrence', *Journal of Strategic Studies* 7:1 (March 1984), pp. 5–28; David J. Lonsdale, 'The 2018 Nuclear Posture Review: A Return to Nuclear Warfighting?', *Comparative Strategy* 38:2, pp. 98–117.

62 Nuclear Posture Review, pp. 66.

63 Gray, *Modern Strategy*, p. 278.

64 Nuclear Posture Review, pp. 65–8.

Further reading

Bracken, Paul, *The Second Nuclear Age*, (New York: St. Martin's Griffin, 2012).

Brodie, Bernard, *Strategy in the Missile Age*, (Princeton: Princeton University Press, 1959).

Freedman, Lawrence, *The Evolution of Nuclear Strategy*, (London: MacMillan Press, 1989).

Gray, Colin S. and Keith B. Payne, 'Victory Is Possible', *Foreign Policy*, Vol. 39 (Summer 1980), pp. 14–27.

Jervis, Robert, *The Meaning of the Nuclear Revolution*, (Ithaca: Cornell University Press, 1989).

Kahn, Herman, *On Escalation: Methaphors and Scenarios*, (London: Pall Mall Press, 1965).

Kissinger, Henry, *Nuclear Weapons and Foreign Policy*, (New York: Harper and Brothers, 1957).

Narang, Vipin, *Nuclear Strategy in the Modern Era: Regional Powers and International Conflict*, (Princeton: Princeton University Press, 2014).

Schelling, Thomas C., *Arms and Influence*, (New Haven, CT: Yale University Press, 1966).

Wohlstetter, Albert J., 'The Delicate Balance of Terror', *Foreign Affairs*, Vol. 37 (1959), pp. 211–34.

Terrorism

13

Reader's guide

Controversies regarding the subject; limits to terrorist capabilities; networks in terrorism and counterterrorism; intelligence in counterterrorism; the new terrorism debate.

Introduction

Terrorist attacks on victims ranging from office workers in New York to schoolchildren in Russia have dominated headlines throughout the twenty-first century. In response, American President George W. Bush committed his nation to a War on Terror – a decision which eminent strategic theorist Michael Howard condemned as a 'terrible and irrevocable error' but which the authors of this book suggest may have had considerable value (see Introduction).[1] Terrorism is, in short, among the most publicised national security issues of our time, and it is also among the most hotly debated. Indeed, one of the main reasons why terrorists prevail in struggles with more powerful opponents is that they confront their foes with situations in which every possible course of action is painful, uncertain, and bitterly controversial. Although terrorists may not be able to overcome their enemies directly, they may confuse them, divide them, isolate them, humiliate them, and demoralise them, breaking down previously existing political relationships and making it possible for the terrorists – or, more commonly, others working alongside them – to impose new ones.

This chapter equips readers such that they can analyse how terrorists and their opponents work to achieve political and military objectives. The first section discusses what terrorists have commonly been able to accomplish, the techniques they have commonly employed, and the resources they have commonly required. The second section considers the methods that state governments and others have commonly used against terrorists and the strategic decisions those who fight terrorists must make. The conclusion considers how terrorists fit into broader struggles in world politics and considers the proposition that an exceptionally vicious new terrorism presents an unprecedented threat in the twenty-first century.

Box 13.1 Defining terrorism

One scholar estimates that academics have formally defined the word 'terrorism' to mean at least 200 different things.[2] The fact that the term conjures such strong emotions almost ensures that attempts to define it will remain controversial. Few wish to define it in a way that will include groups they support as terrorist organisations, while many will wish to define it in a way that allows them to condemn their enemies as terrorists. Moreover, no matter how objective one is willing to be, it is probably impossible to draw a satisfying distinction between terrorism and other forms of warfare. If, for instance, one defines terrorism as an attempt to inflict terror on civilians, one must count strategic bombing as a terrorist activity. But the military and political considerations that, for example, the United Kingdom and its RAF had to take into account when bombing Dresden in 1945 have little in common with the military and political considerations that the IRA had to take into account when bombing Manchester in 1996.

Strategists may find different definitions useful at different times. If one is interested in developing effective methods for capturing members of an organisation that is carrying out bombings within one's cities, one may not care whether one's definition of the word 'terrorist' would also include heroic members of the French Resistance fighting Nazis in World War Two. If, however, one is interested in broader policy issues, one may need to define 'terrorism' in a way that takes legal, moral, and political issues into account. When national leaders decide whether or not to support a particular group of combatants in a conflict, they may well need to consider whether to define those combatants as legitimate resistance fighters or as reprehensible 'terrorists'. The fact that many are cynical about this distinction does not change the fact that national leaders must make decisions of this nature, nor does it change the fact that there are meaningful moral differences between a World War Two–era Resistance organisation that bombs German military installations in Nazi-occupied France and a contemporary terrorist organisation that bombs hotels in democratically governed India.

Since no single definition of terrorism will be appropriate in all situations, this chapter defines the term broadly and discusses special cases as they arise. Except where otherwise noted, this chapter adopts the definition that Alexander Schmid offered the United Nations Crime Branch in 1992:

> Terrorism is an anxiety-inspiring method of repeated violent action, employed by (semi-)clandestine individual, group or state actors, for idiosyncratic, criminal or political reasons, whereby – in contrast to assassination – the direct targets of violence are not the main targets. The immediate human victims of violence are

generally chosen randomly (targets of opportunity) or selectively (representative or symbolic targets) from a target population, and serve as message generators. Threat-based and violence-based communication processes between terrorist (organisation), (imperilled) victims, and main targets are used to manipulate the main target (audience(s)), turning it into a target of terror, a target of demands, or a target of attention, depending on whether intimidation, coercion, or propaganda is primarily sought.[3]

This chapter also distinguishes between terrorism and insurgency. Terrorism, strictly speaking, is an indirect attempt to achieve goals by frightening others into responding in useful ways to the terrorists. Insurgency can involve direct methods, such as physically seizing territory. These distinctions typically blur in practice, since many fighters practise both insurgency and terrorism at the same time. For further discussion, see Chapter 14.

What terrorists can do

George W. Bush and his advisers may have blundered when they termed their struggle with the al-Qaeda network a 'war'. Nevertheless, terrorists have historically performed many of the same functions as state armed forces. To begin with one obvious point of comparison between terrorist groups and more formally recognised fighting organisations, terrorists can most certainly destroy enemy military assets. On October 31, 2000, to pick a well-known example, two members of the al-Qaeda network rammed the American destroyer USS Cole with a small boat loaded with explosives and incapacitated the warship for 18 months.

Terrorists may find it even easier to interfere with enemy military supply lines. During the 1990–1 Gulf War, for instance, terrorists with ties to the Iraqi government attacked a U.S. Air Force base in Turkey.[4] Terrorists can also attack factories, laboratories, and other components of a country's defence industrial base. Such components may include people, and terrorists commonly carry out kidnappings and assassinations. During the 1980s, to pick one example, Communist organisations in Germany and Italy targeted scientists associated with the United States' attempts to develop defences against ICBMs.[5] In a similar vein, terrorists may duplicate the functions of intelligence agencies, covertly gathering information on matters that interest them or their various sponsors.

Not only can terrorists sap their enemies' military capabilities, but they can also damage national economies. Al-Qaeda's September 11 attack on New York City and Washington, DC, prompted the largest property/casualty claim in the history of the insurance industry.[6] Right-wing US organisations such as the Montana Freemen counterfeit the US dollar, not only to fund themselves but also to undermine the currency.[7] In the short term, terrorist attacks can deprive large numbers of people of goods and services. Over the longer term, such attacks – and the cost of guarding against them – contribute to inflation, unemployment, and market crashes.

Terrorist attacks also compel opposing security forces to use money, personnel, and other resources on counterterrorist operations, preventing those forces from attending to other things. During the early 1990s, for instance, the British internal security service MI-5 spent almost half its annual budget contending with terrorists in the United Kingdom and Northern Ireland.[8] In 1995, to note another example, the French police services assigned over 20,000 officers to counterterrorist work.[9] The secretary-general of the Paris police union argued that this undercut their ability to deal with more mundane forms of crime.[10]

Moreover, terrorists may hope to influence political decisions directly. Human beings occasionally compromise to avoid danger, and thus it follows that leaders, officials, and voters will display this human trait. Indeed, there are circumstances in which it is right and prudent for them to do so. The UK government has almost certainly saved lives and achieved valuable social ends by negotiating with the IRA, even though this has involved granting concessions to groups that meet common definitions of terrorist organisations.

All this leads up to the question whether terrorism can replace more traditional types of warfare. To answer this, we must first consider what people have traditionally waged war to accomplish. 'War', Carl von Clausewitz tells us, is 'an act of force to compel our enemy to do our will'.[11] Clausewitz adds that 'to secure that object, we must render the enemy powerless'.[12] For Clausewitz, this primarily meant destroying the enemy's forces. Ultimately, Machiavelli might have added, we may also have to overthrow the enemy's government and reorganise the enemy's society.

Can terrorists compel their enemies to do their will? V.I. Lenin, who was no stranger to the issue, held that they cannot. Even supporters of terrorism, he noted, admit that 'the government cannot now be terrified'.[13] To radicals who hoped that spectacular acts of violence would inspire members of the public to join the revolutionary cause, Lenin responded that those who had not already joined were more likely to 'stand by "twiddling their thumbs", watching a handful of terrorists engaged in single combat with the government'.[14] Although Lenin wrote these words for other Russian revolutionaries in 1902, his warnings hold true for most, if not all, who have contemplated resorting to terrorism in every period of history.

Lenin described terrorist attacks as mere 'drops and streamlets'.[15] This image sums up one of the most important strategic weaknesses of terrorism. Even the most dramatic terrorist attacks tend to be brief, localised, and sporadic. Rarely do terrorists have the resources or organisational capability to follow up even their most successful operations in a sustained or systematic way. Therefore, their targets remain in control of the outcome. One may speculate about what terrorists could accomplish with WMDs, but states survive natural disasters claiming tens of thousands of lives, and the leaders of reasonably stable countries have reason to hope that their societies could survive even nuclear acts of terrorism.

Frightened politicians might offer terrorists concessions. Discontented citizens might rally to the terrorists' cause. Nevertheless, if they do not, the terrorists cannot force them to. Indeed, many of the factors that give terrorists power work only when the victims voluntarily 'injure' themselves.

Carlos Marighella, whose *Minimanual of the Urban Guerrilla* has served as an instruction book for numerous terrorist organisations over the past three decades, advised readers that one of their most potent weapons was their ability to goad their opponents into overreacting. Specifically, Marighella argued that terrorist attacks could drive governments to adopt repressive security measures. These, he argued, would turn ordinary citizens against the government and thus help other types of anti-government revolutionaries win widespread popular support.[16] Marighella dismissed the idea that terrorists might achieve their political goals directly through their own efforts as no more than an egotistical fantasy, one of the 'seven sins of the urban guerrilla'.[17]

The role of the urban guerrilla, Marighella suggested, is to support rural guerrillas as part of a broader insurgency campaign.[18] (For more on insurgency, see Chapter 14.) Lenin expressed similar ideas in more general terms. In his view, 'the most pressing duty' of a revolutionary is to 'organize comprehensive political agitation'.[19] Terrorism can be an invaluable tool for reorganising societies, but if the new organisations are to achieve meaningful strategic purposes, some of their members must be capable of using other tools as well.

Thus, terrorists must work with external groups. Most terrorists need such contacts simply to function. Urban guerrillas require logistical support as much as armed forces of any other kind. Although they may try to make some of their own weapons, forge some of their own fake documents, care for some of their own wounded, maintain safe houses for some of their operatives to hide out in, and the like, they will eventually need money, supplies, and outside assistance.

For these reasons alone, terrorist groups cooperate with apparently unrelated terrorist groups. The IRA, for instance, has allegedly helped the Revolutionary Armed Forces of Colombia (FARC) improve its bomb-making techniques.[20] Neo-Nazi terrorists in Germany have sought alliances with left-wing groups, despite the fact that they supposedly oppose each other's political beliefs.[21] In 1972, members of Japan's Red Army killed 28 passengers at Israel's Lod airport on behalf of the Popular Front for the Liberation of Palestine.[22] Terrorists find partnerships with street gangs, drug smugglers, human traffickers, money launderers, illegal arms dealers, organised crime families, and other elements of the criminal underworld invaluable as well.

Terrorists also work with superficially legitimate organisations. Charities, for instance, may provide terrorists with money, legal advice, and other forms of support. Political activist groups may be even more forthcoming. Legally operated businesses may sell terrorists a wide range of goods and services. Terrorists who lack such support in their home countries may be able to find it elsewhere. The IRA, for instance, notoriously solicits contributions from Irish-Americans, and groups as internationally obscure as Peru's *Sendero Luminoso* have developed networks of donors throughout Western Europe and the United States.[23]

State governments are the most valuable friends that any terrorist organisation can have. States can provide terrorists with far more money, far more useful information, far greater access to weapons, and far more connections to other possible allies throughout the world than supporters of any other type can. States can offer terrorists safe places to train, organise, deposit money, stockpile supplies, and regroup after operations, all without fear of arrest. States can even provide terrorists with well-trained personnel from their intelligence services and military special forces.

Even small states can support ambitious terrorist campaigns. During the 1960s and 1970s, for instance, Cuba trained members of the left-wing organisation known as the Weather Underground to strike against no less an opponent than the United States of America.[24] According to *Janes Intelligence Review*, the Syrian government has sponsored over a dozen terrorist organisations operating in countries ranging from Turkey to Japan.[25] During the Cold War, the smaller Warsaw Pact nations actively promoted terrorist organisations throughout the West. Just as terrorists themselves often prove willing to cooperate with those who nominally oppose their political beliefs, communist countries such as East Germany proved willing to support Neo-Nazis along with left-wing groups.[26]

Not only do relationships with external groups make it possible for terrorist organisations to survive and carry out attacks, but they also help them to produce – or at least facilitate – lasting political change. The secretive groups that perform terrorist attacks may not be able to control public responses to their actions, but larger and more widely supported organisations such as labour unions and political parties may be able to manipulate popular opinion more dextrously. Once terrorists have excited large numbers of people through spectacular violence, broad-based organisations may find it easier to rally supporters for strikes, street demonstrations, guerrilla armies, or even elections. Terrorists may help such organisations suppress rivals, and they may frighten those who would prefer to remain neutral into choosing sides.

Most state governments officially refuse to negotiate with enemy terrorists. Although many governments quietly compromise this principle, few are willing to set a precedent for doing so openly or on major issues, and few are willing to accept the humiliation that would typically come from doing so. Governments are normally a great deal more forthcoming with political organisations that have some claim to legitimacy, even if those organisations also have well-known ties to militants. This is yet another reason why terrorist cells are more likely to achieve their goals if they can work alongside more broadly based organisations.

As earlier paragraphs have noted, terrorists have a vast potential to disrupt people's lives, interfere with public institutions, undermine national economies, and even inflict losses on full-fledged military organisations. Those paragraphs went on to note that, by themselves, none of these capabilities offer terrorists a reliable means to overcome state governments. Once terrorists have tacitly recognised political organisations to speak on their behalf, they can use these capabilities to pressure governments into offering those organisations concessions and to punish them when they refuse. This process may work differently in different countries with different political systems: terrorists may, for instance, achieve more from negotiations with democracies where significant numbers of voters sympathise with their cause than they will achieve by negotiating with strongly led governments representing societies where their cause is widely despised, but the principle remains the same.

For this reason, violent movements typically separate into numerous organisations, ranging from tiny groups of vicious fanatics to ostensibly peaceful 'political wings' that function as much like legal parties (or independent state governments), as their circumstances allow. All of these groups are free to merge, split, or change their methods as they wish. Different groups may pursue different policies simultaneously, and if one ceases to function, another may take its place. The leaders of these various groups may – or may not – turn out to be the same people. Often, many members are only dimly aware of their connection to the terrorist campaign.

This means, among other things, that few members have much useful information to betray. Some clandestine groups deliberately organise themselves into so-called cells, in which no individuals in any group know any more about the other groups than necessary, but terrorist movements that rely on semi-formal relationships among semi-independent groups often achieve a similar effect without even trying. In recent decades, management theorists and strategic thinkers have become increasingly interested in the idea that loose 'networks' consisting of cooperative but largely independent 'nodes' may prove more resourceful, more resilient, more adaptable, and harder for their opponents to understand than rigidly structured institutions are. The art of achieving political objectives through terrorism is largely the art of forming such networks.

The organisation known as the Islamic State (IS) provides a twenty-first-century example of such a network. IS traces its history to Abu Musab al-Zarqawi, an adventurer who oversaw terrorist attacks in Jordan and Spain before ending his career of attempting to organise a revolution in Coalition-occupied Iraq.[27] Although al-Zarqawi was acquainted with Osama bin Laden and went so far as to name his own organisation al-Qaeda in Iraq, he appears to have planned and supported his operations independently.[28] Since he was able to, this allowed both terrorist leaders to reap propaganda rewards from each other's actions without the risk, logistical difficulties, and internal political conflict that they would have experienced if they had tried to merge their similarly named organisations.

Al-Zarqawi's career as a pure terrorist was dramatic but self-limiting. Although he perpetrated such historically significant attacks as the 2004 Madrid train bombings, he died in a 2006 US air strike, and his organisation dwindled as Iraqi citizens organised to resist its cruel practices.[29] Al-Qaeda in Iraq did, however, survive under the new name of Islamic State in Iraq (ISI).[30] Both Iran and Syria's Assad regime allegedly provided it with limited amounts of aid, although they presumably withdrew this support as the terrorist network began to threaten their own interests.[31] By 2013, ISI had recovered enough to resume regular attacks against the Iraqi government. Perhaps of equal significance, it expanded its network by forming an alliance with rebels fighting Assad in Syria.[32]

Later that year, ISI's new leader joined the Syrian and Iraqi factions into a group called Islamic State in Iraq and Syria (ISIS). Some chose to refer to the organisation as Islamic State in Iraq and al-Sham (also abbreviated ISIS) or Islamic State in Iraq and the Levant (ISIL), terms which encompass larger geographical regions. Both Iraqi and Syrian members resisted the merger and broke away to form their own combatant groups.[33] Although these groups fought ISIS in battles that took an estimated 3000 lives, reports suggest that they have occasionally joined forces with it to fight the Syrian and Iraqi governments.[34] Meanwhile, other insurgent groups throughout the Middle East and Africa either allied themselves to ISIS or merged with the ISIS organisation.[35]

Thus, ISIS acquired a mix of assets and a level of organisational efficiency that allowed it to dominate a region the size of Great Britain.[36] In 2014, after capturing the valuable Iraqi city of Mosul, the organisation underscored its goal of expanding beyond Iraq and Syria to create a global Muslim polity by shortening its name to Islamic State (IS). IS achieved its territorial gains by using an approach that Mao (see Chapter 14) would have found familiar. As successful raids permitted the organisation to accumulate resources, attract members, and acquire a fearsome reputation, it formed larger units and used them to hold land. IS then took advantage of the goods, infrastructure, and people of the conquered territory to develop its capabilities further.

Meanwhile, IS appealed to admirers abroad, making full use of twenty-first-century modes of communication such as social media. Thus, from its earliest days, the IS network included state-like institutions fielding relatively large military units, franchise insurgent organisations in distant countries, allied insurgent organisations that insisted on varying levels of independence, hostile insurgent groups who would occasionally help it against shared enemies, even more hostile national governments that were temporarily willing to make common cause, and a global community of individual supporters. Some of these supporters took it upon themselves to independently attack the organisation's perceived enemies. Tens of thousands more travelled to Syria and Iraq to fight with IS forces.[37] IS sent some of these back to their home countries, where they entered using legitimate passports and exploited their personal networks of friends and relatives to form terrorist cells abroad.

Bin Laden's organisation selected recruits carefully, favouring those without criminal records who could blend into Western society.[38] The original al-Qaeda preferred to use these presumably high-quality operatives to strike symbolic targets in memorable ways, the 9/11 attacks being the defining example.[39] IS, by contrast, accepted almost everyone who could be induced to join and used them in less demanding operations.[40] The latter approach proved successful, not only because it allowed IS to build up larger forces but also because recruits with a criminal past had skills and contacts that made them more effective as terrorists.[41] The same skills and contacts allowed experienced criminals to carry out attacks more independently.

In this way, IS acquired new nodes in its network and new capabilities in its repertoire. Like the IS supporters who independently carried out attacks, the new operatives could work with minimal support. Those who had fought in Syria and Iraq, however, had skills and experience that spontaneous volunteers typically did not. Moreover, since the IS leadership in the Middle East knew the identities of the fighters that it had dispatched abroad, it could direct them to carry out attacks at times and in ways that it believed would be most helpful rather than wait for purely autonomous supporters to act spontaneously.

Although IS terrorist cells required little support, when compared to other clandestine groups, the central IS organisation had ample resources for projects that required them. IS's capture of banks, oil wells, and other valuable assets made it the wealthiest terrorist group in history.[42] Moreover, it harvested wealth from those who live in the territory under its control, both through an orderly process of taxation and through more arbitrary acts of extortion, notably kidnapping.[43] Due to the financial side of the terrorist organisation's operations, the IS network came to include a wide range of business and financial institutions, many within IS territory but some outside it.

Although the IS network included a wide range of elements and although this allowed IS to fight back against a wide range of challenges, old-fashioned military thinkers are entitled to note that some parts of its network proved more crucial than others. IS managed to acquire significant amounts of land and money only when it succeeded at generating large military units. Its ability to attract international support also depended at least partially on those units' ability to hold and expand its territory in Syria and Iraq. Since both large units and the economic assets that IS used to sustain them were relatively easy for the terrorist organisation's numerous and powerful enemies to find and attack, IS lost much of what it gained. In 2019 its opponents overran the last of its territorial enclaves, but some of its captured fighters subsequently escaped and its global network of terrorists may remain lethal for as long as their members are willing to fight.

Box 13.2 How large is large?

When discussing terrorist and insurgent organisations, it is useful to distinguish between large units capable of fighting to control territory and smaller bands which can carry out raids but must hide to survive. Nevertheless, the word 'large' is relative. Estimates collected by Stanford University's Mapping Militant Organisations project suggest that ISIS had an overall force of between 6000 and 31,500 in 2014.[44] Journalists writing for Al Jazeera estimated that the organisation deployed 1300 fighters in the critical 2014 battle for Mosul.[45] One of the reasons why these troops won is that they had vehicles and heavy weapons, but they were not armed as well or as systematically as soldiers in most state-organised armies. The Communist Vietnamese revolutionary organisation known as the People's Liberation Armed Force (PLAF) combined large-unit and small-unit tactics in ways that might remind one of ISIS, but it had 400,000 troops in 1968.[46] So-called Main Force PLAF units were equipped to the same formidable standards as the North Vietnamese state's regular army, and when Vietnamese Communist commanders chose to launch a major offensive, they deployed these soldiers tens of thousands at a time.

Box 13.3 Brought to you by your local terrorists

Most successful terrorist organisations devote great effort to public relations. Since the invention of the printing press, political agitators have tried to win support by surreptitiously handing out propaganda leaflets on city streets. This tactic remains effective today. Newspapers, broadcast media, and the Internet allow agitators to reach larger audiences faster – and sensational acts of violence help them capture those audiences' attention. Terrorists commonly ensure themselves of favourable media coverage by publishing their own newspapers. Lenin himself operated a paper known as *Iskra* (Spark). Better yet, from the radicals' perspective, mainstream journalists have been known to pick up material from terrorist publications and use it in more widely respected papers and news programmes.

Fighting back

Those who wish to fight back against terrorists must dismember the networks that make terrorism strategically effective. The first step is often that of forming an opposing network mirroring the terrorists' own. Terrorists support their operations through activities ranging from raising money by hawking compact discs of illegally recorded music to indoctrinating future recruits by founding schools in countries that lack adequate public education. The institutions that have the information, skilled personnel, and legal authority necessary to interfere with terrorists' activities are equally diverse. To neutralise the terrorists in the previous example, for instance, state security forces not only will need to cooperate with police and international aid workers but also may need to liaise with music retailers.

To complicate matters further, most governments deliberately divide responsibility for internal security among multiple military, intelligence, and law enforcement agencies, both for administrative convenience and to prevent any one of those agencies from becoming dangerously powerful. Much of the time, no one counterterrorist organisation will be in a position to disrupt more than a small part of the terrorists' operations. To stop terrorists from achieving their overall goals, the various organisations that oppose various elements of their operations must work together. Governments that wish to resist terrorists must pass laws mandating cooperation and members of the relevant organisations must work to cooperate effectively in practice.

Moreover, most successful terrorist groups are adept at spreading their operations throughout a wide area so that no single government has jurisdiction over more than a few of their activities. Although state police and security forces are normally terrorists' most dangerous enemies, this practice also helps militants minimise the damage that other regionally based opponents might cause them. When terrorists use this technique, those who wish to strike against them – or even to uncover their activities – must normally find partners abroad. When terrorists operate in more troubled parts of the world, those who wish to pursue them may have to become involved in those regions' disputes – with all the risk, violence, and political complexity that that entails. Thus, the business of forming counterterrorist networks often raises foreign policy questions of the highest order, such as which countries or other political organisations one is willing to associate with and what one is prepared to do to gain their confidence.

Having joined forces, the counterterrorists must determine precisely what they are going to do. Once again, the fact that terrorist networks include members of so many types involved in such a wide variety of activities complicates this problem. To think sensibly about counterterrorist strategy, one must come up with general approaches for addressing the mind-boggling range of issues that may become relevant. One useful way to begin is to distinguish between strategy and tactics. Just as a general planning strategy in land warfare is normally well advised to leave tactical problems, such as the best way to overcome a particular enemy bunker, to the troops who must solve them, those who plan counterterrorist strategy may want to leave problems, such as the best way to raid a bomb-making factory or the best way to reform a certain country's banking regulations, to specialists.

Since this book focuses on strategy, it will not attempt to catalogue the kaleidoscopic range of 'tactical' policy issues that may become relevant to a contemporary counterterrorist campaign. Strategists must, however, remain conscious of the fact that their decisions affect tacticians' ability to do their jobs and of the fact that their plans can succeed only if tacticians succeed at putting them into effect. These are among the reasons why the process of establishing cooperative relationships and freely flowing communications among members of counterterrorist networks is so critical. General Charles Krulak of the U.S. Marine Corps observed that there are occasions when a low-ranking soldier who happens to be in a critical place at a critical moment may make decisions that affect the outcome of an entire campaign.[47] Krulak referred to this soldier as the 'strategic corporal'. Not only may counterterrorist campaigns involve strategic corporals, but they may also involve strategic customs inspectors, strategic intelligence analysts, and strategic clerks in firms that supply explosives to the construction industry.

The foundation of counterterrorist strategy is intelligence. Some of the reasons for this are obvious. To attack terrorists, one must find them. Without warning of their activities, it becomes far more difficult to defend one's society against their attacks. Moreover, intelligence gives other aspects of counterterrorist strategy their definition. When one considers common strategic-level approaches to counterterrorism, one sees why this is necessary.

Researcher Christopher Hewitt has classified high-level counterterrorist policies into six categories:

1   Ceasefires and negotiations.[48]
2   Economic conditions.[49]
3   Making reforms.[50]
4   Collective punishments.[51]
5   Emergency powers and anti-terrorist legislation.[52]
6   The use of security forces.[53]

More recently, the US government articulated its anti-terrorist strategy in terms of four Ds

1   Defeat terrorists and their organisations.[54]
2   Deny sponsorship, support, and sanctuary to terrorists.[55]
3   Diminish the underlying conditions that terrorists seek to exploit.[56]
4   Defend US citizens and interests at home and abroad.[57]

Other analysts may prefer other lists. All of these general approaches to counterterrorism – and most others that one can imagine – are conceptually vague. What sort of 'reforms' does Hewitt have in mind? How does he imagine that governments will make 'use of security forces'? The US government's list states its objectives more directly, but many of its methods are so broad that they are equally difficult to apply. Few will be surprised to learn that US authorities hope to 'deny sponsorship, support and sanctuary to terrorists' – the question is how?

One would expect vaguely conceived methods to produce inconsistent results. Hewitt's research confirms that the outcomes of broadly defined anti-terrorist policies are varied at best. When, for instance, he investigated instances in which governments negotiated ceasefires with terrorists, he found that the terrorist groups in his study normally moderated their attacks when the truces first took effect – only to resume them viciously later.[58] Hewitt's statistical analysis provided no evidence to suggest that governments could reduce terrorist activity by improving economic conditions and, in fact, identified instances in which terrorists became more aggressive during periods of prosperity.[59] Terrorist attacks decreased after political reforms in some cases but increased in others.[60] The same was true of collective punishments, new laws granting authorities emergency powers and deployments of security forces in troubled regions.[61]

The U.S. State Department claimed that the number of terrorist incidents worldwide fell by 50% in the two years after the US president called for 'war' on terrorism – but critics discredited these statistics, and the State Department eventually revised them.[62] Independent research provides some evidence that the number of terrorist attacks declined in this period, but not as much as the State Department data seemed to suggest. The British Home Office and the United States Department of Justice (DOJ) have also claimed clear-cut success for their twenty-first-century counterterrorist strategies – only to encounter similar criticism.[63] Syracuse University's Transactional Records Access Clearinghouse, for instance, has noted that although the DOJ identified an impressive 6400 alleged terrorists between September 11, 2001, and September 30, 2003, it filed charges against only one-third of them and noted that the length of time convicted terrorists spent in prison actually declined to a median figure of 14 days.[64]

The fact that statistical data about the results of anti-terrorist strategies are ambiguous does not mean that such measures always fail. To the contrary, Hewitt's research identified circumstances in which wisely implemented counterterrorist strategies achieve worthwhile results. Strategies to reduce popular support for violent political movements by introducing political reforms, for instance, may initially encourage more attacks, especially when politicians appear to be giving in to radical demands.[65] Thus, when one studies reforms in the aggregate, they appear worse than useless. Nevertheless, when states have introduced reforms specifically designed to grant ethnic minorities and other alienated groups a greater stake in society, and when states have maintained those policies despite continuing terrorist attacks over the course of years, the level of terrorist activity has often dwindled over time.[66]

In a similar fashion, although Hewitt found little evidence to suggest that curtailing civil liberties, deploying large numbers of security forces, or carrying out aggressive crackdowns reduces terrorist activities, he did find that security forces that actually succeed at imprisoning larger numbers of militants – with or without resorting to such measures – reduce levels of terrorist violence accordingly.[67] In most cases, the idea that turning terrorist fighters into martyrs will merely inspire others to take up their cause appears to be a myth. States that adopt authoritarian policies, however, are no more certain to succeed at neutralising terrorists than those that uphold liberal democratic principles. Benjamin Franklin reputedly stated that those who would give up essential liberty to purchase a little temporary safety deserve neither liberty nor safety, and data from counterterrorist campaigns in Cyprus, Uruguay, Ireland, Spain, and Italy suggests that Franklin was right.

More recent Western approaches to counterterrorist strategy have also succeeded when effectively matched to appropriate cases. Jacobson details numerous French, British, German, and American victories over terrorists in the early twenty-first century.[68] German authorities, for instance, appear to have arrested one of al-Qaeda leader Osama bin Laden's personal bodyguards.[69] Meanwhile, despite Hewitt's research indicating that attempts to compromise with terrorists typically fail, the UK government appears to have successfully taken advantage of circumstances that permitted it to negotiate a lasting peace with the IRA. (By the same token, one might say that the IRA appears to have successfully taken advantage of circumstances that permitted it to negotiate a lasting peace with the UK government.)

To develop a generally defined strategic concept such as 'making reforms' or 'deny sponsorship, support, and sanctuary to terrorists' into a course of action that will prove effective in a real conflict, one must understand the terrorist network and the environment in which it operates. This kind of knowledge helps one to determine whether the terrorists' fighting cells receive assistance from a disaffected portion of the population that might eventually respond to specific and acceptable political changes. This kind of knowledge helps one determine whether a particular group of terrorists finds 'sanctuary' in states where governments wish to control them but cannot or states in which the government is deliberately assisting them. A strategy for denying terrorists sanctuary in the first case might mean foreign aid, whereas a strategy for denying terrorists sanctuary in the second case might mean war.

Under excellent circumstances, a well-informed, well-selected, and well-implemented anti-terrorist strategy may extinguish a terror organisation in its entirety. Unfortunately, as earlier sections have noted, terrorist movements that succeed at organising themselves into diverse and well-compartmentalised networks may have no single 'head' to cut off. France and Spain, for instance, contend with a terrorist organisation known as Euskada Ta Askatasuna (ETA). ETA is a Marxist-inspired group that wishes to detach territory from northern Spain and southern France in order to form an independent state for the Basque ethnic group.[70] During the 1970s, Spain introduced political reforms that dramatically reduced the Basque population's willingness to support ETA activities.[71] By the twenty-first century, Spanish security services appeared to have developed exceptionally effective methods for collecting information on ETA activities.[72] Spanish authorities went on to arrest several hundred ETA members, including, in 2008, the head of ETA's military wing.[73]

ETA, however, includes a wide variety of semi-independent groups, of which the military wing is only one. These groups, in turn, include different types of members, some of whom fight as full-time terrorists and others of whom support the fighters in an assortment of ways while living as ordinary citizens. ETA also distributes its members across both sides of the border between Spain and France in order to make it as difficult as possible for authorities in either country to apprehend them. Therefore, ETA was able to replace its arrested military leader – and the four successive military leaders whom the Spanish also arrested – and launch a lethal new bombing campaign against Spain's police stations.[74]

Despite the fact that ETA remains active, the Spanish government's offensive appears to have reduced the terrorist organisation's capabilities. In 2000, ETA killed 23 people.[75] In the six years between 2003 and 2009, it has killed nine.[76] Although anti-terrorist forces cannot normally crush their opponents with a single decisive blow – or even a large number of decisive blows – they can progressively wear away terrorist networks' ability to function. A successful anti-terrorist strategy destroys important nodes in the terrorist network, forces the others to operate more cautiously, discredits the terrorists' cause, deprives terrorists of opportunities to cooperate with other types of political organisations, reduces fighters' access to all forms of support, empowers citizens to go about their lawful business with minimal terrorist interference, and otherwise frustrates terrorists in their attempts to do what they must do to achieve meaningful objectives. Under this treatment, Lenin's drops and streamlets gradually dry up.

Box 13.4 Intelligence in counterterrorism

Writers commonly observe that some intelligence assets are more useful for monitoring terrorist networks than others are. Many technologies that have proven invaluable for spying on state military forces are less useful for watching small groups that operate in secret. Satellite photography, for instance, is unlikely to reveal terrorist plans and even less suitable as a means for identifying the various groups that make up terrorist networks. Human agents are widely acknowledged to be the most useful sources for intelligence in counterterrorism.

Human sources commonly include informers, agents who manage to infiltrate terrorist networks, and captured terrorists who reveal information under interrogation. Such sources may also be bystanders who notice terrorist activities and choose to report them, often without fully understanding what they have observed. Since HUMINT sources are so critical to fighting terrorists, decisions that affect their use assume strategic-level importance in anti-terrorist planning. These decisions often raise difficult moral and political issues, which may in turn assume grand strategic and constitutional importance for entire states. To use informers, for instance, one may have to strike bargains with certain terrorists to monitor others. For agents to infiltrate terrorist organisations successfully, they may have to participate in terrorist activities. If one is fortunate enough to capture terrorists alive, one must decide whether to question them under torture – a process that may involve deciding how to define 'torture'.

Important as human sources are, other techniques of gathering intelligence may be useful as well. One may, for instance, eavesdrop on terrorists by tapping telephones, opening mail, intercepting Internet messages, and otherwise monitoring their communications. Since most competent terrorists are prudent enough to encrypt sensitive messages, cryptanalysis plays an important role in counterterrorism. Not only may intercepted communications contain important information, but also those who fight terrorists can benefit simply from knowing whom known terrorists seem to be communicating with. Such information helps counterterrorists map terrorist networks.

Yet another proven method for gathering intelligence on terrorists is known as data mining or grid searching. This involves using computers to sort through large volumes of information on people's everyday activities in order to detect questionable patterns. Both COMINT and data mining can involve controversial issues as well, notably regarding privacy. Data mining may also raise questions concerning racial and other forms of discrimination. The intelligence analysts who design data-mining software and interpret its outputs may believe that members of a certain minority group are particularly likely to become involved in terrorism, but this may merely reflect the analysts' prejudice. Even if the analysts are correct, the other members of that minority group have a right to insist on being treated as innocent until there is specific evidence to suggest that they are guilty.

The previous examples might suggest that the most ruthless policies are the most effective ones. Even from the narrow perspective of counterterrorist operations, this is not always the case. For instance, those who hope to encourage bystanders to volunteer information must craft their overall anti-terrorist strategy in such a way as to retain maximum levels of public support. At a minimum, they must work to make members of the public feel safer cooperating with them than they feel cooperating with the terrorists.

Moreover, as Marighella's *Minimanual* suggests, the terrorists may find it easier to achieve their political objectives when governments resort to brutal, unjust measures. There are other reasons to adhere to ethical strategies as well. Counterterrorist planners must, ultimately, ask themselves why they are fighting the terrorists in the first place and what sort of society they wish to preserve. Intelligence is vital to counterterrorist operations, but it remains only a means to an end.

Conclusion: everything new is old

During the 1990s, certain researchers suggested that the nature of terrorism had changed. The scholar Antony Field identifies Bruce Hoffman, Walter Laqueur, and Ian O'Lesser as pioneers of the so-called new terrorism school of thought.[77] Earlier generations of terrorists – Hoffman, Laqueur, and O'Lesser suggested – used violence in a measured way to achieve well-defined political objectives.[78] 'New' terrorists, these researchers argued, indiscriminately strike as many victims as they can.[79]

The 'new' terrorists' goals are vague and grandiose. Indeed, 'new' terrorists have no clear plans for achieving those goals: they kill simply to express the intensity of their feelings, which usually have to do with their religious beliefs. For these reasons, it is impossible to negotiate any kind of satisfactory compromise with 'new' terrorists. 'New' terrorists are also much more likely to seek and use WMDs. Researchers from the new terrorism school of thought went on to claim that terrorist organisations were becoming more international in scope and that terrorists were making greater use of semi-formal network systems of organisation.

The concept of a new terrorism certainly seemed to account for many of the prominent events that took place around the end of the twentieth century. During that period, widely quoted studies suggest, the total number of terrorist incidents throughout the world declined, but the attacks that took place became, on average, more lethal.[80] Many of the left-wing terrorist groups which had been active in the 1970s and 1980s dwindled. Two of the world's older and better-known terrorist groups – the Palestinian Liberation Organisation and the IRA – did negotiate for more realistic political objectives than they had demanded in the past, whereas religiously inspired groups such as Aum Shinrikyo and al-Qaeda did carry out vicious attacks for reasons many outsiders perceived as irrational. Al-Qaeda, in particular, used the network system of organisation effectively.

In response, the United States adopted what one might call a strategy of new counterterrorism. The US government enacted laws to make it easier for the security services to investigate and detain suspected terrorists. This was controversial, since many believed that the new regulations eroded important principles of human rights. The United Kingdom, Germany, and numerous other states adopted similar legislation and experienced similar controversies.

Moreover, the United States went beyond many of its allies by publishing a National Security Strategy, in which it resolved to wage preventive war against potential terrorists and their supporters. According to this strategy, the United States would 'proceed deliberately, weighing the consequences of [its] actions'. But it would not 'remain idle while dangers gather'; rather, it would strike first.[81] The National Security Strategy justified this policy by noting that more restrained policies 'will not work against a terrorist enemy whose avowed tactics are wanton destruction' and went on to describe those terrorists in much the same way as Hoffman, Laqueur, and O'Lesser did.

As the twenty-first century has gone on, researchers have begun to question the hypothesis of new terrorism. Researchers such as Hoffman were right to note that twenty-first-century terrorists are cruel, fanatical, and adept at forming network-type organisations on a global scale – but all this has been true of numerous other militant groups throughout history. Field takes up each of the supposed characteristics of 'new terrorism' in turn, listing extensive twenty-first-century research that shows that all of them are actually quite old.[82] Even the figures indicating that individual terrorist attacks have become more lethal may be less significant than they initially appear, because the researchers who produced them focused on international terrorist attacks.[83] Since most terrorist attacks are domestic, the researchers have, as Field notes, simply failed to consider the 'vast majority' of all terrorist incidents, including many of the most deadly ones.[84]

The changes of the 1990s and 2000s may have less to do with the terrorism as an activity than with specific people and institutions that make up specific terrorist groups' extended networks. When the Communist governments of Central and Eastern Europe fell or reorganised themselves, left-wing terrorists throughout the world lost both their most generous sources of support and their most prominent sources of ideological inspiration. Meanwhile, terrorists who claimed to represent Islam succeeded at forming a global network of supporters. Organisations such as the IRA had not always followed a conciliatory approach. To the contrary, specific members of these organisations chose to change their older and more aggressive strategies during the 1990s and 2000s in response to specific circumstances and specific actions by their opponents. Members of these groups that preferred to continue more traditional forms of armed struggle broke away to form new organisations, which claimed to be truer to their movements' original purposes – thoroughly muddling any attempt to distinguish between 'new' and 'old' versions of terrorism.

If the apparent change in terrorist methods reflects specific political changes rather than a general change in terrorism itself, one may ask whether early-twenty-first-century approaches to counterterrorism have addressed these changes effectively. To an important extent, it has. Whatever frustrations NATO has faced since it invaded Afghanistan, it has deprived one of the world's most dangerous terrorist networks of sanctuary, training camps, substantial amounts of resources, and many of its leaders. Throughout the world, states have stiffened their own counterterrorist policies and coordinated their anti-terrorist efforts with one another. Nevertheless, these counterterrorist methods have been costly in terms of lives and money. They have occupied the military forces of most Western states, reducing those forces' availability for other purposes. Aggressive counterterrorist policies have been politically divisive in many ways, and states that have pursued them will find that this also affects their capabilities and relationships in far-reaching ways. The so-called War on Terror may have succeeded as strategy in the narrow sense of the word, but its consequences in the realm of grand strategy are, at best, more complex.

Key points

1 It is practically impossible to define 'terrorism' precisely or to draw an absolute line between terrorism and other methods of using force.
2 Nevertheless, the fighters commonly referred to as terrorists play a significant role in world politics. Thus, as long as we remember that concepts such as 'terrorist' and 'terrorism' are imprecise, it is useful to study the topic.
3 Terrorist fighters can degrade state armed forces, sap national economies, inflict widespread suffering, and indeed influence political processes.
4 Nevertheless, terrorists seldom succeed at achieving broad political objectives on their own.
5 The strategy of using terrorism effectively consists largely of organising effective networks among a diverse range of groups.
6 Counterterrorist strategy depends on a similar process of network building.
7 Intelligence is even more critical to counterterrorism than it is to other strategic activities.

Questions

1 Can we expect terrorists to refrain from using WMDs?
2 Pick a terrorist movement. How great a role do state sponsors appear to play in its network?
3 Are suspected terrorists entitled to the same rights as other criminal suspects?

Notes

1 Michael Howard, 'What's in a Name? How to Fight Terrorism', in James F. Hoge and Gideon Rose (eds.), *Understanding the War on Terror* (New York, Council on Foreign Relations, 2005), p. 318.
2 Richard Jackson, 'The Study of Terrorism after 11 September 2001: Problems, Challenges and Future Developments', *Political Studies Review* 7:2 (May 2009), pp. 171–84.
3 Alex Schmid, *Definitions of Terrorism*, 1992, www.unodc.org/unodc/terrorism_definitions.html (accessed June 12, 2007).
4 Christopher Harmon, 'Five Strategies of Terrorism', *Small Wars and Insurgencies* 12:3 (Autumn 2001), p. 58.
5 Ibid., pp. 57–8.

6 Gail G. Makinen, *The Economic Effects of 9/11: A Retrospective Assessment* (Washington, DC, Library of Congress, 2002), p. 4.

7 Harmon, 'Five Strategies of Terrorism', p. 51.

8 Ibid., p. 54.

9 Ibid., p. 55.

10 Ibid.

11 Carl von Clausewitz, *On War*, trans. Michael Howard and Peter Paret (New Haven, Princeton University Press, 1976), p. 75.

12 Ibid.

13 Vladimir Lenin, *What Is to Be Done*, trans. Anonymous (Peking, People's Publishing House, 1973), p. 95.

14 Ibid.

15 Ibid.

16 Carlos Marighella, 'Minimanual of the Urban Guerrilla', Anonymous (trans.), appendix to Robert Moss, *Urban Guerrilla Warfare, Adelphi Paper No. 79* (London, International Institute for Strategic Studies, 1971), p. 40.

17 Ibid., p. 39.

18 Ibid.

19 Lenin, *What Is to Be Done*, p. 96.

20 Jeremy McDermott, 'IRA Influence in FARC Attacks', *BBC News*, May 9, 2005, http://news.bbc.co.uk/1/hi/world/americas/4528109.stm (accessed September 2, 2009).

21 R. Jogshies, 'Changing Political Mould of Terror Groupings', *The German Tribune* 1090 (July 3, 1983), p. 15.

22 Marc Celmer, *Terrorism, U.S. Strategy and Reagan Policies* (London, Mansell Publishing Ltd, 1987), p. 6.

23 William Long, 'Peru Orders Anti-Sendero Effort in U.S'., *Los Angeles Times*, September 18, 1992, p. A13.

24 Anonymous, 'Weatherman Links Traced to Cuba, Hanoi', *Christian Science Monitor* (February 18, 1975), p. 8.

25 M. Eisenstadt, 'Syria and the Terrorist Connection', *Janes Intelligence Review*, January 1993), p. 33.

26 Roger Boyes, 'Stasi Supported West German Neo-Nazi Groups', *The Times* 66905 (August 14, 2000), p. 15.

27 Lee Hudson Teslik, 'Profile: Abu Musab al-Zarqawi', *Council on Foreign Relations* (June 8, 2006), www.cfr.org/iraq/profile-abu-musab-al-zarqawi/p9866#p4 (accessed April 26, 2017).

28 Teslik, 'Profile'; Anonymous, 'What Is "Islamic State?"', *BBC News*, www.bbc.com/news/world-middle-east-29052144 (accessed April 26, 2017).

29 Ibid.

30 Anonymous, 'What Is "Islamic State?"'

31 Anonymous, 'The Islamic State', *Stanford University Mapping Militants Project* (April 14, 2017), http://web.stanford.edu/group/mappingmilitants/cgi-bin/groups/view/1#locations (accessed April 26, 2017).

32 Anonymous, 'What Is "Islamic State?"'

33 Ibid.

34 Anonymous, 'The Islamic State'.

35 Ibid.

36 Anonymous, 'What Is "Islamic State?"'

37 Ibid.

38 Clint Watts, 'Terror in Europe: Safeguarding U.S. Citizens At Home and Abroad', *Foreign Policy Research Institute* (April 5, 2016), www.fpri.org/article/2016/04/terror-europe-safeguarding-u-s-citizens-home-abroad/ (accessed April 28, 2017).

39 Ibid.

40 Ibid.

41 Ibid.

42 Colin Clarke, Kimberly Jackson, Patrick Johnston, Eric Robinson, and Howard Shatz, *Financial Futures of the Islamic State of Iraq and the Levant: Findings from a RAND Corporation Workshop* (Santa Monica, RAND, 2017), p. iii, www.rand.org/pubs/conf_proceedings/CF361.html (accessed April 28, 2017).

43 Ibid., p. 9.

44 Anonymous, 'The Islamic State'.

45 Anonymous, 'Iraqis Flee Mosul after Fighters Seize City', *Aljazeera* (June 11, 2014), www.aljazeera.com/news/middleeast/2014/06/thousands-iraqis-flee-after-mosul-seized-201461023449883723.html (accessed April 28, 2017).

46 Douglas Pike, *PAVN: People's Army of Vietnam* (Novato, Presidio Press, 1986), p. 48.

47 Charles Krulak, 'The Strategic Corporal: Leadership in the Three-Block War', *Marines Magazine*, January 1999, www.au.af.mil/au/awc/awcgate/usmc/strategic_corporal.htm (accessed July 29, 2009).

48 Christopher Hewitt, *The Effectiveness of Anti-Terrorist Policies* (Lanham, University Press of America, 1984), p. v.

49 Ibid.

50 Ibid.

51 Ibid.

52 Ibid.

53 Ibid.

54 Anonymous, *National Strategy for Combating Terrorism* (Washington, DC, The White House, 2003), p. 15.

55 Ibid., p. 17.

56 Ibid., p. 22.

57 Ibid., p. 24.

58 Hewitt, *The Effectiveness of Anti-Terrorist Policies*, pp. 36–41.

59 Ibid., p. 45.

60 Ibid., pp. 52–3.

61 Ibid., p. 58; Hewitt, *The Effectiveness of Anti-Terrorist Policies*, p. 66; Hewitt, *The Effectiveness of Anti-Terrorist Policies*, p. 89.

62 Thomas Kane, *Theoretical Roots of US Foreign Policy: Machiavelli and American Unilateralism* (Abingdon, Routledge, 2006), p. 142.

63 Michael Jacobson, *The West at War: U.S. and European Counterterrorism Efforts, Post-September 11* (Washington, DC, The Washington Institute for Near East Policy, 2006), pp. 16–17.

64 Ibid., p. 119; Anonymous, *Criminal Terrorism Enforcement since the 9/11/01 Attacks*, TRAC Special Report, December 8, 2003, http://trac.syr.edu/tracreports/terrorism/report031208.html#figure1 (accessed August 3, 2009).

65 Hewitt, *The Effectiveness of Anti-Terrorist Policies*, p. 54.

66 Ibid.

67 Ibid., p. 89.

68 Jacobson, *The West at War*, pp. 79–80.

69 Ibid.

70 Hewitt, *The Effectiveness of Anti-Terrorist Policies*, p. 18.

71 Ibid., p. 19.

72 Giles Tremlett, 'Miracle Escape for Civil Guard Families in Massive Barracks Blast Blamed on ETA', *The Guardian*, July 29, 2009, www.guardian.co.uk/world/2009/jul/29/eta-car-bomb-burgos (accessed August 11, 2009).

73 Ibid.

74 Ibid.

75 Ibid.

76 Ibid.

77 Antony Field, 'The "New Terrorism": Revolution or Evolution?', *Political Studies Review* 7:2 (May 2009), p. 96.

78 Ibid., pp. 197–200.

79 Ibid.

80 Ibid., p. 204.

81 Anonymous, *National Security Strategy of the United States of America* (Washington, DC, The White House, 2002), pp. 15–16.

82 Field, 'The "New Terrorism"', pp. 200–5.

83 Ibid., p. 204.

84 Ibid.

Further reading

Anonymous, *National Strategy for Combating Terrorism*, (Washington DC: The White House, 2003).

Harmon, Christopher C., 'Five Strategies of Terrorism', *Small Wars and Insurgencies*, Vol. 12, No. 3 (Autumn 2001), pp. 39–66.

Hoge, James F. and Gideon Rose (eds.), *Understanding the War on Terror*, (New York: Council on Foreign Relations, 2005).

Jacobson, Michael, *The West At War: U.S. and European Counterterrorism Efforts, Post-September 11*, (Washington DC: The Washington Institute for Near East Policy, 2006).

Lenin, Vladimir Ilyich, *What Is To Be Done*, trans. By Anonymous, (Peking: People's Publishing House, 1973).

Marighella, Carlos, 'Minimanual of the Urban Guerrilla' in appendix to Robert Moss, *Urban Guerrilla Warfare, Adelphi Paper No. 79*, trans. By Anonymous, (London: International Institute for Strategic Studies, 1971), pp. 20–42.

Insurgency and counterinsurgency

14

Reader's guide

Poor performance in COIN; defining the problem – insurgency as strategy; the strategic logic of COIN; coercion in COIN; COIN as war; the character of military operations in COIN.

Introduction

COIN is one of the most challenging and debated of strategic activities. At the time of writing, the war in Afghanistan is in its eighteenth year and shows no sign of reaching a resolution. Part of the problem is the wide diversity of opinions on what constitutes effective COIN practice. For some, COIN campaigns should be guided by the thoughts of theorist/practitioners, such as Robert Thompson's *Defeating Communist Insurgency* and David Galula's *Counterinsurgency Warfare* (exemplified in contemporary doctrine, as in *U.S. Army Field Manual 3–24*). Others argue that modern COIN theory is a myth and is no more than tactical and operational procedures masquerading as strategy.[1] One of the fiercest debates centres on the question of whether COIN constitutes a distinct form of strategy and thereby requires its own particular theory and doctrine. Or perhaps COIN has been overthought. Perhaps *war is war*, and regardless of its character, it can be understood within the familiar Clausewitzian framework. The army chief of staff during the Vietnam War, General George Decker, was certainly unimpressed by the novelty of insurgency: 'any good soldier can handle guerrillas'.[2] Even if one accepts some level of distinctness for COIN, debate rages over how best to classify different approaches to the subject. Readers will encounter works that use the population-centric versus enemy-centric dichotomy. Other writers reject such an approach, preferring to talk in terms of motive-focused and iron-fist campaigns.[3]

As a strategic activity, insurgency certainly has a long pedigree. History is replete with cases of uprisings aimed at overthrowing the existing order. However, the twentieth century witnessed a substantial development in the theory of both insurgency and COIN. Men such as Mao, Guevara, Thompson, and Galula, all of whom were theorists and practitioners, gave these forms of warfare a more developed, structured appreciation. And yet the practice of irregular warfare has often not matched the conceptual heights to be found in works of theory. This is particularly the case with COIN, which still appears to present a steep strategic challenge. This chapter will define the problem of insurgency, before discussing the reasons for relatively poor performance in COIN, and finally will provide some guidance on good COIN practice.

Despite the vast amount of attention and study COIN has garnered over the years, the practice of it is often flawed, and successes have been few and far between. It is true that each COIN campaign operates in a unique and often-complex setting. Thus, one must be careful when trying to elicit general observations from historical and contemporary practice. Nonetheless, as with many complex sociopolitical phenomena, we can acknowledge the importance of context but still find commonality across cases. With that in mind, one of the primary reasons for the limited success rate of COIN may be a disconnect between the nature of strategy and how states conduct COIN campaigns. While it may be true that COIN is a distinct activity that presents unique challenges to the strategist, it cannot operate outside of the basic tenets of strategy. Thus, with an eye to historical and contemporary practice, this chapter seeks to reconnect COIN theory with some of the core elements of strategy. This is not an easy task, because the historical record throws up a variety of different lessons vis-à-vis the practice of COIN.[4]

A historical analysis of COIN leaves us with the conclusion that, like any other form of strategic behaviour, there is a certain logic to COIN as an act of strategy. As will be discussed later, part of that logic is strongly Clausewitzian: a battle of wills conducted through the threat and application of violence. Invariably, said violence is aimed primarily at the opposing forces. Yet elements of the civilian population, especially those who may be minded to support an insurgency, are also an important constituency vis-à-vis the strategic effect of kinetic force. If one desires success in a COIN campaign, the role of political violence cannot be ignored for the sake of social, legal, moral, or cultural reasons. Indeed, if one tries to operate at variance to this logic, a competent insurgent foe may be able to outwit one's attempts.

This creates something of a problem for the practitioner. It is generally accepted that how a state wages war is to some degree a reflection of its culture. Similarly, the methods used by the armed forces should be generally acceptable to the society that they serve. Thus, a dilemma arises if the norms and values of said society are at variance with the nature of war and strategy. In such circumstances, should a war be waged in a manner that is less effective but is at least morally and culturally acceptable? Or does a society have to accept a method of war that causes ethical and cultural discomfort? Indeed, can a state conduct war in a manner that is at odds with its culture? These questions raise a number of intellectual and practical challenges. These issues, as they relate to strategy as a whole, are discussed at length in Chapter 3. The current chapter deals specifically with the challenges relating to COIN.

To better understand the disconnect between theory and practice, once insurgency has been defined, the chapter will analyse the current accepted wisdom on the conduct of COIN.

In particular, those elements that are at variance with the nature of war and strategy will be discussed. To provide an alternative perspective and approach, the chapter will then discuss the most important elements that are missing from modern COIN doctrine. The elements in question will be constructed from both a theoretical basis and a historical basis. The theoretical aspect is, in part, provided by Thomas Schelling's work on 'the power to hurt', which is rarely, if ever, discussed in relation to COIN. The historical evidence is drawn from a range of different case studies, going as far back as Alexander the Great, covering the many important conflicts during the Cold War, and incorporating recent and ongoing COIN campaigns in Syria, Iraq, and Afghanistan.

The work will conclude that modern COIN theory and doctrine is flawed since it does not take adequate account of the power to hurt and also has increasingly neglected the fact that COIN is still war, in which offensive military operations against insurgents form an essential ingredient of strategy. To use the common phraseology, modern COIN theory and COIN practice have become too population-centric. Thus, this chapter outlines an approach to COIN that while respecting many of the positive elements of modern thought on the subject, does place a greater emphasis on the role of offensive military operations and the coercive use of force. When challenging the findings of this study, it may be easy to portray its central message as a rather simplistic, heavy-handed approach to COIN. However, not only would this be a misrepresentation of the work, but also such a criticism would also overlook the spirit of Clausewitz's comment that the absolute use of force is not incompatible with use of the intellect.[5] Indeed, a counterargument can be made that modern COIN doctrine has become overly convoluted, giving military forces far too many complex sociopolitical tasks to fulfil.

Insurgency as strategy

Before discussing the solution, we must define the problem. In contrast to terrorism, which seeks to effect political change indirectly by the use of force, insurgency is more direct in how it uses military power. Although terrorism and insurgency are discussed separately in this book (each has a chapter devoted to it), they are not mutually exclusive. Indeed, it is often the case that a group will conduct a campaign of terror in support of their insurgency goals. This creates a complex security challenge for those involved in COIN. Irregular conflicts are rarely straightforward; indeed, their character tends to fluctuate and evolve over time. This is typified by ISIS, which at various times, and sometimes simultaneously, was a terror group, an insurgency, a mesh of city-states, and a state-like entity conducting quasi-conventional warfare. To add further to the complexity, ISIS operated at the local, regional, and global levels. At its height, ISIS controlled 88,000 km² and eight million people. At the same time, it promoted a global campaign of terror through lone-wolf attacks committed by individuals with no direct link to territorially defined ISIS.[6]

Such a merging of the terrorism and insurgency is commonplace. The Viet Cong, Liberation Tigers of Tamil Eelam (LTTE), Malayan Communist Party (MCP), Front de Liberation Nationale (FLN), Castro's rebels in Cuba, to name just five, all conducted campaigns of terror in support of more ambitious insurgency goals. That being said, there are conceptual and actual differences between terrorism and insurgency, and they are significant. Most importantly, unlike terrorism in its pure strategic form, insurgency seeks direct and physical control over an area/population. Thus, insurgent forces are used both to disrupt government activities (military and civil) and to establish insurgent control. Put more simply, terrorists seek political change, whereas insurgents seek governance. Thus, even if an insurgency uses terror tactics, the objective of direct political control will always remain. In this sense, terrorism is a tactic used in support of a strategy of insurgency. In a distinctly terrorism campaign, terror is both the tactic and the strategy.

Another notable consideration, well noted by James Kiras, relates to the strategic objectives and ambitions of irregular war. While it is sometimes the case that irregular actors have clearly defined objectives and strategies to achieve them, it is not always so. Rather, it may be that an irregular force has only a vague idea of how their strategy will function. Violence may be introduced into a political process not with any clear idea of how it will effect change but rather as a means to undermine the established order. A clearly defined strategy may not exist. Additionally, over time, political objectives may come to play second fiddle to financial ones. Irregular warfare can be quite lucrative for those involved, described by Kilcullen as 'conflict entrepreneurs'.[7] That being the case, an insurgent force may aspire to control, not to effect political change but rather to maintain and increase its income.[8] These are important points for COIN practitioners, who have to understand the motivations, objectives, and strategies of their opponents.

The history of irregular warfare is essentially as old as war itself. Jewish uprisings against Roman rule around the time of Christ (the biggest rebellion coming in 66 CE) are but one ancient example of a group taking up arms against the ruling authority. Despite this long heritage, it is not unreasonable to claim that modern insurgency began its long road to maturity during the eighteenth century and matured fully during the last century. Radical political ideas of liberation underpinned the American Revolution, which in turn inspired a wave of uprisings throughout Europe in the late eighteenth to mid nineteenth centuries (1848 being the year of revolutions across Europe). The large conflicts that sometimes emerged from the spread of these ideas, most notably the French Revolutionary and Napoleonic Wars, also witnessed their fair share of insurgencies. Under French rule, rebellions flared up across Europe, with perhaps the most significant being the Iberian Peninsula, from which we gained the term 'guerrilla' – the diminutive form of 'war'.

From a theoretical standpoint, one of the most significant contributions is the work of T.E. Lawrence. Based on his account of leading the Arabs in their revolt against the Turkish Empire during the First World War, Lawrence's work, *Seven Pillars of Wisdom*, identified some of the most important elements of a successful insurgency. In particular, Lawrence identified the balance of forces relative to the geographic environment and from this concluded that hit-and-run tactics conducted by small, mobile forces were the most appropriate operations for a rebel force. He also wrote on the primacy of the psychological aspects of insurgency. In other words, Lawrence understood that the primary function of an insurgent force was to undermine the will of the enemy rather than defeat them in battle. To diminish the will of a stronger enemy, Lawrence understood that insurgents needed time and an unassailable base (both physically and psychologically).

Further development of theory and practice came about through the merging of communist ideology and national liberation movements. Particularly noteworthy careers in this period are those of Mao, Régis Debray, and Che Guevara. Aside from developing the three stages of revolutionary war (strategic defensive, stalemate, and strategic offensive), Mao is notable for discussing the essential but complex relationship between force and politics. Mao understood the essential Clausewitzian principle that all use of military force must be perceived as a political action. Thus, it is essential to use violence in a manner that did not undermine one's other political activities. Indeed, Mao perceived military force as a means of protection for the Communist insurgents, so that they could undertake their political education of the masses. Just as importantly, Mao took Marxist-Leninist ideology, based as it was on the plight and support of the urban working class, and adapted it to serve the interests of a rural, peasant-based society. This latter development had important implications for many under colonial rule. Thus, Mao's insurgency theory was exported to various countries, albeit with differing degrees of success and failure.

Box 14.1 Mao's three stages of revolutionary war

Strategic defence
Guerrilla warfare.
Avoiding set-piece battles.
Small tactical offensives to stretch enemy resources.
Political activities to gain popular support and establish a political base.

Stalemate
Attrit the government's will and capability.
Destroy government control in rural areas.
Establish political and military control over countryside.

Strategic offence
Shift to regular warfare.
Large battles of manoeuvre.
Overwhelming force to destroy enemy forces.

Perhaps the most successful export of Maoist theory was that by Ho Chi Minh, Giap, and Le Duan in Vietnam. Although not an exact replica of Mao's theory and practice in China, the Communists in Vietnam did wage a protracted campaign, which developed over time from a guerrilla-based insurgency to something more akin to a regular invasion of South Vietnam. Less successful was the insurgency in Malaya, which suffered from a lack of outside backing and was eventually defeated by a coherent and patient British COIN campaign. In contrast to Mao's emphasis on the education and politicisation of the masses, Che Guevara and Régis Debray based their theories on small groups of dedicated revolutionaries (the foco), who through their actions could create the necessary conditions for a general uprising. The value of this idea is perhaps reflected in the failures and deaths of both of these men.

As the Cold War has receded, the ideological motivations driving insurgency have changed. Where once communism and decolonisation were the ideological motivators of insurgents, radical Islam now appears to be the main driver. Aside from an increased emphasis on certain tactics, particularly suicide attacks, the cause of radical Islam has also given insurgency a more global character. Although it is true that different communist revolutionary movements aided one another during the Cold War, contemporary Islamic insurgents (especially groups like al-Qaeda and ISIS) have a more developed global network. This network is not just sustained by a common ideology but also enabled by information-age technology.

Global insurgent networks complicate the task of COIN campaigns, in that the latter must include operations at global, national, and even local levels. Moreover, while the global character of modern insurgency must be recognised, the local circumstances of each case must not be overlooked. External support is important for irregular campaigns, but solving local problems is often the key to success in contemporary COIN. This was evident, at various times, in Iraq, where the influence of foreign al-Qaeda fighters receded as Iraqis witnessed an improvement in their local conditions (economic, security, political). Although underwritten by US forces and aid, improvements were often due to changes enacted by local actors. These include the Anbar Awakening, in which Iraqi Sunni militias played an increasing role in providing security for their own communities. Contrastingly, local issues can feed an insurgency. David Kilcullen reports that by 2009 al-Qaeda in Iraq was essentially defeated. However, as the United States withdrew under Obama, the corruption of Prime Minister Maliki came to the fore and undermined much of the political progress that had been made. Moreover, Maliki's politicisation of the Iraqi military rendered it incapable of holding its ground against the ISIS offensive in 2014.[9]

Regardless of the time period or the motivating ideology, there are a number of methods common to insurgencies. Political mobilisation is an essential ingredient of most insurgencies. Both to garner support for their campaign and to establish the foundation for the forthcoming political order, insurgent groups engage in educating and proselytising the local population. Since a degree of popular support is essential, insurgents often offer substantial inducements to the local population. These may include measures such as land reform or the provision of services (e.g. in health and education). Alternatively, an insurgency may simply offer an opportunity to make money and/or increase one's social position. This is particularly important for young men in areas where employment and opportunities for social empowerment are limited.

Despite the significance of these nonviolent political activities, an insurgency also relies on the application and threat of violence. By definition, insurgents are not engaged in a peaceful political process. Thus, an insurgency's nonviolent methods are supported by military actions that seek to undermine trust in the state's ability to provide security and prosperity for the population. A certain degree of coercion is also often evident in many insurgent campaigns. Those in the population who do not willingly accept the coming order may be threatened, tortured, or eliminated. The efficacy of coercion is a debated subject within the insurgency literature. Guevara considered its use problematic for fear of delegitimising the insurgents' cause. This was certainly the case in Greece 1945–9 and the Philippines 1946–56, when acts of brutality undermined the insurgent cause.[10] In contrast, both Mao and Carlos Marighella saw coercion as a method of dissuading the population from lending their support to the governing authorities.[11]

The Viet Cong were particularly adept at violent measures. Often, upon entering a village for the first time, they would murder the village elders to neutralise the established political order before replacing it with their own. In some respects, then, insurgencies are not competitions in popularity. Rather, they are about the imposition of a political system on a largely apolitical population. In this sense, legitimacy and coercion run side by side. The issue is not one of popularity but one of authority. Clearly, from the perspective of both insurgents and counterinsurgents, the use of violence has to be finely balanced. Although violence (especially in its coercive form) may be required to control the population, if used too freely or in the wrong context, it will merely alienate those whose support/acquiesce one requires. A recent example of this can be seen in Iraq. Participants in The Awakening were motivated to act in response to the indiscriminate and/or brutal use of violence by their former insurgent allies.[12] It seems that in terms of violence, al-Qaeda overplayed their hand in Iraq.

Assuming that the campaign goes well, insurgent military operations tend to evolve. Characterised initially by guerrilla hit-and-run tactics, insurgent campaigns are normally protracted affairs designed to weaken the resolve of their enemies over time. As the enemy retreats, insurgent forces and operations may increase in scale and indeed become more regular in form. In Maoist theory, the final stage of revolutionary war, strategic offensive, shifts to larger, regular operations. South Vietnam did not fall to irregular Communist guerrillas but to conventional North Vietnamese divisions. However, a number of insurgencies have switched to conventional operations too quickly, making them vulnerable to the firepower of counterinsurgency forces. This was the case in the aforementioned insurgencies in Greece and the Philippines. Likewise, in Sir Lanka, the LTTE became increasingly conventional, even sporting an air force and naval forces. This worked reasonably well until the Sir Lankan military boosted its own efforts with an aggressive enemy-centric campaign that eventually led to the total defeat of the rebels in 2009.[13]

Clearly, like all forms of strategy, insurgency is challenging. On the one hand, the objective of governance dictates that an insurgency must grow and take on increasingly conventional aspects and scale to challenge the forces of the state and its allies. At the same time, growing too quickly, becoming conventional too early, potentially plays into the hands of counterinsurgency forces. As a consequence, insurgencies must adapt. Alongside the ability to slowly morph into regular forces, insurgencies sometimes must also downscale when put under sufficient pressure. As Kiras notes, so long as the political organisation remains intact, the insurgency has the opportunity of re-emerging at some point.[14] Castro understood this point well when he fled into the Sierra Maestra in Cuba; first to survive, and then to reorganise and launch a new coordinated campaign against the Batista government. As will be discussed later, adaptability is an important characteristic for COIN forces also.[15]

The population is usually of central importance to the outcome of an insurgency. Since insurgent groups normally begin their campaigns at a substantial disadvantage relative to government forces, they must compensate for this in some way. By winning the support, or at best the acquiescence, of the local population (normally via a combination of the carrot and the stick), insurgents can gain an important intelligence advantage over their foes and gain access to regular supplies and areas to hide. The latter consideration is essential for insurgents in the early to middle stages of their campaign. Due to the material superiority of their enemies, insurgents require secure bases from which to conduct their guerrilla operations. Ideally, these bases can be established in secure geographic areas. In some cases, security may be provided by terrain (mountains, jungle, etc.) or by a friendly neighbouring ally who provides sanctuary. However, at times, neither of these options may be available. In this case, the insurgents may need to operate from within the populous and rely on their ability to hide among the locals for their security. In turn, this requires some degree of successful political engagement with the population.

Taken together, these characteristics of insurgency produce the following challenges for COIN forces. They must offer a plausible political alternative to the insurgents. In turn, this requires establishing a secure environment to enable sociopolitical life to function and development projects to flourish. Thus, COIN forces must neutralise the physical threat posed by insurgents. Importantly, defeating the enemy not only enables nonviolent sociopolitical action to function but also has political consequences of its own. Political authority emanates, at least in part, from military prowess. To adapt the language of the RAND study, *Paths to Victory*, a strategy for COIN must be both motive and kinetic force focused.[16] Although history suggests that insurgents can often be contained, achieving victory against them is frequently elusive. Sometimes, this is because the important political issues are not adequality addressed. Alternatively, and often in addition, insurgent forces cannot be defeated. Bringing small, mobile guerrilla forces into battle is difficult, especially if they enjoy sanctuaries (internal or external) to which they can retreat.

At the same time as defeating the insurgents, COIN forces must also protect the population from insurgent influence and harm. For regular forces, which are normally less mobile than insurgents and often rely on the delivery of significant levels of firepower, these challenges can be extremely hard to overcome. This is especially the case in the modern environment, when the media and human rights organisations are ever on the watch. Excessive use of force, or errors that lead to civilian casualties, will likely undermine the legitimacy of a COIN campaign. COIN is such a challenging undertaking because it requires a carefully balanced exercise of military force in delicate and complex political circumstances. Counterinsurgents must use enough force to defeat the enemy but not so much to delegitimise the broader campaign. Over time, doctrine and special forces have been developed to cope with this strategic challenge. Despite such adaptation and development, success in COIN is often costly or missing in action. This chapter will now turn its attention to why this is the case. In particular, it will discuss the need for COIN campaigns to respect the nature of strategy.

The logic of COIN as strategy

Although certainly not without merit, modern doctrine and thought on COIN has in some important respects become disconnected from the strategic logic of counterinsurgency or at least underestimated important parts of it. In this sense, there is a fundamental flaw in modern doctrine, in that it misunderstands some of the key relationships in strategy. In particular, there is misapprehension concerning the relationship at the heart of strategy, namely that between military force and policy objective. Too often, COIN is seen as primarily a political issue, in which military force is often regarded as a hindrance. For example, one COIN theorist discusses the need to transition from 'combat' to 'political' soldiers.[17] In contrast, Clausewitzian theory teaches us that combat is a political act. The killing of the enemy, or an act of coercion, is the use of force in the service of policy.

Box 14.2 Thompson's five principles of counterinsurgency

1　Have a clear political objective: establish a stable and unified country.
2　Follow a coherent plan: coordinate actions in economics, social, security, and so on.
3　Secure government base areas.
4　Operate within the rule of law.
5　Prioritise defeating political subversion.

The problem with modern COIN theory and doctrine is evident in one of the most revered texts on the subject, Thompson's *Defeating Communist Insurgency: Experiences from Malaya and Vietnam*. In this work, Thompson identified 'five basic principles which must be followed and within which all government measures must fall'. Three of Thompson's five principles represent sensible advice for any COIN campaign: have a clear political objective of establishing a stable and united country; the government must have an overall plan, which takes account of a range of factors, including economic, social, security, administrative, and so on; and finally, the government must secure its base areas. It is difficult to argue with the wisdom of these three principles. However, the remaining two principles are more problematic, and they may explain some of the difficulties facing modern COIN practice. In the first instance, Thompson states that the government must always operate within the law. While it is true that operating within a legal framework is often an important component of establishing legitimate authority, as noted in Chapter 3, an overly strict adherence to a legal regime may hamper the process of strategy. More problematic still is Thompson's principle that 'the government must give priority to defeating the political subversion, not the guerrillas'.[18]

We see some something similar in the United States' seminal doctrine manual on the subject, *FM 3–24 Insurgencies and Countering Insurgencies*, which is often credited with leading a resurgence in US COIN performance. To be sure, there is much to admire in this document, most recently updated in 2014. For example, FM 3–24 espouses the shape-clear-hold-build-transition framework for COIN; the need to isolate insurgents from support; the superiority of simple, flexible plans; the value of air power; the need to seek and maintain the initiative; the challenges of assessing progress in COIN; the need to find host nation answers to problems and security; and the fact that long-term solutions must include progress in the economy and polity. Despite these positive elements, FM 3–24 displays a somewhat confused understanding of strategy.

It would be going too far to suggest that FM 3–24 denigrates the role of military power in COIN campaigns. To its credit, when discussing the different elements of an insurgency (leadership, guerrillas, auxiliary, underground), FM 3–24 advises that focus should be given to enemy guerrilla forces, since they introduce violence into the political equation.[19] This is important, because it is crucial to remember that COIN is still a form of war. Nonetheless, FM 3–24 is at heart a population-centric doctrine, which perceives the role of military power as a support to other actions (political, economic, etc.) that address the root cause of an insurgency.[20] Indeed, the doctrine puts a great deal of emphasis on information operations and is at pains to make the point that military force should not undermine them. It clearly states that 'counterinsurgents often achieve the most meaningful success in garnering public support and legitimacy for the host-nation government with activities that do not involve killing insurgents'.[21] In this sense, the doctrine overplays the notion of popularity in political authority and thereby ignores an inescapable logic of COIN as an act of strategy.

The logic in question is constructed of two elements. First, military power must be perceived as the continuation of political intercourse, not as something used in support of, or perhaps even detrimental to, politics. In this sense, strategy must be perceived as a gestalt, in which all of the expressions of political intercourse are given their due in a coherent campaign.[22] In COIN, military power does not *support* political action; it *is* a political action, working in concert with other sociopolitical activities. Of course, military power can be used inappropriately; but that would be bad strategy, not military force spoiling politics. Too often, modern writings on COIN (including FM 3–24 to some degree) focus on the competition in governance and downplay the military expression of political intercourse. Yet defeating the insurgents has political consequences.

This feeds into the second element of the logic of COIN. Where there is political competition between the insurgent and COIN forces, it is a competition in authority, not popularity.[23] Insurgency is rarely about an expression of the will of the people; rather, it is about imposing a political system on them. This is not to suggest that legitimacy has no place in politics and thereby in COIN. Rather, it is to suggest that legitimacy is misunderstood. The concept of legitimacy is too often mistaken for popularity. In contrast, in fact, legitimacy is more closely related to authority. In turn, a sense of authority often emanates from military pre-eminence and the ability to provide security. The British irregular warfare theorist Charles Callwell was clear about this: 'Prestige is everything in such warfare'.[24] To this end, during the successful British COIN campaign in Dhofar, military force was used 'to focus their [local population] minds. The population had to be convinced of the power of the government and of the ability of the security forces to inflict punishment if support and assistance is extended to the rebels'.[25] Similarly, Julian Paget, in his work *Counter-Insurgency Campaigning*, concludes that to win the support of the local population, 'the Government must demonstrate its determination and its ability to defeat the insurgents'.[26] Steven Metz concurs: 'it is less an assessment of a preferred future that drives insurgents or insurgent supporters than an assessment of who will prevail – the insurgents or the regime'.[27] Thus, being militarily successful in a conflict will inspire support, or at least acquiescence, from the population. Equally, it may deter those contemplating adding their active support to the insurgents.

To be sure, FM 3–24 understands the importance of neutralising the physical insurgent threat. However, it does so in the context of enabling socioeconomic development. Thus, according to contemporary US doctrine, military power is a supporting element. In contrast, the argument put forward in this chapter is that military power is on an equal footing with the other political instruments. To reiterate, the exercise of military power is an important ingredient of authority and political legitimacy. Politics is primarily concerned with power (the ability to influence others). Whether that power comes from peaceful means or violent methods is, at one level, irrelevant. In an insurgency, power is exercised through both violent and nonviolent means. As a general theory, between these two categories, there is no real hierarchy, as each situation is unique and requires a different blend. At times, and in certain circumstances, violent expressions of politics will dominate; the opposite is also true. In most circumstances, a range of violent and nonviolent forms of political intercourse will be active, ideally operating in a mutually supportive manner.

Wylie convincingly claimed that control is exercised by the man on the scene with a gun. Control can of course be exercised by nonviolent means, but in situations where political violence is extant or threatened, Wylie's theory must be respected. What does this all mean for COIN? Essentially, it means that neutralisation of the enemy's military forces is an essential political action, because it reduces their power while increasing the power and authority of the COIN actor. Of course, in the same way, gaining public support via good governance also reduces the relative power of the insurgents.

To extend this final point, when giving due recognition to the violent political instrument, we must avoid the opposite trap of seeing everything through a military lens and thereby undervaluing the nonviolent political components of COIN. Alongside reducing violence, providing security, and displaying authority through military potency, it is essential to address underlying political issues that may be feeding the insurgency. In this sense, FM 3–24 is correct to discuss the importance of rectifying root causes. This certainly aided the COIN campaigns in Malaya and the Philippines. The promise of independence took much of the wind out of the sails of the MCP. Likewise, Magsaysay's reforms in the Philippines undermined the message of the Huk rebellion. In contrast, the American campaigns in Vietnam, Iraq, and Afghanistan all suffered as a consequence of a disconnect between sections of the populous and the government. In Algeria, the French never really offered a viable solution to the political issues in the colony.

When considering nonviolent means, in general terms, it is impossible to state what reforms and development projects are necessary for successful COIN. Each context is unique and complex. So, for example, in Malaya, political independence was a key ingredient of the strategy. In Angola, the Portuguese largely contained the rebellion without going that far. However, they did enact a number of important reforms, including increased political representation for the colony in Lisbon; an end to forced labour; increased educational opportunities; and substantial economic development. In Sri Lanka, an aggressive military offensive was supported by socioeconomic measures to help alleviate poverty. At a theoretical level, we are left to conclude that the logic of COIN as strategy is composed of military and non-military actions on an equal footing. The application of them in practice depends on the particular circumstances of the context in question. This final point may not be definitively helpful for those charged with countering an insurgency; but it is where the theory and the history lead us.

The power to hurt in COIN

Although it may be something of a cliché, successful COIN is best characterised by the carrot-and-stick approach. However, in recent years, Western powers appear to have increasingly focused on the carrot and have underestimated the significance of the stick. This particular approach may reflect social attitudes as well as the misplaced belief that success emanates from being popular with the public. This creates something of a problem, as identified by Major General Robert H. Scales: 'Non-Western enemies understand Western military vulnerabilities: aversion to casualties and collateral damage, sensitivity to domestic and world opinion'.[28]

Such attitudes to the role of the stick (power to hurt) appear to reflect cultural and social norms, and they somewhat misinterpret the available historical evidence. Despite his claim to be working from the historical record, Lynn is at variance with some past practice of COIN when he states that 'Morality should guide us'.[29] In fact, however unpalatable the historical evidence may be, it suggests that carefully managed use of the stick against local populations can produce results. As Colin S. Gray notes,

> The winning of 'hearts and minds' may be a superior approach to quelling irregulars, but official, or extra-official but officially condoned, military and police terror is swifter and can be effective. The proposition that repression never succeeds is, unfortunately, a myth. Half-hearted repression conducted by self-doubting persons of liberal conscience certainly does not work.[30]

As with much in strategy, the strategic application of coercion in COIN requires careful balance and judgement.

In many respects, these thoughts open up a key debate on the nature of war, in particular whether it has its own internal logic beyond the influence of culture. On one side of the argument, Anthony Coates claims that 'war is not a natural necessity, driven by its own internal and unchanging logic, but a cultural and normative reality, for if culture is a prime determinant of war, then so too is morality'.[31] However, war does have its own internal nature, and that nature, among other things, is by definition competitive and violent and acts in the service of policy. Thus, if one treats cultural and moral concerns as the prime consideration in war, then one may cede the advantage and initiative to an enemy who is in harmony with the nature of war. An example of this is the battle of Chaeronea in 338 BCE, at which Macedonia defeated the Greek city-states to establish hegemony over the Greek world. To use Plato's distinction, the Greek city-states facing Macedonia thought they were engaged in a conflict of 'discord', in which the conduct and violence of operations is moderated among similarly minded foes. However, Macedonia waged, again in Plato's terms, 'war', in which the conduct of operations is far more total. The result of this cultural, and therefore operational, mismatch was a crushing victory for Macedonia.

One can also challenge Coates's position on the basis that strategy may at times call for an approach that is at variance with one's cultural and moral preferences. The deliberate firebombing of German civilians in World War Two was perceived as a necessary ingredient of victory against Nazi Germany, yet it would be difficult to argue that this reflected a cultural preference of British and American society.

To illustrate the utility of the power to hurt in COIN, we can look to a host of historical case studies. In Bactria and Sogdiana, Alexander was able to quell resistance to his rule partly through a brutal campaign against the local population. This campaign included economically devastating the rebellious regions. More recently, in their analysis of the British effort in the Boer War, which is regarded as a 'sophisticated pacification strategy', Ian F. W. Beckett and John Pimlott conclude that 'The Boers' support was also totally eroded by the incarceration of their women and children in concentration camps and the systematic destruction of their farms, crops and livestock'.[32] Similarly, in 1864 the Navajo people surrendered in large numbers to the U.S. Army. This capitulation was due to the combined effects of the attrition of their warriors and the economic deprivation inflicted by their enemy. Colonel Kit Carson, who led the campaign against the Navajos, reported that 'owing to the operations of my command they are in a complete state of starvation, and that many of their women and children have already died from this cause'. In a similar example, Robert M. Utley cites the battle at Wounded Knee, in which 150 Indigenous people were killed (including women and children), as the event that broke the will of the Sioux to further resist the reservation system. Indeed, from this period in US history, we are provided with a concise summary of the relationship between the carrot and the stick. When President Grant discussed his peace policy towards the Native Americans, he warned, 'Those who do not accept this policy will find the new administration ready for a sharp and severe war policy'.[33] Or as the COIN theorist David Galula notes, the population should be cognisant of the following warning: 'Stay neutral and peace will return to the area. Help the insurgent, and we will be obliged to carry on more military operations and thus inflict more destruction'.[34]

Thus, the conclusion to be drawn is that rather than merely hoping that the population will support the government, mainly as a result of its hearts-and-minds policy, the power to hurt can act as an influencing factor. The famous Briggs Plan in Malaya, which is often regarded as the model of a modern COIN campaign, also witnessed a considerable use of the stick against the local population. A notable element of the campaign was the resettlement of 400,000 people into secure new villages as a way of isolating them from the insurgents. Importantly, as Newsinger comments, 'Resettlement was not accomplished freely, but by the application of overwhelming force in order to prevent any attempt at escape or resistance'.[35]

As a side note, resettling the population amply demonstrates the complexity of COIN, the significance of local context, and the importance of how pacification methods are enacted. To clarify, resettling civilians is designed to remove them from insurgent threat and influence. To put it in Maoist terms, the objective is to drain the sea and leave the fish isolated and struggling for support and resources. Not surprisingly, uprooting people from their homes is often unpopular. Therefore, it is imperative that the conditions in new villages/strategic hamlets be tolerable, secure from insurgent infiltration, and imposed by a strong authority. If these conditions are met, resettlement can play an important positive role in COIN. Equally, if poorly handled, they can damage the COIN cause.

Historically, the record is mixed on resettlement. Such an approach appears to have had a positive impact in certain areas of Angola and Greece, but it was counterproductive in Algeria and Vietnam. Indeed, the Portuguese example illustrates the difficulties involved in these projects. In Angola, the Portuguese resettled one million people (20% of the population). However, context played a major role in whether the *aldeamentos* system proved successful or not. In the north, where 130 strategic hamlets were established, *aldeamentos* were generally well received, primarily because the population was suffering significantly from the effects of insurgent violence and food shortages. However, the system did not translate so well in the east of the country. Often, the new villages lacked adequate security, were infiltrated by the guerrillas, and were sometimes badly sited and had poor facilities.[36] When such conditions exist, the resettlement programme can become counterproductive. That being said, even though they often proved controversial, van der Waals concludes that the *aldeamentos* played an important role in the defeat of the Movimento Popular de Libertacao de Angola (MPLA). By 1972, 75% of the Angolan population was free from rebel influence.[37] Again, we are left to conclude that context and application are crucial in determining the success or otherwise of COIN methods.

To return to our discussion on coercion, we can do no better for a theoretical basis than to turn to Thomas C. Schelling's work on the subject. Schelling regarded the coercive use of force as one of the most potent means by which to achieve one's objectives: 'The power to hurt can be counted among the most impressive attributes of military force'. Coercion can often achieve significant policy effect with limited effort. It is, therefore, an efficient use of force and may be especially important in COIN campaigns, which tend not to be especially well resourced or heavy on forces.[38] By carefully employing the power to hurt in COIN, one can negate an advantage that Metz notes is often held by the insurgents: the ability to seize the initiative and practice greater flexibility and 'absence of ethical or legal constraints'.[39] The implications of this were evident in Iraq for a time, where 'the insurgency has won support – or at least neutrality – through a combination of terror and robust propaganda'.[40]

Not only is coercion recognised as an advantage for insurgents, but there is also a further recognition in the modern literature that a more aggressive approach to COIN can be effective: 'Regime after Regime fighting determined insurgents has found that the most effective methods, sometimes the only effective methods, violate human and civil rights'. However, the author of these words, Metz, rightly also recognises that a brutal approach can sometimes be counterproductive. He cites the case of Slobodan Milošević's Serbian regime in its campaign in Kosovo against the KLA.[41] One would also cite the example of the French in Algeria and the fact that insurgents can also overplay their hand in dishing out coercion. Al-Qaeda in Iraq, the Huks in the Philippines, and the Democratic Army of Greece (DSE), all lost support as a consequence of their respective brutality.

This latter point serves once again to illustrate that in strategy, context is everything and that judgement over the use of force is critical. The point to be made here is not that coercion will work on every occasion but that it may be effective and therefore should be on the strategic table. Thus, from a strategic perspective, one has to ask whether at times a greater emphasis on the power to hurt should be contemplated. The quest for strategic efficacy inevitably forces us to consider such a possibility.

Of course, strategy is the art of the possible. As a consequence, the citation of historical examples should not be taken as a call for outright brutality against local populations. COIN, like strategy in general, calls for balance and judgement in the application of force

To this end, Julian Paget is correct when he argues that the stick must be used with finesse. Specifically, certain sections of the populace (who Paget describes as active and willing supporters of the insurgents) may well be subjected to harsh punishment, perhaps being treated in the same manner as the insurgents themselves. In contrast, those who either are undecided in their loyalty, or support the insurgents out of fear, can be persuaded through collective forms of punishment such as fines, curfews, and detentions.[42] Likewise, Callwell demonstrates an acute grasp of strategy in his analysis of how military operations against the population can contribute to success. He calls for a balance between clemency and firmness. In his discussion of how to come to grips with an irregular enemy who refuses to fight, Callwell notes that 'the regular troops are forced to resort to cattle lifting and village burning and that war assumes an aspect which may shock the humanitarian'. He continues,

> Still, there is a limit to the amount of licence in destruction which is expedient. . . . Expeditions to put down revolt are not put in motion merely to bring about a temporary cessation of hostility. Their purpose is to ensure a lasting peace'.[43]

In this case, amnesties and clemency, alongside socioeconomic development projects and other nonviolent political initiatives, can often prove adept at reducing insurgent numbers and support.

Thus, we can conclude that within a balanced campaign, punishments aimed at the civilian population, in particular those willing to support the insurgents, can have a role to play. This can be seen in the success of measures used in the British campaign against the MCP. During the campaign, thousands of people were detained without trial; others were deported from the country; and the death penalty was introduced for offences such as the possession of explosives. Newsinger concludes that these repressive measures were very successful in limiting the efficacy of the MCP.[44] At the same time, applying the rule of law and addressing the grievances of the population can engender support. Once again, we are left to conclude that the defining factor is authority. Legitimate governance is based not only on the power to provide security and basic services but also on the ability to punish those who transgress against the established order and the common good.

The military dimension in COIN

A problem with some of the literature on COIN is that it underestimates the role of the military and thus misunderstands the nature of strategy. For example, in an important 1965 article, *The Theory and Practice of Insurgency and Counterinsurgency*, Bernard B. Fall writes,

> the kill aspect, the military aspect, definitely always remained the minor aspect. The political, administrative, ideological aspect is the primary aspect. Everybody, of course, by definition, will seek a military solution to the insurgency problem, whereas by its very nature, the insurgency problem is military only in a secondary sense, and political, ideological, and administrative in a primary sense.[45]

Contemporary writers are also guilty of this error. Commenting on Iraq, Andrew Krepinevich called for an approach 'that focuses on providing security to Iraqis rather than hunting down insurgents'.[46] The most obvious response to Krepinevich's comment is, why not do both? Indeed, one theme of this chapter is that the counterinsurgent *must* do both.

While not wholly inaccurate, these comments tell only half of the story. In the first instance, to disassociate the military from the political is to fundamentally misunderstand the nature of strategy. Military action taken against the insurgents and/or their supporters is an act in support of the political objective. In addition, to take the aforementioned views too seriously could lead one to assume that COIN is not war. As a consequence, COIN gets downgraded to something akin to a 'police action' or 'stability operations', to use some of the favoured nomenclature. Although nonviolent political, social, and economic programmes may be an important element of a COIN campaign, military action against the insurgents and their supporters is essential. Such a thought is clearly in line with Clausewitz's central point: 'it is evident that destruction of the enemy forces is always the superior, more effective means, with which others cannot compete'.[47] In this sense, the insurgents have to be defeated. Kitson notes that 'because the very fact that a state of insurgency exists implies that violence is involved which will have to be countered to some extent at least by the use of force'.[48] At the very least, insurgents have to be kept under sufficient military pressure to prevent them from gaining the initiative and setting a violent agenda.

In Vietnam, U.S. Military operations were successful in preventing the Viet Cong from establishing proto-states in the South, from where they could spread their insurgency.[49] Although South Vietnam was eventually lost to the Communists, it was not taken by the insurgent forces of the Viet Cong but rather by the regular NVA. Similarly, the LTTE in Sri Lanka were defeated, at least in part, by an aggressive enemy-centric military campaign that enabled the COIN forces to seize the initiative.[50] In Angola, the Portuguese developed effective offensive operations against the insurgents. 'Static garrisons' would exert control over important regions; the PIDE and DSG (secret police) largely prevented insurgent attacks in the main urban areas (such as the capital Luanda); and Special Operations Forces (SOF) and elite forces (with air power support) conducted deep raids against insurgent bases and infiltration routes. As a consequence, between 1970 and 1972, over 2000 MPLA insurgents were killed, including 43% of their leadership, reducing their operational strength by half.[51] Indeed, one can conclude that the war was largely won in Angola but was subsequently lost in Lisbon. As a general point, then, one can conclude that enemy forces must remain an important focus for a COIN campaign. In contrast, an overly population-centric approach is problematic because it gives insurgent forces too much breathing space and cedes the initiative to them. Moreover, such a method also focuses conflict in and around the population and thus often leads to higher civilian casualties and disruption to civilian life.

It is interesting that much of the literature on insurgency makes the claim that one of the most important considerations for the insurgents is not to lose the war, merely to keep it ticking over, hopefully to a point at which the government forces or their allies lose the will to continue. Yet this same literature often does not draw the obvious conclusion from this thought: from a COIN perspective, the objective therefore has to be to ensure that the insurgents do lose the war. To cite an important work by Brian Bond, *The Pursuit of Victory*, strategy, even in its COIN guise, must be characterised by the pursuit of victory.[52] One of the main contributions to British success in Malaya was the fact that the insurgents were 'remorselessly ground down by attrition'.[53] Likewise, in Vietnam, the Viet Cong 'were militarily crushed in the 1968 Tet Offensive and saw their political underground decimated by the Phoenix Program'.[54] The conclusion from this evidence seems to be clear; insurgents must be constantly harassed and ground down through attrition. Unfortunately, much modern thinking on COIN assumes that major and/or prolonged military operations against the insurgents are counterproductive, especially because they may hinder hearts-and-minds efforts. Bruce Hoffman notes that in Iraq the USMC learned to regard heavy weapons as a last resort, precisely because they believe their use undermines the hearts-and-minds campaign.[55] History would suggest that this is not necessarily the case.

It is, therefore, a critical mistake in COIN to merely attempt to 'contain' the insurgents while the political process is developed. Despite the inherent problems of a containment strategy, such an approach is still being advocated in the modern literature: 'In liberation insurgencies, though, a strategy of victory is a very long shot, hence a strategy of containment is the more logical one'.[56] This advice is contrary to much of the historical evidence. In Mozambique, the initial Portuguese response was limited and merely tried to contain the insurgency. All that this approach achieved was to cede the initiative to the insurgents. In contrast, an early forceful response by the government can seriously retard the development of an insurgency.[57] After this initial mistake, the Portuguese successfully went on the offensive with Operation Gordian Knot. This broad offensive involved 35,000 troops and made use of artillery and air power to engage in the heavy bombardment of guerrilla bases. Unfortunately, the initial success of Operation Gordian Knot was eventually undermined by the political leadership in Lisbon, who, concerned with growing casualty rates, began to restrict the campaign.

Thus, it is evident that certain self-imposed restraints in the conduct of a COIN campaign can be problematic. During Portugal's campaigns in Africa, it refused to pursue guerrillas into neighbouring states such as Zaire, Congo, and Zambia.[58] The United States made a similar blunder in Vietnam by not engaging in substantial ground operations in North Vietnam, Laos, or Cambodia. Indeed, Harry G. Summers laments the missed opportunities that this policy decision resulted in. Commenting on the period following the US success in the Ia Drang Valley in 1965, Summers concludes that

> Now was the time for the United States to take the offensive. Although in theory the best route to victory would have been a strategic offensive against North Vietnam, such action was not in line with US strategic policy which called for the containment rather than the destruction of communist power.[59]

The result of this policy left the United States in 'an untenable strategic position where the enemy's territory was inviolable while the territory of our ally was open to attack'.[60] Such a policy creates the significant problem of permitting one's opponents the luxury of external sanctuaries, from which they can prepare and launch raids. As Henriksen notes of Mozambique, 'Across the border sanctuaries were of prime importance. . . . Contiguous states furnished training sites, conduits for armaments, and havens from all but a few Portuguese retaliatory strikes'.[61]

External sanctuaries are often tolerated for fear of conflict escalation. However, this again may partly reflect the fact that states increasingly do not regard COIN as war proper. Thus, they place limits on their actions that are out of kilter with the scale of the conflict and the approach of the enemy. This is perhaps most clearly evident in the US war in Vietnam. While the United States was waging a limited war, North Vietnam had a different approach: 'Like us, Hanoi had failed to win the hearts and minds of the South Vietnamese peasantry. Unlike us, Hanoi's leaders were able to compensate for this failure by playing their trump card – they overwhelmed South Vietnam with a twenty-two division force'.[62] Such thoughts do not denigrate a more nuanced COIN approach; rather they merely show that the aggressive/offensive use of military operations may have a part to play in a conflict that is, partly, characterised as an insurgency.

The character of military operations in COIN

So if military force should play a more prominent role in COIN than is often advocated, how should it be applied? Population-centric theories argue that because access to the population is the key to success, the territory in which the majority of the population live will become the main battleground. It is on this basis that the United States' military strategy in Vietnam is often heavily criticised. Krepinevich is damning in his critique of the U.S. Army's approach against the VC. He claims that the chosen strategy of attrition, which led the United States to focus on the larger VC concentrations in the more remote areas, played into the hands of their opponents. Not only did this draw US forces away from areas of higher population, which left them more vulnerable to the VC; it also meant that large US search-and-destroy operations often failed to engage their more mobile and wily foes. Thus, the United States failed to effectively protect the population and at the same time failed to attrit sufficient numbers of the enemy.[63]

From this perspective, the evidence from Vietnam suggests that large sweeps designed to engage an insurgent foe are largely ineffective as a use of force in a COIN campaign. There is certainly further historical evidence to support this approach. Having previously defeated the Persian army in large regular battles, Alexander the Great needed to reorganise his forces into smaller mobile detachments to successfully engage rebellious forces in Central Asia.[64] Similarly, in the successful COIN campaign in the Philippines, government forces were based on small, self-sufficient patrols that constantly harassed the guerrillas. Likewise, the 1870 campaign by the U.S. 5th Cavalry in Arizona is instructive of how to use forces against a mobile insurgent foe:

> The campaigns in Arizona did not owe their success to any particular Waterloo-like victory, as much as they did to the covering of a great deal of ground by a comparatively small number of men, permitting the Indians no rest and rendering any and every hiding place insecure.[65]

Too often, the U.S. Army lacked imagination in its operations against the Indians, relying on cumbersome regular formations that were limited in their mobility.

However, while it is often true that small mobile operations are preferable against guerrillas, there are examples where larger-scale operations have produced some successes. Aside from Operation Gordian Knot, another successful Portuguese example was Operation Attila in 1972, which eliminated half of the guerrillas in Eastern Angola.[66] Moreover, in Sri Lanka, the government forces were able to better protect population centres (and important targets within them) via an aggressive enemy-centric approach. Before this Eelam IV War, initiated in mid 2006, the LTTE had been able to strike at will across the country, including suicide attacks against population targets and prominent government and military officials. This changed only once the LTTE was forced to go on the defensive. For the Sri Lankan government, the best defence was an aggressive offence.[67]

Thus, the historical evidence suggests that a successful COIN campaign is based on two complementary forms of military operation. Certainly, the population needs protection and reassurance from COIN force presence. A successful version of this is evident in the Portuguese static garrisons in Angola and the aggressive actions of the secret police in urban areas. In contrast, the detrimental effects of not providing adequate security to the population were evident for the British during the American War of Independence. Loyalists were often reluctant to publicly declare their support for the existing order, since they often could not rely on the presence of British troops to protect them from Patriot militia groups. Similarly, the Portuguese lost a degree of popular support in Mozambique because they struggled to prevent the indiscriminate use of landmines by the insurgents.[68]

Population protection, then, is clearly vital. However, an overly population-centric approach cedes the initiative to the guerrillas. In this case, COIN forces must pay practical homage to Clausewitz's adage that defeating the enemy's forces is normally the most sensible focus for military operations. For the most part, in COIN, this will consist of aggressive, mobile patrols by small units, who employ some of the guerrillas' own tactics against them. This type of operation is designed to seize and maintain the initiative against the insurgents, to keep them on their toes, to limit their movement/infiltration, and to slowly reduce their capabilities through attrition and attacks against their supplies and bases. One can consider the drone attacks of recent years to function in this way. However, when circumstances permit, a COIN actor must not be afraid to engage in large campaigns aimed at destroying irregular forces, their bases, and their supplies. Indeed, to return to U.S. Army operations against Native Americans, where the larger operations did bring some success was through the pressure that they could exert on the Indigenous population, who were of course less mobile than the warriors: 'the army set forth to find the enemy in their winter camps, to kill or drive them from their lodges, to destroy their ponies, food, and shelter, and to hound them mercilessly across a frigid landscape until they gave up'.[69] Thus, we see that over time this combined approach is aimed at fulfilling another of Clausewitz's ideas: to degrade the will of the enemy through the medium of physical force.

Before we leave the subject of military operations in COIN, we note that, where possible, indigenous forces must have a role in providing military security to their own communities. Without local involvement, COIN forces may be seen as imperialists or external oppressors – merely replacing one unwanted outside influence with another. As the war in Angola progressed, the Portuguese increased the black Africanisation of their military forces. By 1973, approximately 40% of forces fighting the rebels were recruited from the black African population (23,000 in total).[70] Likewise, it has already been established that conditions in Iraq improved starting in 2007, when local Iraqi militias became increasingly important in providing local security.

However, a major headache for external COIN actors is often the low quality of indigenous forces. US COIN efforts suffered from this problem in Vietnam, Afghanistan, and Iraq. The quality of government forces (ARVN) in Vietnam suffered as a consequence of Diem's corruption and focus on preventing coups. Similarly, in Iraq, Maliki's politicisation of the Iraqi military left them weak and unable to withstand the ISIS offensives in 2014.[71] As a consequence, much time and effort must be put into improving the COIN combat capabilities of indigenous forces. At the same time, because these forces are often unable to reach the required levels of efficacy, external COIN actors must be prepared to maintain their presence and commitment over the long term. The US failed in this respect in Afghanistan and Iraq. US Elite and Special Forces were withdrawn too early from Afghanistan to support the ill-judged war in Iraq in 2003. Likewise, Obama withdrew US forces too early from Iraq in 2011. As a consequence, in both cases, much good work was undone.

Conclusion

Box 14.3 Elements of successful COIN practice

Context is everything (adapt doctrine and practice).
Seize the military initiative; defeat the enemy.
Small agile units normally work best, but sometimes large offensives are required.
Secure the population (which may require resettlement).
Address underlying sociopolitical issues.
Establish political authority (through military force and persuasion).

Having considered COIN campaigns from a range of theoretical perspectives and historical periods, what conclusions can we draw? In the first instance, irregular forms of warfare are still subject to the constant nature of strategy. In this sense, military force is still a tool of policy; and the particular policy in question, allied to the context, should dictate how the force be used. Second, it is a false dichotomy to distinguish between population-centric and enemy-centric approaches to COIN. Neither of these exclusive approaches represents the best form of COIN strategy.

COIN is clearly a complex form of strategy, and the historical record serves merely to illustrate this point. To take the issue of population control as an example, the historical record throws up various possible options. At one end of the spectrum, an unsupportive population can be massacred to the point at which they cease to pose a viable support base for the insurgents. A similar effect can be achieved in a more humane fashion, by simply relocating the local populace in large numbers to safe, controlled areas that isolate them from the insurgents. If neither of these methods are desirable or possible, the locals must be persuaded to cease supporting the insurgency. For the most part, modern practice on COIN seeks to achieve this through a competition in popularity with the insurgents. Thus, through economic, political, and social actions, the government actor can hope to win the support of the locals. Alternatively, a more coercive approach can be taken. In this sense, the insurgents and government may engage in a competition in intimidation. Those more able to inflict pain on the population may gain their begrudging 'allegiance'.

A more effective and acceptable approach can be constructed from this discussion. At the risk of being predictable, this third option can be described as the carrot-and-stick approach, albeit one that places more emphasis on the stick than has been common in recent campaigns. History clearly reveals that people can be coerced into supporting a government through the fear of reprisals. However, this approach does not have to rely on outright brutality. Indeed, the punishments envisaged may take the form of detentions, fines, and curfews. In combination with good works, this approach provides the population with a clear choice: support for the government brings benefits, while opposition leads only to punishments. Also, the power to hurt can be overused by both sides in a conflict, to the point at which it ceases to provide the desired effect. If acts of reprisals become too random and frequent, the population may feel that their acquiescence will not save them from brutality. In such circumstances, they may resist, since they feel that their slaughter does not depend on their behaviour. This error can be seen in Alexander's campaign in India, when his use of force became too brutal and random.

For the population to be controlled and/or persuaded through good works, the government must ensure that it limits the influence of the insurgents. It is at this point that military and security operations play their vital part. From the security perspective, many measures need to be taken. These include the creation of secure areas for the population and perhaps an effective ID system. Of critical importance is the recognition that COIN is still war, in which the enemy has to be defeated. By bringing the enemy to battle, the enemy can be defeated materially and psychologically. COIN forces must not simply go on the defensive to protect population centres and key assets. Thus, while being based and patrolling among the population, COIN forces must seize the initiative with aggressive operations against insurgent forces, their bases, and their means of supply. More often than not, offensive COIN operations are best performed by small mobile detachments, preferably recruited from locals, perhaps with the support of specially trained external forces and their attendant firepower. Such forces should be employed in deep raids against insurgent forces, their bases, and their sanctuaries. The war must be taken to the insurgents. This not only serves the objective of defeating the foe in a military sense but also helps to engender a perception of success for the government.

COIN should be regarded as a competition in authority rather than a competition in popularity. Legitimacy is important but seems to garner much of its potency from authority rather than popularity. What seems absolutely clear from the historical evidence is that at all costs one should avoid the temptation to merely contain the insurgency. Also, one should not allow the insurgents the luxury of external sanctuaries. The enemy must be pursued across borders whenever possible. As noted in RAND's *Paths to Victory*, the key to insurgent success is usually to be found in 'tangible', rather than popular, support. The Communist insurgency in South Vietnam would undoubtedly have failed were it not for massive amounts of Soviet and Chinese aid. Likewise, the Angolan insurgencies would surely have dissipated without substantial support from neighbouring African countries, the superpowers, China, and Cuba.

The lessons outlined in this chapter on COIN form a general picture of how best to conduct this type of strategy. However, each insurgency is unique and calls for a response appropriate to the situation. To reiterate a common theme in this book, context is everything. And as strategy is the art of the possible, certain actions will be out of the question simply on political grounds. However, COIN operations also cannot be out of kilter with the nature of strategy or the internal logic of COIN itself. Thus, although at times there may be social, cultural, and moral opposition to some elements of a COIN campaign discussed here, from a strategic perspective, such options need to be available in some form. This is not to suggest that modern Western armies should engage in the wholesale slaughter or brutal coercion of local populations. Rather, it is merely to note that the power to hurt must be in play, whether to be threatened or used in some manner. Merely being popular does not make COIN campaigns successful; being more successful and powerful than the enemy is a key element of achieving one's objective. Authority must be won and enforced.

Strategy is a complex, multidimensional activity. However, as Clausewitz wisely observes, it is a mistake to attempt to counteract this complexity with complex operations. Simple actions are often the best approach.[72] Unfortunately, modern COIN theory is often overly complex and demands convoluted actions from the strategist. Note this comment on the Coalition's responsibilities in Iraq. Aside from combat operations, 'Part of the Coalition's sociological mission is instantiating important concepts into the Iraqi collective conscious, including mercy, restraint, proportional force, and just war'.[73]

It seems that the West is left with three possible approaches to how it conducts COIN campaigns. The first approach is to eschew the power to hurt and therefore accept that modern COIN potentially remains a more complicated and difficult undertaking. Such an approach does have the positive outcome that it is more socially and politically acceptable. The second option is to accept the words of General Sherman, that war is hell, and thereby adopt an approach that ignores the ethical dimension to COIN and thus uses the power to hurt without constraints, except those imposed by strategy. However, there is a third approach that may represent a compromise between the first two. This third option accepts the role of the power to hurt but uses it in a modern guise. Thus, local populations can be punished and coerced but are done so in ways that stop short of slaughter, torture, and executions. In such a situation, punishments may take the form of detention without trial, fines, and other sanctions.

Above all, what seems clear from the historical and theoretical evidence is that COIN must be considered as war. If this position is taken, then the nature of war must be the context within which a COIN campaign is conducted. Thus, the struggle between the insurgents and government forces is characterised by competitive, violent behaviour in the service of policy objectives. In such an environment, alongside social and economic acts designed to gain the support of the local populous, the power to hurt and offensive military operations must play a significant part. To use Clausewitzian language, the 'centres of gravity' in insurgencies are the enemy forces and the perception and exercise of legitimate authority. To reiterate, perceptions of legitimate authority come, at least in part, from the exercise of military power.

Key points

1 Modern COIN performance has been poor.
2 Insurgency seeks to achieve its objectives primarily through protracted, irregular operations designed to disrupt and weaken the government.
3 COIN has its own strategic logic but is also bound by the logic of strategy.
4 COIN is an act of war, in which the enemy must be defeated.
5 The local population is an important ingredient of success, and they must be controlled through legitimate authority.

Questions

1 Why has modern COIN been so difficult?
2 How does insurgency function as an instrument of strategy?
3 Should COIN be considered as an act of war?
4 What are the key characteristics of a successful COIN campaign?

Notes

1 See, for example, Douglas Porch, *Counterinsurgency: Exposing the Myths of the New Way of War* (Cambridge, Cambridge University Press, 2013).
2 Ibid., p. 206.
3 Christopher Paul, Colin P. Clarke, Beth Grill, and Molly Dunigan, *Paths to Victory: Detailed Insurgency Case Studies* (Santa Monica, RAND, 2013).
4 This work is conscious of the words of caution contained in the work of James Kiras, who quite correctly warns against the temptation to draw simple lessons from history and transpose them directly onto today's problems. Nonetheless, history is an important teacher. James Kiras, 'Irregular Warfare', in David Jordan et al. (eds.), *Understanding Modern Warfare* (Cambridge, Cambridge University Press, 2008), p. 265.
5 Carl von Clausewitz, *On War* (Princeton, NJ, Princeton University Press, 1976), p. 75.
6 For an analysis of the rise of ISIS, see David Kilcullen, *Blood Year: Islamic State and the Failures of the War on Terror* (London, Hurst and Company, 2016).
7 Ibid., p. 28.
8 Kiras, p. 273.
9 Kilcullen.
10 Paul et al., pp. 14–22, 31–9.
11 Kiras, p. 174.
12 Sam Collyns, 'Iraq's Militia Leaders Reveal Why They Turned on al-Qaeda', *BBC News*, www.bbc.co.uk/news/world-middle-east-11417211
13 See Paul et al., pp. 423–39; Peter Layton, 'How Sri Lanka Won the War: Lessons in Strategy from an Overlooked Victory', *The Diplomat*, April 9, 2015, https://thediplomat.com/2015/04/how-sri-lanka-won-the-war/

14 Kiras, p. 236.

15 David J. Lonsdale, 'Alexander the Great and the Art of Adaptation', *The Journal of Military History* 77:3 (July 2013), pp. 817–35.

16 Paul et al. actually use the terms 'motive-focused' and 'iron-fist'.

17 Robert R. Tomes, 'Relearning Counterinsurgency Warfare', *Parameters* (Spring 2004), p. 26. Later in the article, Tomes uses a more appropriate distinction, by describing the difference in such actions as 'a confluence of military and non-military operations'.

18 Robert Thompson, *Defeating Communist Insurgency: Experiences from Malaya and Vietnam* (London, MacMillan Press, 1966), pp. 50–5.

19 Department of the Army, *FM 3–24/ MCWP 3–33.5: Insurgencies and Countering Insurgencies* (Washington, DC, Department of the Army, 2014), pp. 10–28.

20 Ibid., pp. 3–24.

21 Ibid., pp. 7–8.

22 Colin S. Gray, *Perspectives on Strategy* (Oxford, Oxford University Press, 2013), p. 155.

23 John Newsinger, *British Counterinsurgency: From Palestine to Northern Ireland* (Houndmills, Palgrave, 2002), p. 49.

24 Charles E. Callwell, *Small Wars: A Tactical Textbook for Imperial Soldiers* (London, Greenhill Books, 1990), p. 79.

25 Newsinger, p. 144.

26 Julian Paget, *Counter-Insurgency Campaigning* (London, Faber and Faber, 1967), p. 176.

27 Steven Metz and Raymond Millen, *Insurgency and Counterinsurgency in the 21st Century: Reconceptualising Threat and Response*, SSI Monograph, November 2004, p. 5, www.au.af.mil/au/awc/awcgate/ssi/insurgency21c.pdf.

28 Robert H. Scales, Jr., 'Adaptive Enemies: Achieving Victory by Avoiding Defeat', *Joint Force Quarterly* (Autumn/Winter 1999/2000), pp. 7–14, 12.

29 John A. Lynn, 'Patterns of Insurgency and Counterinsurgency', *Military Review*, July/August 2005, p. 25.

30 Colin S. Gray, *Another Bloody Century* (London, Weidenfeld & Nicolson, 2005), p. 223.

31 Anthony Coates, 'Culture, the Enemy and the Moral Restraint of War', in Richard Sorabji and David Rodin (eds.), *The Ethics of War: Shared Problems in Different Traditions* (Farnham, Ashgate, 2006), p. 209.

32 Ian F.W. Beckett and John Pimlott, 'Introduction', in Ian F.W. Beckett and John Pimlott (eds.), *Armed Forces and Modern Counter-Insurgency* (London, Croom Helm, 1985), p. 3.

33 All of the above references to the American frontier wars are taken from Robert M. Utley, *The Indian Frontier of the American West 1846–1890* (Albuquerque, University of New Mexico Press, 1984), pp. 84, 261, 130.

34 Quoted in Tomes, p. 24.

35 Newsinger, p. 50.

36 See W.S. van der Waals, *Portugal's War in Angola 1961–1974* (Pretoria, Protea Book House, 2011); Ian F.W. Beckett, 'The Portuguese Army: The Campaign in Mozambique, 1964–1974', in Ian F.W. Beckett and John Pimlott (eds.), *Armed Forces and Modern Counterinsurgency* (London, Croom Helm, 1985), p. 147.

37 Van der Waals, p. 220.

38 Thomas C. Schelling, *Arms and Influence* (New Haven, CT, Yale University Press, 1966), p. 2.

39 Metz and Millen, p. 6.

40 C.M. Ford, 'Targeting a Population's Neutrality to Defeat an Insurgency', *Parameters*, 2005, p. 54.

41 Metz and Millen, p. 32.

42 Paget, pp. 168–9. For example, in Malaya, villages that harboured guerrillas were collectively fined or had curfews imposed.

43 Callwell, pp. 40–2.

44 Newsinger, pp. 41–6.

45 Bernard B. Fall, *The Theory and Practice of Insurgency and Counterinsurgency*, www.nwc.navy.mil/press/Review/1998/winter/art5-w98.htm

46 Andrew F. Krepinevich, 'How to Win in Iraq', *Foreign Affairs*, September/October 2005, www.foreignaffairs.org To be fair, Krepinevich does later note that small, mobile patrols should be used to keep the insurgents on their toes and thereby deny them sanctuary.

47 Clausewitz, p. 111.

48 Quoted in Bruce Hoffman, *Insurgency and Counterinsurgency in Iraq* (Santa Monica, RAND, 2004), p. 10.

49 Thomas H. Henriksen, 'Some Notes on the National Liberation Wars in Angola, Mozambique, and Guinea-Bissau', *Military Affairs* 41 (February 1977), p. 33.

50 Credit must also be given to the Sri Lankan campaign to minimise international and regional support for the LTTE, and the fact that in 2004 the Tamil Tigers lost control of the East of the Peninsula when Colonel Karuna and his forces defected to the government side. See Layton and Paul et al.

51 Van der Waals, p. 215.

52 Brian Bond, *The Pursuit of Victory* (Oxford, Oxford University Press, 1998).

53 Newsinger, p. 57.

54 Metz and Millen, p. 10. Similarly, the Portuguese secret police, the PIDE, were successful in creating significant divisions within Frelimo. William C. Westfall, *Mozambique: Insurgency against Portugal, 1963–1975*, p. 24, www.globalsecurity.org/military/library/report/1984/WCW.htm.

55 Hoffman, p. 9.

56 Metz and Millen, p. vii.

57 Westerfall, p. 16.

58 Beckett, 'The Portuguese Army . . .', p. 139.

59 Harry G. Summers, *On Strategy: A Critical Analysis of the Vietnam War* (New York, Ballentine Books, 1995), p. 55.

60 Ibid., pp. 87, 69.

61 Henriksen, p. 33.

62 Lieutenant Colonel Stuart A. Herrington, quoted in Summers, p. 91.

63 Andrew Krepinevich, *The Army and Vietnam* (Baltimore, The John Hopkins University Press, 1988), p. 167.

64 David J. Lonsdale, *Alexander the Great: Lessons in Strategy* (Abingdon, Routledge, 2007).

65 Utley, p. 155.

66 Beckett, pp. 144–5.

67 Layton.

68 Westfall, p. 28.

69 Utley, pp. 157, 169.

70 Van der Waals, p. 212.

71 D. Michael Shafer, *Deadly Paradigms: The Failure of US Counterinsurgency Policy* (Princeton: Princeton University Press, 1988); Kilcullen.

72 Clausewitz, p. 271.

73 Tomes, p. 24.

Further reading

Callwell, Charles E., *Small Wars: A Tactical Textbook for Imperial Soldiers*, (London: Greenhill Books, 1990).

Department of the Army, *FM 3–24/ MCWP 3–33.5: Insurgencies and Countering Insurgencies*, (Washington, DC: Department of the Army, 2014).

Galula, David, *Counterinsurgency Warfare: Theory and Practice*, (Westport: Praeger, 2006).

Lawrence, T.E., *Seven Pillars of Wisdom*, (Ware: Wordsworth, 1997).

Metz, Steven and Raymond Millen, *Insurgency and Counterinsurgency in the 21st Century: Reconceptualising Threat and Response, SSI Monograph*, (Carlisle: SSI, November 2004), www.au.af.mil/au/awc/awcgate/ssi/insurgency21c.pdf

Paul, Christopher, Colin P. Clarke, Beth Grill and Molly Dunigan, *Paths to Victory: Detailed Insurgency Case Studies*, (Santa Monica: RAND, 2013).

Porch, Douglas, *Counterinsurgency: Exposing the Myths of the New Way of War*, (Cambridge: Cambridge University Press, 2013).

Robert Thompson, Defeating Communist Insurgency: Experiences from Malaya and Vietnam, (London: Macmillan Press, 1966), p. 50.

Steven Metz & Raymond Millen, Insurgency and Counterinsurgency in the 21st Century: Reconceptualizing Threat and Response, (Carlisle: Strategic Studies Institute, 2004), p. 32.

Summers, Harry G., *On Strategy: A Critical Analysis of the Vietnam War*, (New York: Ballentine Books, 1995).

Thompson, Robert, *Defeating Communist Insurgency: Experiences from Malaya and Vietnam*, (London: MacMillan Press, 1966).

Tse-Tung, Mao, *Selected Military Writings of Mao Tse-Tung*, (Peking: Foreign Language Press, 1966).

Conclusion: patterns in grand strategy today

What, then, are the patterns in grand strategy today? A thorough answer to that question would require volumes. What remains of this book will sketch the outlines of a response and reflect on how studying the contemporary grand strategic environment can help us to understand the broader topic of twenty-first-century strategy. As of 2019, relations among the great powers in world politics remain protean – capable of assuming a variety of forms.

Geography continues to exert a relatively consistent influence on strategy over relatively long periods of time. The Horn of Africa, to pick but one example, is a watery crossroads connecting Asia, Europe, southeast Africa, and the Middle East. Therefore, it is invaluable to any power in any one of those areas that wishes to act beyond its immediate neighbourhood. Admiral Zheng He of China's Ming dynasty visited that region in the 1400s, and he would undoubtedly have been pleased to learn that his twenty-first-century successors have established a base in the Horn nation of Djibouti.[1] Although journalists for *The New York Times* allege that American diplomats have tried to block Russia from acquiring similar facilities, the Russian publication *TASS* notes that Russian warships already undergo maintenance and take on fuel in Djibouti.[2] France, Japan, and the United States have a military presence in Djibouti as well, while the chief of staff of the Iranian armed forces has expressed a desire for a base on the other side of the Gulf, in Yemen.[3]

Thus, the scholar C. Dale Walton has revived geopolitics for the present day.[4] Walton notes that a variety of new powers are rising in international politics. Many of these are in parts of the world that remained relatively undeveloped during the great struggles of the twentieth century. As new powers arranged in new geographical patterns seek to consolidate their growing influence, Walton suggests that they will turn to innovative forms of military technology and innovative ways of using it. This will precipitate both future revolutions in military affairs and a more comprehensive 'revolution in strategic perspective'.

Other geopolitical analysts may offer alternative interpretations. Meanwhile, as the chapter on grand strategy noted, strategists must pay particular attention to the political dimension of geopolitical analysis. Those who wish to understand contemporary strategy will wish to know what goals the political actors of the twenty-first century might seek and how they might organise themselves to achieve them. The answers to such questions remain ambiguous. Whereas the strategic relevance of geography remains stable, the strategic relevance of political thought appears to have lost definition.

Fewer than 30 years ago, strategists had to consider the possibility that conflict between liberal states and communist states might lead to nuclear war. Thankfully, the ideological disputes between twenty-first-century powers remain less apocalyptic. One must acknowledge that there are exceptions to this statement. In 2016, for instance, the North Korean official news agency threatened to turn South Korea into a 'pile of ashes' and a 'sea of fire'.[5] Terrorist leaders make extreme threats as a matter of course.

Some analysts argue that contemporary terrorists are becoming increasingly willing to act on such statements. The increasing possibility that radicals may obtain WMDs makes it unwise to overlook terrorist rhetoric. Not only are groups with al-Qaeda's determination to hurt its enemies likely to detonate such weapons purely for the sake of causing harm, groups with ISIS's ambition to found states could benefit from deterrence. As Chapters 13 and 14 have noted, militarily powerful nations proved reluctant to use force against ISIS. If ISIS had been able to make a credible threat that it had smuggled nuclear weapons into Western countries and had been prepared to use them to retaliate for strikes against its own territory, those countries would find responding to the terrorist organisation even more difficult.

Even if ISIS acquired had more readily available WMD such as toxic gases and used them only on Middle Eastern battlefields, such armaments would have strengthened the group's ability to drive back attacks on its territory. Thus, ISIS would have probably been able to pursue its ambitions more aggressively and for longer. The possibility that similar scenarios might take place in real life is, if nothing else, a reason for state governments to act decisively against potentially hostile political organisations. This in turn reminds one of the fact that state governments themselves will often have conflicting interests in such disputes. Russia, for instance, clearly perceives the civil war in Syria differently from many Western nations, and both sides are using military force to pursue their differing agendas.

At the dawn of the twenty-first century, many scholars, commentators, and political leaders spoke optimistically about the prospects for increasing cooperation among states. The so-called globalisation of the world's economy gave governments, businesses, and other powerful actors material incentives to cooperate. Violent opponents of the status quo such as al-Qaeda threatened almost everyone but themselves and thus even they seemed to contribute to the trend towards unity. Even then, however, it was clear that certain political actors, including such powerful states as Russia, the PRC, and the United States remained firm in their commitment to lead the emerging world order or to emancipate themselves from it. The author has explored these developments and their implications in his book *Emerging Conflicts of Principle: International Relations and the Clash between Cosmopolitanism and Republicanism*.

As the century's second decade wanes, the trend towards cooperation appears to have reversed. In 2016, British voters approved a referendum calling on the United Kingdom to withdraw from the European Union. That same year, American voters elected a president who questioned many of his country's alliances and treaty commitments. Meanwhile, as the global economic crisis that began in 2008 reached its tenth year, several states that curtailed their military spending to cope with the Great Recession have resolved to increase their defence budgets.

The United States and the United Kingdom stand out as countries that have committed themselves to expanding their armed forces.[6] The PRC invested increasing sums into its military even during the worst years of the crisis and, as of 2019, continues to do so.[7] Russia's economy remains volatile, and its government has allowed this to affect its defence budget. In 2017, analysts for Janes reported that the Russian armed forces had lost one-quarter of their funding, although other observers suggested that the actual cut was closer to 6%–7%.[8]

Despite declines in international cooperation and rises in military spending, the prospects for large-scale war remain more distant in the twenty-first century than in any previous historical era. For as long as we can rely on the great powers to remain at peace, strategy will remain one important political concern among many. States waged war throughout the first decade of the twenty-first century, and they will continue to do so. Terrorists, pirates, and other violent non-state actors will remain active. All the issues discussed throughout this book will remain relevant. Nevertheless, responsible political leaders will not necessarily give these issues the highest priority.

If, on the other hand, Colin Gray is right to suggest that we are living at the beginning of 'another bloody century', then we must anticipate a moment when strategy once again becomes a matter of life and death for every one of us.[9] Historical episodes such as Frederick William I's grand strategic ruses of the eighteenth century remind us that we may not recognise the rise of powerful opponents as early as we might hope. For both the Western powers and their potential opponents, then, the strategic challenge of the next decade may be that of securing the resources that they may need to address sharper challenges later in the century. This book has sought to detail what those resources might be.

Notes

1 Andrew Jacobs and Jane Perlez, 'U.S. Wary of Its New Neighbor in Djibouti: A Chinese Naval Base', *New York Times*, February 25, 2017, www.nytimes.com/2017/02/25/world/africa/us-djibouti-chinese-naval-base.html?_r=0 (accessed May 1, 2017).

2 Ibid.; Anonymous, 'Russian Warship Yaroslav Mudry Starts Anti-Piracy Mission in Gulf of Aden', *Tass* (August 18, 2016), http://tass.com/defense/894901 (accessed May 1, 2017).

3 Dubai Newsroom, 'Iran May Seek Naval Bases in Yemen or Syria: Chief of Staff', *Reuters* (November 27, 2016), www.reuters.com/article/us-iran-navy-yemen-syria-idUSKBN13M08M (accessed May 1, 2017).

4 C. Dale Walton, *Geopolitics and the Great Powers in the Twenty-First Century: Multipolarity and the Revolution in Strategic Perspective* (Abingdon, Routledge, 2007).

5 Anonymous, 'N Korea Vows to Turn South Into "Sea of Fire": Pyongyang Reacts to Moves by the US and South Korea to Deploy a New Missile Defence System', *Sky News* (Monday July 11, 2016), http://news.sky.com/story/n-korea-vows-to-turn-south-into-sea-of-fire-10498501 (accessed May 5, 2017).

6 Michael Shear and Jennifer Steinhauer, 'Trump to Seek $54 Billion Increase in Military Spending', *The New York Times*, February 27, 2017, www.nytimes.com/2017/02/27/us/politics/trump-budget-military.html?_r=0 (accessed May 5, 2017); Ministry of Defence and The Rt Hon Sir Michael Fallon, 'Defence Budget Increases for First Time in Six Years', April 1, 2016, www.gov.uk/government/news/defence-budget-increases-for-the-first-time-in-six-years (accessed May 5, 2017).

7 'What Does China Really Spend on Its Military?', *Center for Strategic and International Studies*, http://chinapower.csis.org/military-spending/ (accessed May 5, 2017).

8 Craig Caffrey, 'Russia Announces Deepest Defence Budget Cuts since the 1990s', *Janes Defence Weekly*, March 16, 2017, www.janes.com/article/68766/russia-announces-deepest-defence-budget-cuts-since-1990s (accessed May 5, 2017); D. Majumdar, 'Did Russia Just Cut Its Defense Budget by a Whopping 25%', *The National Interest*, March 20, 2017, http://nationalinterest.org/blog/the-buzz/did-russia-just-cut-its-defense-budget-by-whopping-25-19831 (accessed May 5, 2017).

9 Colin Gray, *Another Bloody Century: Future Warfare* (London, Weidenfeld & Nicolson, 2005).

Further reading

Gray, Colin, *Another Bloody Century: Future Warfare*, (London: Weidenfeld & Nicolson, 2005).

Kane, Thomas M., *Emerging Conflicts of Principle: International Relations and the Clash Between Cosmopolitanism and Republicanism*, (Aldershot: Ashgate, 2008).

Walton, C. Dale, *Geopolitics and the Great Powers in the Twenty-First Century: Multipolarity and the Revolution in Strategic Perspective*, (Abingdon: Routledge, 2007).

Index

Printed in Great Britain
by Amazon

58902031R00212